Issues in Heterodox Economics

Issues in Heterodox Economics

Edited by
Donald A.R. George

Chapters © 2008 The Author(s)
Book compilation © 2008 Blackwell Publishing Ltd

First published as a special issue of the *Journal of Economic Surveys* (volume 21, issue 3)

BLACKWELL PUBLISHING
350 Main Street, Malden, MA 02148-5020, USA
9600 Garsington Road, Oxford OX4 2DQ, UK
550 Swanston Street, Carlton, Victoria 3053, Australia

First published 2008 by Blackwell Publishing Ltd

1 2008

Library of Congress Cataloging-in-Publication Data

Issues in heterodox economics/edited by Donald A. R. George. p. cm.
   "First published as a special issue of the *Journal of Economic Surveys* (volume 21, issue 3)"–
T. p. verso.
   Includes bibliographical references and index.
   ISBN: 978-1-4051-7961-4 (pbk.: alk. paper) 1. Economics. I. George, Donald A. R., 1953-II.
Journal of Economic Surveys.
HB171.I94 2007
330–dc22

                                                        2007040261
A catalogue record for this title is available from the British Library.

Set in 10.5pt Times
by aptara, New Delhi, India

For further information on
Blackwell Publishing, visit our website at
www.blackwellpublishing.com

CONTENTS

CONSOLATIONS FOR THE ECONOMIST: THE FUTURE OF ECONOMIC ORTHODOXY[1]

Donald A.R. George

Edinburgh School of Economics, University of Edinburgh

1. Introduction

There are thousands of economists around the world devoting a large quantity of human capital to an enterprise, about which many of them are developing serious doubts. Modern economics has a tightly defined mainstream 'orthodoxy' and a fragmented 'heterodoxy' (Sheila Dow explores the distinction between 'orthodoxy' and 'heterodoxy' in her paper 'Variety of Methodological Approach in Economics'). Many economists are concerned that the mainstream of their subject has become far too narrow: more a brackish puddle of techniques than a sparkling torrent of ideas. Several features of this orthodoxy can be identified.

- It involves a particular approach to theory, based on the idea of a 'mathematical model' (utilising a limited range of mathematical techniques).
- It entails empirical work based on a limited range of econometric techniques. This empirical material has little or no connection with economic theory.
- It only acknowledges a limited range of theoretical approaches and is antithetical to pluralism. Orthodox economists often extol the benefits of economic competition, but they much prefer unregulated monopoly in the market for ideas. Mathematical modelling, discussed in Section 2, provides a handy barrier to entry to this market.
- It is largely technique-driven rather than issue-driven: valuing difficult technique and formalism above work of applied or policy relevance.
- It has an 'imperialist' attitude to cognate disciplines such as politics, sociology and economic history, seeking to incorporate them safely into economics, rather than learning from them.
- It has a tightly defined professional structure which, for example, dictates a narrow range of publication outlets (the so-called core journals) which, exclusively, lead to career development. This is reinforced in the UK by

the Research Assessment Exercise (RAE), which links financial reward with conformity to the mainstream approach.[2]

Many economists feel that, unless things change, their subject will end up in utter sterility, with rewards going to those who can count the number of Bayes–Nash equilibria that can dance on a locally compact pin-head. Apart from intellectual vacuity and irrelevance there is also the prospect that, in countries where academic research is state funded,[3] the tax-payer may object to her taxes being spent on sterile formalism and seek to withhold further contributions.

Mainstream economists are herd animals and are aware of the dangers of egregious (outside the herd) behaviour. They have therefore developed effective mechanisms of enforcement to ensure conformity to orthodoxy. So-called core journals and their role in appointments and career development have been mentioned above, as has the British RAE. Any economist specialising in the history of economic thought, methodology or radical economics would never get appointed or promoted to an academic job in the UK today. Development economists, applied labour or industrial economists would have serious difficulty.

Mainstream economists may well reply that they are simply following an obvious example, namely the natural sciences. Feyerabend (1970, p. 198) remarks:

> More than one social scientist has pointed out to me that now at last he has learned to turn his field into a 'science' – by which of course he meant that he had learned how to *improve* it. The recipe, according to these people, is to restrict criticism, to reduce the number of comprehensive theories to one, and to create a normal science with this one theory as its paradigm. Students must be prevented from speculating along different lines and the more restless colleagues must be made to conform and 'to do serious work'.

and later (p. 209):

> The sciences especially are surrounded by an aura of excellence which checks any inquiry into their beneficial effect.

It is surely better to emulate the white-coated miracle workers of physics and biology than bearded, woolly minded sociologists. Physicists and biologists get their hands on a far larger chunk of public money than economists and they are revered by the public as 'experts'. Alas this line of argument has some obvious flaws. First, the methodology of the natural sciences may simply not work in a social science such as economics (this point is explored in Thomas Boylan and Paschal O'Gorman's paper 'Axiomatization and Formalism in Economics' and in Sheila Dow's paper 'Variety of Methodological Approach in Economics'). Second, most economists are woefully ignorant of the natural sciences and how research in those subjects actually proceeds (it is far more pluralist and takes empirical testing far more seriously than most economists realise). Third, public approbation of the natural sciences is on the wane, largely because the public do not distinguish science from technology (various assorted public policy disasters such as BSE[4] are blamed, perhaps unfairly, on 'scientific experts').

2. Mathematical Models

The most important skill an economist can have (and this includes undergraduates and postgraduates) is a good command of a relatively narrow range of mathematical techniques, largely dating back to the eighteenth and nineteenth centuries. (The mathematisation of economics is discussed in Vela Velupillai's paper 'Variations on the Theme of Conning in Mathematical Economics'.) These techniques provide the means to construct those objects which are central to the professional life of every orthodox economist (and some heterodox ones), namely mathematical models. At the simplest, such models start from mathematical assumptions and, after several pages of tortured mathematics, arrive at some conclusions. The laws of logic dictate that these conclusions were embodied in the assumptions, so the precise purpose of such an exercise is not immediately obvious. It does, however, provide a good opportunity for economists to demonstrate how clever they are, and simultaneously to provide a useful barrier to entry to the market for ideas.

The orthodox economist will often argue that mathematics is essential to make their arguments 'rigorous' or 'deep'. But it is not clear what sort of rigour or depth they are talking about. If asked 'do you subscribe to the Zermelo–Frankel axioms or the Axiom of Choice?', the orthodox economist will typically supply no answer. But, as any mathematician will tell you, these questions require an answer if mathematical rigour is to have any chance of survival. The argument for 'depth' must not be taken too far.

Mainstream economists are clearly strongly committed to their mathematical models but it would be a mistake to assume that economics research is more likely to gain acceptance the more mathematical it is. It is quite possible for economists to produce research which is 'too mathematical' or, more accurately, uses the 'wrong kind' of mathematics. Mainstream economists have invested heavily in a very narrow and limited range of mathematical techniques (calculus, linear algebra, game theory). So, for example, research involving topological techniques such as catastrophe theory or chaos theory is often rejected by the mainstream, because those techniques are not part of the standard mainstream toolkit. There is a striking contrast here with the natural sciences where many new areas have been developed using such topological techniques.

3. Empirics

A genuinely useful role for mathematical models would be to present economic theory in a form suitable for empirical testing. If any implication of a theory can be empirically refuted then the theory is refuted, and can be rejected or modified. The mainstream economist often argues that, despite appearances to the contrary, economics is an empirical subject. Surely the elaborate mathematical models, beloved of the theorist, are continually subject to empirical testing and will be cast into the dustbin of history as soon as they are refuted by empirical evidence. The example to follow is, once again, the natural sciences where, it is claimed, experimenters confront theory with evidence and reject it if it is found wanting. Experiments in economics are usually impossible[5] (Jinkwon Lee's paper

'Repetition and Financial Incentives in Economics Experiments' discusses some of the difficulties with experimentation) so economists typically use statistical data and econometric methods. But, as with economic theory, techniques have come to dominate ideas. The orthodox econometrician is rewarded for developing new and demanding techniques but not for assembling useful data sets. Most statistical data used by economists has been collected for purposes quite different from theirs (e.g. tax collection) and is riddled with inaccuracy and bias. The refined and sophisticated techniques of the econometricians are useless without reliable data to apply them to.

It may be that the underlying assumptions of a theory are not themselves open to empirical test but that testable implications can be drawn from them. However, there immediately arises the problem of verisimilitude. The underlying assumptions of any theory are unlikely to be exactly true descriptions of the real world but, one hopes, are close approximations to it. Under such circumstances it is important that the implications of a scientific theory are robust with respect to small variations in the underlying assumptions. Such variations should only produce small variations in the theory's implications, not wild and dramatic ones. Without this property empirical testing of theories becomes impossible, because of random environmental perturbations in the conditions under which observations are made. Consider, for example, a chemical theory which predicts the outcome of a particular chemical reaction under conditions of constant ambient temperature. Whatever care the experimental chemist may take, she will not be able to hold the ambient temperature exactly constant; it is bound to fluctuate slightly during the course of the experiment. Suppose the outcome of the experiment is substantially different from what the theory predicted. Is the theory refuted? The theorist can always reply that the ambient temperature was not exactly constant, as his theory requires, and that the experiment does not therefore constitute a refutation. This would not be the case if the robustness property, discussed above, had been required of the theory *ab initio*. Had the theory satisfied this property, the experimenter could be sure that, according to the theory, small fluctuations in the ambient temperature could only generate small fluctuations in the outcome of the reaction. An experimental outcome substantially different from the theory's predictions would then constitute a genuine refutation of the theory. Non-robust theoretical predictions are, in practice, non-observable, and therefore of no scientific interest.

This kind of problem clearly arises in economics as well as chemistry. The theory under test is typically expressed as a model involving some parameters which are assumed to be constant. The marginal propensity to consume or the interest elasticity of the demand for money might fall into this category. Of course no one actually believes that parameters such as these are exactly constant over time: they are bound to vary slightly, just as the ambient temperature would in the chemical example discussed above. It is clear then that the robustness property should be required as a necessary (though not sufficient) property of any economic theory, if that theory is to be regarded as scientifically valid. There are many economic theories which fail this robustness test (for example, most models involving saddlepoint dynamics; see Oxley and George (2007) for an elaboration of this argument) and cannot, therefore, even be considered candidates for empirical refutation.

A further problem arises for those who wish to transplant empirical testing from the natural sciences to economics. Experiments are typically replicable, whereas the statistics used by economists are usually generated in particular, non-replicable, historical circumstances. They more closely resemble the data of the economic historian or sociologist than those of the physicist. Given these data restrictions, perhaps economists should drop their attempts at grandiose, all-encompassing theories and accept that they can only offer theories which are restricted to particular historical and political circumstances. The theory of gravity may hold as good on the moon as on the earth, but the theory of inflation does not.

It may be that economists will have to abandon their attachment to complex but irrelevant econometric techniques, and embrace less grandiose empirical methods. For example, case studies, usually dismissed as the preserve of business studies or sociology, provide a potentially useful alternative approach. Whether orthodox economists will forever find it beneath their dignity to acknowledge that remains to be seen. In fact most orthodox economic theorists have little or no interest in empirical testing, especially not empirical refutation. When asked 'what feasible observation would refute your theory?', the orthodox economist usually responds with blank incomprehension.

4. Pluralism

Clearly appeal to empirical evidence is not the primary means by which the 'good' theories are separated from the 'bad' ones: most mainstream economics is not susceptible to empirical refutation, even in principle. Nonetheless there appears to be remarkable agreement as to which theories shall be accepted and gain currency. Marxian economics, institutional economics and radical economics, for example, are all classified as 'heterodoxy' and ignored. But the mainstream rejection of pluralism operates at a much more detailed level than that. Most published articles in economics involve minute variations on already published material: adopting non-standard assumptions or criticising currently fashionable techniques is usually enough to get your paper rejected, especially by the so-called core journals.

The mainstream maintains its homogeneity, not by appeal to evidence but by appeal to authority. The discipline has a tightly defined professional structure, an 'invisible college' which controls publication, appointments and promotions. No other discipline maintains such a sharp discontinuity between its 'core' journals and all other forms of publication.[6] In major UK universities a tiny number of core journal publications can lead to appointment and promotion in economics, whereas extensive non-core publication and scholarship is treated with contempt. It is widely believed that the RAE uses the proportion of core journal publications as a key measure of research quality in economics, and this in turn impacts on the allocation of large sums of public money. Recent empirical research by Oswald (2006) casts serious doubt on the Core Journal Doctrine.[7] Oswald remarks:

In universities all over the world, hiring and promotion committees regularly hear the argument: 'this is important work because it is about to appear in prestigious journal X'. Moreover those who allocate levels of research funding, such as in the multi-billion pound Research Assessment Exercise in UK universities, often come under pressure to assess research quality in a mechanical way by using journal prestige ratings. The results in this paper suggest that such tendencies are dangerous.

Given the tendency of mainstream economists to ignore empirical evidence, Oswald's findings are unlikely to weaken the malign and anti-intellectual effects of the CJD. The difficult mathematical techniques required of modern economists provide a useful barrier to entry to the profession and help to keep alarming pluralism at bay. The mainstream economists place a huge premium on technique and abstract theory but nonetheless some applied or policy content may occasionally leak into the mainstream. It is even possible that rival disciplines such as politics, sociology or economic history may offer alternative accounts of topics which economists had hitherto considered their territory. (Alex Preda's paper 'The Sociological Approach to Financial Markets' provides an example.) As discussed above, these disciplines may also have a lot to teach economists. However, mainstream economists are wary of close involvement with cognate disciplines. There are essentially two approaches to these subjects. The first, and most popular, is to ignore them altogether. The second is to incorporate them safely into economics. This second approach involves flooding the rival discipline with formalism borrowed from economics: mainstream economists sneer at political science papers with no equations. Mainstream economics does not learn from the other social sciences, something it desperately needs to do, but rather attempts to colonise them.

But does not all this pre-suppose some kind of conspiracy theory? Is it not simply paranoia to imagine an invisible college controlling economics? First, conspiracies do happen: conspiring is not particularly costly and the development of electronic communication has made it even cheaper. Cronyism is widespread in economics and has a significant impact on publication, citation, appointments, promotions and access to research grants. Mainstream economists are herd animals and the herd offers many forms of security, not least financial security. In virtually all countries economics research is dependent on some form of state funding,[8] and if the tax-payer discovers that eminent professors of economics are spending her tax-pounds (or dollars) proving that a countably infinite number of equilibrium contracts exist in a convex, locally compact economy,[9] she may be disinclined to supply future contributions. In the United States, Senator William Proxmire founded in 1975 the Golden Fleece award, often given for ludicrous money-wasting research in the natural sciences. How long will it be before another enterprising politician does something similar for economics? This possibility provides a powerful incentive for mainstream economists to set up barriers to entry to their profession. They do not need to conspire in too much detail: all have a common interest in shading their subject from prying eyes.

At the level of teaching, the homogeneity of economics is often advanced as a positive feature of the subject: mainstream economists frequently explain with pride that in an economics lecture, on any particular branch of the subject, the diagrams and equations will be the same all over the world, though the words may be in different languages. With the advent of space travel, no doubt the Martians will soon catch on too. Unfortunately, however, students are increasingly rejecting this sort of sterile formalism, turning instead (perhaps disappointingly) to subjects such as business studies. Since, in most countries, students generate the income necessary to pay for economics research, this presents a series of problems. For example there is an emerging dichotomy between the needs of teaching and the needs of research. Students like interesting courses which are related to real-world problems, whereas high prestige research involves lots of difficult maths. It is becoming increasingly difficult to hire academics who can supply both. For some UK universities a possible solution is to focus on postgraduate students who can be charged high fees and who are sufficiently acculturated to mainstream economics that they are willing to embrace its sterile formalism without too much complaint.

5. A Future for Economic Orthodoxy?

Economics should deal with topics of huge importance: economic growth, employment, production, world poverty, inequalities of wealth and power, crises and environmental degradation to name a few (aspects of this agenda are discussed in Brian Lin's paper, 'A New Vision of the Knowledge Economy', Fulvio Castellacci's paper, 'Evolutionary and New Growth Theories: Are They Converging?' and Donald A. R. George's paper 'Workers' Savings and the Right to Manage'). Young people studying the subject for the first time often believe that it will supply, if not the answers, then at least the intellectual tools to tackle these issues. They are usually shocked to discover that a large part of their studies involves mastering difficult and ultimately sterile mathematical formalism, which has virtually nothing to say about these matters. Rarely has so much human capital been so seriously misallocated. Should they go on to undertake academic research in economics, they will realise that this sterile formalism, published in core journals, is the only route to career success. Deviation from this route is ruthlessly punished. Mainstream economists are usually untroubled by their academic critics: after all, controlling publication, appointments, promotions and research grants provides much of the power[10] necessary to keep interlopers out. But, as mentioned above, most economics research depends on public funding. So far 'peer review' has kept the tax-payers' noses out of the thorny question of value for money in research funding. The implicit contract is that, provided the universities continue to provide the tax-payers' offspring with high status qualifications, there will be little scrutiny of what research funds are being spent on. This happy situation may not continue indefinitely and mainstream economists may lose their professional fig leaves sooner than they think.

If such an awful day of judgement were to arrive, could economists recover their professional dignity (not to mention their salaries)? There is an intellectually valid future for economics, and economists could contribute to analysing some of the most pressing issues of today. But the path to this sunlit intellectual upland is strewn with obstructions and diversions. To reach it economists will have to:

- Abandon sterile formalism and start judging research quality from its content not its place of publication.
- Stop invoking notions of 'rigour' which they do not understand.
- Understand that theories are only interesting if they are in principle open to refutation: their purpose is to explain the world, not to show how clever their author is.
- Realise that techniques are a means to an end, not an end in themselves.
- Realise that their theories can only be limited to specific historical and political conditions.
- Value applied and policy work as highly as theory.
- Learn from cognate disciplines instead of trying to colonise them.
- Abandon futile 'ranking' exercises such as the RAE
- Adopt a pluralist attitude to theory and settle disputes, where possible, by appeal to evidence not appeal to authority.
- Learn some history of economic thought and stop re-inventing the wheel.

Notes

1. The title acknowledges Paul Feyerabend's (1970) paper 'Consolations for the Specialist' and his lectures at the University of Sussex, which provided me with great inspiration and an understanding of methodological anarchism. Feyerabend's ideas are developed in his (1975) book *Against Method*.
2. Orthodox British economists often argue that the UK needs an RAE to keep 'standards' closer to those of the United States. They miss the obvious fact that the United States does not have an RAE: no American academic would accept a committee of state bureaucrats telling them how good they are at research.
3. This category includes the United States, where large sums of public money enter the universities via research grants, etc.
4. Popularly known as 'mad cow disease' and the probable cause of the fatal human disease vCJD.
5. Though some economists have attempted to emulate psychologists and set up experiments with human subjects to 'test' certain propositions based on game theory. These experiments are never interpreted as rejections of the theory; any apparent rejection is typically explained away, for example by arguing that the rewards on offer were not large enough to induce the subjects to play the game 'properly'.
6. For the benefit of any non-economists who may inadvertently be reading this paper, it should be explained that mainstream economists subscribe to a proposition known as the 'Core Journal Doctrine' (CJD: no relation to the CJD of note 4, though possibly another form of madness). This asserts that there exists a small group (around 10) of journals ('core' journals) with the property that anything published in a core journal is of high quality and all other publications are of low quality.
7. See note 6.
8. See note 3.
9. I made that up, but you know what I mean.

10. Despite possessing so much of it, mainstream economists are surprisingly poor at understanding power. The usual formulation is to 'model' it as the exponent in a von Neumann/Morgenstern utility function, traditionally assigned the value 0.5, for 'ease of exposition'.

References

Feyerabend, P.K. (1970) Consolations for the Specialist. In I. Lakatos and A. Musgrave (eds), *Criticism and the Growth of Knowledge*. Cambridge: Cambridge University Press.

Feyerabend, P.K. (1975) *Against Method*. London: NLB.

Oswald, A.J. (2006) An examination of the reliability of prestigious scholarly journals: evidence and implications for decision-makers. *Economics Department Discussion Paper*, University of Warwick.

Oxley, L. and George, D.A.R. (2007) Economics on the edge of chaos: some pitfalls of linearizing complex systems. *Environmental and Modelling Software*, Vol. 22.

2

AXIOMATIZATION AND FORMALISM IN ECONOMICS

T.A. Boylan and P.F. O'Gorman

National University of Ireland, Galway

1. Introduction

In recent years the malaise within economics is increasingly identified with the dominance of a particular mode of mathematical theorizing and modelling, both buttressed by a methodological framework which purports to provide a foundationalist defence of this particular approach. While we do not propose to review the expanding but variegated literature emerging from various constituencies within the economic community, three broad strands of thinking can be distinguished.[1] The first is a group of commentators represented by such writers as Blaug (2002) and Hutchison (1977, 2000) who have voiced a sustained and stringent critique of the excessive use of formalism. For these commentators this development has reached a stage where it is now perceived as an inhibiting influence, which is alienating the discipline from engaging real-world problems on any meaningful scale. Not that these writers represent a particularly 'heterodox' position within economics. On the contrary they speak from within the orthodox fold, but their dissatisfaction and source of critique is the dominance of the increasing formalization of the discipline. For these writers, this is particularly represented in the model of general equilibrium arising from the neo-Walrasian programme with, in their view, its excessive degree of abstraction and empirical vacuousness.

A second strand of critique is represented by economic methodologists who present a more fundamental heterodox engagement with the methodological foundations of economics. Arguably the most articulated and institutionally organized is represented by the Cambridge critical realists centred on the work of Tony Lawson and his co-workers in Cambridge and elsewhere (Lawson, 1997, 2003; Fleetwood, 1999; Lewis, 2004). The centrality of ontology and its methodological implications for economic theorizing and modelling along with their critique of deductivism, or a particular version of it, represent two of the principal pillars of the critical realist critique of orthodoxy. Deductivism has provided the accommodating methodological cover for the application of mathematics on an indiscriminate

level to the detriment of the discipline. Not that critical realists eschew the use
of mathematics or mathematical modelling *per se*; the issue may be the type of
mathematics to be used.

Similarly in our methodological work, we sought to reformulate the methodological framework of economics based on developments in twentieth-century philosophy
of science with the aim of re-establishing the centrality of empirical content in the
context of economic theory construction and testing (Boylan and O'Gorman, 1991,
1995, 1997a, b, 2001, 2005). While our starting methodological point differs from
that of critical realism, we share with them the same methodological concerns of
critique and re-orientation of orthodox methodology and by implication economic
theorizing and modelling. As in the case of the critical realists, we do not eschew
the use of mathematics in economics or the enormous benefits to be gained
from the use of mathematical modelling. We do, however, seriously question
the philosophical genealogy and trajectory by which economics came to adopt
the particular methodological framework that legitimates the current mathematical
mode of theorizing and modelling. A central component of our argument is that
given the hegemony of orthodox practice in this domain, if there is to be a coherent
heterodox response it will have to address complex issues at a number of different
levels and in a number of different dimensions. As part of that heterodox response
we address in this paper a particular set of issues located in the intersection of
developments in the philosophy of mathematics and mathematical economics at a
particular juncture. It represents the intersection of historiography and methodology
with a view to challenging orthodoxy's self-referential interpretative narrative of its
development and claim to legitimacy.

This brings us to the third strand of contributions to this topic, and is the
one that is of most concern to us in this paper. This is the work of a number
of scholars who have engaged the historiography of formalism in twentieth-
century economics. The historiography of formalism involves intellectual discourse
between a number of academic disciplines, including the history of mathematics,
the philosophy of mathematics and the history of economic thought. It also involves
a number of evolving interpretative narratives within each of these disciplines in an
attempt to render a coherent account of major shifts within economics, particularly
from the 1930s. It has focused on developments in mathematical economics and
more particularly the theorizing of general equilibrium. Illustrative of work in the
historiography of formalism in economics would include Mirowski (1989), Ingroa
and Israel (1990), Punzo (1991), Golland (1996) and in particular Weintraub (1979,
1985, 1998a, b, 2002) who has chronicled in detail the growth of formalism in
economics in the course of the twentieth century.

A central figure, we argue, in attempting to understand the current status of
mathematical theorizing in contemporary economics comes from mathematics, that
of David Hilbert and more particularly the ramifications of the Hilbert programme
of 1900. Clarification of the relation between axiomatization, formalization and
the pursuit of what came to be termed the finitistic programme in Hilbert's work is
central to our interpretation and understanding of how contemporary economics has
come to be dominated by the particular mode of mathematical theorizing currently

in use. The conventional story of the mathematization of economics traces a line from the Hilbert formalist programme through the contributions of the Viennese group of mathematicians and economists of the 1930s, along with the influence of the Bourbakist programme and its migration to the United States as represented by Gerard Debreu, and his pivotal contributions in the 1950s, who is the quintessential formalist in the post World War II period.

However, in Weintraub (2002), which represents one of the most comprehensive accounts of the emergence of economics as a mathematical science, the argument is advanced that there is 'little sense to be made of the Hilbert Formalist Program'. Rather Hilbert's views are argued to contain two intertwined lines of what was an evolving research programme. One line involved the quest for certainty in mathematics, linked to Hilbert's Second Problem of 1900, which pursued a proof of the consistency of arithmetic, logic or set theory. This part of the Hilbert formalist programme is termed by Weintraub the 'Finistic Program for the Foundations of Arithmetic (FPFA)'. Complementing this is the second line identified by Weintraub as the search to develop axiomatic formulations not only of mathematical theories but of all scientific theories, in line with Hilbert's Sixth Problem of 1900. This Weintraub has designated Hilbert's Axiomatic Approach (AA) (Weintraub, 2002, p. 90).

The distinction between the 'Finistic Program for the Foundations of Arithmetic' and the 'Axiomatic Approach' is important for Weintraub, since he argues that there is a problem of historiographic interpretation in that the FPFA has been identified with 'Hilbert's formalist programme' by historians of the philosophy of mathematics, who have been accepted as the authoritative interpreters of these developments by historians of economics. Weintraub insists that it is the 'historians of mathematical practice, like Corry (1996) and Giorgio Israel' who should receive the attention of historians of economics. In any event, for Weintraub the FPFA, as a result of Godel's theorem of the 1930s, was demonstrated to be incapable of completion. Notwithstanding this undermining of the quest for certainty in mathematics in Hilbert's programme, Godel's theorem paved the way for what Weintraub calls 'relative certainty' in that for any system truth as consistency was relative to the structure in which the system was embedded. Central to this process was Hilbert's AA, and for Weintraub as between the two components of Hilbert's thinking, the FPFA and AA, it 'is my contention that only the latter was to play a role in the development of a mathematical economics' (2002, p. 90). Alternatively stated, Weintraub's thesis is that the 'image of mathematics' within economics shifted from a model of 'mechanical reductionism' in the nineteenth century to a model of 'mathematical reductionism' as a result of developments in the philosophy of mathematics, or metamathematics, by the 1930s, and the latter view was embedded in the AA.[2] This new image of mathematics is argued to have shaped a new emergent mathematical economics, where rigour and truth (identified with consistency) was linked to the axiomatic development of economic theory.

Our central concern in this paper is to contribute to the hermeneutical debate on our understanding of the current status of economics and in particular the issues surrounding the process by which its formalization was achieved, and how this process might have pursued a different trajectory at a critical juncture in time. In this connection we can concur with Weintraub that the mathematization of economics occurred in two phases. The first, initiated by Walras and others, was largely based on analogies to the mathematical science of mechanics. The second phase, associated with the neo-Walrasian programme, appealed to Cantorian set theory and exploited the formidable mathematical tools of the latter, as reflected in the work of Debreu and others. By focusing on the axiomatic dimension of the Hilbert programme, Weintraub has certainly contributed to our understanding of the formalization process in its present form.

However, and contra to Weintraub, we contend that his analysis of the process is truncated arising from his exclusive concentration on the AA. We argue that in order to provide a more adequate hermeneutical understanding of the mathematization of economics, we must also engage Hilbert's foundational programme in order to enhance our insight into both the historiographical process and methodological implications arising from Hilbert's programme and its influence on economics. Hilbert's foundational programme was both formalist and finitist. We propose to elucidate the specific notion of formalism used by Hilbert and show how this was taken up by Debreu. Next we look at Hilbert's finitism, which includes what he called 'Cantor's paradise'. In this connection we show how, by espousing a Hilbert-type finitism, Debreu was able to exploit the novel range of mathematical tools associated with Cantorian set theory in his development of general equilibrium theory. Finally we argue that if Debreu had espoused a different finitist programme, for instance that suggested by Poincaré, he would have effected the mathematization of economics along totally different lines: the mathematical resources of Cantor would not have been exploited. Instead he would have been confined to constructivist mathematics, such as Church's lambda calculus or Turing machines, giving us a totally different picture of a complex economy than that furnished by general equilibrium theory. This represents, we believe, one of the critical developments in the historiography of the mathematization of contemporary economics. These developments must be critically re-examined if the processes of current modes of mathematical theorizing and modelling along with their supporting methodological principles are to be adequately understood and challenged with a view to facilitating, à la Kant, the conditions of the possibility of articulating alternative frameworks of analysis.

The structure of the paper is as follows. In Section 2 we provide a brief overview of Hilbert's axiomatic system, highlighting both its formalist and finitist dimensions. This acts as a prelude to Section 3 which examines Debreu's approach to formalism, whose work was central to imposing a particular type of formalism on twentieth-century economics, through his implementation of Hilbert's particular version of finitism. In this section we also discuss the concept of the Walrasian 'propaedeutic', a concept taken from Frege, and go on to examine a different version of finitism, that produced by Poincaré, which would have provided a different perspective for economics, had it been adopted. In Section 4 we examine the process of how mathematical economics got 'locked-in' to the Hilbertian version of finitism along with its methodological implications for economics. In Section 5 we examine the implications for economics if Poincaré's finitism had been adopted rather than Debreu's Bourbakist version of Hilbert's finitism, while in the final Section 6 we provide some methodological reflections based on our own methodological work, which would facilitate and advocate Poincaré finitism as the proper methodological basis for economics in response to the current orthodoxy.

2. Hilbert's Axiomatic System: Formalist and Finitist

In her paper on 'Formalism in Economics', Golland (1996) points out that axiomatization and formalism are two distinct concepts. This is certainly correct: one can axiomatize, without being committed to a formalist reading of the axiomatic system. Axiomatization is as old as Euclid, whereas formalism is a much later development. For instance the German founder of the logicist programme, Frege, at the turn of the twentieth century, associates formalism with Thomae in Jena and Korselt who defended Hilbert's 1899 Festschrift, *Foundations of Geometry*, on formalist grounds. In this connection Frege is worth quoting:

> For it seems to me that Mr. Korselt wants to give a peculiar turn to Mr. Hilbert's doctrine in that he understands it as a formal theory, as a purely formal system. Whether this explication quite corresponds to Mr. Hilbert's intentions is another question; for all that a lot speaks in favour of it. (Frege, 1971, p. 52)

Clearly Korselt reads Hilbert's axiomatization in a purely formalist way and Frege has some sympathy with this reading though not with formalism. We leave it to the Hilbert scholars to decide when finally Hilbert espoused pure formalism. For Golland this occurred between 1918 and 1922. Our concern here is with the impact of Hilbert's formalism on Debreu. Golland uses Kleene's account of Hilbert's formalism which we extend. In this extended account we attempt to show how formalism, finitism and axiomatics are inextricably linked in the Hilbert programme.

In a purely formalist setting, any axiomatic system has a finite list of primitive, undefined symbols. For instance, 'p', 'q', '~', '&'. These are empty signs, without any signification or meaning. They do not stand for, or refer to, anything. They are not signs. Rather they are meaningless strokes on paper. Next, one has a finite list of rules of syntax. These rules unambiguously determine the well-formed formulae (wffs) of the system. Any wff is finite in length, e.g. 'p' is a wff, '~p' is a wff, 'p~' is not a wff. The finite rules of syntax, when applied to the primitive signs, result in a potentially infinite number of wffs: one can go on indefinitely to construct new finite wffs.

Next one has the process of nominal definition. This enables one to introduce new symbols into the system. Any new symbol (definiendum) must be definable in terms of the primitive symbols or an already constructed wff. For instance $p \rightarrow q$ is defined as $\sim(p \& \sim q)$. Thus any definiendum can in principle be eliminated and replaced by its definiens. The formalist point is that none of these symbols is given any interpretation. To repeat, they are meaningless strokes on paper.

We now proceed with axiomatization in this formalist setting. A short finite list of wffs are selected as axioms. This list is the starting point of the axiomatic process. Once again there is no question of these axioms being intuitively true. On the contrary, not only does the issue of truth not arise, the axioms, being wffs, are meaningless. This chosen list is the basis of the axiomatic system in the following sense. A finite set of rules of inference are specified. By the systematic and unambiguous application of these rules to the axioms, theorems are derived from the axioms. In this way a deductive proof is an effective, mechanical procedure whereby a theorem is derived from the axioms (or previously established theorems) according to these rules of inference. The rules of inference when applied to the axioms can generate a potentially infinite number of theorems. The axioms and theorems form a subset of the wffs. Finally, as Kleene points out, any axiomatic system must meet a number of requirements or constraints, especially consistency and completeness.[3] These conditions are also defined formalistically.[4]

In this fashion, axiomatization, formalism and finitism are inextricably linked in the Hilbert programme. The finitism is evident in the commitment to a finite set of primitive terms, a finite set of rules of inference, a finite set of axioms and a potentially infinite set of theorems. What is of crucial importance to our reading of Debreu is the fact that this finitism was extended by Hilbert to include what he called 'Cantor's paradise'.[4] Cantor's paradise extended mathematics beyond the confines of potential infinity to actual infinity. In Cantorian set theory, with its recourse to actual infinity, a vast range of theorems can be proved which are not provable in the traditional, potentially infinite, mathematical domain. Thus Hilbert's finitism, which includes the paradise of Cantorian infinity, gives the pure mathematician a range of powerful resources not available when one is limited to potential infinity. Contrary to, for instance, the finitism of Poincaré, who limits infinity to potential infinity, Hilbert's finitist dream aims to render the powerful mathematical resources of Cantorian set theory compatible with a strictly finitist base. In short, the Hilbert programme in the 1920s included a deep-seated commitment to what we call the 'Hilbert dream' in a formalist axiomatic setting: the dream of combining finitism with Cantorian infinitist set theory.

Thus far our focus is on pure mathematics. Applied mathematics consists of an interpretation of the formal axiomatic system. It does this by giving its primitive signs specific interpretations. Indeed the same empty, primitive symbol may receive different interpretations. For instance, the symbol 'p' and the symbol 'q' could be interpreted as Boolean sets or as propositional variables. Then the symbol 'p & q' could be interpreted as the intersection of two sets or as the proposition p and q.[5] These specific interpretations are of no concern to the pure mathematician. Pure mathematics operates without them: its mathematical logic is purely formal. In the next two sections we see how Debreu subscribes to this formalist view and in the subsequent sections we will see how Hilbert's finitism is indispensable to Debreu's economics.

3. Debreu and the Hilbert Programme

Weintraub (2002) is certainly correct in noting that the term formalism as used in economics frequently has little to do with the above logico-mathematical notion of formalism. Rather it is usually used to signal the mathematization of economics, a move which was indispensable for Walras, Pareto and other theoretical economists at the turn of the twentieth century. Moreover, Weintraub is correct in emphasizing the major shift in this process of mathematization, which occurred in the 1950s, effected by Debreu and others. This shift hinges on the movement away from the exploitation of differential calculus and from analogies between mechanics and economics to the AA, pioneered by Debreu and others, in their articulation of the neo-Walrasian, general equilibrium theory. However, we differ from Weintraub's analysis of this shift. He excludes the foundational, finitist dimension of the Hilbert programme and analyses the shift in terms of its axiomatic dimension. In our opinion this analysis is incomplete as a reconstruction of the mathematization of economics in the post World War II period, which has important interpretative consequences as we will argue. Our thesis is that Hilbert's formalism along with his finitism, which includes the Hilbert dream of pure mathematicians not being expelled from Cantor's paradise, is closely interwoven with his axiomatization and that this trinity played an indispensable role in the Debreu shift in the mathematization of economics (Debreu, 1984, 1991). Firstly, we argue that if the analysis of the Debreu mathematization of economics is limited to an axiomatic system, there is nothing distinctively Hilbertian to this axiomatizion. Secondly, by recourse to Debreu's own work and as borne out by Ingrao and Israel's (1990) scholarly analysis, we show how a Hilbert-type formalism informs Debreu. Thirdly, we show how his use of mathematics, particularly his use of Cantorian set theory, is rooted in the Hilbert finitist programme which incorporates Hilbert's dream. If Debreu were to follow his celebrated countryman's dream of a different finitist programme, namely that of Poincaré, he would have developed an altogether different shift in the mathematization of economics.

The first point is relatively easy to establish. Numerous logicians, philosophers of mathematics and practising mathematicians who do not share Hilbert's formalism fully acknowledge the indispensable role of the axiomatic method for pure mathematics. For instance, Poincaré, the most outstanding mathematician at the turn of the twentieth century, while acknowledging the value of axiomatic systems, rejected Hilbert's formalism. Similarly Frege, the leading logician of the period, while rejecting Hilbert's formalism, extensively used the AA. Thus Weintraub's emphasis on axiomatic systems, to the utter neglect of foundational finitism, certainly draws our attention to the value of the AA. However, there is nothing distinctively Hilbertian in acknowledging this value. Thus Debreu, in stressing the contribution that axiomatization makes to logical rigour and clarity, is merely acknowledging this value, which was recognized by the most eminent mathematicians and logicians of the first third of the twentieth century. There was virtually no debate on the value of axiomatization, rather the debate ranged over whether or not a strictly formalist account of axiomatization was adequate to the whole of pure mathematics – a thesis which became central to the Hilbert programme and in that sense is more distinctively Hilbertian than axiomatization normally understood.[6]

Debreu is fully aware of the numerous advantages of axiomatization. In Debreu
(1986) he identified some of these advantages. They include 'the pursuit of logical
rigour', 'generality', 'exactness of formulation', 'clarity' and 'simplicity' (1986,
pp. 1265–1266). In this context he gives a brief 'schema' of an axiomatized
economic theory and adds:

> According to this schema, an axiomatized theory has a mathematical form that
> is *completely separated from its economics content. If one removes the economic
> interpretation of the primitive concepts* ... its bare mathematical structure must
> still stand. ... The divorce of form and content immediately yields a new theory
> whenever a novel interpretation of a primitive concept is discussed. (Debreu,
> 1986, p. 1265)

In this passage we see the formalist usage of key terms like 'primitive concept',
'axioms', 'interpretation of primitive concepts', 'a novel interpretation' and
'separation of form from content'. According to Debreu, axiomatization, understood
in the formalist way, 'contributed powerfully to the rapid expression of mathematical
economics after World War II' (1986, p. 1265).[7]

This same formalist understanding is introduced in his 1959 monograph *The
Theory of Value.* Here he asserts:

> Allegiance to rigor dictates the axiomatic form of the analysis where the theory,
> in the strict sense, is logically entirely disconnected from its interpretations. In
> order to bring out fully this disconnectedness all the definitions, all the hypotheses
> and the main results of the theory, in the strict sense, are distinguished by italics;
> moreover the transition from the informal discussion of interpretations to the
> formal construction of the theory is often marked by one of the expressions 'in
> the language of the theory', 'for the sake of the theory', 'formally'. (Debreu,
> 1959, p. x)

Moreover this formalist agenda is repeated by Debreu in his speech on the occasion
of being conferred with an honorary doctorate by the Friedrich Wilheim University
of Bonn in 1977, which is quoted by Hildenbrand in the introduction to his
collection of Debreu's writings (Debreu, 1983). Clearly Ingrao and Israel (1990)
are correct in summing up Debreu's formalism as follows:

> Debreu's view is the theory's formal structure must be constructed axiomatically
> and with no reference to the interpretative values of the concepts. The axiomatic
> system is... to adopt the Bourbaki viewpoint and language of *an empty scheme
> of 'possible realities'.* (p. 285)

They go on to add:

> Debreu's approach ... involves – in accordance with the canons of the axiomatic
> approach – emptying the theory radically and uncompromisingly of all empirical
> reference... Empirical meaning and interpretation may be attached only *a
> posteriori.* (p. 303)

Later when discussing the issue of the existence of equilibrium they insist that:

> Debreu not only pursues the axiomatic approach suggested by von Neumann but
> pushes it to its extreme consequences by his adherence to the canons of 'the
> modern formalist school of mathematics'. (p. 303)

Our thesis is that by insisting only on the AA and ignoring the foundational finitism
of the Hilbert programme, Weintraub is severely limiting our understanding of
Debreu's contribution to the mathematization of economics. Weintraub's reading,
solely through the lenses of an axiomatic system, fails to give due acknowledgement
to the radical formalist nature of Debreu's axiomatization of economics. From the
point of view of economics, why is such a purely formalist conception so important
for Debreu? The answer lies in his view of what it is to do economics in a way
which attains the highest standards of rigour outlined by logic and mathematics. If
one does not do economics in a purely formal way one is confused and lacking in
mathematical rigour.

3.1 Debreu's Formalistic Approach to Economics: The Walrasian Propaedeutic

One important difference between Debreu and Weintraub's Debreu is that Weintraub
reads the strict formalist approach as part of 'the image' of science, whereas for
Debreu it is 'a severe test', which much of economics in its historical setting fails to
pass (Debreu, 1986, p. 1265). In other words Debreu takes strict formalism seriously
and sees in it more than an image. In this connection one might be inclined to agree
with Weintraub: like the just man of the gospels who falls seven times daily, strict
formalists will inevitably fail to adhere to their image of science. For instance, for
the strict formalist, any formal system is as 'good' as any other, provided it is
consistent. Thus the formalist, at the level of pure theory, cannot account for what
is geometric in a formal system of geometry or what is economic in a purely
formal axiomatization of economics. Mathematically, both are simply different
purely formal axiomatic systems, with neither geometric nor economic content.

Undoubtedly the purely formalist demands are very exacting. As we have already
seen, Hilbert's *Foundations of Geometry* of 1899 was taken as the clearest exemplar
of a purely formal AA and thus served as the practical guide for its implementation.
Given this, it is useful to see how Frege, in his correspondence with Hilbert, raised
the issue of the proper geometic 'content' of Hilbert's axiomatization of geometry.
In this connection Frege draws a sharp distinction between definitions, axioms and
a third kind of proposition. For our present purposes we focus on this third kind of
proposition. These are

> the explicatory propositions which, however, I should not like to consider as
> belonging to mathematics itself but instead should be relegated to the preamble
> or propaedeutic. (Frege, 1971, p. 8)

In this propaedeutic case, mathematicians are, strictly speaking, neither defining nor
asserting axioms. Rather in the propaedeutic, the mathematician works by 'hints'
based on 'co-operative understanding'. Thus these propaedeutic sentences cannot
be used in proofs 'for they lack the requisite precision and because of this I should
like to relegate them to the preamble'. These propaedeutic assertions guide the

choice of geometric primitive terms and axioms used by Hilbert. Thus, as a piece of pure geometry, Hilbert's axiomatic system is purely formal in that its proofs depend solely on its formal axioms and formal rules of inference. However, it is geometric because of its geometric propaedeutic. Geometry inspired it.

Our thesis is that the Walrasian programme serves as a propaedeutic in Debreu's axiomatization of economics and that this approach is compatible with the exemplar of formal axiomatization, namely Hilbert's axiomatization of geometry. We are not claiming that Debreu intentionally followed Frege. Rather we are saying that the manner in which the axiomatization is actually carried out is accurately described as using a propaedeutic strategy. His *Theory of Value* is, as Ingrao and Israel point out,

> consciously inspired by a group of well-defined economic themes, and its explicit reference to the 'tradition of the Lausanne school' is proof of this. However, from the moment in which the theory is born and develops all links with its empirical starting point are severed. (Ingrao and Israel, 1990, p. 284)

We would prefer to say that from the moment in which mathematical theory is operable, its propaedeutic links to Walras and the Lausanne school are mathematically inoperable; they belong to the preamble. Indeed Debreu suggests this when he says 'although an axiomatic theory may flaunt the separation of its mathematical form and its economic content in print, their interaction is sometimes close in the discovery and elaboration phases' (Debreu, 1986, p. 1266). As already noted in the previous section, in his *Theory of Value* he explicitly notes such a distinction: he uses various phrases to indicate 'the transition from the *informal* discussion of the *formal* construction of the theory' (Debreu, 1959, p. x; italics ours). Clearly Debreu's axiomatization of economics is based on the propaedeutic role of Walrasian themes and, as Frege noted, these propaedeutic themes do not form part of the axiomatic system. However, they are required to show what is economic in the formal axiomatic system.

3.2 *Debreu and Two Conflicting Finitisms*

We now turn to Debreu's finitism. As is well known, the crisis in the foundations of arithmetic arose from a series of paradoxes which emerged in the use of Cantorian set theory in the logicist, foundational programme. In light of these paradoxes some, such as Frege, abandoned the logicist programme, while others, such as Russell, sought to resolve the paradoxes. Mathematicians and logicians frequently diverged in their diagnosis of the source of the paradoxes and in their proposed solutions. Poincaré, however, regarded Cantorian set theory, with its recourse to novel methods of proof and infinities of infinity, the source of the paradoxes. For Poincaré there was a crucial difference between saying the sequence of natural numbers is potentially infinite, in the sense that this sequence can be continued on indefinitely, and saying, with Cantor, that these are different actual infinities: for instance since the infinite set of rational numbers is a proper subset of the infinite set of real numbers, there is more than one infinity. In philosophy of mathematics it is often said that this difference hinges on whether mathematical infinity is, *à la* Poincaré, merely potential, i.e. one can continue on indefinitely, or whether, *à la* Cantor, infinity is actual.

For epistemological reasons which we will discuss in the next section and, in order to resolve the paradoxes, Poincaré proposed a specific finitist solution, which included what we call Poincaré's finitist principle for doing mathematics. This principle reads as follows:

> A theorem must be capable of proof, but since we ourselves are finite, we can only deal with finite objects. Thus, even though the notion of infinity plays a role in the statement of a theorem, *there must be no reference to it in the proof:* otherwise the proof is impossible. (Poincaré, 1963 p. 66; italics ours)

He communicates his principle by means of an example. According to Poincaré, the Cantorians are charmed by the rigour of the proof of Zermelo's theorem proving 'that space is capable of being transformed into a well-ordered set' (Poincaré, 1963, p. 67). Poincaré, however, is not impressed. He responds 'you say you can transform space into a well-ordered set. Well! Transform it.' The Cantorians respond: 'it would take too long'. Poincaré in turn responds: 'Then at least show us that someone with enough time and patience could execute the transformation'. But Cantorians reply: 'No, we cannot, *because the number of operations to be performed is infinite,* it is even greater than aleph zero' (1963; italics ours). Poincaré terminates the dialogue with 'the theorem is not proved; because any genuine proof must be carried out in a finite number of steps' (1963, p. 67).

In this fashion Poincaré's finitism is not simply pruning the trees in the domain of pure mathematics. Rather it is transforming what Hilbert later calls 'Cantor's paradise' into a mathematical slum in need of ruthless clearing for the development of genuine pure mathematics. In particular, it rules out recourse to theorems like that of Zermelo in pure mathematics. In contemporary terminology, Poincaré is advocating a constructivist approach to the methods of pure mathematics. In line with his finitism, any proof is an effective procedure, which implies that it must consist of a finite number of steps. However, the subsequent use of any theorem like that of Zermelo in a proof are illegitimate because they presuppose actual infinities which in principle cannot be cashed out in a finite number of steps.

Hilbert, on the other hand, felt that any such finitist solution was too high a price to pay. Hence his famous statement in his 1925 address 'No one shall drive us out of the paradise that Cantor has created for us'. In this connection he appears to agree with Poincaré's diagnosis of the crisis in the foundations of arithmetic:

> We must establish throughout mathematics the same certitude for our deductions as exists in elementary number theory, which no one doubts and where contradictions and paradoxes arise only through our own carelessness. (Hilbert, 1925, p. 51)

In Poincaré's terminology the paradoxes are avoided when we limit ourselves to potential infinity. Nonetheless, despite his commitment to this kind of finitism, Hilbert insisted that Cantorian mathematics can be incorporated into this finite framework. In Hilbert's finitism, as Brown puts it: 'we want to keep the extraordinary beauty, power and utility of classical (Cantorian) mathematics but we also want to incorporate it in such a way that we can have full confidence that no paradoxes will arise' (Brown, 2002, p. 66).

Brown, like most other scholars, points out that Hilbert's solution was ingenious. The Cantorian part of pure mathematics can be added to finite mathematics as an 'ideal element' which rounds off the finite in the sense that the Cantorian part can be used to derive new, but finite, results. The introduction of ideal elements is not entirely novel in the history of mathematics. For instance, to use Brown's example, in projective geometry almost every pair of lines intersect at a point. However, there are exceptions, namely parallel lines. Projective geometry is rounded off by the introduction of ideal points, namely the points at infinity. Now even parallel lines intersect at a point, namely a point at infinity. The introduction of points at infinity in projective geometry 'eliminates the need to state exceptions to theorems. In general it simplifies theorems and proofs.... Points at infinity are taken to be mere fictions, justified by their enormous power and utility' (Brown, 2002, p. 66).

Of course one cannot add ideal elements whenever one feels like it. As Epstein and Carnielli (2000) point out: Hilbert's criteria for adding ideal elements were '(1) they must not lead to any contradiction and (2) they must be fruitful' (Epstein and Carnielli, 2000, p. 153). In this fashion Hilbert, contrary to Poincaré, dreams of retaining 'Cantor's paradise' and, in the course of attempting to realize this dream, ingenious developments occurred in the foundations of mathematics.

The question is how, if at all, Hilbert's finitism is relevant to economics. As we have already seen according to Weintraub, Hilbert's axiomatics are crucial but his finitism is irrelevant. We now challenge this conclusion.

4. Path Dependence and Lock-in: A Methodological Analysis of Debreu's Mathematization of Economics

The process of the mathematization of economics, initiated at the turn of the twentieth century by Walras and others, emerged under the influence of analogies drawn between theoretical economics and theoretical mechanics. These analogies facilitated, on one hand, the conception of an economic agent as a utility maximizer and, on the other, the exploitation of calculus as a means of formalizing, in a rigorous mathematical way, this notion of a rational economic agent. The mathematization of economics took a novel turn with the construction by Debreu and others of general equilibrium theory. In this connection we emphasize, with Debreu, the role of the novel mathematical tools, based on Cantorian set theory, crucial to this turn. Methodologically, this turn is rooted in the Hilbert finitist programme which, despite the crisis in earlier foundational programmes, retained the dream of reconciling finitist mathematics with Cantor's paradise. In particular, Debreu developed economic theory along a particular line, namely Hilbert's finitism. If Debreu had developed the mathematization of economics along the lines pointed to by Poincaré's finitism, in particular Poincaré's finitist principle, his theoretical reflections and mathematical tools would be completely different. Poincaré's finitism would, negatively, have excluded recourse to many of the mathematical tools acceptable within Cantor's paradise and, positively, would have exploited the novel mathematical tools of finitist mathematics developed by Church, Turing and others. This difference is succinctly summed up in Vélupillai (2000) which in our view is an excellent and sustained effort at economic theorizing utterly faithful to the Poincaré finitist principle.

> Analogously, as Debreu (1984, p. 268) points out 'one can describe the action of an economic agent by a vector in the commodity space R^l. The fact that the commodity space has the structure of a real vector space is a basic reason for the success of the mathematization of economic theory. In particular convexity properties of sets in R^l, a recurring theme in the theory of general equilibrium, can be fully exploited.' As we will see in what follows 'one can also describe the action of an economic agent' as if 'it' were a Turing machine; in this case the commodity space would have an appropriate recursive structure in which computable and combinatorial properties would be exploited (Velupillai, 2000, p. 2, fn 5).

One may counter-claim that the differences in mathematical tools noted by Velupillai is exaggerated, since Debreu himself welcomes the computable economics of Scarf and others. To quote Debreu:

> In an unanticipated, yet not unprecedented, way greater abstraction brought Walrasian theory closer to concrete applications. When different areas of the field of computable general equilibrium were opened to research at the University of Oslo, at the Cowles Foundation and at the World Bank, the algorithms of Scarf included in their lineage proofs of existence of general economic equilibrium by means of fixed point theorems. (Debreu, 1986, p. 1268)

Thus Debreu sees no incompatibility between his work and computable general equilibrium, based on algorithms, which would render computable economics compatible with the Poincaré finitist principle. However, in Scarf's case this is not the case: Scarf's computable analysis violates the Poincaré finitist principle. As Velupillai demonstrates and as Scarf himself acknowledges, Scarf's analysis is non-constructive and thus violates the Poincaré finitist principle. Vellupillai lets Scarf (1973) speak for himself:

> When applying the algorithm it is, in general, impossible to select an even finer sequence of grids and a convergent sequence of subsimplices. *An algorithm for a digital computer must be basically finite and cannot involve an infinite sequence of successive refinements.* . . . The passage to the limit is the non-constructive aspect of Brouwer's theorem. . . . (Velupillai, 2002, p. 315)

The sentence in italics shows the necessity of rigorously and systematically applying the Poincaré finitist principle but the following sentence concedes that it is not applied. The Poincaré finitist principle demands eternal vigilance with any and every so-called algorithm to ensure that no non-constructive element is smuggled in or tacitly assumed. There are no exceptions to the principle.

Thus Velupillai maintains that 'the claims of some applied computable general equilibrium (CGE) theorists, regarding the constructivity and effectivity of CGE models are unsubstantiated' (Velupillai, 2002, p. 307). In our view, Velupillai's *Computable Economics* is the clearest attempt at the mathematization of economics compatible with the Poincaré finitist principle. Contrary to Debreu, the two programmes are quite divergent: recursion theoretic decision problems replace standard optimization procedures and this leads to undecideable choices, where there 'is no effective procedure to generate preference orderings' (Velupillai, 2000, p. 38). 'Guaranteeing the existence of an optimum is one thing; finding it is another thing; and finding it *tractably* is yet another thing' (p. 61, fn 6). A similar negative result holds for general equilibrium: 'The Walrasian equilibrium will also, in general, be nonconstructive or noneffective (or both). In plain economic terms, this means that the 'price signals' can not be effectively encoded to lead agents in any *systematic* way to make decisions that are necessarily mutually compatible' (Velupillai, 2002, p. 311).

Thus our thesis still stands. At a particular, crucial juncture, Debreu developed economic theory along a particular line, namely the Hilbert finitist way which embraced Cantor's paradise. If he had developed the mathematization of economics along the path pointed to by the Poincaré finitist principle, like Velupillai, he would have ended up with a radically different vision of an economy. To quote Velupillai:

> It is, surely, just an accident of history and the special training of a particular class of individuals, who happened to be interested in the formalization of the subject at crucial junctures in the development of the subject that determined and locked it into choosing the real number system as its domain and set theory as the foundation. (Velupillai, 2002, p. 309)

Debreu, with his practice of the Hilbert finitist programme enshrining Hilbert's dream of Cantor's paradise, was a central figure in this lock-in of theoretical economics. Regrettably Weintraub's analysis in terms of Hilbert's axiomatics without Hilbert's finitism unduly limits the correct interpretation of Debreu's influential contribution to the mathematization of economics.

We can discern a number of parallels or analogies between the success of Debreu's mathematization of economics and Brian Arthur's analysis of technologies in his *Increasing Returns and Path Dependence in the Economy*. In Arthur's words:

> First, *a priori*, we cannot say with accuracy *which* technological structure will 'win' the market.... Second the technology which comes to dominate – the structure that emerges – does not necessarily have to be the 'best' or most efficient; events early on can lock the system into an inferior technological path.... Third once a single-technology structure emerges and becomes self-reinforcing, it is difficult to change it. (Arthur, 2000, p. 46)

In the case of the Debreu mathematization of economics, we cannot *a priori* say which class of mathematical tools will win out in the future. Secondly, at any time the range of mathematical tools that comes to dominate need not necessarily have to be the best; events early on can lock a mathematization programme into an inferior path. Thirdly, once a specific mathematization programme emerges and becomes self-enforcing it is difficult to change. In the next section we address what we consider to be a crucial methodological reason to effect this change.

5. Theoretical Economics and Poincaré Finitism

According to Poincaré, the divergence between his finitism and any other kind of finitism which seeks to locate itself in Cantor's paradise is rooted in a fundamental 'difference of mentality which engenders such divergent views' (Poincaré, 1963, p. 65). This deep-seated difference springs from 'two tendencies among mathematicians in their manner of considering infinity' (1963). Poincaré's finitism is rooted in what we call his anthropological–epistemological principle, namely that we human beings are conceptually bounded in the sense that 'we ourselves are finite and can only deal with finite objects'. In particular, for Poincaré each human mind is subject to the constraint of operating with a finite number of words. 'A man, however talkative he may be, will never in his lifetime utter more than a billion words.' Poincaré envisages a Cantorian objecting on the grounds that such a finitism will illegitimately 'exclude from science the objects whose definition contains a billion and one words'. In other words, the halting point for finitists is arbitrary and thus there is no point excluding Cantorian infinities which are not finitistically, i.e. algorithmically, definable. This Cantorian argument leaves Poincaré 'cold. . . . However talkative a man may be, mankind will still be more talkative and, since we do not know how long mankind will last, we cannot limit beforehand the field of its investigation' (1963). In this sense the Cantorian insight is correct. Nonetheless, according to Poincaré, the field of human research past, present and future 'will always remain limited'. Indeed Poincaré readily concedes that his finitism has no difficulty 'in imagining a mankind much more talkative than ours but still retaining something human'. Despite this, his finitism *refuses to argue on the hypothesis of some infinitely talkative divinity capable of thinking of an infinite number of words in a finite length of time'* (Poincaré, 1963; italics added). Human beings simply do not have the mental capacity of an infinitely knowing divinity, the imaginary creator of Cantor's paradise. To use the terminology of Herbert Simon, for Poincaré, we are bounded rational agents, in that our cognitive abilities are limited by the constraints of finite time and, in particular, our finite linguistic abilities.

Plausible as these arguments may be, one may feel that these profound differences in the philosophy of mathematics have no relevance for economic methodology. Disputes about finitism in the philosophy of pure mathematics have nothing to do with the genuine concerns of economic methodologists who encounter contemporary economic reality, including economic practice or the history of economic thought. Our thesis is that these disputes are relevant and the relevance is evident in the use of mathematical models, especially in the mathematical model of general equilibrium as articulated by Debreu.

As we have already seen, this model is a piece of applied mathematics. In our view, whatever the merits or otherwise of Poincaré finitism for pure mathematics, his anthropological–epistemological principle is a most coherent basis for the *application of mathematics* to economics. This principle, when applied to the domain of the mathematical modelling of a complex economic system of millions of agents operating in overlapping local, national and international institutions, implies that any recourse to the powerful mathematical tools of Cantorian mathematics, which are not restricted to Poincaré's finitism, simply gives us a God-like view of the economy. This infinite god-like conception, however, is of no pragmatic use to us human beings. Its picture of the economic world is not conveyable in finitist terms. It is merely the ideology of an infinitely knowing God which has no practical use to us human beings, except perhaps serving the ideological purposes, in the Marxist sense, of interested parties.

Moreover, it should be noted that the Poincaré anthropological–epistemological principle does not imply any message of doom for the mathematical modelling of a complex economic system. We know from the history of twentieth-century mathematics that since the 1930s a host of intriguing, finitist mathematical tools have been developed, ranging from a universal Turing machine to Church's lambda calculus. These developments offer mathematical economists an extensive range of alternative tools to those of Cantorian mathematics, exploited by Debreu and others in their endeavours in constructing a mathematical model of a complex economy. In our opinion, Velupillai's work represents a pioneering and innovative project in mathematical economics which is compatible with the Poincaré anthropological–epistemological principle.

In this connection one may speculate that this was part of Poincaré's reasons for responding in a less than an enthusiastic way to Walras's request to him to endorse his programme of the mathematization of economics. As is clear from Poincaré's very brief correspondence, he had no objections in principle to the mathematization of economics but expressed reservations about Walras's specific programme.[8] Be that as it may, the Poincaré anthropological–epistemological principle, while rendering the Debreu articulation of the neo-Walrasian programme pragmatically useless, opens up a host of challenges to theoretical economists who wish to construct finitist mathematical models of economic systems and rational economic agents.

6. Concluding Reflections

In this paper we have critically examined the role of formalism in orthodox economics by concentrating on the work of one of the central architects of mathematical economics and general equilibrium theory, Gerard Debreu. We have shown how Debreu's conception of formalism is closely aligned to that of Hilbert, where axiomatization and Hilbertian finitism which incorporates Cantor's infinite paradise and formalism are inextricably linked. Economically speaking, for Debreu, recourse to formalism is demanded at the theoretical level in order to avoid confused thought on one hand and to attain the highest degree of logico-mathematical rigour on the other. Moreover, by recourse to Frege's notion of propaedeutic, we have shown how the neo-Walrasian vision of theoretical economics informs Debreu's axiomatization: the neo-Walrasian propaedeutic is given a rigorous formulation in Debreu's work.

Heterodox economists fully agree that economic theorizing should not be confused and should avoid logical inconsistency. However, economic theorizing has other indispensable roles, such as enabling economists to describe as accurately and precisely as possible economic systems, including economic agents and institutions, and to analyse how these operate and interact with each other and to analyse how external institutions influence these. The formalist approach to economics as exemplified in the work of Debreu appears not to be very relevant to these other indispensable tasks of pure economics and hence the frustration of heterodoxy and the search for a methodological critique of orthodox formalism. Against this, the orthodox methodologist could argue that economic formalism is not irrelevant to these additional roles of economic theorizing. On the contrary, it provides a coherent framework for the construction of models in the economic analyses demanded above and thereby enables economists to avoid confused or incoherent analyses. In this way orthodox formalism is indispensable to economic models analysing real economics. Methodologically, however, it is precisely at this juncture that we, as causal holists,[9] raise fundamental methodological objections to this indispensability argument. The orthodox framework cannot act as an indispensable constraint in the construction of models in economic analyses of actual economics. Neither can it supply economists with adequate resources for describing actual economics. The orthodox framework, *as a piece of pure mathematics,* certainly provides a coherent framework, but this framework is limited to the infinitist parameters of Cantor's paradise. *As a piece of pure economic theory*, this orthodox framework is inadequate in any economic analysis which recognizes the finite dimensions of the rationality of economic agents on one hand and the finite dimensions of economics, economic institutions and economic resources on the other. Economically, as distinct from mathematically, the orthodox framework 'is as idle as a painted ship upon a painted ocean'; it is incapable of serving the economic analysis of finite economic agents and finite economies. The framework is only operable, in Poincaré's words, for 'some infinitely talkative divinity capable of thinking an infinite number of words in a finite length of time' (Poincaré, 1963, p. 65). For us finite human beings, with finite mental capacities, there is no way of rendering the orthodox framework pragmatically operable in the real finite world of bounded rational economic agents operating in open-ended, but finite, economic systems. The domain of application of the orthodox framework is the non-constructivist domain of Cantor's paradise, which cannot be given any interpretation in our finite world of rational economic agents operating in real, finite historical time frames. History does matter to economic theory, economic time is finite and economic rational agents are thereby limited. Consequently, as pointed out by Poincaré, any recourse to the non-constructivist dimension of Cantor's paradise is impossible in this historical time perspective. The orthodox framework, as pioneered by Debreu and other non-constructivist mathematical economists and theoreticians, fails to meet this finite time requirement.

In particular, because of its recourse to the non-constructivist dimension of Cantor's paradise, the orthodox notion of equilibrium cannot be given an economic interpretation in a finite, economic world. The Debreu proof of the existence of general equilibrium merely establishes the existence of a non-constructive element in a Cantorian infinite set. Precisely because it is non-constructive, this equilibrium *cannot be given an economic interpretation as an entity in a finite economic world which either initiates or undergoes change in finite historical time or indeed acts in any regulative or causal fashion.* General equilibrium theory is merely a mathematical idealization which is populated by non-historical agents, with rational capacities beyond the bounds of our limited time frames. Its usefulness as a tool of analysis for real economics in actual historical time is therefore negligible to non-existent.

In this fashion causal holism furnishes heterodoxy with the methodological means of correctly analysing the role of formalism in economics and thereby liberates heterodoxy to explore, in a non-formalist way, bounded finite economic agents operating in a complex world in real historical time. The causal holist opposition to formalism, however, does not imply that causal holism is in principle opposed to the use of mathematical models in heterodox analyses of actual economies. For causal holists, the acceptance of a mathematical model depends on two factors: firstly, its epistemological–methodological presuppositions, and secondly, whether or not it is descriptively adequate. We have argued that orthodox equilibrium theory meets neither of these requirements: it is not adequate to the task of describing complex economic systems located in actual historical time. Time matters to economics and a crucial challenge for heterodoxy is to systematically and objectively explore the complexity of economic systems in actual, finite, historical time. In this connection we have argued that Davidson's non-ergodicity is a paradigm example of such research (Davidson, 1996). It challenges the economist to analyse in a non-reductionist way rational decisions in the circumstances of radical uncertainty. Causal holism has attempted to construct a methodological framework which recognizes that there is no essence to economic rationality: just as there are different games with different rules, there are different economic domains with different criteria of rationality. The challenge facing heterodoxy is to identify these domains and to construct models of rationality descriptively adequate to the rationalities of the decisions in these domains. Formalism as characterized in orthodox neoclassical economics is of no avail in this central challenge.

Acknowledgements

We would like to thank Donald George for his invitation to contribute to the special issue, and our colleague Vela Velupillai for all his generosity, friendship and support.

Notes

1. There has been a long tradition of critical discussion about the role of mathematics in economics, but this has intensified since the 'formalist revolution' in the post World War II period. For a representative sample of critical comment since the 1970s, see Leontief (1971), Phelps Brown (1972), Worswick (1972), Ward (1972), Kaldor (1972, 1975), Woo (1986), McCloskey (1994), Dennis (1995), Blaug (2002), Hutchison (1977, 2000). A number of economic journals in recent years have also

devoted special issues or part of particular issues to addressing formalism or the relation of mathematics to economics – see for instance *Economic Journal* (108, November 1998, pp. 1826–1869), *Journal of Economic Studies* (27, No. 4–5, 2000, Special Issue), *Journal of Post Keynesian Economics* (25, Summer 2004, pp. 527–598).

2. The concept of the 'image of mathematics' as used by Weintraub is borrowed from the historian of mathematics, Leo Corry, who in turn acknowledges its source in the work of the historian of science Yehuda Elkana (1981). See Weintraub (2002, p. 2).

3. The axioms must be shown to be independent of one another, i.e. the simplest set of axioms is preferable. This is another condition.

4. In an address delivered to the congress of the Westphalian Mathematical Society, in June 1925, held in Münster in honour of Weierstrass, Hilbert proclaims 'no one shall drive us out of the paradise that Cantor has created for us'. This address is a beautiful summary of what we call Hilbert's dream in a strictly formalist setting.

5. Again logically one should be more precise: p and q is the form of a conjunctive proposition.

6. Despite the fact that formalism is associated with others, it is nonetheless intimately associated with the Hilbert programme of the 1920s.

7. Having made the point that formalism is a severe test Debreu goes on to state 'the pursuit of logical rigor *also* contributed powerfully to the rapid expansion of mathematical economics after World War II' (p. 1265, italics ours). Clearly the word 'also' justifies our claim.

8. The authors are currently working on an analysis of the Poincaré–Walras correspondence related to the themes of this paper.

9. Causal holism is the term we use to refer to our methodological position.

References

Arthur, W.B. (2000) *Increasing Returns and Path Dependence in the Economy*. Ann Arbor, MI: University of Michigan Press.

Blaug, M. (2000) Ugly currents in modern economics. In U. Maki (ed.), *Facts and Fiction in Economics*. Cambridge: Cambridge University Press.

Boylan, T.A. and O'Gorman, P.F. (1991) The critique of equilibrium theory in economic methodology. *International Studies in the Philosophy of Science* 5: 131–142.

Boylan, T.A. and O'Gorman, P.F. (1995) *Beyond Rhetoric and Realism: Towards a Reformulation of Economic Methodology*. London: Routledge.

Boylan, T.A. and O'Gorman, P.F. (1997a) Kaldor on method: a challenge to contemporary methodology. *Cambridge Journal of Economics* 21: 503–518.

Boylan, T.A. and O'Gorman, P.F. (1997b) Critical realism and economics: a causal holist critique. *Ekonimia* 1: 9–21. Reprinted in S. Fleetwood (ed.), *Critical Realism in Economics: Development and Debate* (pp. 137–150). London: Routledge.

Boylan, T.A. and O'Gorman, P.F. (2001) Causal holism and economic methodology: theories, models and explanation. *Revue Internationale de Philosophe* (Special Issue) 55: 395–405.

Boylan, T.A. and O'Gorman, P.F. (2005) Fleetwood on causal holism: clarification and critique. *Cambridge Journal of Economics* 30: 123–135.

Brown, J.R. (2002) *Philosophy of Mathematics: An Introduction to the World of Proofs and Pictures*. London: Routledge.

Corry, L. (1996) *Modern Algebra and the Rise of Mathematical Structures*. Boston, MA: Birkhauser.

Davidson, P. (1996) Economics and reality. *Journal of Post Keynesian Economics* 18: 479–508.

Debreu, G. (1959) *Theory of Value: An Axiomatic Analysis of Economic Equilibrium*. New York: Wiley.

Debreu, G. (1984) Economic theory in the mathematical mode. *American Economic Review* 74: 267–278.

Debreu, G. (1986) Theoretical models: mathematical form and economic content. *Econometrica* 54: 1259–1270.

Debreu, G. (1991) The mathematization of economic theory. *American Economic Review* 81: 1–7.

Dennis, K. (1995) A logical critique of mathematical formalism in economics. *Journal of Economic Methodology* 2: 181–199.

Elkana, Y. (1981) A programmatic attempt at an anthropology of knowledge. In E. Mendelsohn and Y. Elkana (eds), *Sciences and Culture*. Dordrecht: Reidal.

Epstein, R.L. and Carnielli, W.A. (eds) (2000) *Computability, Computable Functions, Logic and the Foundations of Mathematics* (2nd edn). Belmont, CA: Wadsworth/Thomson Learning.

Fleetwood, S. (ed.) (1999) *Critical Realism in Economics: Development and Debate*. London: Routledge.

Frege, G. (1971) *On the Foundations of Geometry and Formal Theories of Arithmetic* (trans. E.H.W. Kluge). New Haven, CT: Yale University Press.

Golland, L.A. (1996) Formalism in economics. *Journal of the History of Economic Thought* 18: 1–12.

Hilbert, D. (1899) *Foundations of Geometry* (trans. L. Unger). La Salle, IL: Open Court.

Hilbert, D. (1925) On the infinite. In R.L. Epstein and W.D. Carnielli (eds) (2000) *Computability, Computable Functions, Logic, and the Foundations of Mathematics* (pp. 44–58). Belmont, CA: Wadsworth/Thompson Learning.

Hutchison, T.W. (1977) *Knowledge and Ignorance in Economics*. Oxford: Basil Blackwell.

Hutchison, T.W. (2000) *On the Methodology of Economics and the Formalist Revolution*. Cheltenham: Edward Elgar.

Ingrao, B. and Israel, G. (1990) *The Invisible Hand: Economic Theory in the History of Science*. Cambridge, MA: MIT Press.

Kaldor, N. (1972) The irrelevance of equilibrium economics. *Economic Journal* 82: 1237–1255.

Kaldor, N. (1975) What is wrong with economic theory. *Quarterly Journal of Economics* 89: 347–357.

Lawson, T. (1997) *Economics and Reality*. London: Routledge.

Lawson, T. (2003) *Reorienting Economics*. London: Routledge.

Leontief, W. (1971) Theoretical assumptions and nonobserved facts. *American Economic Review* 62: 1–7.

Lewis, P. (ed.) (2004) *Transforming Economics: Perspectives on the Critical Realist Project*. London: Routledge.

McCloskey, D.N. (1994) *Knowledge and Persuasion in Economics*. Cambridge: Cambridge University Press.

Mirowski, P. (1989) *More Heat than Light*. Cambridge: Cambridge University Press.

Phelps Brown, E.H. (1972) The underdevelopment of economics. *Economic Journal* 82: 1–10.

Poincaré, H. (1963) *Mathematics and Science. Last Essays* (trans. J.W. Boduc). Dover: New York.

Punzo, L. (1991) The school of mathematical formalism and the Viennes circle of mathematical economics. *Journal of the History of Economic Thought* 13: 1–18.

Scarf, H. (1973) *The Computation of Economic Equilibria*. New Haven, CT: Yale University Press.

Velupillai, K. (2000) *Computable Economics*. Oxford: Oxford University Press.

Velupillai, K. (2002) Effectivity and constructivity in economic theory. *Journal of Economic Behaviour and Organization* 49: 307–325.

Ward, B. (1972) *What's Wrong with Economics?* London: Macmillan.

Weintraub, E.R. (1979) *Microfoundations: The Compatability of Microeconomics and Macroeconomics*. Cambridge: Cambridge University Press.

Weintraub, E.R. (1985) *General Equilibrium Analysis: Studies in Appraisal*. Cambridge: Cambridge University Press.

Weintraub, E.R. (1988a) Axiomatisches mißverstandnis. *Economic Journal* 108: 1837–1847.

Weintraub, E.R. (1988b) From rigour to axiomatics: the marginalization of Griffith C. Evans. In M. Morgan and M. Rutherford (eds), *On the Transformation of American Economics: From Interwar Pluralism to Postwar Noeclassicism* (pp. 227–259). Durham, NC: Duke University Press.

Weintraub, E.R. (2002) *How Economics became a Mathematical Science*. Durham, NC: Duke University Press.

Woo, H.K. (1986) *What's Wrong with Formalization in Economics? An Epistemological Critique*. Newark, CA: Victoria Press.

Worswick, G.D.N. (1972) Is progress of economic science possible? *Economic Journal* 82: 73–86.

3

VARIETY OF METHODOLOGICAL APPROACH IN ECONOMICS

Sheila C. Dow

University of Stirling

1. Introduction

The discipline of economics is continually changing, requiring a re-examination of the concepts of orthodox economics and heterodox economics. The particular feature of recent change which this paper examines is the appearance of increasing variety, or plurality, in economics, in particular in economic theory, and what this implies for heterodox economics.

In this exercise, we can benefit from the unusual degree of reflection on the state of economics during the recent millennium. Weintraub's (1999) approach to the subject explicitly drew on modern developments in historiography, which acknowledge that different histories can be written from different perspectives; no historical account can claim to be the one 'true' account. The emphasis therefore was on the variety of perspectives in economics and, by implication, variety in economics itself. Indeed, such an account provides implicit support for pluralism, i.e. the argument for, or celebration of, variety. But if economics is pluralistic, how are we to understand it as a discipline? And does plurality spell the end of methodology on one hand, or set out an agenda for a new methodological discourse on the other? Does plurality mean that criticism has no role ('anything goes'), or does it require a redrawing of the framework for criticism? What opportunities are offered by pluralism?

The role for plurality had already arisen in earlier exercises in looking forward to the future of economics. In 1991, the *Economic Journal* marked the occasion of the first issue of its second century by inviting leading economists to reflect on what the future held for the discipline. Among the prescient themes which emerged were the following, each of which was explored by several contributors:

- the opening of economics to input from, as well as input to, other disciplines, notably sociology and psychology (see also Allen, 2000);
- increasing specialisation within economics (and thus of conferences, journals, etc.) leading to fragmentation of the community of economists;

- increasing cohesion around methodological and theoretical principles, with a move away from the type of divide seen in the monetarist–Keynesian debates.

John Pencavel (1991) concluded that these seemingly opposing trends would be compatible if we think of economic ideas as being diverse and competing freely in competitive markets. He used the term 'pluralistic' to describe the outcome, which he welcomed as reducing the scope for '[p]rofessional tyranny' (Pencavel, 1991, p. 87), by implication an imperfection in the market for ideas. But plurality is not universally welcomed, since it raises concerns as to how the different types of theory can be put together. Blanchard and Fischer (1989, p. 505), for example, had referred to it as being 'logically uncomfortable'.

The concept of plurality has been explored more widely in recent years, both within and beyond economics. It is conventional now to remark that we live in a pluralist society, for example. Since economics is a social science, and particularly given the greater interface with sociology, it would not be surprising to find evidence of plurality also in economics. But there has further been the development in the economic methodology literature of the argument for plurality, i.e. pluralism. This literature, further, has clarified the different meanings of the term, out of which we might understand the different identifications of, and attitudes towards, plurality, as well as its implications. These developments in the field of methodology are just part of the increasing specialisation within fields in economics, which itself raises issues of meaning, and thus of communication.

The purpose of this paper is to try to overcome some of the communication difficulties across specialisations (including methodology) in order to consider variety in economics. First we review the evidence on variety. We then probe further what is meant by plurality at different levels which need to be distinguished (reality, methodology, method, theory), and then consider the arguments for and against pluralism, starting with Caldwell's (1982) seminal contribution to the modern discourse. This discussion throws the spotlight on a range of important issues, including the relation between mathematical formalism and plurality. We also consider schools of thought as a particular form of plurality. Here it is relevant to consider the role of Kuhn's analysis in relation to plurality and pluralism. In particular, while the arguments for plurality are strong, it is argued further that unstructured pluralism or eclecticism, understood as an absence of selection criteria, or 'anything goes', is antithetical to the building up of knowledge.

It is concluded that it would be helpful (for our understanding of the current state of economics with its variety of approaches to theory and evidence, for communications between different approaches and for future developments in the discipline) for the scope for both openness and constructive critique to be more widely discussed. This would imply that more economists be aware of, and discuss more, the architecture of the discipline. Indeed, it will be argued that, while we observe variety at the level of theory and evidence, the reasons for such variety also justify variety at the level both of method and of methodology. While their characteristics may change, the concepts of orthodox economics and heterodox economics are still relevant as a way of capturing variety at the meta-methodological level.

2. Evidence of Plurality in Economics

We start by considering how far, and in what way, economics may be said to be pluralistic, drawing on the wide range of commentaries which have appeared in the recent literature. In order to consider how far modern economics is fragmented, it is useful to compare it with the recent history of economics, and indeed most of these commentaries have taken such an approach.

The conventional account (see for example Colander, 2000a; Goodwin, 2000) characterises the 1970s–1980s as a period of fierce debate between different schools of thought, often epitomised by the monetarist–Keynesian debates. The differences are characterised as being policy-focused and, ultimately, ideological. But contemporary accounts from that period identified a wider range of schools of thought, which were differentiated more by methodological approach than by ideology alone: mainstream economics, post-Keynesian economics, institutionalist economics, neo-Austrian economics, Marxian economics and so on. There were differences as to how to characterise mainstream economics. Weintraub (1985) and Backhouse (1991) saw it as being unified in terms of the principles of general equilibrium theory (see also Dow, 1985). But Phelps (1990), Mair and Miller (1991) and later Snowdon *et al.* (1994) could identify schools of thought within mainstream economics (such as monetarism, new classical economics, real business cycle theory and new Keynesian economics).

The most notable change identified in the literature some 20 years later has been a process of increasing fragmentation within mainstream economics, going beyond the schools of thought identified earlier. Colander (2000b) for example focused on the movement of economics in the direction of handling increasing complexity. He noted a growing divergence from formal general equilibrium models for policy purposes, which was inevitably a force for fragmentation, and predicted a move towards more contextual microfoundations, which would reinforce that trend. He had already announced the 'death' of neoclassical economics as a useful category (Colander, 2000a). As predicted in the centennial *Economic Journal* issue, the growth of game theory, experimental economics, evolutionary economics, behavioural economics, complexity economics and so on had meant that the mainstream of economics could no longer be identified as a single theoretical system.

Davis (2006) offers an explanation for this development in terms of a cyclical process of trade in ideas, whereby variety emerges when imports exceed exports. Thus, many of these developments in mainstream economics can be seen as an adaptation designed to incorporate ideas from other approaches in economics (which had been questioning the rational economic man concept, for example) or other disciplines (such as psychology and biology). Since many of these developments have encroached on the middle ground between mainstream economics and non-mainstream schools of thought, Goodwin (2000) questions whether there is any continuing relevance in these two categories (see further Coats, 2000). The character of plurality in economics had changed.

This plurality of theories is also evident in their content, and the changing nature and scope of evidence, reflecting an increasing understanding of plurality in the subject matter. Thus, by considering the possibility of different information sets among different categories of economic actor, rational expectations theory generated multiple equilibria. This outcome jeopardised the clear implications which had earlier been drawn from the strong rational expectations hypothesis. Similarly, behavioural economics took on board different attitudes to risk in order to explain more complex behaviour in financial markets. Game theory took on the implications of interaction between different interest groups and so on. This increasing focus on heterogeneous agents reflects a movement away from the idea of the representative agent in an effort to capture more effectively a complex reality (see for example Kirman, 1992). Thaler (2000) predicts a continuation of this trend. In the meantime, theory change has been prompted by new types of evidence that have been gathered on the basis of experiments (Morgan, 2005; Sugden, 2005). Further, happiness studies have gathered new survey evidence which challenges conventional utility theory (Frey and Stutzer, 2002). Survey evidence similarly has also opened up labour market analysis to concepts (such as self-worth) outside the conventional framework (Bewley, 1995).

Nevertheless some see the resulting complexity of the disciplinary landscape as being unified by the shared purpose of a general systematisation of agents' rational behaviour (however defined) under certainty and uncertainty conditions, including interactive behaviour (Giocoli, 2003). Indeed, while there is a consensus that there has been fragmentation in terms of theory and evidence, there is also a consensus in the literature that there has been a growing cohesion at the level of approach, specifically in terms of method selection. Thus Blanchard, who with Fischer had drawn attention to the plurality within macroeconomics in 1989, as we noted above, had by 1997 come to emphasise the commonality at the level of framework (Blanchard, 1997, p. 582). More generally, Goodwin and Colander point to the increasing requirement for theory to be expressed in terms of formal mathematics, which at the level of method reduces significantly the degree of plurality. Indeed the consensus identified by commentators (such as Morgan and Rutherford, 1998; Blaug, 1999) has been that constructing, analysing and testing formal models is the core activity of mainstream economics. Indeed, as Becker (1976, p. 5) put it: 'what distinguishes economics as a discipline from other disciplines in the social sciences is not the subject matter but its approach'.

Thus game theory has evolved by formalising different notions of rationality (Samuelson, 2004). In behavioural economics, the notion of 'rational' behaviour has been extended to incorporate what had once been dubbed 'irrational', such as time-inconsistency and self-control. But the outcome is still expressed in terms of optimising behaviour subject to constraints such that it is amenable to formal treatment (e.g. Samuelson and Swinkels, 2006). The conventional mainstream notion of uncertainty (i.e. risk) has been refined, now incorporating experienced uncertainty, as well as decision uncertainty (e.g. Kahnemann and Sugden, 2005), but again still applied within a utility maximisation framework. Institutional and conventional considerations are being given more prominence in labour market analysis. For example Thomas (2005) analyses labour market behaviour focusing on the idea of the fair wage (and thus wage relativities). But the analysis still rests on a utility-maximising framework where such considerations do not appear in the utility function. Similarly it is not clear how the evidence on happiness will be translated into theory, not least because of the subjective nature of the evidence. We seem still to be in Blanchard and Fischer's 'logically uncomfortable' territory.

Samuelson (2005) explains the challenges such developments pose for a formalist approach, exploring in detail the difficulties in combining the apparently conflicting insights from experimental economics with theory. For example, how far are surprising results from experiments still conditioned by the abstractions of the theory to which they related, and therefore do not constitute independent evidence? How should preferences be modelled when going beyond a narrow conception of self-interest? The importance of addressing such difficulties is emphasised when he concludes that 'at some point some connections must be made between theory and behaviour if economic theory is not to fade into either philosophy or mathematics' (Samuelson, 2005, p. 100). The key question will therefore be how far the requirements of mathematical modelling are given priority in resolving the emerging incompatibilities between theory and evidence. There are after all other approaches available outside the optimising-individual framework, as in Davis (2003) on rational behaviour, and the two different treatments of the labour market in Chick (1983) and Nelson (1996). These approaches differ in giving formal models a partial role alongside other methods of analysis (or even no role). Unlike conventional theory, the model solution is not regarded as necessarily the definitive solution. One critical consequence of defining economics by a particular methodology, as in mainstream economics, is that such alternatives may not be recognised as even falling within economics. The homogeneity of methodological approach is then self-reinforcing.

Given the importance, therefore, of unity of method (alongside plurality of theory and evidence), we turn now to analyse its justification, as well as significance and implications. In particular it is important, given the diverging trends in terms of theory/evidence and method, that it be clarified what is entailed by plurality at different levels. We do this in the next section, and at the same time consider the arguments put forward for plurality, i.e. for pluralism.

3. Variety at Different Levels

We have already seen evidence of a consensus that there is increasing plurality in the practice of mainstream economics and unity in terms of methodology. So we also need to consider the relations between the levels, the meaning of plurality at the level of reality, and distinguish between a plurality of methodologies, or approaches, on the one hand and a methodology which advocates a plurality of methods on the other (Dow, 2001).

We start with the subject matter of economics: reality, and the nature of social systems, of which the economy is a part. The nature of reality in turn determines what kinds of knowledge are possible. It is difficult definitively to separate the level of reality from the level of our knowledge about it. Nevertheless, it is possible to make statements about what we understand as the nature of reality, and about what that implies for possibilities for knowledge. The question at issue here is whether or not there is an underlying unity to social systems. If there is, then behaviour is law-like, and it is the task of economics to uncover those laws. There is little scope for diversity of opinion, or plurality in terms of knowledge, except in the transitional state during which laws are being uncovered. Put another way, closed social systems allow for the identification of laws on the basis of which predictions can be made with confidence.

On the other hand if there is diversity in nature, i.e. behaviour is not law-like, then there is scope for variety of opinion (i.e. plurality of knowledge), and thus a range of possible explanations for economic outcomes (Runde, 1998). This would also be the case, even if there is unity in nature, if there are difficulties in observing nature. Open systems, which allow for human agency (creativity, the non-deterministic exercise of choice, etc.) and the (indeterminate) evolution of the institutional structure within which individuals exercise agency, do not have the invariant kind of causal mechanisms which yield up laws, and allow instead for a plurality of explanations and modes of explanation (Davis, 2003; Chick and Dow, 2005). Many economists would agree with Popper (1982) that reality is an open system (or at least, if a closed system, that signals are too noisy to allow us to identify it). For example, such thinking lies behind Colander's (2000b) prediction that economics will increasingly focus on the particularity of institutional context, so that we can expect increasing variety in knowledge.

For world-truth realists, reality is the arbiter of opinion: knowledge can only be regarded as true or false by reference to reality (Mäki, 1988). Positivism saw world-truth realism as ensuring unity of knowledge through empirical testing (only one opinion could be correct). But it became clear that empirical testing was not definitive in settling disputes in science more generally or in economics in particular. The problems ranged from the difficulty of identifying precisely which element of a hypothesis accounted for falsifying evidence and should be abandoned (the 'Duhem–Quine problem'), to the inability to test all theoretical statements, to more practical issues such as data compatibility. In charting the decline of positivism in philosophy of science, Caldwell (1982, p. 244) concluded that '[t]he most significant contribution of the growth-of-knowledge philosophers was the demonstration that the quest for a single, universal, prescriptive scientific methodology is quixotic'.

Different methodologies can be seen to follow from different understandings of reality. Thus, for example, market economies can be understood to be inherently stable (such that deviations from trend are understood as resulting from shocks, as in the new growth theory) or inherently unstable (as in the Keynes/Minsky theory of the business cycle). From each view of reality follows a different view of how best to build knowledge about it. A stable new Keynesian system with all variables, including shocks, identified (a closed system) lends itself to mathematical modelling which yields a precise conclusion. On the other hand, the focus of the Keynes/Minsky approach on the indeterminate nature of the timing and amplitude of the cycle, and the central role given to unquantifiable risk, explains the more partial role for formal models (without optimising behaviour) alongside other methods of analysis (see for example Dow (1998); see Lucas (1980), for a different view). From these different methodologies stem different selection and use of methods, and different theories.

We can identify four arguments for variety in methodological approach, which we will discuss in turn below. The first is to accept its existence as a feature of knowledge systems on ethical grounds, whether or not it is justified. The second is to argue that no mechanism exists for unifying knowledge about reality, so we have no choice but to accept plurality of approach. The third is to argue that plurality of approach inevitably follows from the nature of the subject matter, and the fourth is positively to advocate plurality on the grounds that variety is essential to the survival of the discipline in the face of an evolving subject matter.

The ethical argument rests on what is seen as a fundamental aspect of knowledge (McCloskey, 1994; Mäki, 1997; Screpanti, 1997). If at a basic level we can construct knowledge in different ways, for whatever reason, and there is no agreed basis for identifying one best approach to knowledge, then there can be no justification in presuming that others' approach to knowledge will be the same as our own. To recognise this requires an awareness that reality may be understood differently, terms may be used with different meanings, different criteria employed for deciding what is a good argument and so on. The ethical argument then is to develop sufficient awareness of difference, first to recognise other approaches, and second not to reject them simply because they are different. This is not at all to rule out criticism. On the contrary, it is argued that critical analysis which is as 'objective' as possible requires some mutual understanding (of methodological principles, meaning, etc.).

When Morgan and Rutherford (1998, p. 8) identified a change in the professional ethos of American economics away from interwar pluralism, they characterised it in terms of a move away from associating objectivity with even-handedness with respect to different arguments (and different types of argument). Even-handedness requires awareness of 'otherness'. Morgan and Rutherford identify modern economics with the rise of technocracy, and an association of objectivity instead with the adoption of a particular range of techniques. These techniques facilitate direct comparability of argument, but at the cost of precluding arguments which cannot be expressed in terms of these techniques. This approach is monist (i.e. discourages variety) with respect to methodological approach. Further the particular methodology itself is monist in content in making mathematical modelling the one general core method.

This increasing monism in terms of methodological approach has therefore allowed the emergence of a plurality of theoretical approaches, using different subsets of formal techniques. But at the same time, it has created a dualistic divide between theories which conform to these norms of development and expression and those which do not, discouraging mutual understanding and communication. There is an asymmetry in that, for mainstream economics, the formalist methodological approach defines the discipline, and thus excludes heterodox economics; for other approaches, economics is defined by subject matter, and thus includes orthodox economics. The ethical argument for pluralism suggests that even-handedness of treatment of different arguments should allow, not only for different theories within one definition of objectivity, but also for other concepts of objectivity. The partial role given to mathematical modelling (or even its absence), along with other methods of analysis, in other approaches indicates variety of methodological approach but also variety within those approaches.

In society at large, awareness of variety of approach to knowledge (as part of a more general awareness of otherness) rose in the 1960s, encouraged by Kuhn's philosophy of science, and later in more extreme form with postmodernism. Kuhn's (1962) paradigm framework was part of the movement away from positivism laying down the principles of best practice in science. Kuhn's history of science demonstrated that science evolves within communities with shared understandings of reality, shared views as to how to construct knowledge and shared understandings of terms. Interestingly, he suggested that the initial spur to his work came from the realisation that later astronomers claimed that Aristotle's reasoning was nonsense because they were applying their own, different, meanings to his terms; to understand Aristotle required an understanding of his different knowledge framework (Kuhn, 1990). According to Kuhn, science progresses within dominant paradigms, which are replaced with new paradigms when anomalies with respect to reality become insupportable. With the new paradigm, terms take on new meanings and criteria for good arguments change. Knowledge drawn from different paradigms is thus 'incommensurate'.

Kuhn was generally disregarded by those economists who misunderstood him as a relativist, advocating 'anything goes' (although the concept of paradigm shift has been widely used in accounts of economics in the twentieth century). The difficulty was that, if it is accepted that positivism does not provide a secure basis for knowledge, and there is no other incontestable candidate for the best approach, then it did indeed seem that 'anything goes'.

But there has recently been a revision to the view that Kuhn therefore had very limited impact on economics. Fuller (2000, 2003) argues that this extreme relativist (mis)understanding of Kuhn encouraged a withdrawal from methodological discussion altogether. Such a move was advocated most publicly by Friedman (1953), who argued that theories should be judged only by their predictive power. Making the case for an end to prescriptive methodology, McCloskey (1983) argued that economists persuade by means of rhetoric rather than methodological principle. The implication was that economists did not need to reflect on methodology, nor to justify their theories with reference to any methodological principles. This may have proved to be telling for the subsequent fragmentation of mainstream economics, as well as the relative lack of discussion about it, but does not explain the increasing homogeneity at the level of general method.

In the meantime, postmodernism also influenced to some extent the content of economic theory. For those who understand knowledge of reality as being socially constructed, there is no independent account of reality which would allow a return to an empirical criterion, reinforcing the view that pluralism of approach is the only option (Samuels, 1998). Thus Phelps (1990) for example identified the rational expectations approach with postmodernism, because of the subjective nature of expectations, something explored more thoroughly with respect to Sargent's thought by Sent (1998). Along with the view that there was no one incontestable understanding of the economy by economists, the practice developed of understanding the expectations of economic agents as also being subjective and thus open to variety, or plurality.

But there was also an argument for a more limited form of plurality of approach which did not adopt the methodological agnostic view (inappropriately) associated with Kuhn (Dow, 2004b). The emphasis here was on the limitations on variety imposed by the social nature of science, i.e. focusing on Kuhn's emphasis (following Popper) on scientific communities. There is a limit to how far there can be plurality of understandings of the nature of reality, approaches to knowledge and meaning, when knowledge needs to be developed within groups of researchers and communicated to others. Plurality in practice cannot be infinite.

Further, the emphasis on the social nature of scientific activity has encouraged attention on the sociology of the discipline, so that much of the activity within economic methodology now is some form of science study, concerned with understanding the choices made by economists in developing theory and the means by which they persuade others to accept their theories. This work draws on a rich seam in what is generally classified as the Sociology of Scientific Knowledge (SSK; see Hands (2001, Ch. 5) for a survey). A key concept in this literature, which has caused considerable problems for its application, is reflexivity. In particular, no commentary on an approach to economics can be objective in the sense of not itself employing an approach. The notion of a market for economic ideas, for example, is not objective, given the range of understandings of markets in the literature (see for example Vickers, 1995; Mäki, 1999; Milberg, 2001). Thus it is highly problematic to contemplate a market for ideas as a satisfactory arbiter of ideas about markets. Nevertheless the SSK approach provides a vehicle for analysing the community of economists as a society, including the way in which methodological norms are adopted and propagated.

The third argument for a plurality of approaches rests on a specific argument about the nature of the subject matter as an open system (King, 2002; Chick and Dow, 2005). The argument then is not just that there are limitations to the human capacity for knowledge which prevent us from identifying a single best approach to knowledge which would satisfactorily explain law-like behaviour. The argument is further that the nature of individual behaviour (with its social and creative aspects) is too complex to be predictable (even stochastically). Formal specification of the conventions and institutions which condition their behaviour to evolve in indeterminist ways, and of creativity which by definition cannot be known beforehand, cannot alone be expected to be adequate to the task. Further, while it is argued that it is part of the human condition not to have certain knowledge (or certainty equivalence), this in turn influences behaviour and the evolution of institutions. Policy-makers are then better equipped to understand that behaviour, and its consequences, if knowledge is built up from a variety of approaches, and indeed a variety of questions asked.

The fourth and perhaps strongest argument for variety of approach to economic knowledge comes from application of the biological metaphor. The argument refers to the subject matter only in the sense that theory has to adapt to new developments. In nature, diversity of species provides protection against unforeseen threats, such that if one strain succumbs to a threat, others are available to take its place. In other words, without diversity, the one dominant strain of ideas is highly vulnerable to unanticipated developments for which it cannot generate an explanation.

Within that diversity of approach, one possibility is a pluralist methodology, i.e. reliance on a range of different methods, on the grounds that no one method is sufficient. These methods must be incommensurate, otherwise they would collapse into one method. Explicit adoption of this type of methodology typifies economics outside the mainstream, although there are differences with respect to the range and focus of methods employed. But McCloskey (1983) has demonstrated that, while the 'official discourse' of mainstream economics conforms to formalism in terms of a particular range of mathematical techniques for formulating theory and assessing evidence, the 'unofficial discourse' relies on a much wider range of methods of argument. And indeed variety of methods is implied by Colander's (2000b) prediction of greater context-specificity of economics, and greater focus on institutional variety. Nevertheless the SSK approach emphasises the important sociological role played by official discourse.

The benefits of plurality of method have been promoted in the monetary policy arena by the Bank of England (1999) and the European Central Bank (2000), following the conclusion that single large formal macro-models had proved to be an unsatisfactory basis for decision-making in the face of the complexity (or openness) of economic reality. This conclusion finds support and elaboration, not only in looking forward to future developments in economics (as in Colander, 2000b), but also looking back to Keynes's economic methodology. This was based on his study of probability in the sense of uncertain knowledge (Keynes, 1921) (see Dow, 2004a). Keynes argued that in general the confidence we have in particular conclusions increases, the more different types of argument, and sources of evidence, support it.

The relative benefits of a pluralist methodology can be understood in terms of a metaphor used by the pragmatist Peirce (Wimsatt, 1981). A pluralist methodology is represented by a rope, which is stronger than each individual strand; it is over-determined in that any one strand breaking will not bring down the edifice of a pluralist argument. A monist methodology (i.e. reliance on one broad method which is necessary and sufficient for good argument, and which involves a shared set of terms and shared meanings) is another possibility within the range offered by variety of approach. The increasing reliance on mathematical formalism in economics in the mainstream can be classified as a monist methodology, and can be compared to a pluralist methodology in terms of relative costs and benefits. In Peirce's symbolism, a monist methodology is represented by a single chain, which is only as strong as its weakest link.

The mathematical formalist methodology clearly has strong attractions for many economists. One of the main advantages of a monist methodology is that all arguments are commensurate. The appeal of mathematical formalism is that it puts all arguments on an equal footing, allowing direct comparison, and a straightforward check on consistency (Allen, 2000). However, in an applied discipline (and even within pure mathematics) mathematical systems cannot be closed, so that internal mathematical consistency is insufficient; there inevitably remains scope for variety of opinion (Weintraub, 1998, 2002). And indeed charges of logical inconsistency (as in the Cambridge controversies of the 1960s (see Harcourt, 1972) or with respect to the no-trade theorem (see Sent, 2006)) in practice have not proved decisive. This suggests an increasing need for a different justification for arguments to be expressed exclusively in terms of mathematical modelling, if this approach is to be sustained.

The issue of justifying choice of methodology is just one of the issues which are associated with variety in economics. In the next section we consider these issues, starting with mathematical formalism.

4. Some Issues

4.1 *Mathematical Formalism*

A discussion of mathematical formalism, in pure theory or as the basis for empirical work, can benefit from considering plurality at different levels, as above. At the level of choice of methodology, the preference for mathematical formalism which came to dominate economics from the 1950s is generally tacit among practising economists. Indeed where it is still discussed, as in Allen (2000), it is generally in terms of the matter being settled. Yet the attitude to mathematical formalism could prove decisive for how the theoretical difficulties are resolved that we noted above as arising from experimental and survey evidence.

At the level of choice of specific method (within a monist, formalist, method-ology), there is a range of techniques which could be employed. The reason for any particular choice of technique is also generally left tacit; this is particularly so at the general level of choosing, say, differential calculus rather than set theory. But inevitably such choice requires argument which is in some sense outside mathematics. The choice requires reference to the nature of the subject matter and a weighing of the costs and benefits of possible methods of analysis in relation to that subject matter. The methodology then cannot itself be fully defined by mathematical formalism.

Similarly, we have drawn attention to something else which lies outside mathematics itself: the issue of meaning. The scope for different meanings itself is a source of variety, but one which is concealed if meaning is presumed to be held in common. Mathematical expression is often treated in terms of translation from verbal language to mathematical language, which is internally precise. Mathematical argument has the advantage that it can achieve more complex operations than verbal argument, retaining precision throughout. But while mathematical argument is internally precise, giving meaning to mathematics is not (Coddington, 1975). The vagueness of verbal language allows it to encompass shades of meaning, to evolve in meaning and to combine a plurality of types of argument. But if there is variety in meaning of verbal terms and variety in methods of argument, both are lost in an effort of translation into mathematics. Mathematical expression is therefore not neutral, but rather puts particular limits on the scope of subject matter and of argument (Chick and Dow, 2001). Most importantly, meaning in application of theory further remains imprecise and open to variety of opinion. The rigour required for application is different from the rigour of mathematical argument, but no less important.

But, while inspection of the leading journals supports the view that mathematical expression is indeed a common feature of mainstream economics (Backhouse, 1998), this is embedded to a greater or lesser extent within verbal argument, as McCloskey (1983) has pointed out. Indeed, the verbal content generally contains a range of types of argument. Nevertheless, since the requirement for mathematical expression is non-neutral as far as the content of argument is concerned, the verbal argument too is constrained.

But if mathematical argument needs to be supplemented by other types of argument, non-mathematical argument is required to explain why one method-ological approach has nevertheless become the common source of homogeneity in mainstream economics. The explanation may be that the growing heterogeneity at the theoretical level can be counteracted by a common mode of expression, with sufficient commonality of meaning (of concepts like 'rationality') to allow understanding across subfields. This would be a particular form of the more general sociological explanation that scientific communities adopt a methodology which becomes an identifying feature (and we have seen that it is conventional now to say that mainstream economics is defined by its method). The community is perpetuated by means of education through textbook exemplars, by peer review, by hiring decisions and so on. While there is a deep background to knowledge which evades articulation (Searle, 1995), a community can serve to create and perpetuate a common background among its members and recruits to support a continuation of the methodological approach. All of this is the meat of Kuhn's analysis of paradigms.

4.2 'Anything Goes'

The background to this growing homogeneity of method was the collapse of positivism, and thus of the possibility of setting up methodological principles for all of economics. The troubling implication was that the only alternative was that 'anything goes' (Salanti, 1997). It is natural for economists to seek firm foundations, and to be concerned at the sense that the discipline is developing in an *ad hoc* manner (Blanchard and Fischer, 1989; Colander, 2000a). In particular there is a concern to be able to settle on criteria by which to gauge progress (Backhouse, 2000).

But one implication of pluralism is that it is not reasonable to expect to establish common criteria for progress. What is an acceptable explanation to one may not be acceptable to others, not just because there may be different preferred methods, but also because the nature of the subject matter is understood differently, and terms are being used in different ways. A 'pure' pluralist response would indeed be 'anything goes', but then it is not clear that we would be left with anything which could be called knowledge.

But in practice, since most economists tend to operate mostly in one of a limited range of (shifting, open) networks with shared underpinnings, the scope for plurality is limited. There is therefore a discrete number of approaches in economics. It is therefore feasible for any economist to learn enough about alternative approaches to engage in some communication, and indeed criticism, to good effect. Indeed it could be argued that most great developments in economics occur as a result of cross-fertilisation across school-of-thought boundaries (as in rational expectations theory growing out of an encounter with behavioural economics; Kantor, 1979).

Communication is not perfect, as across language barriers, but can nevertheless achieve some mutual understanding (Rorty, 1979). There is some common basis to all of economics (as in the structure of language, to continue the metaphor) which provides the basis for communication. This hermeneutical argument supports the ethical argument for recognising plurality, and not rejecting simply on the basis of difference. But successful communication requires understanding not only of others' approaches to economics, but also of one's own approach.

If there is a limit to the scope for substantive over-arching principles which apply to all of economics, then each approach to economics is incommensurate in the sense of not being directly comparable. But this should not be confused with internal inconsistency. As Hodgson (1997, pp. 148–149) put it: 'The role of diversity is not to sanctify or foster contradiction. Tolerance of the right of the scientist to practise, even when we may disagree with his or her views, does not imply tolerance of any method and proposition.... Pluralism does not mean that "anything goes".... We have to recognise the immense and enduring value of pluralism within the discipline without abandoning precision and rigour in our own work.'

Surely most economists would agree with the necessity for precision and rigour. But the significance of methodological pluralism is that the meaning and application of precision and rigour may differ from one approach to another (just as Weintraub (2002) has shown that they have changed within mathematics itself). In particular there is a trade-off between different notions of precision and rigour in application. Consider a precise projection arising from a formal model with precise assumptions, within which classical logic has been rigorously applied. Precision and rigour in this sense need to be weighed against precision and rigour as they are understood in the exercise of judgement, e.g. in relaxing assumptions which are unsustainable in practical policy application, such as *ceteris paribus*. Such matters are critical for example in making monetary policy decisions (see for example Bank of England, 1999).

4.3 *Schools of Thought*

If economics is to operate as a collection of loose communities, rather than an inchoate plurality, then it would seem that we would be returning to the configurations of the 1970s and 1980s. That period has been identified with ideological difference, distinguished from what is seen as the more open plurality which prevails now (Colander, 2000a; Goodwin, 2000).

Goodwin (2000) identifies the declining significance of ideology in economics with a growing disengagement from the policy process, which he regrets. But this does not address the role of values more generally. Values are an inherent part of Searle's (1995) deep background, which influences the way in which we understand the nature of reality, and build knowledge about it, and is thus endemic to our economic theorising. It is therefore inconceivable that differences in schools of thought would not have some value component. But there are different kinds of values, and it is arguably methodological values which are of greatest importance if we understand schools of thought in terms of methodological approach. As Backhouse (2005) argues, ideology may be understood quite differently in terms of the set of values which determine choice of methodology (in addition to ideology understood in terms of political preference). Mathematical formalism was seen by many as a mechanism for promoting pluralism while getting away from ideological debate. Yet mathematical formalism itself reflects what might be called an ideological choice.

Within this general methodology, it is possible to identify groupings, around endogenous growth theory, experimental economics, behavioural economics, complexity theory and so on. Each is developing a different set of mathematical tools which effectively separates the discourse into schools of thought. The dividing lines are not strictly drawn, not least because of the agreed adherence to mathematical formalism. Implicit here also is a shared view of human nature. While the old idea of fully informed, rational, atomistic agents is increasingly being replaced by the idea of complex (learning, emotional, etc.) heterogeneous agents (Thaler, 2000), the requirement to model behaviour mathematically is an effective constraint on what can be addressed. There are other methodological approaches in economics which can also be regarded as schools of thought, e.g. the older forms of behavioural economics and institutionalism which quite explicitly chose an alternative to mathematical formalism in order to get round these constraints. These approaches too of course suffer from (different) constraints, yet they add to the plurality of methodology, of theory and method in economics.

The divisions between schools of thought are not rigid or impermeable, and indeed individual economists may be seen to work across such divides. But clarification of broad-brush differences in approach is a prerequisite for addressing difference (in meaning, etc.) in a constructive manner. It is also useful to use the basic classification of orthodoxy/heterodoxy to capture the distinction between economics being defined by mathematical formalism and adoption of different methodological approaches, respectively (see Dow, 2007).

What is being portrayed here is what could be termed 'structured pluralism' (Dow, 2004b). McCloskey (1994) has been concerned that we get away from structuring the discipline around schools of thought on the grounds that they inhibit discourse. But on the contrary it can be argued that it aids discourse if there is some basis, first for identifying, and second for understanding, the principles and perceptions underpinning others' thought, something which is impossible with an unlimited range of methodologies. It also provides the basis for effective criticism. Awareness of methodological difference is a precondition for engagement with ideas. Criticism inevitably comes from some perspective or other, without recourse to absolute principles. But, as Popper (1963) argued, it is through criticism that knowledge progresses.

5. Conclusion

We have seen evidence that there are forces for heterogeneity in mainstream economics (at the level of theory and evidence) but much less at the level of methodology. Whether or not there is agreement as to the precise account of change within the discipline, it cannot be denied that there has been change. Yet this has attracted remarkably little critical scrutiny within the mainstream of economic discourse, as if whatever change occurs must be socially optimal.

One possible explanation which can be imputed from such methodological statements as have emerged (such as Pencavel, 1991) is that there is the presumption of some sort of invisible hand at work in a market for ideas. This is a powerful metaphor to use in economics, but one which itself requires further examination, not least because ideas are not traded; there is no price mechanism through which markets might adjust. Indeed this metaphor illustrates well its own limitations. Because, given the plurality in economics, there are different understandings of market processes within different schools of thought, each would understand the operation of a market for ideas differently. In particular, those who identify limitations to the social benefits of free markets, and thus intervention (including intervention to promote increased competition), would be inclined to question whether the unfettered production of ideas in economics did indeed produce the optimal outcome. While this argument is ultimately circular (depending on the perspective of market adopted), so is the argument that rests on the invisible hand. Indeed the scope for different understandings of key terms is central to the nature of plurality in economics.

It has been argued here that the growing plurality in mainstream theory and evidence, prompted by the desire to capture more of the complexity of the economy, raises questions about the sufficiency of mathematical formalism as a methodological approach. In other words, there is room also for non-formalist argument, with the mainstream methodological approach only one of a range of possible approaches. In particular, the issues posed for formal modelling by plurality in mainstream theory and evidence suggest that there is scope for more plurality at the methodological level. Economic theory is facing exciting new challenges which are open to a range of methodological treatments. The scope to take up these challenges would be severely limited if there were an overriding requirement to express all theory in terms of the kind of individual behaviour which can be captured in formal mathematics (i.e. in deterministic form).

In practice any discipline can only function with a limited range of approaches (within which there are understandings of the economic process, shared meanings, shared views as to what constitutes good theory, etc.). An absence of universal methodological principles therefore does not mean that 'anything goes', but rather a limited range of sets of such principles. This implies that there is a continuing role for schools of thought as a way of categorising these difference approaches, aiding mutual understanding, and providing the variety on which economics can build.

But the main purpose has been to draw attention to the issues posed by current trends in economics and to encourage wider attention to them. To leave such issues unexamined is arguably to opt for 'anything goes'.

Acknowledgements

This paper has benefited from discussions following presentation of related work at Queen's University, Belfast, at the University of Ljubljana, at the 'Dissent in Science' Seminar at the LSE, at the University of Bath and the University of Liverpool and comments from Victoria Chick, John Davis, Alexander Dow, Miguel Duran, Tatiana Kornienko and Warren Samuels. A sister paper arising from this work is Dow (2006).

References

Allen, B. (2000) The future of microeconomic theory. *Journal of Economic Perspectives* 14: 143–150.

Backhouse, R.E. (1991) The neo-Walrasian research programme in macroeconomics. In N. de Marchi and M. Blaug (eds), *Appraising Economic Theories*. Cheltenham: Edward Elgar.

Backhouse, R.E. (1998) The transformation of U.S. economics, 1920–1960. In M.S. Morgan and M. Rutherford (eds), *From Interwar Pluralism to Postwar Neoclassicism. History of Political Economy* (Annual Supplement) 30: 85–108.

Backhouse, R.E. (2000) Progress in heterodox economics. *Journal of the History of Economic Thought* 22: 149–156.

Backhouse, R.E. (2005) Economists, values and ideology: a neglected agenda. *Revue de Philosophie Economique* 11: 49–73.

Bank of England (1999) *Economic Models at the Bank of England*. London: Bank of England.

Bewley, T.F. (1995) A depressed labor market as explained by participants. *American Economic Review, Papers and Proceedings* 85: 250–254.

Blanchard, O. (1997) *Macroeconomics* (3rd edn). Upper Saddle River, NJ: Prentice Hall.

Blanchard, O. and Fischer, I. (1989) *Lectures in Macroeconomics*. Cambridge, MA: MIT Press.

Blaug, M. (1999) The formalist revolution or what has happened to orthodox economics after World War II. In R.E. Backhouse and J. Creedy (eds), *From Classical Economics to the Theory of the Firm*. Cheltenham: Edward Elgar.

Caldwell, B.J. (1982) *Beyond Positivism*. London: Allen & Unwin.

Chick, V. (1983) *Macroeconomics after Keynes: A Reconsideration of the General Theory*. Oxford: Philip Allen.

Chick, V. and Dow, S.C. (2001) Formalism, logic and reality: Keynesian analysis. *Cambridge Journal of Economics* 25: 705–722.

Chick, V. and Dow, S.C. (2005) The meaning of open systems. *Journal of Economic Methodology* 12: 363–381.

Coats, A.W. (2000) Opening remarks for roundtable on the progress of heterodox economics. *Journal of the History of Economic Thought* 22: 145–148.

Coddington, A. (1975) The rationale of general equilibirum theory. *Economic Inquiry* 13: 539–558.

Colander, D. (2000a) The death of neoclassical economics. *Journal of the History of Economic Thought* 22: 127–143.

Colander, D. (2000b) New millennium economics: how did it get this way, and what way is it? *Journal of Economic Perspectives* 14: 121–132.

Davis, J.B. (2003) *The Theory of the Individual in Economics*. London: Routledge.

Davis, J.B. (2006) The turn in economics: neoclassical dominance to mainstream pluralism? *Journal of Institutional Economics* 2: 1–20.

Dow, S.C. (1985) *Macroeconomic Thought: A Methodological Approach*. Oxford: Blackwell.

Dow, S.C. (1998) Knowledge, information and credit creation. In R.J. Rotheim (ed.), *New Keynesian Economics/Post Keynesian Alternatives*. London: Routledge.

Dow, S.C. (2001) Modernism and postmodernism: a dialectical analysis. In S. Cullenberg, J. Amariglio and D.F. Ruccio (eds), *Postmodernism, Economics and Knowledge*. London: Routledge.

Dow, S.C. (2004a) Uncertainty and monetary policy. *Oxford Economic Papers* 56: 539–561.

Dow, S.C. (2004b) Structured pluralism. *Journal of Economic Methodology* 11: 275–290.

Dow, S.C. (2006) Plurality in orthodox and heterodox economics. Presented to the Annual Conference of the Association for Heterodox Economics, London.

Dow, S.C. (2007) Heterodox economics: a common challenge to mainstream economics? In E. Hein and A. Truger (eds), *Money, Distribution and Economic Policy – Alternatives to Orthodox Macroeconomics*. Cheltenham: Edward Elgar.

European Central Bank (2000) The two pillars of the ECB's monetary policy strategy. *ECB Monthly Bulletin*, November, 37–48.

Frey, B.S. and Stutzer, A. (2002) What can economists learn from happiness research? *Journal of Economic Literature* 60: 402–435.

Friedman, M. (1953) The methodology of positive economics. *Essays in Positive Economics*. Chicago, IL: University of Chicago Press.

Fuller, S. (2000) *Thomas Kuhn: A Philosophical History of Our Times*. Chicago, IL: University of Chicago Press.

Fuller, S. (2003) *Kuhn vs Popper*. Cambridge: Icon Books.

Giocoli, N. (2003) *Modelling Rational Agents: From Interwar Economics to Early Modern Game Theory*. Cheltenham: Edward Elgar.

Goodwin, C. (2000) Comment: it's the homogeneity, stupid! *Journal of the History of Economic Thought* 22: 179–184.

Hands, D.W. (2001) *Reflection without Rules: Economic Methodology and Contemporary Science Theory*. Cambridge: Cambridge University Press.

Harcourt, G.C. (1972) *Some Cambridge Controversies in the Theory of Capital*. Cambridge: Cambridge University Press.

Hodgson, G.M. (1997) Metaphor and pluralism in economics: mechanics and biology. In A. Salanti and E. Screpanti (eds), *Pluralism in Economics*. Cheltenham: Edward Elgar.

Kahnemann, D. and Sugden, R. (2005) Experienced utility as a standard of policy evaluation. *Experimental and Resource Economics* 32: 161–181.

Kantor, B. (1979) Rational expectations and economic thought. *Journal of Economic Literature* 17: 1422–1441.

Keynes, J.M. ([1921] 1973) *A Treatise on Probability. Collected Writings,* Vol. 8. London: Macmillan for the Royal Economic Society.

King, J.E. (2002) Three arguments for pluralism. *Journal of Australian Political Economy* 50: 1–7. Reprinted in *Post-Autistic Economics Review* 23: 5, 2004.

Kirman, A.P. (1992) Whom or what does the representative individual represent? *Journal of Economic Perspectives* 6: 117–136.

Kuhn, T.S. (1962) *The Structure of Scientific Revolutions.* Chicago, IL: University of Chicago Press.

Kuhn, T.S. (1990) Remarks on incommensurability and translation. In R. Favretti, G. Sandri and R. Scazzieri (eds), *Incommensurability and Translation.* Cheltenham: Edward Elgar.

Lucas, R.E., Jr (1980) Methods and problems in business cycle theory. *Journal of Money, Credit and Banking* 12: 696–715.

Mair, D. and Miller, A.G. (eds) (1991) *A Modern Guide to Economic Thought.* Cheltenham: Edward Elgar.

Mäki, U. (1988) How to combine rhetoric and realism in the methodology of economics. *Economics and Philosophy* 4: 89–109.

Mäki, U. (1997) The one world and the many theories. In A. Salanti and E. Screpanti (eds), *Pluralism in Economics.* Cheltenham: Edward Elgar.

Mäki, U. (1999) Science as a free market: a reflexivity test in an economics of economics. *Perspectives on Science* 7: 486–509.

McCloskey, D.N. (1983) The rhetoric of economics. *Journal of Economic Literature* 31: 434–461.

McCloskey, D.N. (1994) *Knowledge and Persuasion in Economics.* Cambridge: Cambridge University Press.

Milberg, W. (2001) Decentering the market metaphor in international economics. In S. Cullenberg, J. Amariglio and D.F. Ruccio (eds), *Postmodernism, Economics and Knowledge.* London: Routledge.

Morgan, M.S. (2005) Experiments versus models: new phenomena, inference and surprise. *Journal of Economic Methodology* 12: 317–329.

Morgan, M.S. and Rutherford, M. (1998) American economics: the character of the transformation. In M.S. Morgan and M. Rutherford (eds), *From Interwar Pluralism to Postwar Neoclassicism. History of Political Economy* (Annual Supplement) 30: 1–26.

Nelson, J. (1996) *Feminism, Objectivity and Economics.* London: Routledge.

Pencavel, J. (1991) Prospects for economics. *Economic Journal* 101: 81–87.

Phelps, E.S. (1990) *Seven Schools of Thought in Macroeconomic Thought.* Oxford: Oxford University Press.

Popper, K. (1963) *Conjectures and Refutations.* London: Routledge.

Popper, K. (1982) *The Open Universe: An Argument for Indeterminism.* London: Routledge.

Rorty, R. (1979) *Philosophy and the Mirror of Nature.* Oxford: Basil Blackwell.

Runde, J. (1998) Assessing causal economic explanations. *Oxford Economic Papers* 50: 151–172.

Salanti, A. (1997) Introduction. In A. Salanti and E. Screpanti (eds), *Pluralism in Economics.* Cheltenham: Edward Elgar.

Salanti, A. and Screpanti, E. (eds) (1997) *Pluralism in Economics.* Cheltenham: Edward Elgar.

Samuels, W.J. (1998) Methodological pluralism. In J.B. Davis, W. Hands and U. Mäki (eds), *The Handbook of Economic Methodology.* Cheltenham: Edward Elgar.

Samuelson, L. (2004) Modelling knowledge in economic analysis. *Journal of Economic Literature* 62: 367–403.
Samuelson, L. (2005) Economic theory and experimental economics. *Journal of Economic Literature* 43: 65–107.
Samuelson, L. and Swinkels, J. (2006) Information, evolution and utility. *Theoretical Economics* 1: 119–142.
Screpanti, E. (1997) Afterword. In A. Salanti and E. Screpanti (eds), *Pluralism in Economics*. Cheltenham: Edward Elgar.
Searle, J.R. (1995) *The Construction of Social Reality*. London: Free Press.
Sent, E.-M. (1998) *The Evolving Rationality of Rational Expectations*. Cambridge: Cambridge University Press.
Sent, E.-M. (2006) Pluralisms in economics. In S. Kellert, H. Longino and K. Waters (eds), *Scientific Pluralism*. Minneapolis, MN: Minnesota Studies in Philosophy of Science.
Snowdon, B., Vane, H. and Wynarczyk, P. (1994) *A Modern Guide to Macroeconomics: An Introduction to Competing Schools of Thought*. Cheltenham: Edward Elgar.
Sugden, R. (2005) Introduction to the symposium on the role of experiments in economics. *Journal of Economic Methodology* 12: 177–184.
Thaler, R.H. (2000) From homo economicus to homo sapiens. *Journal of Economic Perspectives* 14: 133–142.
Thomas, J. (2005) Fair pay and a wage-bill argument for low real wage cyclicality and excessive employment variability. *Economic Journal* 115: 833–859.
Vickers, D. (1995) *The Tyranny of the Market*. Ann Arbor, MI: University of Michigan Press.
Weintraub, E.R. (1985) *General Equilibrium Analysis*. Cambridge: Cambridge University Press.
Weintraub, E.R. (1998) Axiomatisches missverständnis. *Economic Journal* 108: 1837–1847.
Weintraub, E.R. (1999) How should we write the history of twentieth-century economics? *Oxford Review of Economic Policy* 15: 139–152.
Weintraub, E.R. (2002) *How Economics Became a Mathematical Science*. Durham, NC: Duke University Press.
Wimsatt, W.C. (1981) Robustness, reliability and overdetermination. In M.B. Brewer and B.E. Collins (eds), *Scientific Inquiry and the Social Sciences*. San Francisco, CA: Jossey Bass.

4

VARIATIONS ON THE THEME OF *CONNING*[a] IN *MATHEMATICAL ECONOMICS*

K. Vela Velupillai

University of Trento and Girton College, Cambridge

1. Preamble

It has been correctly said that mathematical economics is flying high these days. So *I come, not to praise mathematics, but rather to slightly debunk its use in economics*. I do so out of tenderness for the subject, since I firmly believe in the virtues of understatement and lack of pretension. (Samuelson, 1952, p. 58; italics added)

Edward Leamer's eloquent critique (1983) of the dissonance between the practice of econometric research and its public dissemination via articles in peer-reviewed journals brought to the forefront the dilemmas faced by an econometrician who was also an experimenter. Alvin Roth (1994), a little over a decade after Leamer, took up a similar issue confronting the experimental economist, as that subject itself came of age – warning of the pitfalls inherent in the divergence between 'the way we report experiments ... and the way an experiment is actually conducted'. Leamer, however, concluded that 'the atmosphere of econometric discourse would be sweetened', if serious attention was paid to two words: *whimsey* and *fragility*:

In order to draw inferences from data as described by econometric texts, *it is necessary to make whimsical assumptions*. The professional audience consequently and properly withholds belief until an inference is shown to be

---

[a]I am invoking three meanings of this word, simultaneously: firstly, in the sense of one of the meanings given in *The Shorter Oxford English Dictionary on Historical Principles* as an '*argument* or *arguer against*' (orthodox mathematical economics); secondly, in the sense of '*to swindle, trick*' (given in *Longman's Concise English Dictionary*); thirdly, in the sense of a '*confidence trick*', as used in US English slang. The second and third senses are, of course, closely related. I suspect it is the third sense that is invoked in the justly celebrated articles by Leamer (1983) and Roth (1994) on econometrics and experimental economics, respectively.

adequately insensitive to the choice of assumptions. The haphazard way we individually and collectively study the fragility of inferences leaves most of us unconvinced that any inference is believable. If we are to make effective use of our scarce data resource, it is therefore important that we study fragility in a much more systematic way. If it turns out that almost all inferences from economic data are fragile, I suppose we shall have to revert to our old methods.... (Leamer, 1983, p. 43; italics added)

In this paper I aim to point out that the dilemmas discussed by Leamer and Roth for econometrics and experimental economics are alive and well also in mathematical economics. I will, in analogy with Leamer, discuss this dilemma paying close attention to the two words *whimsey* and *fragility* but, implicitly in the case of the latter, also in terms of the 'fragility of deduction'[1] in addition to the 'fragility of inferences'. In fact, the way I will discuss and demonstrate the role of *whimsey* and *fragility* in the *conning* that is mathematical economics, it will become evident that the 'fragility of inferences' is a by-product of the whimsical assumptions of mathematical economics.

It may not be out of place, given the nature of this paper, to point out that Sir Michael Atiyeh's 'Fields Institute Lecture' in Toronto, given in June 2000, was titled 'Mathematics in the 20th century' (Atiyeh, 2002). Significantly, he began with an important *caveat emptor*[2](p. 1):

I will say nothing... about the great events in the area between logic and computing associated with the names of people like Hilbert, Gödel and Turing.

I will, however, try to dissect *conning* in mathematical economics primarily on the basis of 'the great events in the area between logic and computation', in particular mathematical logic and theories of computation, thus encompassing both recursion theory and constructive mathematics in the latter and some non-classical logics in the former.

I will illustrate the role and mode of *conning* in mathematical economics by discussing three famous examples in economics: the role, functions and claims made for the *Walrasian auctioneer*;[3] the various formulations and conclusions about the scope for formal policy, particularly in macroeconomics; and the formalization of the notion of a *rational expectations equilibrium* (REE) using topological fixed-point theorems and then, separately, the devising of learning mechanisms to determine it.

The paper is therefore structured as follows. In the next section I discuss, formally, the meaning and (extravagant) claims on economic dynamics by the mathematical economists and show the nature of cons involved in the various formal exercises. In Section 3, a similar exercise is attempted for the formalized theory of economic policy. The kind of conning implicit and explicit in the fix-point approach to REE is the subject matter of Section 4. In the concluding section, Section 5, speculative hints are discussed on how a *conless mathematical economics* might be devised, paying close attention to the interaction between the ontology of economic entities and their quantitative realizations and verifications.[4] I include a substantial discussion of an alternative tradition in game theory, unfortunately quite unfamiliar to most economists – even those who may well be fairly competent in mathematics – with the purpose of debunking the *con* that is implied in uncritical invoking of and reliance on the *axiom of choice*.

In a sense the main theme of the paper is the attempt to disabuse economic theorists in general, and mathematical economists in particular, of uncritical reliance on, and unwarranted acceptance of, certain kinds of mathematical formalizations and uncritical or ignorant acceptance of controversial or meaningless mathematical axioms. Such mathematical formalizations, I argue in terms of the main three examples, lead to the cons that are replete in a kind of mathematical economics that relies on them for formalizations, theorizing and inferences. Reliance on them leads to whimsical assumptions, entirely determined and dictated by the mathematics and not by the ontology of economic entities, institutions and behaviour. As a consequence the inferences are inherently fragile or even senseless, since they require impossible approximations from uncomputable entities and undecidable propositions.

The main – but not the sole – culprit is easy to identify. It is best identified in terms of a programmatic assertion – not a proof or an inference from empirical or experimental observations – by the doyen of twentieth century mathematical economics, Gerard Debreu. In his Frisch Memorial Lecture, delivered at MIT in August, 1985, he asserts the following:[5]

> Thus von Neumann's lemma, reformulated in 1941 as Kakutani's fixed point theorem, was an accident within an accidental paper.[6] But in a global historical view, *the perfect fit between the mathematical concept of a fixed point and the social science concept of an equilibrium* stands out.... In this view, fixed point theorems were slated for the prominent part they played in game theory and in the theory of general economic equilibrium after John Nash's one-page note of 1950. (Debreu, 1986b, p. 1262; italics added)

He may well be right about the 'mathematical concept of a fixed point', but his unawareness of the existence of different kinds of 'fixed-point theorems' – especially recursion theoretic fixed-point theorems – shunted the formalization of economic theory in a direction that made it prone to *conning*, particularly about dynamics, in general, and processes, such as learning, in particular.

As a result of this monomaniacal reliance and belief in the validity of the assertion that there is a 'perfect fit between [particular kinds of] fixed point theorems and the social science concept of equilibrium', all kinds of problems in economics have been forced into a formalization that can exploit the use of such theorems. A whole subject has been conned into believing this 'perfect fit' on no empirical, experimental or even historical grounds or necessity. It was not an economist but an eminent applied mathematician who had the courage, hindsight and foresight to point out that

> We return to the subject of equilibrium theory. The existence theory of the static approach is **deeply rooted to the use of the mathematics of fixed point theory**. Thus one step in the liberation from the static point of view would

be to **use a mathematics of a different kind**. Furthermore, proofs of fixed point theorems traditionally use difficult ideas of algebraic topology, and this has obscured the economic phenomena underlying the existence of equilibria. Also the economic equilibrium problem presents itself most directly and with the most tradition not as a fixed point problem, but as an *equation*, supply equals demand. **Mathematical economists have translated the problem of solving this equation into a fixed point problem**.

I think it is fair to say that for the main existence problems in the theory of economic equilibrium, **one can now bypass the fixed point approach and attack the equations directly to give existence of solutions, with a simpler kind of mathematics** and even **mathematics with dynamic and algorithmic overtones**. (Smale, 1976, p. 290; bold emphasis added)

Smale could have added that there is a 'simpler kind of mathematics' that combines the notion of fixed points and algorithms – hence dynamics – in one fell swoop. The implications are that we have not only been *conned* into formalizing unnaturally, but have also been *conned* into using a more complex mathematics.[7]

2. Exposing the Dynamics *Con* in Economic Theory

We have got accustomed to referring to computable and constructive methods of algorithmic analysis in the *digital mode* in economic theory. However, at the outset, our neoclassical masters, when they referred to the market as an equation solver, were thinking in terms of *analogue devices*.[8] It is worth pointing out then, at the outset, that the explicit computing tradition in economics can be said to have begun with Walras's fertile idea of *tâtonnement* and Pareto's famous invoking of the analogy of the market's dynamics as a solver of an equilibrium system of equations. The key distinction between the two great neoclassical pioneers of general equilibrium theory is that Walras envisaged *tâtonnement* to be a *gedankenexperiment* to organize his thoughts about equilibrium solutions to a multi-market system of equations;[9] Pareto, on the other hand, was explicit that market dynamics was acting as a solver for the equilibrium of a system of simultaneous equations:

It may be mentioned here that this [analytic] determination has by no means the purpose to arrive at a numerical calculation of prices. Let us make the most favourable assumption for such a calculation, let us assume that we have triumphed over all the difficulties of finding the data of the problem and that we know the ophelimités of all the different commodities for each individual, and all the conditions of production of all the commodities, etc. This is already an absurd hypothesis to make. Yet it is not sufficient to make the solution of the problem possible. We have seen that in the case of 100 persons and 700 commodities there will be 70,699 conditions (actually a great number of circumstances which we have so far neglected will further increase that number); we shall therefore have to solve a system of 70,699 equations. This exceeds practically the power of algebraic analysis, and this is even more true if one contemplates the fabulous number of equations which one obtains for a population of forty millions and several thousand commodities.

In this case the rôles would be changed: it would not be mathematics which would assist political economy, but political economy would assist mathematics. In other words, if one really could know all these equations, *the only means to solve them which is available to human powers is to observe the practical solution given by the market.* (Pareto, 1927/1971, pp. 233–234; italics added)

The pioneers, therefore, were trying to supplement their formalizations of the supply–demand equilibrium nexus with a mechanism for solving for equilibrium. The separation between proving the existence of an equilibrium and finding methods to solve for it was not part of the tradition of nineteenth (or earlier) century mathematics (as mentioned earlier). However, a natural formalization of the problem of 'supply equals demand', without *conning* us into believing that the real numbers are the adequate, ideal or the default domain, is as a *Diophantine decision problem*.[10] This suggests that the market *mechanism*, in seeking and, perhaps, finding equilibrium prices, is *solving* the formally *unsolvable*! This would imply hypotheses or thought experiments on plausible economic processes suggesting that they might, in fact, be formal algorithms, not necessarily subject to the strictures of the Church–Turing thesis. Any such thought experiment on feasible economic processes not subject to the strictures of the Church–Turing thesis raises the question of the formal meaning of *mechanism* and whether or not the economic system is to be viewed as a *non-mechanism*. I will use the term relying on the classic definition given by Gandy (1980) and a series of exceptionally suggestive questions and tentative answers broached by Kreisel on the question of *mechanism* (see, for example, Kreisel, 1974, 1982). Clearly the market system functions in ways that violate these definitions and characterizations, and hence any claims about constructing mechanisms or algorithms to depict its smooth and successful functioning, as made by orthodox economic theorists, is an unadulterated *con*.

In his characteristically prescient fashion, Steve Smale, although not an economist, hit upon the central problem confronting the dynamic economic theorist by stating, as the eighth of 18 'Mathematical Problems' for the twenty-first century – in 'Hilbertian Mode' – the following:[11]

Extend the mathematical model of general equilibrium theory to include price adjustments. (Smale, 1998, p. 10; italics in original)

The analogy of the dynamics of a market mechanism in search of an equilibrium of supply and demand[12] with the paradigmatic actions and functions of a computer[13] has a long and distinguished tradition in economics. The changing mathematical underpinnings and formalisms, with the evolution not only of the sophistication of mathematical economics but also of the development of mathematics, has brought the question of price adjustments of a market *mechanism* within the formal ambit of both recursion theory and constructive analysis. It is reasonably well known that the hypotheses of economic theory imply non-recursive outcomes even if the input data are computable. Against the backdrop provided by this theory, and assuming as usually done in economics that economic activity takes place in continuous time and market decisions are, in general, asynchronous, it is easy to show, experimentally, how Turing machine constructions can be devised to show the generation of non-computable economic data.

The tricky question of how such uncomputable data can be used for inference and in which way they become inputs again into the dynamic economic system is one important aspect of the conning exercise in this part of economic theory. How can one infer anything in a quantitative mode from uncomputable data? By definition uncomputable data cannot even be represented in any meaningful finite mode.

In a perceptive review of the important papers by Pour-El and Richards (1979), Kreisel (1982, p. 900) observed

> The [papers by Pour-El and Richards] add to the long lists of operations μ in analysis with some recursive 'input' I for which no output in $\mu(I)$ is recursive. ... Familiar examples are provided by (i) Brouwer's fixed point theorem in dimension >1... where I ranges over (i) continuous maps of the unit circle into itself ... and where $\mu(I)$ is the set of (i) fixed points....

Contrast this with the fundamental theorem of computable general economic equilibrium theory:

Theorem 1. *The Walrasian equilibrium existence theorem (WEET) is equivalent to the Brouwer fixed-point theorem.*[14]

Now, mathematical equivalence between two propositions entails not just that each implies the other, but it also means that the 'objects' defined by each of the propositions are, mathematically, identical. In other words, in the world of mathematical objects, the two objects defined by the two propositions are, ostensibly, simply the same items with two different names. Kreisel's perceptive point, therefore, means that the Walrasian economic equilibrium is *non-recursive*. This means that whatever economic process is devised, observed or inferred to locate or reach the equilibrium must, at some point in its path – perhaps just at the 'final' step – *transform a recursive input into a non-recursive output*. How can a realistic or meaningful mechanism be devised, at least as a thought experiment, to perform this transformation? Even a die-hard orthodox mathematical economist or economic theorist must admit that only some form of serious conning can achieve this – i.e. a fictitious mechanism which, even if postulated to possess ideal properties, can achieve the transformation only by conning.

I have demonstrated, in Velupillai (2006), how the hypotheses underlying WEET, together with the naive *tâtonnement* dynamics of

$$\frac{dp}{dt} = z(p) \tag{1}$$

can be shown to be consistent with the following theorem in Pour-El and Richards (1979, p. 61).

Theorem 2. *There exists an ordinary differential equation with initial condition*

$$\varphi'(t) = F(t, \varphi(t)), \quad \varphi(0) = 0 \tag{2}$$

such that $F(x, y)$ is computable on the rectangle $\{0 \le x \le 1, -1 \le y \le 1\}$, but no solution of the differential equation is computable on any interval $[0, \delta], \delta > 0$.

Using the recursive construction deftly used by Pour-El and Richards it can be shown how a mechanism can be envisaged for *tâtonnement* dynamics to generate the *equilibrium uncomputable solutions.* The best that an applied, empirical or experimental economist can do under these circumstances is to assume disequilibria, since approximating uncomputable equilibrium solutions is a meaningless activity. The whole exercise shows the fundamental dissonance between reckless mathematical theory and impossible empirical and experimental inferences.

To put the nature of the task facing the *Walrasian Demon*[15] in complete perspective let me also state the problem in terms of mappings (discrete time). The naively equivalent *mapping* for the dynamics of *tâtonnement*, as given in textbooks for example, is

$$p_{t+1} = \frac{p_t + \Theta(p_t)}{[p_t + \Theta(p_t)]e} \tag{3}$$

where $\Theta(P_t)$ is mapping depending on the excess demand function $z(p)$; e is the appropriately dimensioned normalizing column vector.

The economic significance and mathematical purpose of this mapping are encapsulated in Scarf's lucid description of what exactly is accomplished by this mapping.

> The particular mapping is a modification of the fundamental price adjustment mechanism in which *prices are revised* in proportion to excess demand – the discrepancy between demand and supply. If the mapping *is iterated,* we obtain a sequence of price vectors, each one responsive to the excess demand evaluated at the previous price vector. While economic intuition might suggest that this sequence of price vectors converges to an equilibrium price vector, this need not be the case. Unless some restrictive assumptions are placed on the excess demand functions, the price sequence may oscillate and approach no limit at all. On the other hand, the fixed point implied by Brouwer's theorem does indeed serve as an equilibrium price vector. [This] illustrates quite well *the role that Brouwer's theorem has played in providing existence proofs,* rather than a constructive and computationally oriented procedure, *for obtaining an equilibrium price vector.* (Scarf, 1973, p. 30; italics added)

Note two standard infelicities in this otherwise impeccably orthodox observation: *'prices are revised'*, but *who* by?; secondly, *'the mapping is iterated'* by *what mechanism* and *who* keeps account of the process? This is where the omniscience and omnipotency of the *Walrasian Demon* is implicitly invoked in the analysis of market dynamics. Omniscience, omnipotent or omni whatever notwithstanding, the basic task of the *Walrasian Demon* is to find a way of processing recursive inputs to produce (at least one) non-recursive output. This means somehow, somewhere, the *Walrasian Demon* will have to violate one or the other of Gandy's (1980) defining criteria for *mechanisms*. Let me suggest another way – in addition to the one suggested above via the Pour-El and Richards theorem – the *Walrasian Demon* might devise a strategy to locate the non-recursive equilibrium.

For concreteness and simplicity I will only consider the scalar case. Generalizing it to a vector equilibrium is conceptually immediate although technically much more complicated. Let the non-recursive Walrasian economic equilibrium be ϑ. Consider

$$\Psi(p) = (p + \vartheta)(\mathrm{mod}\ 1) \quad \text{for} \quad \Psi\colon [0,1) \to [0,1) \tag{4}$$

Ψ is therefore given by

$$\Psi(p) = \begin{cases} p + \vartheta & 0 \le p < 1 - \vartheta \\ p + \vartheta - 1 & 1 - \vartheta \le p < 1 \end{cases} \tag{5}$$

To generate a binary sequence using the techniques of symbolic dynamics, define

$$\Xi(p) = 0 \quad \text{for} \quad x \in [0, 1 - \vartheta) \tag{6}$$

$$\Xi(p) = 1 \quad \text{for} \quad x \in [1 - \vartheta, 1) \tag{7}$$

Now, apply Ξ to Ψ, initializing it on 0, and generate the binary sequence $\{\pi_n\}$, i.e.

$$\pi_n = \Xi(\Psi(0)), \quad n \in \mathbb{Z}_+ \tag{8}$$

It is easy to show that the long-term average of the sequence $\{\pi_n\}$ is ϑ which, by construction, is the Lebesgue measure of that part of the interval that maps to 1 under Ξ; i.e.

$$\text{if } N_v \equiv \text{number of 1's in } \{\pi_n\colon 1 \le n \le v\} \tag{9}$$

$$\text{then } \lim_{v \to \infty} v^{-1} N_v = \vartheta \tag{10}$$

Thus, the best that the *Walrasian Demon* can generate is the non-recursive equilibrium value as a long run equilibrium outcome.[16]

But do we need this extra-territorial being, the *Walrasian Demon*, to perform this task? Does it possess any special knowledge or skills that ordinary mortals do not (thinking, again, analogously to the special characteristic of being a tiny, molecular, size being the *Maxwell Demon* was, to perform the task of a gatekeeper to disorderly molecules)? Seemingly not. Therefore, we can actually dispense with any and all assumptions of such a being and assume, hereafter, that any rational economic agent can perform the same task, given the necessary mathematical and computing skills. This is precisely what is assumed in any mathematical economic framework where assumption of the representative agent is fundamental. So, there is no point in exorcizing the *Walrasian Demon* since it is embodied in the person of the omniscient representative agent, where conning is supremely dominant via the embodiment of attributes that go *beyond mechanism* (in the Gandian[17] sense).

3. Dissecting *Conning* in the Mathematical Theory of Economic Policy

I will assume that 'elementary characterizable[18] attractors' are the standard limit points, limit cycles and 'strange' (i.e. 'chaotic') attractors. All known dynamical systems in economic theory belong to one of these attractors. In particular, macroeconomic growth and cycle theories (including 'growth cycle' theories) can be shown to be one of the 'elementary attractors'. Then, given the observable trajectories of a dynamical system, say computed using simple Poincaré maps or the like, an 'elementary characterizable attractor' is one that can be associated with a finite automaton.[19] Thus, limit points, limit cycles and strange attractors are *effectively characterizable* in a *computably trivial sense*. This means that every dynamical system encapsulating or representing any kind of dynamics in economic theory, particularly in macrodynamics, is computably trivial. I need not emphasize the nature of the conning exercise perpetrated by the purveyors of dynamics in economics, if this notion of 'trivial' is to be taken seriously.

Only dynamical systems capable of 'computation universality' are non-trivial in a computable sense. However, dynamical systems capable of computation universality have to be associated with Turing machines. Such dynamical systems, by a formal process of elimination, can be shown to be those that are poised delicately at the boundaries of the elementary characterizable dynamical systems. Constructing them is as delicate a task as constructing a dynamical system to generate equilibrium uncomputable solutions.

Thus, trajectories that are generated by dynamical systems poised on the boundaries of the basins of attractions of simple attractors may possess *undecidable* properties due to the ubiquity of the *halting problem for Turing machines*, the emergence of *Busy Beavers* (i.e. uncomputabilities), etc. Any theory of policy, i.e. any rule – fixed or discretionary – that is a function of the values of the dynamics of an economy formalized as a dynamical system capable of computation universality, will share these exotic properties.

I will assume, simply for the sake of the discussion in this paper, an abstract model of a 'complex economy', or of an 'economy capable of complex behaviour', to be a dynamical system capable of *computation universality*. By implication, then, the converse – i.e. a 'simple economy' – is one whose dynamics is formalizable as a finite automaton. This means that we have been *conned* by the purveyors of economic dynamics in the mathematical mode into accepting the formalization of complex economic dynamics by simple attractors! Is any act of *conning* more treacherous than this? Perhaps the two mentioned above are candidates?

I will now assume familiarity with the formal definition of a dynamical system (cf. e.g. the obvious and accessible classic (Hirsch and Smale, 1974) or the more modern (Brin and Stuck, 2002)), the necessary associated concepts from dynamical systems theory and all the necessary notions from classical computability theory (for which the reader can, with profit and enjoyment, go to a classic like Rogers (1987) or, at the frontiers, to Cooper (2004)). Just for ease of reference the bare bones of relevant definitions for dynamical systems are given below in the usual telegraphic form.[20] An intuitive understanding of the definition of a 'basin of attraction' is probably sufficient for a complete comprehension of the main result – provided there is reasonable familiarity with the definition and properties of Turing machines (or *partial recursive functions* or equivalent formalisms encapsulated by the Church–Turing thesis).

Definition 1. *The initial value problem (IVP) for an ordinary differential equation (ODE) and flows. Consider a differential equation*

$$\dot{x} = f(x) \tag{11}$$

where x is an unknown function of $t \in I$ (say, t is time and I an open interval of the real line) and f is a given function of x. Then, a function x is a solution of (11) on the open interval I if

$$\dot{x}(t) = f(x(t)), \quad \forall t \in I \tag{12}$$

The IVP for (11) is then stated as

$$\dot{x} = f(x), \quad x(t_0) = x_0 \tag{13}$$

and a solution x(t) for (13) is referred to as a solution through x_0 at t_0. Denote x(t) and x_0, respectively, as

$$\varphi(t, x_0) \equiv x(t) \quad \text{and} \quad \varphi(0, x_0) \equiv x_0 \tag{14}$$

*where $\varphi(t, x_0)$ is called the **flow** of $\dot{x} = f(x)$.*

Definition 2. Dynamical system. *If f is a C^1 function (i.e. the set of all differentiable functions with continuous first derivatives), then the **flow** $\varphi(t, x_0)$, $\forall t$, induces a **map** of $U \sqsubset \mathbb{R}$ into itself, called a C^1 **dynamical system on** $\mathbb{R}$*

$$x_0 \longmapsto \varphi(t, x_0) \tag{15}$$

if it satisfies the following (one-parameter group) properties:

1. *$\varphi(0, x_0) = x_0$;*
2. *$\varphi(t + s, x_0) = \varphi(t, \varphi(s, x_0))$, $\forall t$ and s, whenever both the left-hand- and right-hand-side maps are defined;*
3. *$\forall t$, $\varphi(t, x_0)$ is a C^1 map with a C^1 inverse given by $\varphi(-t, x_0)$.*

Remark 1. *A geometric way to think of the connection between a **flow** and the induced **dynamical system** is to say that the flow of an **ODE** gives rise to a dynamical system on $\mathbb{R}$.*

Remark 2. *It is important to remember that the **map** of $U \sqsubset \mathbb{R}$ into itself may **not** be defined on all of $\mathbb{R}$. In this context, it might be useful to recall the distinction between partial recursive functions and total functions in classical recursion theory.*

Definition 3. Invariant set. *A set (usually compact) $S \sqsubset U$ is **invariant** under the flow $\varphi(.,.)$ whenever $\forall t \in \mathbb{R}$, $\varphi(.,.) \sqsubset S$.*

Definition 4. *Attracting set.* *A closed invariant set $A \sqsubset U$ is referred to as the* **attracting set** *of the flow $\varphi(t, x)$ if $\exists$ some neighbourhood V of A such that $\forall x \in V$ and $\forall t \geq 0$, $\varphi(t, x) \in V$ and*

$$\varphi(t, x) \to A \text{ as } t \to \infty \tag{16}$$

Remark 3. *It is important to remember that in dynamical systems theory contexts the attracting sets are considered the* **observable** *states of the dynamical system and its flow.*

Definition 5. *The basin of attraction of the attracting set A of a flow, denoted, say, by Θ_A, is defined to be the following set:*

$$\Theta_A = \cup_{t \leq 0} \varphi_t(V) \tag{17}$$

where $\varphi_t(.)$ denotes the flow $\varphi(., .)$, $\forall t$.

Remark 4. *Intuitively, the basin of attraction of a flow is the* **set of initial conditions** *that eventually leads to its attracting set – i.e. to its limit set (limit points, limit cycles, strange attractors, etc.). Anyone familiar with the definition of a Turing machine and the famous halting problem for such machines would immediately recognize the connection with the definition of basin of attraction and suspect that my main result is obvious.*[21]

On the policy side, my formal assumption is that by 'policy' is meant 'rules' and my obvious working hypothesis – almost a thesis, if not an axiom – is the following.

Claim 1. *Every rule is reducible to a recursive rule.*[22]

Remark 5. *This claim and the results below are valid whether by 'rule' is meant an element from a set of preassigned rules (i.e. the notion of policy as a fixed 'rule' in the 'rules vs discretion' dichotomy) or a rule as a (partial recursive or total) function of the current state of the dynamics of a complex economy (discretionary policy).*[23]

Remark 6. *If anyone can suggest a rule which* cannot *be reduced to a recursive rule, it can only be due to an appeal to a* non-algorithmic principle *like an* undecidable disjunction *(which are routinely invoked in mathematical economics), magic, ESP or something similar.*

Definition 6. *Dynamical systems capable of computation universality.* *A dynamical system capable of computation universality is one whose defining initial conditions can be used to program and simulate the actions of any arbitrary Turing machine, in particular a universal Turing machine.*

Proposition 1. *Dynamical systems characterizable in terms of limit points, limit cycles or 'chaotic' attractors, called 'elementary attractors', are not capable of universal computation.*

Proposition 2. *Only dynamical systems whose basins of attraction are poised on the boundaries of elementary attractors are capable of universal computation.*

Theorem 3. *There is no effective procedure to decide whether a given observable trajectory is in the basin of attraction of a dynamical system capable of computation universality.*

Proof. The first step in the proof is to show that the basin of attraction of a dynamical system capable of universal computation is recursively enumerable but not recursive. The second step, then, is to apply Rice's theorem to the problem of membership decidability in such a set.

First of all, note that the basin of attraction of a dynamical system capable of universal computation is *recursively enumerable*. This is so since trajectories belonging to such a dynamical system can be effectively listed simply by trying out, *systematically*, sets of appropriate initial conditions.

On the other hand, such a basin of attraction is not recursive. For, suppose a basin of attraction of a dynamical system capable of universal computation is recursive. Then, given arbitrary initial conditions, the Turing machine corresponding to the dynamical system capable of universal computation would be able to answer whether (or not) it will halt at the particular configuration characterizing the relevant observed trajectory. This contradicts the unsolvability of the halting problem for Turing machines.

Therefore, by *Rice's theorem*, there is no effective procedure to decide whether any given arbitrary observed trajectory is in the basin of attraction of such recursively enumerable but not recursive basin of attraction. ∎

Given this result, it is clear that *an effective theory of policy is impossible in a complex economy*. Obviously, if it is effectively undecidable to determine whether an observable trajectory lies in the basin of attraction of a dynamical system capable of computation universality, it is also impossible to devise a policy – i.e. a recursive rule – as a function of the defining coordinates of such an observed or observable trajectory. Just for the record, I will state it as a formal proposition.

Proposition 3. *An effective theory of policy is impossible for a 'complex' economy.*

Remark 7. *The 'impossibility' must be understood in the context of effectivity and does not mean specific policies cannot be devised for individual complex economies. This is similar to the fact that non-existence of general purpose algorithms for solving arbitrary Diophantine equations does not mean specific algorithms cannot and have not been found for special, particular, such equations.*

What if the realized trajectory lies outside the basin of attraction of a dynamical system capable of computation universality and the objective of policy is to drive the system to such a basin of attraction? This means the policy maker is trying to design a dynamical system capable of computational universality with initial conditions pertaining to one that does not have that capability. Or, equivalently, an attempt is being made, by the policy maker, to devise a method by which to make a finite automaton construct a Turing machine, an impossibility. In other words, an attempt is being made endogenously to construct a 'complex economy' from a 'non-complex economy'. Much of this effort is, perhaps, what is called 'development economics' or 'transition economics' and various principles of institution design are attempting the recursively impossible. Essentially, my claim is that it is recursively impossible to construct a system capable of computation universality using only the defining characteristics of a finite automaton. To put it more picturesquely, a *non-algorithmic step* must be taken to go from systems incapable of self-organization to ones that are capable of it. This is why 'development' and 'transition' are difficult issues to theorize about, especially for policy purposes. It must be remembered, however, that this does not mean that the task is impossible in any absolute sense. There may well be non-recursive methods to 'seek out the boundaries of the equivalent of the basins of attractors of dynamical systems'. There may also be *ad hoc* means by which recursive methods may be discovered for such a task. The above theorem seeks only to state that there are no *general purpose effective methods* for such a policy task. Hence the admonition by some of the pioneers of economic theory – Hayek, above all – to be modest about policy proposals for a complex economy may have been motivated by concerns about being *conned* by pseudo-mathematical economists, trained in one kind of convenient but irrelevant mathematics.

I should emphasize that no reading of the above framework and results justifies the widespread belief that the New Classicals have made a formal case for rules against discretion. The framework and results above make a case for an enlightened approach to policy, where poetry and prose may well be the better guides than one-dimensional mathematics.

Perhaps this is the reason for Hayek's lifelong scepticism on the scope for policy in economies that emerge and form spontaneous orders! It is not for nothing that Harrod's growth path was on a knife-edge and Wicksell's cumulative process was a metastable dynamical system, located on the boundary defined by the basins of attractions of two stable elementary dynamical systems (one for the real economy, founded on a modified Austrian capital theory; the other for a monetary macroeconomy underpinned by a pure credit system).

When policy discussions resort to reliance on special economic models the same unease that causes disquiet when special interests advocate policies should be the outcome. Any number and kind of special dynamic economic models can be devised to justify almost anything – all the way from policy nihilism, the fashion of the day, to dogmatic insistence on rigid policies, justified on the basis of seemingly sophisticated, essentially *ad hoc*, models. Equally, studying patterns by simulating complex dynamical models and inferring structures, without grounding them on the mathematics of the computer, is a dangerous pastime. A *fortiori*, suggesting policy measures on the basis of such inferred structures is doubly dangerous. Nothing in the formalism of the mathematics underlying the digital computer, the vehicle in which such investigations are conducted and simulations by it, justifies formal inferences on implementable effective policies.

Impossibility and undecidability results do not mean paralysis. Arrow's impossibility theorem did not mean that democratic institution design was abandoned forever; Rabin's powerful result that even though there are *determined* classical games, it is not possible to devise effective instructions to guide the theoretical winner to implement a winning strategy has not meant that game theory cannot be a useful guide to policy. Similarly, the above results do not mean that the poets in our profession cannot devise enlightened policies that benefit a complex economy. Perhaps the growth of the complexity of economies calls forth more than intuition based on a thorough familiarity of the institutions of an economy and its behavioural underpinnings. Neither poetry nor prose are algorithmic endeavours – either in their creation or in their appreciation; nor is policy, especially in a complex economy.

Justification for policy – either positively or negatively – cannot be sought in mathematical formalisms. One must resort to poetry and classical political economy, i.e. rely on imagination and compassion, for the visions of policies that have to be carved out to make institutions locate themselves in those metastable configurations that are defined by the boundaries in which dynamical systems capable of universal computation get characterized.

4. *Conning* about Rational Expectations Equilibrium and its Learning

In standard mathematical economics, *topological* fixed-point theorems have been used routinely to encapsulate and formalize *self-reference* (*rational expectations* and policy ineffectiveness), *infinite regress* (*rational expectations*) and *self-reproduction* and *self-reconstruction* (growth) in economic dynamic contexts. This is in addition to, and quite apart from, their widespread use in proving existence of equilibria in a wide variety of economic and game theoretical contexts. The mathematical foundations of topology are, in general, sought in axiomatic set theory. Set theory, however, is only one of four branches of mathematical logic, the other three being model theory, proof theory and recursion theory.[24] One can associate, roughly speaking, real analysis, non-standard analysis, constructive analysis and computable analysis with these four branches of mathematical logic. Economists, in choosing to formalize economic notions almost exclusively in terms of real analysis, may not always succeed in capturing the intended conceptual underpinnings of economic notions with the required fidelity. My claim in this section is that the use of topological fix-point theorems to formalize rational expectations does not capture the two fundamental behavioural notions that are crucial in its definition: *self-reference* and *infinite regress*. I try, therefore, to reformalize the notion of rational expectations using a recursion theoretic formalism such that fundamental theorems from this field can be invoked and utilized.[25] The idea of self-referential behaviour is formalized, for example, by considering the *action of a program* or an *algorithm* on its *own description*. Infinite regress is, of course, short-circuited, in the usual way, by a fix-point theorem.

Thus, I formalize the notion of *rational expectations equilibria* recursion theoretically, eschewing all topological assumptions. The emphasis is on suggesting an alternative modelling strategy that can be mimicked for other concepts and areas of economic theory. The implicit claim is that the dominance of topological fix-point theorems in mathematical economics was – indeed is – a particularly insidious *con*, perpetrated by the usual one-dimensional approach to mathematics and mathematical logic by the mathematical economists.

All recursion theoretic formalizations and results come, almost invariably, 'open ended' – meaning, even when uniqueness results are demonstrated there will be, embedded in the recesses of the procedures generating equilibria and other types of solutions, an *indeterminacy*. This kind of indeterminacy is unfamiliar to economists with a mathematical bent simply because it is not common in the mathematics of real analysis. These indeterminacies are due to the generic result in computability theory, referred to and invoked in the previous section: the *halting problem for Turing machines*. It is a kind of generic *undecidability* result, a counterpart to the more formal, and more famous, Gödelian *undecidability* results. It is this fact that makes it possible to claim that seeking economic theoretic foundations for policy may not be an easy task. To be categorical about policy – positively or negatively – on the basis of mathematical models is a dangerous sport.

4.1 *Background*

In a critical discussion of the use of the Brouwer fixed-point theorem by Herbert Simon (1954) that presaged its decisive use in what became the definition of a rational expectations equilibrium, Karl Egil Aubert, a respected mathematician, suggested that economists – and political scientists – were rather cavalier about the domain of definition of economic variables and, hence, less than careful about the mathematics they invoked to derive economic propositions. I was left with the impression, after a careful reading of the discussion between Aubert and Simon (Aubert, 1982a, b; Simon, 1982a, b), that the issue was not the use of a fixed-point framework but its *nature, scope* and *underpinnings*. However, particularly in a rational expectations context, it is not only a question of the nature of the domain of definition but also the fact that there are *self-referential* and *infinite regress* elements intrinsic to the problem. This makes *the appropriate choice of the fixed-point theorem* within which to embed the question of a rational expectations equilibrium particularly sensitive to the kind of mathematics and logic that underpins it. In this section, I trace the origins of the 'topologization' of the mathematical problem of rational expectations equilibrium and discuss the possible infelicities inherent in such a formalization.

There are two crucial aspects to the notion of rational expectations equilibrium – henceforth, REE – (Sargent, 1993 pp. 6–10): an individual optimization problem, subject to *perceived constraints,* and a system-wide, autonomous, set of constraints imposing consistency across the collection of the perceived constraints of the individuals. The latter would be, in a most general sense, the accounting constraint, generated autonomously, by the logic of the macroeconomic system. In a representative agent framework the determination of REEs entails the solution of a general fix-point problem. Suppose the representative agent's *perceived law of motion* of the macroeconomic system (as a function of state variables and exogenous 'disturbances') as a whole is given by H.[26] The system-wide autonomous set of constraints, implied partially, at least, by the optimal decisions based on perceived constraints by the agents, on the other hand, imply an *actual law of motion* given by, say, H^0. The search for fixed points of a mapping, T, linking the individually perceived macroeconomic law of motion, H, and the actual law of motion, H^0, is assumed to be given by a general functional relationship subject to the standard mathematical assumptions:

$$H^0 = T(H) \tag{18}$$

Thus, the fixed points H^* of T[27]

$$H^* = T(H^*) \tag{19}$$

determine REEs.

What is the justification for T? What kind of 'object' is it? It is variously referred to as a 'reaction function', a 'best response function', a 'best response mapping', etc. But whatever it is called, eventually the necessary mathematical assumptions are imputed to it such that it is amenable to a topological interpretation whereby appeal can be made to the existence of a fix point for it as a mapping from a structured domain into itself. So far as I know, there is no optimizing economic theoretical justification for it.

There is also a methodological asymmetry in the determination of H and H^0, respectively. The former has a self-referential aspect to it; the latter an infinite regress element in it. Transforming, mechanically, the former into the latter hides this fact and reducing it to a topological fixed-point problem does little methodological justice to the contents of the constituent elements of the problem. These elements are brought to the surface at a second, separate, step in which ostensible learning mechanisms are devised, in *ad hoc* ways, to determine explicitly the *uncomputable* and *non-constructive* fixed points. But is it really impossible to consider the twin problems in one fell swoop, so to speak?

This kind of tradition to the formalization and determination of REEs has almost by default forced the problem into a particular mathematical straitjacket. The mapping is given topological underpinnings, automatically endowing the underlying assumptions with real analytic content.[28] As a consequence of these default ideas the problem of determining any REE is dichotomized into two sub-problems: a first part where non-constructive and non-computable proofs of the existence of REEs are provided; and a subsequent, quite separate, second part where mechanisms – often given the sobriquet 'learning mechanisms' – are devised to show that such REEs can be determined by individual optimizing agents.[29] It is in this second part where standard economic theory endows agents with varieties of 'bounded rationality' postulates, without modifying the full rationality postulates of the underlying, original, individual optimization problem.

Now, how did this *topological fixed-point REE tradition* come into being? Not, as might conceivably be believed, as a result of Muth's justly celebrated original contribution (Muth, 1961), but from the prior work of Herbert Simon on a problem of predicting the behaviour of rational agents in a political setting (Simon, 1954) and an almost concurrent economic application by Emile Grunberg and Franco Modigliani (1954). Let me explain, albeit briefly, to the extent necessary in the context of this essay.[30]

Simon, in considering the general issue of the feasibility of public prediction in a social science context, formalized the problem for the particular case of investigating how 'the publication of an election prediction (particularly one based on poll data) might influence [individual] voting behaviour, and, hence – ... – falsify the prediction'. Simon, as he has done so often in so many problem situations, came up with the innovative suggestion that the self-referential and infinite regress content of such a context may well be solved by framing it as a mathematical fixed-point problem:

> Is there not involved here a vicious circle, whereby any attempt to anticipate the reactions of the voters alters those reactions and hence invalidates the prediction?
>
> *In principle*, the last question can be answered in the negative: there is no vicious circle.
>
> ...
>
> We [can prove using a 'classical' *theorem of topology* due to Brouwer (the 'fixed-point' theorem)] that it is always possible in principle to take account of reactions to a published prediction in such a way that the prediction will be confirmed by the event. (Simon, 1954, pp. 82–84; italics added)

Grunberg and Modigliani recognized, clearly and explicitly, the *self-referential* nature of the problem of consistent individually rational predictions in the face of being placed in an economic environment where their predictions are reactions to, and react upon (*ad infinitum* – i.e. *infinite regress*), the aggregate outcome, but also were acutely aware of the technical difficulties of infinite regress that were inherent in such situations (cf. in particular, Simon, 1954, pp. 467, 471). In their setting an individual producer faced the classic problem of expected price and quantity formation in a single market, subject to public prediction of the market clearing price. It was not dissimilar to the crude cobweb model, as was indeed recognized by them (Grunberg and Modigliani, 1954, p. 468, footnote 13). Interestingly, what eventually came to be called *rational expectations* by Muth was called a *warranted expectation*[31] by Grunberg and Modigliani (1954, pp. 469–470). In any event, their claim that it was '*normally* possible' to prove the *existence* of 'at least one correct public prediction in the face of effective reaction by the agents' was substantiated by invoking Brouwer's fixed-point theorem (1954, p. 472). To facilitate the application of the theorem, the constituent functions[32] and variables – in particular, the *reaction function* and the conditions on the domain of definition of prices – were assumed to satisfy the necessary *real number* and *topological* conditions (continuity, boundedness, etc).

Thus it was that the tradition in the rational expectations literature of 'solving' the conundrums of self-reference and infinite regress via *topological fixed-point theorems* was etched in the collective memory of the profession. And so, four decades after the Simon and the Grunberg–Modigliani contributions, Sargent, in his influential Arne Ryde Lectures (1993), was able to refer to the fixed-point approach to rational expectations, referring to equation (19):

> A rational expectations equilibrium is a fixed point of the mapping T. (Sargent, 1993, p. 10)

Now, 50 years after that initial introduction of the topological fixed-point tradition by Simon and Grunberg–Modigliani, economists automatically and uncritically accept that this is the only way to solve the REE existence problem – and they are not to be blamed. They have been conned for so long, and bamboozled, too, by the ubiquity of fixed-point theorems in economic theory that yet another application to a domain of economic theory causes no apparent dissonance, cognitive or otherwise. After all, the same somnambulent complacency, equally due to conning by one-eyed mathematical economists, dominates the fundamentals of general equilibrium theory, as if the equilibrium existence problem can only be framed as a fixed-point solution. Because of this complacency, the existence problem has forever been severed of all connections with the problem of determining – or finding or constructing or locating – the processes that may lead to the non-constructive and uncomputable equilibrium.

On the other hand, the recursion theoretic fixed-point tradition not only preserves the unity of equilibrium existence demonstration with the processes that determine it; but it also retains, in the forefront, the self-referential and infinite regress aspects of the problem of the interaction between individual and social prediction and individual and general equilibrium.

4.2 Recursion Theoretic Formalisms

There is nothing sacrosanct about a topological interpretation of the operator T, the reaction or response function. It could equally well be interpreted recursion theoretically, which is what I shall do in the sequel.[33] I need some unfamiliar, but elementary, formal machinery – concepts, definitions, new or alternative connotations for familiar words, etc. – not normally available to the mathematical economist.

Definition 7. *An **operator** is a function*

$$\Phi: \mathcal{F}_m \longrightarrow \mathcal{F}_n \qquad (20)$$

where $\mathcal{F}_k$ $(k \geq 1)$ is the class of all partial (recursive) functions from $\mathbb{N}^k$ to $\mathbb{N}$.

Definition 8. *Φ is a **recursive operator** if there is a computable function ϕ such that $\forall f \in \mathcal{F}_m$ and $\mathbf{x} \in \mathbb{N}^m, y \in \mathbb{N}$:*

$$\Phi(f)(\mathbf{x}) \simeq y \text{ if } \forall f \exists \text{ a finite } \theta \sqsubseteq f \text{ such that } \phi(\widetilde{\theta}, \mathbf{x}) \simeq y$$

where[34] $\widetilde{\theta}$ *is a standard coding of a finite function* θ, *which is extended by* f.

Definition 9. *An operator* $\Phi\colon \mathcal{F}_m \longrightarrow \mathcal{F}_n$ *is* **continuous** *if, for any* $f \in \mathcal{F}_m$, *and* $\forall \mathbf{x}$, y:

$$\Phi(f)(\mathbf{x}) \simeq y \ \text{if} \ \forall f \ \exists \ a \ \text{finite} \ \theta \sqsubseteq f \ \text{such that} \ \Phi(\theta)(\mathbf{x}) \simeq y$$

Definition 10. *An operator* $\Phi\colon \mathcal{F}_m \longrightarrow \mathcal{F}_n$ *is* **monotone** *if, whenever* $f, g \in \mathcal{F}_m$ *and* $f \sqsubseteq g$, *then* $\Phi(f) \sqsubseteq \Phi(g)$.

Theorem 4. *A recursive operator is continuous and monotone.*

Example 1. *Consider the following* **recursive program** Þ *(also a recursive operator) over the integers:*

$$\text{Þ}\colon F(x, y) \Longleftarrow \ \text{if} \ x = y \ \text{then} \ y + 1, \ \text{else} \ F(x, F(x - 1, y + 1))$$

Now replace each occurrence of F in Þ *by each of the following functions:*

$$f_1(x, y)\colon \text{if} \ x = y \ \text{then} \ y + 1, \ \text{else} \ x + 1 \tag{21}$$

$$f_2(x, y)\colon \ \text{if} \ x \geq y \ \text{then} \ x + 1, \ \text{else} \ y - 1 \tag{22}$$

$$f_3(x, y)\colon \ \text{if} \ \left(x \geq y\right) \wedge (x - y \ \text{even}) \ \text{then} \ x + 1, \ \text{else} \ \text{undefined} \tag{23}$$

Then, on either side of $\Longleftarrow$ *in* Þ *we get the* **identical** *partial functions:*

$$\forall i \ (1 \leq i \leq 3), \ f_i(x, y) \equiv \ \text{if} \ x = y \ \text{then} \ y + 1, \ \text{else} \ f_i(x, f_i(x - 1, y + 1)) \tag{24}$$

Such functions f_i ($\forall i$ ($1 \leq i \leq 3$)) *are referred to as* **fixed points** *of the recursive program* Þ *(recursive operator).*

Note that these are fixed points of functionals.

Remark 8. *Note that* f_3, *in contrast to* f_1 *and* f_2, *has the following special property.* $\forall \langle x, y \rangle$ *of pairs of integers such that* $f_3(x, y)$ *is defined, both* f_1 *and* f_2 *are also defined and have the same value as does* f_3.

- f_3 *is then said to be* **less defined than or equal to** f_1 *and* f_2 *and this property is denoted by* $f_3 \sqsubseteq f_1$ *and* $f_3 \sqsubseteq f_2$.
- *In fact, in this particular example, it so happens that* f_3 *is* **less defined than or equal to** *all fixed points of* Þ.
- *In addition,* f_3 *is the* **only** *partial function with this property for* Þ *and is therefore called the* **least fixed point** *of* Þ.

We now have the minimal formal machinery needed to state one of the classic theorems of recursive function theory, known variously as the *first recursion theorem, Kleene's theorem* or, sometimes, as the *fixed-point theorem for complete partial orders.*

Theorem 5. *Suppose that* $\Phi\colon \mathcal{F}_m \longrightarrow \mathcal{F}_m$ *is a recursive operator (or a recursive program* Þ*). Then there is a partial function* f_ϕ *that is the least fixed point of* Φ:

$$\Phi\bigl(f_\phi\bigr) = f_\phi$$

$$\textit{If } \Phi(g) = g, \ \textit{then } f_\phi \sqsubseteq g$$

Remark 9. *If, in addition to being partial,* f_ϕ *is also total, then it is the **unique least fixed point**. Note also that a recursive operator is characterized by being continuous and monotone. There would have been some advantages in stating this famous theorem highlighting the domain of definition, i.e. complete partial orders, but the formal machinery becomes slightly unwieldy.*

Remark 10. *Although this way of stating the (first) recursion theorem almost highlights its non-constructive aspect – i.e. the theorem guarantees the **existence** of a fixed point without indicating a way of finding it – it is possible to use a slightly stronger form of the theorem to amend this 'defect' (cf. Moret, 1998, p. 59).*

4.3 Recursion Theoretic REE

Before stating formally, as a summarizing theorem, the main result (i.e. Theorem 6) it is necessary to formalize the rational agent and the setting in which rationality is exercised in the expectational domain in recursion theoretic formalisms, too. This means, at a minimum, the rational agent as a *recursion theoretic agent*.[35]

The topological fix-point theorems harnessed by a rational agent are, as mentioned previously, easily done in standard economic theory where the agents themselves are *set-theoretically* formalized. There is no dissonance between the formalism in which the rational agent is defined and the economic setting in which such an agent operates. The latter setting is also set-theoretically defined.

The recursion theoretic formalism introduced in the previous subsection presupposes that the rational agent is now recursion theoretically defined and so too the setting – i.e. the economy. Defining the rational agent recursion theoretically means defining the preferences characterizing the agent and the choice theoretic actions recursion theoretically. This means defining, firstly, the domain of choice for the agent number theoretically and, secondly, the choice of maximal (sub)sets over such a domain in a computably viable way. Such a redefinition and reformalization should mean equivalences between the rational choice of an agent over well-defined preferences and the computing activities of an ideal computer, i.e. Turing machine (or any of its own formal equivalences, by the Church–Turing thesis). Since a complete formalism and the relevant equivalences are described, defined and, where necessary, rigorously proved in Chapter 3 of my Ryde Lectures (Velupillai, 2000),

I will simply assume that the interested reader can be trusted to refer to it for any detailed clarification and substantiation.

It is now easy to verify that the domain over which the recursive operator and the partial functions are defined is weaker[36] than the conventional domains over which the economist works. Similarly, the continuity and monotonicity of the recursive operator is naturally satisfied by the standard assumptions in economic theory for the reaction or response function, T. Hence, we can apply the *first recursion theorem* to equation (19), interpreting T as a recursive operator and not as a topological mapping. Then, from Theorem 5, we know that there is a partial function – i.e. a computable function – f_t that is the least fixed point of T. Thus, we can summarize the desired result in the form of the following theorem.

Theorem 6. *Suppose that the reaction or response function* $T: H_m \longrightarrow H_m$ *is a recursive operator (or a recursive program* Γ*). Then there is a computable function* f_t *that is a least fixed point of* T:

$$T(f_t) = f_t$$
$$\text{If } T(g) = g, \text{ then } f_t \sqsubseteq g$$

Remark 11. *Theorem 6 can be used directly to show that* $\exists$ *a (recursive) program that, under any input, outputs exactly itself. It is this program that acts as the relevant reaction or response* **function** *for an economy in REE. The existence of such a recursive program justifies the New Classical methodological stand on the ubiquity of REEs. However, since Theorem 6 is stated above in its non-constructive version, finding this particular recursive program requires a little effort. Hence, the need for learning processes to find this program, unless the theorem is utilized in its constructive version. Even with these caveats, the immediate advantage is that there is no need to deal with non-recursive reals or non-computable functions in the recursion theoretic formalism. In the traditional formalism the fix point that is the REE is, except for flukes, a* **non-recursive real; constructing learning processes to determine non-recursive reals** *is either provably impossible or formally intractable (computationally complex).*

What are the further advantages of recasting the problem of solving for the *REE recursion theoretically* rather than retaining the traditional topological formalizations?

An advantage at the superficial level but nevertheless not unimportant in policy-oriented economic theoretic contexts is the simple fact that, as even the name indicates, recursion encapsulates, explicitly, the idea of self-reference because functions are defined, naturally, in terms of themselves. Secondly, the existence of a least fix point is a solution to the infinite regress problem. Thus the two 'birds' are encapsulated in one fell swoop – and, that too, with a computable function.

Think of the formal discourse of economic analysis as being conducted in a programming language; call it $\mathfrak{F}$. We know that we choose the underlying terminology for economic formalisms with particular meanings in mind for the elemental units: preferences, endowments, technology, information, expectation and so on; call the generic element of the set ς. When we form a compound economic proposition out of the ς units, the meaning is natural and clear. We can therefore suppose that evaluating a compound expression in $\Im$ is immediate: given an expression in $\Im$, say $\lambda(\varsigma)$, the variables in λ, when given specific values α, are to be evaluated according to the *semantics* of $\Im$. To actually *evaluate* a compound expression, $\lambda(\varsigma)$, we write a *recursive program* in the language $\Im$, the language of economic theory.

But that leaves a key question unanswered: what is the computable function that is implicitly defined by the recursive program? The first recursion theorem answers this question with the answer: the least fixed point. In this case, therefore, there is a direct application of the first recursion theorem to the semantics of the language $\Im$. The artificial separation between the syntax of economic analysis, when formalized, and its natural semantics can, therefore, be bridged *effectively*.

If the language of economic theory is best regarded as a very high-level programming language, $\Im$, to understand a *theorem* in economics, in recursion theoretic terms, represent the *assumptions* – i.e. *axioms* and the *variables* – as *input data* and the *conclusions* as *output data*. State the theorem as an expression in the language $\Im$. Then try to convert the proof into a program in the language $\Im$, which will take in the inputs and produce the desired output. If one is unable to do this, it is probably because the proof relies essentially on some infusion of non-constructive or uncomputable elements. This step will identify any inadvertent infusion of non-algorithmic reasoning, which will have to be resolved – sooner or later – if computations are to be performed on the variables as input data. The computations are not necessarily numerical; they can also be symbolic.

In other words, if we take algorithms and data structures to be fundamental, then it is natural to define and understand functions in these terms. If a function does not correspond to an algorithm, what can it be? The topological definition of a function is not naturally algorithmic. Therefore, the expressions formed from the language of economic theory, in a topological formalization, are not necessarily implementable by a program, except by flukes, appeal to magic or by illegitimate, intractable and vague approximations. Hence the need to dichotomize every topological existence proof. In the case of REE, this is the root cause of the artificial importance granted to a separate problem of learning REEs.

In all of these – and many more – senses, the REE and its learning literature are noble purveyors of indiscriminate *conning*.

5. Concluding Notes

The human mind is not a purely logical entity. The complex manner in which it functions is *often at variance with the logic of mathematics*. It is not always pure logic which gives us insight, nor is it chance that causes us to make mistakes. To understand how these processes occur, both successfully and erroneously, we must formulate a distinction between the *mathematical concepts as formally defined* and *the cognitive processes by which they are conceived*. (Tall and Vinner, 1981, p. 151; italics added)

What guarantee is there, then, that economic concepts can be mapped unambiguously and subjectively – to be terribly and unnecessarily mathematical about it – into mathematical concepts? The belief in the power and necessity of formalizing economic theory mathematically has thus obliterated the distinction between cognitively perceiving and understanding concepts from different domains and mapping them into each other. Whether the age-old problem of the equality between supply and demand should be mathematically formalized as a system of inequalities or equalities is not something that should be decided by mathematical knowledge or convenience. Surely it would be considered absurd, bordering on the insane, if a surgical procedure was implemented because a tool for its implementation was devised by a medical doctor who knew and believed in topological fixed-point theorems? Yet, weighty propositions about policy are decided on the basis of formalizations based on ignorance and belief in the veracity of one kind of one-dimensional mathematics.

5.1 *A Mathematical Excursion*

Thus, consider Hildenbrand's attempt at characterizing 'an axiomatic theory of a certain economic phenomenon as formulated by Debreu' (1986a). This attempt leads to two precepts for formalizing in economics:

> First, the primitive concepts of the economic analysis are selected, and then, each of these primitive concepts is represented by a *mathematical object*.
>
> . . . .
>
> Second, assumptions on the mathematical representations of the primitive concepts are made explicit and are fully specified. Mathematical analysis then establishes the consequences of these assumptions in the form of theorems. (Debreu, 1986a, p. 4; italics added)

Even if we grant Hildenbrand the first precept, accepting orthodox characterizations of the 'primitive concepts of economic analysis', there are a variety of mathematics, each with different kinds of mathematical object, onto which these can be mapped. Surely, many economic concepts are naturally combinatorial. The mapping from such combinatorial 'primitive concepts of economics' to an appropriate mathematics is, even at the simplest level, as different as ordinary linear programming as against integer programming. One cannot solve an 'equivalent' linear programming problem, defining economic variables to range over the reals, and then approximate the solution to the integer programming problem by taking the nearest integer solution to the real solution of the linear programming problem. Non-standard mathematical analysis is quite comfortable with infinitesimal objects. Constructive mathematics does not accept the Church–Turing thesis and, hence, the nature and scope of allowable algorithms is significantly different from those accepted in recursion theory, which accepts the Church–Turing thesis. The Bolzano–Weierstrass theorem is invalid in constructive analysis; the Heine–Borel theorem has no counterpart in computable analysis. And so on.

Nor is it the case that the 'mathematical analysis' which 'then establishes the consequences of these assumptions in the form of theorems' independent of the nature of the mathematical objects and the logic of mathematical reasoning allowed in that particular mathematical analysis. In most forms of constructive mathematics undecidable disjunctions are eschewed, particularly when they are implications of invoking the *tertium non datur*.

Let me give a famous example from the very heart of number theory, which in its conception and formulation is also elementary: *the prime number theorem*. I choose this example to illustrate the fact that *the nature of the mathematical object*, in this case ordinary numbers, about which a conjecture was made belongs to one particular type of mathematics, i.e. number theory; but the conjecture itself belongs to a different kind of mathematics, i.e. analysis, and its proof, therefore, was sought after in the latter branch of mathematics.

The saga that led to what I like to call the 'prime number nut' began with the famous conjectures, independently made, by Euler, Legendre and Gauss that $\pi(x)$, the number of primes less than x, approaches, asymptotically, the quotient $x/\log x$, or

$$\lim_{x \to \infty} \frac{\pi(x)}{x/\log x} = 1 \tag{25}$$

As Shanks (1978, p. 16; last italics in original)) observed perceptively:

No easy proof of the [prime number theorem] is known. The fact that it took a century to prove is a measure of its difficulty. *The theorem is primarily one of analysis. Number theory plays only a small role.* That some analysis must enter is clear from [the above equation] – a *limit* is involved. The extent to which analysis is involved is what is surprising.

But surely the object about which the conjecture was made was combinatorial and therefore techniques of proof belonging to some variant of combinatorial mathematics may well result in a proof that was as simple as it was to state the conjecture? Consider, therefore, the following proof of a bound for $\pi(x)$. Denote by p_i ($\forall i = 1, \ldots, m$) those prime numbers less than the number x. Then:

$$x = p_1^{e_1} \cdot p_2^{e_2} \cdot \ldots p_m^{e_m} \tag{26}$$

Clearly each exponent is at most $\log x$; i.e.

$$e_i \leq \log x \quad \forall i = 1, \ldots, m \tag{27}$$

Thus each e_i can be *effectively*[37] encoded by at most $\log \log x$ bits. On the other hand, a fundamental result in algorithmic complexity theory shows that maximally complex numbers x cannot be encoded by less than $\log x$ bits; i.e.

$$\pi(x) \leq \frac{\log x}{\log \log x} \tag{28}$$

This (provably simpler) proof presupposes some elementary knowledge of *algorithmic complexity theory* which, in turn, presupposes some further elementary grounding in classical recursion theory. But the proverbial buck stops there; the basis is computable and combinatorial and hence entirely consistent with the nature of the mathematical object, about which the conjecture was originally made. In the proof – called *proof by the incompressibility method* – itself I have, implicitly, exploited the fact that we can assume most numbers to be maximally descriptively complex (in a precise sense). Then the required contradiction is obtained by supposing that such a number can be (effectively) encoded by exploiting extractable algorithmic patterns. The key methodological difference between proof by the incompressible method and 'traditional' formalistic proofs (particularly *existence* and *lower–upper bound* proofs) is best described by Li and Vitanyi, the most polished exponents and expositors of the 'incompressible method':

> Traditional proofs often involve all instances of a problem in order to conclude that some property holds for at least one instance. The proof would have proceeded simpler, if only that one instance could have been used in the first place. Unfortunately, that instance is hard or impossible to find, and the proof has to involve all the instances. In contrast, in a proof by the incompressibility method, we first choose a random (that is, incompressible) individual object that is known to exist (even though we cannot construct it). Then we show that if the assumed property would not hold, then this object could be compressed, and hence it would not be random. (Li and Vitanyi, 1993, p. 4)

In the above (sketch of the) proof I have exploited the incompressibility of most numbers by selecting a 'typical x', and the *selection* process is *effective*, i.e no metaphysical *choice axioms* need be invoked at any stage of the demonstration. This remark leads me on to my next point regarding the ubiquity of the axiom of choice in the activities of the mathematical economist. But before that, to continue and close the thread of reasoning involved with the example of the prime number theorem and its proof, let me remind the reader of a wise observation made by Clower and Howitt (1978) in the context of monetary theory with entirely obvious rational number constraints on the domain of traditional supply–demand variables. Clower and Howitt pointed out that *proofs* of propositions in monetary theory with rational number constraints

> [N]ecessarily involve the use of number theory – a branch of mathematics unfamiliar to most economists. (Clower and Howitt, 1978, p. 452)

This perceptive observation and the kind of mathematics I used to prove quite simply the prime number theorem are reminders of the fact that 'the economic problem' is not naturally to be viewed (always) necessarily from the point of view of classical mathematical analysis; nor need propositions have (always) to be proved by analytical methods. The more substantive examples in the main body of the paper are illustrations of these precepts and therefore highlight the problem of the ontology of economic concepts and entities and their unambiguous mapping into mathematical domains.

Then, there is the ubiquity of the *axiom of choice* in the activity of the
mathematical economist and the way it cons us into somnambulance is far more
sinister in many ways than even the blind use of fixed-point theorems and reliance
on classical mathematical analysis for formalizations. Each time an article or a
text in economic analysis contains the unguarded assertion that 'agents are indexed
over the continuum', and a particular 'representative agent' is identified, there is
an implicit reliance on, and explicit invoking of, *the axiom of choice*.[38]

Economically evocative descriptive terms and concepts such as *choice sets*,
selectors, etc. are associated with the use of this axiom in economics, particularly
in discussions about the *foundations of rational choice*. How do mathematical
economists who appreciate its formal power justify its use in deriving economic
propositions despite its blatant violation of any implemental choice? Not, as one
may expect, on the basis of the intuitive richness of its implications; but, peculiarly,
on its apparent acceptance by mathematicians:

> The proof of [Szpilrajn's theorem on the existence of an extension that is an
> ordering] requires an auxiliary proposition called Zorn's lemma [that] is **not
> intuitively clear**, but it is **demonstrably equivalent** to an important *axiom of
> choice* that is accepted today by most mathematicians. (Suzumura, 1983, pp.
> 16–17; bold emphasis added)

Have we been reduced to accepting mathematical axioms also on the basis of
the simple majority rule? Are we, as economists, supposed to accept the use of a
controversial axiom, to put it mildly, to derive important economic propositions,
simply on the basis that it is 'accepted today by most mathematicians'? Even if
we, again as economists, grant this should we not wonder why it was necessary,
in the first place, for mathematicians and mathematical logicians to formulate
such an axiom and, often, to be quite explicit about actually appealing to it –
much more than the half-baked mathematical economists who more often than
not do not even realize they are using it and its dubious underpinnings and
implications?[39]

5.2 *An Excursion into Game Theory*

An important sub-field of mathematical economics that I have not dealt with must
be mentioned in this context of comments about the invoking of the axiom of
choice: *game theory*, a theory which is also heavily dependent, even historically,
on the use of fixed-point theorems.[40]

In the case of game theory the subversion into its subjective vision of economic
behaviour in adversarial situations was a direct consequence of the fixed-point
approach pioneered by von Neumann and Nash. I think I can make a strong case
to substantiate this assertion and thus provide a further example of economists
and social scientists being conned into a particular vision of economic, social and
political processes.[41] My starting point would be Zermelo's celebrated lecture of
1912 (Zermelo, 1912) and his pioneering formulation of an adversarial situation
into an *alternating game* and its subsequent formulation and solution as a mini–

max problem by Jan Mycielski in terms of *alternating the existential and universal quantifiers.*

The Zermelo game has no subjective component of any sort. It is an entirely objective game of perfect information, although it is often considered part of the orthodox game theoretic tradition. Let me describe the gist of the kind of game considered by Zermelo, first. In a two-player game of perfect information, alternative moves are made by the two players, say A and B. The game, say as in chess, is played by each of the players 'moving' one of a finite number of counters available to him or her, according to specified rules, along a 'tree' – in the case of chess, of course, on a board of fixed dimension, etc. Player A, say, makes the first move (perhaps determined by a chance mechanism) and places one of the counters, say $a_0 \in A_0$, on the designated 'tree' at some allowable position (again, for evocative purposes, say as in chess or any other similar board game); player B, then, observes the move made by A – i.e. observes, with perfect recall, the placement of the counter a_0 – and makes the second move by placing, say, $b_1 \in B_1$, on an allowable position on the 'board'; and so on. Let us suppose these alternating choices terminate after player B's n-th move; i.e. when $b_n \in B_n$ has been placed in an appropriate place on the 'board'.

Definition 11. *A **play** of such a game consists of a sequence of such alternative moves by the two players.*

Suppose we label the alternating individual moves by the two players with the natural numbers in such a way that

1. the even numbers, say, $a(0), a(2), \ldots, a(n-1)$ enumerate player A's moves;
2. the odd numbers, say, $b(1), b(3), \ldots, b(n)$ enumerate player B's moves.
   - Then, each (finite) play can be expressed as a sequence, say γ, of natural numbers.

Suppose we define the set α as the set of plays which are wins for player A; and, similarly, the set β as the set of plays which are wins for player B.

Definition 12. *A **strategy** is a function from any (finite) string of natural numbers as input that generates a single natural number, say σ, as an output.*

Definition 13. *A game is **determined** if one of the players has a winning strategy; i.e. if either $\sigma \in \alpha$ or $\sigma \in \beta$.*

Theorem 7. Zermelo's theorem. $\exists$ *a winning strategy for player A, whatever is the play chosen by B; and vice versa for B.*

Remark 12. *This is Zermelo's version of a minimax theorem in a perfect recall, perfect information, game.*

It is in connection with this result and the minimax form of it that Steinhaus observed, with considerable perplexity:

[My] inability [to prove the minimax theorem] was a consequence of the ignorance of Zermelo's paper (1912) in spite of its having been published in 1913. . . . J von Neumann was aware of the importance of the minimax principle (cf. von Neumann, 1928); it is, however, *difficult to understand the absence of a quotation of Zermelo's lecture in his publications.* (Steinhaus, 1965, p. 460; italics added)

Why did not von Neumann refer, in 1928, to the Zermelo-tradition of alternating games? The tentative answer to such a question is a whole research program in itself and I will simply have to place it on an agenda and pass on. I have no doubts whatsoever that any serious study to answer this almost rhetorical question will reap a rich harvest of further cons perpetrated by the mathematical economists, perhaps inadvertently. The point I wish to make is something else and has to do with the axiom of choice and its place in *economic conning.* So, let me return to this theme.

Mycielski (cf. Steinhaus, 1965, pp. 460–461) formulated the Zermelo minimax theorem in terms of alternating logical quantifiers as follows:[42]

$$\sim \left\{ \bigcup_{a_0 \in A_0} \bigcap_{b_1 \in B_1} \ldots \bigcup_{a_n \in A_{n-1}} \bigcap_{b_n \in B_n} (a_0 b_1 a_2 b_3 \ldots a_{n-1} b_n) \right\} \in \alpha$$

$$\implies \left\{ \bigcap_{a_0 \in A_0} \bigcup_{b_1 \in B_1} \ldots \bigcap_{a_n \in A_{n-1}} \bigcup_{b_n \in B_n} (a_0 b_1 a_2 b_3 \ldots a_{n-1} b_n) \right\} \notin \beta$$

Now, summarizing the structure of the game and taking into account Mycielski's formulation in terms of alternating we can state as follows:

1. The sequential moves by the players can be modelled by alternating existential and universal quantifiers.
2. The existential quantifier moves first; if the total number of moves is odd, then an existential quantifier determines the last chosen integer; if not, the universal quantifier determines the final integer to be chosen.
3. One of the players tries to make a logical expression, preceded by these alternating quantifiers *true*; the other tries to make it *false*.
4. Thus, inside the braces the win condition in any play is stated as a proposition to be satisfied by generating a number belonging to a given set.
5. If, therefore, we can extract *an arithmetical form* – since we are dealing with sequences of natural numbers – for the win condition it will be possible to discuss recursive solvability, decidability and computability of winning strategies.

The above definitions, descriptions and structures define, therefore, an *arithmetical game* of length n (cf. Velupillai, 2000, pp. 125–126, for a formal definition). Stating the Zermelo theorem in a more formal and general form, we have:

Theorem 8. *Arithmetical games of finite length are determined.*

The more general theorem, for games of arbitrary (non-finite) length, can be proved by standard diagonalization arguments and is[43]

Theorem 9. *Arithmetical games on any countable set or on any set which has a countable complement are determined.*

Now, enter the axiom of choice! Suppose we allow any unrestricted sets α and β. Then, for example, if they are *imperfect sets*,[44] the game is not determined. If we work within ZFC, then such sets are routinely acceptable and lead to games that cannot be determined – even if we assume perfect information and perfect recall. Surely, this is counter-intuitive? For this reason, this tradition in game theory chose to renounce the axiom of choice and work with an alternative axiom that restricts the class of sets within which arithmetical games are played. The alternative axiom is the *axiom of determinacy*, introduced by Steinhaus:

Axiom 1. The ***axiom of determinacy***. *Arithmetical games on every subset of the Baire line[45] are determined.*

The motivation given by Steinhaus (1965, pp. 464–465) is a salutary lesson for mathematically minded economists or economists who choose to accept the axiom of choice on 'democratic' principles or economists who are too lazy to study carefully the economic meaning of accepting a mathematical axiom:

> It is known that [the axiom of choice] produces such consequences as the decomposition of a ball into five parts which can be put together to build up a new ball of twice the volume of the old one [the Banach–Tarski paradox], a result considered as paradoxical by many scientists. There is another objection: how are we to speak of perfect information for [players] A and B if it is impossible to verify whether both of them think of the same set when they speak of ['α']? *This impossibility is inherent in every set having only [the axiom of choice] as its certificate of birth.* In such circumstances it is doubtful whether human beings will ever play really [an infinite game].
>
> *All these considerations impelled me to place the blame on the Axiom of Choice.* Sixty years of the theory of sets have elapsed since this Axiom was proclaimed, and some ideas have ... convinced me that a purely negative attitude against [the axiom of choice] would be dangerous to propose. Thus I have chosen the idea of replacing [the axiom of choice] by the [above axiom of determinacy]. (italics added)

There is a whole tradition of game theory, beginning at the beginning, so to speak, with Zermelo, linking up, via Rabin's modification of the Gale–Stewart infinite game, to recursion theoretic formulations of arithmetical games underpinned by the *axiom of determinacy* and completely independent of the *axiom of choice* and **eschewing all subjective considerations**. In this tradition notions of *effective playability*, *solvability* and *decidability* questions take on fully meaningful computational and computable form where one can investigate whether it is feasible to instruct a player, who is known to have a winning strategy, to actually select a sequence to achieve the win. None of this is possible in the orthodox tradition, which *cons* us into a somnambulance that there are no alternative mathematics for investigating, mathematically, adversarial situations in the social sciences.

5.3 *A Very Brief Note on Macrodynamics*

In macrodynamics, the current frontiers seem to be dominated by the New Classicals who have gradually begun to refer to this sub-discipline as *recursive macroeconomics*.[46] Their vision for the nature and future of macroeconomics, a field in which computation and dynamics is almost intrinsic to its problems, is best reflected in the way the subject is characterized by a leading proponent, a Nobel Laureate of recent years,[47] along the lines of the predominance of 'tools' in determining the nature of the subject.[48]

> ... I want to emphasize that the methodology that transformed macroeconomics is applicable to the study of virtually all fields of economics. In fact, the meaning of the word *macroeconomics* has changed *to refer to the tools being used*[49] rather than just to the study of business cycle fluctuations. (Prescott, 2004a; second set of italics added)

Moreover, as far as the New Classicals are concerned, the mathematical foundations of neoclassical economics is provided by general equilibrium theory (and, occasionally, game theory). Since their foundations are in orthodox general equilibrium theory – i.e. neoclassical microeconomics – there is no special reason for me to identify the cons that we are subject to, at their hands: they will be the same ones that emanate from the issues discussed in earlier sections of this paper, on dynamics, policy and REE. On the other hand, the New Classical macrodynamic theorist is very explicit about the crucial role of the *computational experiment* in macrodynamics (Kydland and Prescott, 1996). The concept and contents of a computational experiment in a macrodynamic model is a direct generalization of the *static computable general equilibrium framework*, particularly the one having its origins in the work of Shoven and Whalley (1972) which, in turn, is based on the pioneering contributions to the field by Herbert Scarf (1973):

> Shoven and Whalley (1972) were the first to use what we call the computational experiment in economics. The model economies that they used in their experiments are static and have many industrial sectors. (Kydland and Prescott, 1996, p. 69, footnote 2)

But Kydland and Prescott misrepresent the actual theoretical nature of the computational model used in Shoven and Whalley (1972). That model is neither constructive nor computable, contrary to the claims by Shoven and Whalley. So, they could not be carrying out a consistent 'computational experiment' that could be underpinned by any theory. The hollowness of the claims of computability and constructivity – i.e. a computational experiment – is fully described and elucidated in Velupillai (2006).

In the case of New Classical macrodynamics there is also the particular and peculiar reliance on the functional equations of Bellman. Almost the first thing an advanced undergraduate or a beginning graduate student is taught is the way of formulating any given representative agent's dynamic optimization problem in terms of the Bellman equation. The particular forte of this formulation, as claimed by most mathematical macroeconomists, is that it is in 'recursive' form and hence amenable to a fixed-point approach (cf. Adda and Cooper, 2003, p. 12)! So, there we are; back to square one on the *conning* front.

However, this is not entirely correct. It is not necessary to invoke the full force of topological fixed-point theorems (cf. Marsden and Hoffman, 1993, p. 275) and therefore one is not saddled with the many whimsical conning mathematical assumptions that make the computational experiment infeasible. It is 'only' necessary to invoke the *contraction mapping theorem* in metric spaces (cf. Denardo, 1967, pp. 166–167, 177), a paper referred to at almost the very beginning of the Kydland–Prescott research program (cf. Kydland and Prescott, 1980), by them, to codify the idea of the *computational experiment*. But here, too, there are so many whimsical and fragile assumptions at the very recesses of the mathematical framework that I am almost reluctant to saddle the end of this already very long paper with their nature. But here is an ultra-brief hint. The contraction mapping theorem is defined on a complete metric space. This characteristic is a generalization of the idea of **Cauchy completeness**, which is given by the theorem:

Theorem 10. *Every Cauchy sequence in $\mathbb{R}$ converges to an element of $\mathbb{R}$.*

This theorem is, in turn, proved using the Bolzano–Weierstrass theorem, which contains an unconstructifiable – i.e. non-algorithmic and hence impossible to utilize in a consistent 'computational experiment' – undecidable disjunction in its proof! And so we go on and on. Somewhere, buried in the recesses of almost every mathematical result used by conventional mathematical macrodynamics, there are undecidable disjunctions that make a mockery of the idea of computational experiments. Nothing less than whimsey and fragility seem to be the ultimate disciplining criteria for much of the mathematics of New Classical macrodynamics.

I will not even begin to discuss the way recent modelling exercises by the New Classicals have relied on a *continuum of agents* in a way that makes any notion of computation completely nonsensical.

5.4 *Final Remarks*

A continuum of agents populate many whimsical and fragile mathematical macrodynamic models. Non-constructive and uncomputable fixed-point theorems are invoked to prove the existence of uncomputable equilibria which are then computed by uncomputable numerical procedures. Axioms whose implications are illusory are invoked routinely at the foundations of economic theory. Such are the whimsies and fragilities of ordinary, bread-and-butter orthodox mathematical and mathematized economic theory. To weed the whimsies and fragilities out of these frameworks may not be a worthwhile exercise. To be aware of them is, on the other hand, almost imperative – so that related mistakes need not be made by a new generation of mathematically able, numerically literate, computationally able, students of economics.

I should add here, in conclusion, that there are non-orthodox varieties of economic theory with powerful mathematical underpinnings.[50] For the purposes of this paper, I have concentrated on a few themes because it was possible to frame them and tackle them from an almost unified or homogeneous point of view. If this exercise is reasonably successful, I may undertake a broader study, incorporating orthodox and non-orthodox mathematical economics in my quest to 'find' the *con* that they, too, might encapsulate.

I can do no better than conclude this paper by recalling an eloquent admonition by a distinguished mathematician who tried valiantly to construct a mathematical economics without cons:

> The very fact that a theory appears in mathematical form, that, for instance, a theory provided the occasion for the application of a fixed-point theorem ... somehow makes us more ready to take it seriously. ... The result, perhaps most common in the social sciences, is *bad theory with a mathematical passport.* ... The intellectual attractiveness of a mathematical argument, ..., makes mathematics a powerful tool of intellectual prestidigitation – *a glittering deception in which some are entrapped, and some, alas, entrappers.* (Schwartz, 1986, pp. 22–23; italics added)

Acknowledgement

This paper was written during a period of leave from Trento, spent happily as a Fellow and College Lecturer at Girton College, Cambridge. Of course, no one is implicated in any of the errors and omissions that remain in this final version of a paper that has been in embryo for many months. However, I cannot help suspecting that my critical friends Tom Boylan, Bob Clower, Steve Kinsella, Francesco Luna and Stefano Zambelli may have tried, without much success, to ameliorate the infelicities by gentle suggestions. Alas, pure stubbornness is the only reason for my mule-headed refusal, sometimes, to take into account their sensible suggestions, particularly with regard to tone and nuance.

Notes

1. *One aspect* of this 'fragility of deduction' was perceptively noted by Samuelson (1952, pp. 59–60):

> [T]here is for all of us a psychological problem of making correct deductions. That is why pencils have erasers and electronic calculators have bells and gongs.
>
>   I suppose this is what Alfred Marshall must have had in mind when he followed John Stuart Mill in speaking of the dangers involved in *long* chains of logical reasoning. Marshall treated such chains as if their truth content was subject to radioactive decay and leakage .... Obviously, in making such a statement, Marshall was describing a property of that biological biped or computing machine called *homo sapiens*; for he certainly could not be describing a property of logical implication.

My own focus will be on the 'fragility of deduction', whether of long or short 'chains of reasoning', due to the background implicit assumptions in almost every step of any such chains of reasoning and the nature of the deductive process itself. Thus, for example, in assuming a *continuum* of agents and then reasoning as if a particular agent in the continuum can be *identified* requires the explicit assumption of the *axiom of choice*; hence, that particular identification is *algorithmically non-effective*.

2. To be read, instead of 'let the buyer be aware', as 'let the reader be aware'.

3. Alias the *Walrasian Demon*, for the purposes of this paper (see below for the justification for the alias).

4. I choose to use this word quite deliberately and not the more Popperian – *whimsical* – word *falsification*, that is uncritically adopted, particularly in econometric discourse.

5. This is a theme, with minor variations, Debreu has emphasized in various writings since the early 1980s (cf. for example Debreu, 1984, 1991). The other mathematical concept to which he makes reference in a similar fashion is the separating hyperplane theorem (or the Hahn–Banach theorem). My strictures against the particular kind of fixed-point theorems to which he and his followers appeal and invoke for use in economic theory apply equally forcefully and rigorously also to the use, invoking and application of such 'duality' theorems.

6. It is not clear that von Neumann's growth paper (presented, first, in 1932, published in German in 1938 and in English in 1945–46) was, in fact, 'an accident within an accidental paper' (cf. Kaldor, 1989).

7. The kind of uncritical acceptance of a *conning* exercise like that which is here pointed out by Smale leads to further irrelevant cons like the following (Suzumura, 1973, p. 67):

> Some years ago, Professor Uzawa established a remarkable theorem to the effect that the Walras' existence theorem and the Brouwer fixed point theorem are equivalent. The importance of this equivalence theorem lies in the fact that *it accounts for the intrinsic necessity of the fixed point type of topological considerations in the analysis of general economic equilibrium.*

8. I have discussed the possible role of analogue computing in economic dynamics in a recent paper and will not further touch on that topic in this paper (Velupillai, 2003).

9. He did not, as generations of critical mathematical economists have alleged, simply count equations and variables and satisfy himself about the existence of solutions in a facile way; he was, after all, a nineteenth-century scientist, for whom solving an equation still meant devising methods to find the solution. The somnambulance of existence proofs without accompanying constructions had to wait for the twentieth century. Progress and its paradoxes have many facets.

10. In a sense I was inspired to move in this direction as a result of Smale's efforts to 'show how the existence proof for equilibria can be based on Sard's theorem and calculus foundations ...[using] equations such as "supply equals demand"... rather than fixed points' (Smale, 1981). I have dealt with this approach in greater detail in Velupillai (2005).

11. The prelude to the actual statement of the 8th Problem reads as follows:

> The following problem is not one of pure mathematics, but lies on the interface of economics and mathematics. It has been solved only in quite limited situations. (Smale, 1998, p. 10)

12. There is an implicit teleological element in stating 'the dynamics of a market mechanism *in search* of an equilibrium of supply and demand'. From Adam Smith's famous observation that the economic agent is '... led by an invisible hand to promote an end which was no part of his intention' right through all the modern classics – particularly those inspired by Hayek – the teleological element has been kept in a penumbra, so to speak. I hope the reader will not try to place the teleological element in the forefront of my mild distortion of a noble tradition.

13. During the first hundred years of invoking of this analogy, the idea of a computer, in the economists who referred to it, was confined to its *analogue* incarnation. Since then the analogy has exclusively (and often explicitly) referred to the *digital* computer. The emphasis on the mathematics of computation and mathematical logic in my efforts to expose *conning* in mathematical economics is partly due to this latter analogy. If the reader keeps in mind the following perceptive observation, then the main thrust of the arguments in this paper will be clear:

> The badly named *real number system* is one of the triumphs of the human mind. It underlies the calculus and higher analysis to such a degree that we may forget how impossible it is to deal with real numbers in the real world of finite computers. But, however much the real number system simplifies analysis, practical computing must do without it. (Forsyth, 1970, p. 932; italics in the original)

14. For the benefit of readers unfamiliar with either or one of these celebrated theorems, here are two concise statements. Define the unit simplex as

$$S_n^+ \equiv \left\{ p \mid p \in \mathbb{R}_{n+1}^+ \text{ and } \parallel p \parallel = 1 \right\}$$

Theorem A. *Brouwer fixed-point theorem*. *Let* $f: S_n^+ \to S_n^+$, *where f is continuous. Then there is a* $p^* \in S_n^+$ *such that* $p^* = f(p^*)$.

Theorem B. *Walrasian equilibrium existence theorem*. *Let* $z: S_n^+ \to \mathbb{R}_{n+1}^+$ *such that*

(1) $z(p)$ *is continuous* $\forall p \in S$

(2) $p.z(p) = 0$, $\forall p \in S$.

Then:

$$\exists p^* \in S_n^+ \quad \text{such that} \quad z(p) \le 0$$

with $p_i^* = 0$ *for i such that* $z_i(p) < 0$.

15. The 'cognoscenti' would have realized that I am using the term *Walrasian Demon* in analogy with the term *Maxwell's Demon*. Of course it is the *Walrasian Auctioneer* that I am re-naming the *Walrasian Demon*. Some may even know that Axel Leijonhufvud, when he coined the term *Walrasian Auctioneer*, did so in analogy with his (incomplete) understanding of the scope and functions of *Maxwell's Demon*, as gleaned from his reading of the Mr Tompkins books of George Gamov. The tortuous history of false analogies add to confusion and conning, as evidenced by some totally absurd remarks by Robert Axtell regarding the formal computational capabilities of the *Walrasian Auctioneer* (cf. Axtell, 2005).

16. But we in economics are only painfully aware of the great Keynesian aphorism: *In the long run we are all dead*!

17. I hope readers do not think this is a misspelling of '*Gandhian*'!!

18. By 'characterizable' I will understand 'effective characterization of defining basins of attraction', using 'effective' in the strict sense of recursion theory and 'basin of attraction' in the sense in which it is defined in formal dynamical systems theory (but see below, too).

19. The analogy here is like that between the Chomsky hierarchy of formal languages and abstract computing machines. Wolfram (1984) developed these ideas in the direction that I am trying to exploit here.

20. In the definition of a dynamical system given below I am not striving to present the most general version. The basic aim is to lead to an intuitive understanding of the definition of a basin of attraction so that the main theorem is made reasonably transparent. Moreover, the definition given below is for scalar ODEs, easily generalizable to the vector case.

21. In the same sense in which the Walrasian equilibrium existence theorem is obvious for anyone familiar with the Brouwer (or similar) fixed-point theorem(s). The finesse, however, was to formalize the Walrasian economy topologically, in the first place. A similar finesse is required here.

22. Firstly, 'recursive' is meant to be interpreted in its 'recursion theoretic' sense; secondly, this claim is, in fact, a restatement of the Church–Turing thesis (cf. Beeson, 1985, p. 34).

23. It may be useful to keep in mind the following caveat introduced in one of the famous papers on these matters by Kydland and Prescott (1980, p. 169):

   [W]e emphasize that the choice is from a [fixed] set of fiscal policy rules.

24. Some add the *higher arithmetic* (i.e. *number theory*) as an independent fifth branch of modern mathematical logic.

25. One of which is also called a *fix-point theorem*.

26. Readers familiar with the literature will recognize that the notation H reflects the fact that, in the underlying optimization problem, a *Hamiltonian* function has to be formed.

27. In a space of functions.

28. In the strict technical sense, as suggested above, of the mathematics of *real analysis* as distinct from, say, *constructive, computable or non-standard analysis*.

29. Perceptive readers may wonder whether there should not also be an optimization exercise over the set of feasible or perceived learning mechanisms? Carried to its logical conclusion, this would entail the determination of a set of REEs over the collection of learning mechanisms, *ad infinitum* (or *ad nauseum*, whichever one prefers).

30. My aim is to show that the framing of the REE problem as a *topological fixed-point problem* was not necessary. Moreover, by forcing the REE problem as a topological fixed-point problem it became necessary to dichotomize into the proof of existence part and a separate part to demonstrate the feasibility of constructing mechanisms to determine them. This is mainly – but not only – due to the utilization of non-constructive or uncomputable topological fixed-point theorems in the first, 'proof of REE existence', part. In this sense, the *REE learning* research program is very similar to the earlier dichotomizing of the *general equilibrium* problem. In that earlier phase,

a long tradition of using topological fixed-point theorems to prove the existence of economic equilibria was separated from devising *constructive* or *computable* mechanisms to determine them. The later phase resulted in the highly successful *computable general equilibrium* (CGE) models. It remains a melancholy fact, however, that even after over 40 years of sustained and impressive work on CGE models, they are neither constructive nor computable, contrary to assertions by proponents of the theory (cf. Velupillai (2006) for a rigorous demonstration of this claim).

31. I am reminded that Phelps, in one of his early papers introducing the concept of the natural rate of unemployment in its modern forms (Phelps, 1979), first referred to it as a *warranted rate*. Eventually, of course, the Wicksellian term *natural rate*, introduced by Friedman, prevailed. Phelps and Grunberg–Modigliani were, presumably, influenced by Harrodian thoughts in choosing the eminently suitable word 'warranted' rather than 'natural' or 'rational', respectively. Personally, for aesthetic reasons as well as reasons of economic content, I wish the Phelps and Grunberg–Modigliani suggestions had prevailed.

32. The relation between a market price and its predicted value was termed the *reaction function*: 'Relations of this form between the variable to be predicted and the prediction will be called *reaction functions*' (Grunberg and Modigliani, 1954, p. 471; italics in original).

    As became the tradition in the whole rational expectations literature, the functional form for the reaction functions was chosen with a clear eye on the requirements for the application of an appropriate topological fixed-point theorem. The self-reference and infinite regress underpinnings were thought to have been adequately subsumed in the existence results that were guaranteed by the fixed-point solution. That the twin conundrums were not subsumed but simply camouflaged was not to become evident till all the later activity on trying to devise learning processes for identifying REEs.

33. I have relied on the following four excellent texts for the formalisms and results of recursion theory that I am using in this part of the essay: Cutland (1980); Davis *et al.* (1994); Manna (1974); Rogers (1987).

34. If $f(\mathbf{x})$ and $g(\mathbf{x})$ are expressions involving the variables $\mathbf{x} = (x_1, x_2, \ldots, x_k)$, then

$$f(\mathbf{x}) \simeq g(\mathbf{x})$$

means: for any $\mathbf{x}$, $f(\mathbf{x})$ and $g(\mathbf{x})$ are either both defined or undefined, and if defined, they are equal.

35. This should not cause any disquiet in expectational economics, at least not to those of us who have accepted the Lucasian case for viewing agents as 'signal processors' who use optimal filters in their rational decision processing activities (cf. Lucas, 1981, p. 9). Agents as 'signal processors' is only a special variant of being 'optimal computing units'.

36. They are 'weaker' in a very special sense. A domain of definition that is number theoretically defined – i.e. over only the rational or the natural numbers – rather than over the whole of the real number system pose natural diophantine and combinatorial conundrums that cannot easily be resolved by the standard operators of optimization.

37. Of course *effectivity* in the strict mathematical sense of recursion theory.

38. I had the melancholy privilege of listening to a seminar given by a senior colleague of mine, at the University of Trento, where all sorts of silly assumptions about a continuum of agents were made. When I pointed out to him that it was, in fact, not

necessary for him to assume a continuum, but that a countable infinity of agents would suffice, his response was: 'But others using this kind of model assume a continuum of agents'! In exasperation, I finally had to write him as follows (in a letter dated 17 June 2003):

> You cannot start with a continuum assumption and restrict the simulation model to 10 or 20 or 1020 or any number of finite agents; the answers will not correspond to the solution given by the model, except by fluke, and even then one will not be any wiser in an analytical sense.
> Economists do this all the time....

39. Kuratowski and Mostowski (1976), whose monumental text on set theory is often invoked by mathematical economists, alert the reader each time a theorem is established using the axiom of choice. This is not the only classic mathematical or mathematical logic text to do so. Would that economists could also be knowledgeable and sensitive enough to do so!

40. In fact, in a sense, the Arrow–Debreu formalization 'borrowed' the fixed-point approach from Nash. But I am not writing a history of mathematical economics; however, much such an approach would be the ideal way to discuss all the *cons* and *conning* I am interested in. That must wait for a different exercise.

41. In direct analogy with the kind of observation made by Steve Smale about transforming an intrinsic equation approach to the problem of supply–demand equilibrium to one of inequalities formulated as fixed-point problems.

42. Readers who are knowledgeable about mathematical logic – particularly recursion, proof and model theories – will recognize, in this formulation, the way Gödel derived *undecidable sentences*.

43. The real-time paradox of implementing an infinite play is easily resolved (cf. Steinhaus, 1965, p. 465; Velupillai, 2000, ch. 7).

44. A set $\mathcal{F}$ is a *perfect set* if it is a *closed set in which every point is a limit point*.

45. A *Baire line* is an *irrational line* which, in turn, is a line obtainable from a continuum by *removing a countable dense subset*.

46. '*Recursive*', because the *tools* used to formalize macroeconomic concepts and entities are determined by the mathematics of *Markov decision processes* (Wald), *dynamic programming* (Bellman) and (Kalman) filtering, all of which have a 'recursive' structure. The reader should be warned that '*recursive*' in this sense has nothing whatsoever to do with '*recursion theory*' in any sense whatsoever.

47. He goes even further when he points out, pungently and frankly:

> What I am going to describe for you is a revolution in Macroeconomics, a transformation in methodology that has reshaped how we conduct our science. Prior to the transformation, macroeconomics was largely separate from the rest of economics. Indeed, some considered the study of macroeconomics fundamentally different and thought there was no hope of integrating macroeconomics with the rest of economics, that is, with neoclassical economics. Others held the view that neoclassical foundations for the empirically determined macro relations would in time be developed. Neither view has proved correct. (Prescott, 2004b)

Of course, Prescott does not recognize the existence of non-neoclassical economics; sometimes not even varieties of neoclassical economics (Prescott, 2004a).

48. I cannot resist the temptation to add, as a counter-weight to this sanguine view, a trenchant observation made by a previous Nobel Laureate, who may not have been unsympathetic to the New Classicals, when he reviewed the classic of an earlier generation, Paul Samuelson's *Foundations of Economic Analysis* (Stigler, 1948, p. 605):

> ... [W]ho can know what tools we need unless he knows the material on which they will be used.

49. Prescott is, of course, referring to mathematical and computational tools. He does not realize that the mathematical framework in which his theories are couched is intrinsically uncomputable and non-constructive. In fact, the Prescott–Kydland research program, apart from resting on Lucasian foundations, is also underpinned by the framework of CGE theory. Neither the practitioners of CGE nor the second-hand followers have ever investigated whether CGE models are actually constructive or computable. In fact they are neither (cf. Velupillai, 2006).

50. I have, in the first instance, in mind Piero Sraffa's remarkable *Production of Commodities by Means of Commodities* (1961) and Jacob Schwartz's *Lectures on the Analytical Method in Economics* (1960). These two books, each in their own way, extol the virtues of non-orthodox approaches to economics using non-routine mathematical tools, concepts, frameworks and proof techniques. A first pass at studying one of them is in Velupillai (2007).

References

Adda, J. and Cooper, R. (2003) *Dynamic Economics: Quantitative Methods and Applications*. Cambridge, MA: MIT Press.

Atiyeh, Sir M. (2002) Mathematics in the 20th century. *Bulletin of the London Mathematical Society* 34: 1–15.

Aubert, K.E. (1982a) Accurate predictions and fixed point theorems. *Social Science Information* 21(3): 323–348.

Aubert, K.E. (1982b) Accurate predictions and fixed point theorems: a reply to Simon. *Social Science Information* 21(4/5): 612–622.

Axtell, R. (2005) The complexity of exchange. *The Economic Journal* 115(June): F 193–F 210.

Beeson, M.J. (1985) *Foundations of Constructive Mathematics*. Heidelberg and New York: Springer.

Brin, M. and Stuck, G. (2002) *Introduction to Dynamical Systems*. Cambridge: Cambridge University Press.

Clower, R.W. and Howitt, P.W. (1978) The transactions theory of the demand for money: a restatement. *Journal of Political Economy* 86(3): 449–465.

Cooper, S.B. (2004) *Computability Theory*. Boca Raton, FL, and London: Chapman & Hall/CRC.

Cutland, N.J. (1980) *Computability: An Introduction to Recursive Function Theory*. Cambridge: Cambridge University Press.

Davis, M., Sigal, R. and Weyuker, E.J. (1994) *Computability, Complexity and Languages: Fundamentals of Theoretical Computer Science* (2nd edn). London: Academic Press.

Debreu, G. (1984) Economic theory in the mathematical mode. *American Economic Review* 74(3): 267–278.

Debreu, G. (1986a) *Mathematical Economics: Twenty Papers of Gerard Debreu*, with an Introduction by Werner Hildenbrand. Cambridge: Cambridge University Press.

Debreu, G. (1986b) Theoretic models: mathematical form and economic content. *Econometrica* 54(6): 1259–1270.

Debreu, G. (1991) The mathematization of economic theory. *American Economic Review* 81(1): 1–7.

Denardo, E.V. (1967) Contraction mappings in the theory underlying dynamic programming. *SIAM Review* 10(2): 165–177.

Forsyth, G.E. (1970) Pitfalls in computation, or why a math book isn't enough. *American Mathematical Monthly* 77(9): 931–956.

Gandy, R. (1980) Church's thesis and principles for mechanisms. In J. Barwise, H.J. Keisler and K. Kunen (eds), *The Kleene Symposium*. Amsterdam: North-Holland.

Grunberg, E. and Modigliani, F.M. (1954) The predictability of social events. *Journal of Political Economy* LXII(6): 465–478.

Hirsch, M.W. and Smale, S. (1974) *Differential Equations, Dynamical Systems and Linear Algebra*. New York and London: Academic Press.

Kaldor, N. (1989) John von Neumann: a personal recollection, as Foreword. In M. Dore, R.M. Goodwin and S. Chakravarty (eds), *John von Neumann and Modern Economics*. Oxford: Clarendon Press.

Kreisel, G. (1974) A notion of mechanistic theory. *Synthese* 29: 11–26.

Kreisel, G. (1982) Review of 'A computable ordinary differential equation which possesses no computable solution; the wave equation with computable initial data such that its unique solution is not computable'. *Journal of Symbolic Logic* 47(4): 900–902.

Kuratowski, K. and Mostowski, A. (1976) *Set Theory–With an Introduction to Descriptive Set Theory*. Amsterdam: North-Holland.

Kydland, F. and Prescott, E.C. (1980) A competitive theory of fluctuations and the feasibility and desirability of stabilization policy. In S. Fischer (ed.), *Rational Expectations and Economic Policy* (Ch. 5, pp. 169–198). Chicago, IL, and London: University of Chicago Press.

Kydland, F.E. and Prescott, E.C. (1996) The computational experiment: an econometric tool. *Journal of Economic Perspectives* 10(1): 69–85.

Leamer, E.E. (1983) Let's take the con out of econometrics. *American Economic Review* 73(1): 31–43.

Li, M. and Vitanyi, P. (1993) *An Introduction to Kolmogorov Complexity and its Applications*. New York and Heidelberg: Springer.

Lucas, R.E., Jr (1981) *Studies in Business-Cycle Theory*. Oxford: Basil Blackwell.

Manna, Z. (1974) *Mathematical Theory of Computation*. Tokyo: McGraw-Hill Kogakusha.

Marsden, J.E. and Hoffman, M.J. (1993) *Elementary Classical Analysis* (2nd edn). New York: W.H. Freeman.

Moret, B.M. (1998) *The Theory of Computation*. Reading, MA: Addison-Wesley.

Muth, J.F. (1961) Rational expectations and the theory of price movements. *Econometrica* 29(6): 315–335.

von Neumann, J. (1928) Zur theorie der gesellsschaftsspiele. *Mathematische Annalen* 100: 295–320.

von Neumann, J. (1945–46) A model of general economic equilibrium. *Review of Economic Studies* 13: 1–9.

Pareto, V. (1971). *Manual of Political Economy*, translated from the French edition of 1927 by A.S. Schwier and edited by A.S. Schwier and A.N. Page. London: Macmillan.

Phelps, E.S. (1979) *Studies in Macroeconomic Theory, Vol. 1: Employment and Inflation*. New York: Academic Press.

Pour-El, M.B. and Richards, I.R. (1979) A computable ordinary differential equation which possesses no computable solution. *Annals of Mathematical Logic* 17: 61–90.

Prescott, E.C. (2004a) Interview (with Nina Mehta) at http://www.fenews.com/fen41/one_on_one/one_on_one.html

Prescott, E.C. (2004b) The transformation of macroeconomic policy and research. *Nobel Prize Lecture*, 8 December, p. 24.

Rogers, H., Jr (1987) *Theory of Recursive Functions and Effective Computability*. Cambridge, MA: MIT Press.

Roth, A.E. (1994) Let's keep the con out of experimental economics: a methodological note. *Empirical Economics* 19: 279–289.

Samuelson, P.A. (1952) Economic theory and mathematics – an appraisal. *American Economic Review, Papers and Proceedings* 42(2): 56–66.

Sargent, T.J. (1993) *Bounded Rationality in Macroeconomics*. Oxford: Clarendon Press.

Scarf, H.E. (1973) *The Computation of Economic Equilibria* (with the collaboration of Terje Hansen). New Haven, CT, and London: Yale University Press.

Schwartz, J.T. (1961) *Lectures on the Mathematical Method in Analytical Economics*. New York: Gordon and Breach.

Schwartz, J.T. (1986) The pernicious influence of mathematics on science. In M. Kac, G.-C. Rota and J.T. Schwartz (eds), *Discrete Thoughts – Essays on Mathematics, Science, and Philosophy*. Boston, MA: Birkhaüser.

Shanks, D. (1978) *Solved and Unsolved Problems in Number Theory*. New York: Chelsea Publishing.

Shoven, J.B. and Whalley, J.W. (1972) A general equilibrium calculation of the differential taxation of income from capital in the U.S. *Journal of Public Economics* 1(3–4): 281–321.

Simon, H. (1954) Bandwagon and underdog effects of election predictions (1954, 1957). In *Models of Man – Social and Rational*. New York: Wiley.

Simon, H. (1982a) Accurate predictions and fixed point theorems: comments. *Social Science Information* 21(4/5): 605–626.

Simon, H. (1982b) Final comment. *Social Science Information* 21(4/5): 622–624.

Smale, S. (1976) Dynamics in general equilibrium theory. *American Economic Review* 66(2): 288–294.

Smale, S. (1981) Global analysis and economics. In K.J. Arrow and M.D. Intriligator (eds), *Handbook of Mathematical Economics*, Vol. 1 (Ch. 8, pp. 331–370). Amsterdam: North-Holland.

Smale, S. (1998) Mathematical problems for the next century. *The Mathematical Intelligencer* 20(2): 7–15.

Sraffa, P. (1960) *Production of Commodities by Means of Commodities: A Prelude to a Critique of Economic Theory*. Cambridge: Cambridge University Press.

Steinhaus, H. (1965) Games, an informal talk. *American Mathematical Monthly* 72(5): 457–468.

Stigler, G.J. (1948) Review [of *Foundations of Economics Analysis* by Paul Samuelson]. *Journal of the American Statistical Association* 43(244): 603–605.

Suzumura, K. (1973) Professor Uzawa's equivalence theorem: a note. *Economic Studies Quarterly* 8(1): 67–70.

Suzumura, K. (1983) *Rational Choice, Collective Decisions and Social Welfare*. Cambridge: Cambridge University Press.

Tall, D. and Vinner, S.V. (1981) Concept image and concept definition in mathematics with particular reference to limits and continuity. *Educational Studies in Mathematics* 12(2): 151–169.

Velupillai, K. (2000) *Computable Economics*. Oxford: Oxford University Press.

Velupillai, K.V. (2002) Effectivity and constructivity in economic theory. *Journal of Economic Behavior and Organization* 49(3): 307–325.

Velupillai, K.V. (2003) Economic dynamics and computation – resurrecting the Icarus tradition. *Metroeconomica* 55(2–3): 239–264.

Velupillai, K.V. (2005) The unreasonable ineffectiveness of mathematics in economics. *Cambridge Journal of Economics* 29(6): 849–872.

Velupillai, K.V. (2006) Algorithmic foundations of computable general equilibrium theory. *Applied Mathematics and Computation* 179: 360–369.

Velupillai, K.V. (2007) Sraffa's mathematical economics – a constructive interpretation. *Journal of Economic Methodology*, forthcoming.

Wolfram, S. (1984) Computation theory of cellular automata. *Communications in Mathematical Physics* 96: 15–57.

Zermelo, E. (1912) Über ein Anwendung der Mengenlehre auf die Theorie des Schachspiels. *Proceedings of the Fifth International Congress of Mathematicians, Cambridge*, Vol. 2, pp. 501–504.

5

THE SOCIOLOGICAL APPROACH TO FINANCIAL MARKETS

Alex Preda

University of Edinburgh

1. Introduction

For a long time, financial markets have been perceived by social scientists other than economists as too esoteric, as marginal objects of study or both. Perhaps due to their deference towards economists, perhaps to their reticence towards an underestimated area of study, sociologists,[1] cultural anthropologists and political scientists had only occasionally paid attention to financial markets. Since the early 1980s, this situation changed markedly. We witness now growing numbers of sociological and anthropological articles and books, as well as of PhD students concerned with what was not so long ago considered a topic best left to economists. More recently, subdisciplines such as the social studies of finance have emerged, concretized not only in publications and doctoral students, but also in incipient institutional structures. This lively interest of social scientists in an imminently economic domain, perceived as arcane by many, can be attributed to several factors, some of which can be located within the changed social landscape of the late twentieth century, and some within intradisciplinary changes that have emerged relatively recently.

Already in the 1980s, the role of financial markets as fundamental institutions of advanced societies became apparent, as a consequence of deregulation on both sides of the Atlantic, as well as of an increased media presence (among other things, due to several financial scandals, as well as to the financial crashes that had scarred the decade). This increased public presence continued and was amplified in the 1990s, when, after the fall of the Iron Curtain, markets seemed to start a process of relentless, worldwide expansion. This coincided with, and was at least in part fostered by, the growing use of computer technologies, which triggered substantial changes in the organization of market transactions and in the dissemination of financial information. Processes of economic globalization were perceived by many as directly related to (and as partly caused by) the expansion of financial markets, which challenged the established understanding of the links between economic and political institutions. The perception of finance as being at the forefront of economic globalization triggered an increased interest on the part of social scientists other than economists (sociologists, social anthropologists, geographers) towards investigating the broader social impact, ties and organization of financial markets.

In the following, I present an analytical overview of the more recent sociological perspectives on financial markets, hoping to persuade readers that the multifaceted study of financial markets as webs of social interactions can contribute to a better understanding of their position and role in advanced societies, a position that goes well beyond the allocation of scarce resources and the processing of economic uncertainties. In a first step of the argument, I will present and discuss social-structural approaches to financial markets, developed mainly in US sociology and spread since the 1980s under the banner of the 'new economic sociology'. In a second step of the argument, I will discuss a set of approaches usually grouped under the umbrella term of 'neo-institutionalism'. Finally, in the third step I present more recent developments, coming mainly from Europe this time, and called 'social studies of finance'. The discussion is centred on how each approach conceptualizes information and links it to the idea of social relationship or interaction.

It should be stated from the start that these three sociological perspectives do not succeed each other, but coexist; they shed the light on various social aspects of market transactions that complement each other, revealing thus the complexity and empirical richness of finance as a field of inquiry. Sometimes, such diversity has been seen as indicating the absence of a unifying, normative theory of social behaviour, or the existence of several competing theories. With respect to financial markets, however, this diversity points to the complex, multilayered character of markets as social institutions, and as knowledge-producing webs of social relationships.

2. Markets as Networks and as Groups

The 1980s marked not only a renewed prominence of financial markets, but also a series of changes within sociology, relevant for its orientation to financial markets. The first of these shifts is given by the rise of the new economic sociology, viewed by many as connected to the seminal articles published by the sociologists Harrison White and Mark Granovetter (White, 1981; Granovetter, 1985). Albeit in distinct ways, White and Granovetter argued that markets can and should be conceptualized not only as systems of exchange, but also as networks of social relationships.[2] Such networks are characterized by routines and habits that contribute not only to their stability and reproduction, but also to the processing of uncertainties that may arise with respect to the transactions conducted within (Beckert, 1996). One of the consequences derived from this is that markets are grounded in trust relationships, which in their turn are provided by social networks. While Granovetter's general argument sees relationships as external frames for economic exchanges,[3] Harrison White, more radically, argued that exchanges take place within a system of existing relationships, which influence information concerning price, quality and reliability. Producers orient themselves to each other and position themselves in niches according to the information obtained by observing what other producers do. Product pricing is then shaped by social networks; in addition to White's theoretical work, empirical investigations have highlighted how pricing practices are network based (e.g. Uzzi and Lancaster, 2004), influenced by prestige and status (e.g. Podolny, 2005) or by routines (e.g. Velthuis, 2005) and rituals (e.g. Smith, 1989).

White's innovation is that he integrates the notion of information into the treatment of markets as networks of social relationships (White, 2002, p. 2). Market actors (i.e. producers) continuously send signals to each other, signals that play a key role in decision about products, pricing and quality. In order to be able to interpret such signals, producers need to share the same frame of perception (called by White discourse). This is ensured by activities such as going to business conventions, membership in the same clubs or after-work socializing. It follows from this that producers are not so much interested in knowing what consumers want as in knowing what other producers are doing. Producers observe an image of the consumer, created with the help of instruments such as focus groups and surveys, while observing each other directly. It follows from this that markets work as quasi-closed systems,[4] primarily oriented towards internal observations.

White's[5] and Granovetter's approach spawned a flurry of work in economic sociology, some of which (to be discussed in more detail below) focused on financial markets. According to their research programmes, the sociologist's task was to investigate how networks of social relationships shape the dynamics of financial transactions, and how they influence price, volume and volatility. A natural starting place was provided by the floors of financial exchanges, as settings in which the dynamics of interpersonal relationships among traders could be investigated at close range. It is perhaps no accident that, one year before Mark Granovetter's article was published in the profession's flagship journal, another article was published in the same venue, analysing the social structure of a major trading floor (Baker, 1984).

Wayne Baker's article on the dynamics of the trading floor argued that traders did not behave like perfectly rational actors ('hyperrational', in Baker's terminology), but were aware of their own cognitive limitations, as well as of the imperfect character of the information they received, its amalgamation with irrelevant bits and the need to process it in a meaningful way (Baker, 1984, p. 778). Being constantly confronted with uncertainties, but also under pressure to make profits, traders need to use their networks on the floor in order to gather meaningful information that can be put to their advantage. Distinguishing between micro-networks (defined by spatial vicinity on the exchange floor and closer-knit relationships) and macro-networks (given by spatial distance and looser relationships), Baker saw these two types of networks as impacting the traders' information processing as well as their opportunistic behaviour in different ways. While micro-networks exert more social control, keep opportunistic behaviour in check and distribute information more efficiently, macro-networks appear to be less competitive and tend to split into subgroups (Baker, 1984, p. 804).

Micro- and macro-networks have thus specific dynamics: since traders are compelled to widen their search for information by expanding their relationships, small groups of traders grow in size, while larger networks subdivide into smaller groups. These different dynamics have an impact on market performance, which, paradoxically, appears to be low in closed small groups, increases while micro-networks open up and diversify and then decreases again in macro-networks (Baker, 1984, p. 805). Price volatility decreases with increased density of relationships in small trading cliques and increases in large networks. This relationship between volatility and group size, due to the uncertainties inherent in the process of searching for and processing information, runs counter to the assumption that a large number of market participants will tend towards perfect competition and thus diminish volatility.

Baker's study was that of a 'classic' trading floor, on which prices are established in the process of direct, face-to-face interaction among traders. As financial markets have moved towards electronic trading in the past decade or so, a whole series of new questions arise, concerning the role of online trading technologies, the ways in which they shape trading behaviour, and their influence on the pricing process.[6] Recent microeconomic work (e.g. Franke and Hess, 2000, p. 472) suggests that there are differences between electronic and traditional exchanges with respect to patterns of price volatility, requiring a closer examination of the link between technology and trading behaviour. Before examining the shift to electronic trading, however, it is worth asking which social-structural arrangements other than networks may play a role with respect to price movements.

3. The Role of Information Intermediaries

While networks pressure market actors to conform, operating thus within a shared perception frame, this perception does not always come out of direct observations, but is the result of mediation undertaken by specialized groups. An example in this sense is that of securities analysts, whose role is to provide evaluations of financial securities to investors and traders. The mere existence of securities analysts as information intermediaries suggests that financial assets are marred by uncertainties concerning not only their price, but also their status and character. Traders and investors perceive financial securities as belonging to sets or categories (e.g. airline, automotive, energy, etc.) and as competing with each other within a given category. In this perspective, securities analysts act as product critics,[7] classifying securities and comparing them with other 'products' in the same category. This work of classification and comparison processes uncertainties and helps create the perception framework in which traders and investors act. Nevertheless, there can be situations in which the classification of some financial securities is uncertain – they can be seen as belonging to several categories at once or as not belonging to any clear-cut category. In this case, will consistent, clear-cut classifications by analysts lead to less volatile stock prices? This question has been answered in the affirmative by

Ezra Zuckerman (1999), who compared the price performance of securities that were consistently classified by analysts with the performance of securities that had multiple, inconsistent classifications. Inconsistently classified securities trade at a discount compared to the ones whose categorial position is certain (Zuckerman, 1999, p. 1424).

In an expanded, theoretically oriented reformulation, this finding is echoed in an argument about financial markets as structurally incoherent – that is, as being composed both of clear-cut categories and of zones of uncertainty (Zuckerman, 2004). Financial securities are ascribed either to zones of certainty or to areas of uncertainty, and this ascription influences both trading volume and volatility. The price of securities ascribed to zones of certainty (i.e. uncontroversial categories, agreed upon by several analysts) would efficiently incorporate and reflect the information available to market actors; conversely, the prices of securities belonging to areas of uncertainty (classified by analysts in controversial or incoherent ways) would not behave according to the hypothesis of efficiency. Their volatility as well as their trading volume would be higher by comparison and not explainable by other factors (Zuckerman, 2004, p. 427). This empirical finding leads Zuckerman to re-assess the debates among proponents and opponents of the efficient markets hypothesis (EMH) and to suggest that financial markets are actually characterized by 'structural incoherence': that is, they include zones that seem to confirm the EMH, as well as zones that seem to disconfirm it, according to whether we encounter coherent, consensual classifications or not.

4. Networks, Groups and Information

This theoretical position builds upon a crucial argument made by Harrison White and re-worked by Joel Podolny (2001), namely, that markets are inward-oriented networks that channel information both about the objects being traded and about trading partners. Information can be thus seen as processing altercentric (if concerning transacted objects) or egocentric uncertainties (if concerning the actors' status and relationships; Podolny, 2001, p. 37). A way of avoiding egocentric uncertainties would be the clustering of some actors in high-status market zones, in which actors know each other and entertain close relationships. Trust in the partners' quality would lead then to increased trust in the quality of transacted objects. Podolny takes venture capital markets as a case study for investigating how segmentation and stratification affect the market actors' orientation with respect to these two kinds of uncertainty. Venture capital markets are generally characterized by high levels of both egocentric and altercentric uncertainty: the outcome of investments is highly risky (altercentric uncertainty) and the partners' trustworthiness is not always taken for granted (egocentric uncertainty). Venture capital firms with a high status (as measured by peer reputation and success) avoid getting involved in the early stage of the investment process and in enterprises that they do not know well. By contrast, firms with a lower status are not embedded in a close knit of multiple reciprocal relationships, in which trust in the transaction partners grounds trust in the venture. Such firms tend to get involved in the earlier, riskier stages of the investment process and to act in an environment with higher egocentric uncertainty (Podolny, 2001, p. 58).[8]

While starting from the notion that markets can be analysed as networks of social relationships, the structural approach, as illustrated by the authors discussed in the above sections, has tried to incorporate concepts such as uncertainty and information into the analysis of how social relationships influence the pricing of financial securities. Networks are seen not only as uncertainty-processing arrangements that provide market actors with routines and stable perception frames, but also as channelling and even generating transaction-relevant information: a social tie is not only a pipe through which information flows, but, when viewed by a third-party observer, information in itself. One could ask here what the structural concept of information consists of and how it links with the notion of information used in financial economics.

The latter is grounded in two different approaches initiated in the 1930s and 1940s: on the one hand, it views allocation processes as determined by the distribution of information, with markets analogous to telephone switchboards (Mirowski, 2002, p. 37). Information consists then in signals analogous to electric impulses that trigger a reaction in the receiver. On the other hand, signals that are apparently random can be processed with formal tools in order to detect underlying, non-random patterns; this view, initially developed by operations research during WWII (Klein, 2001, p. 131; Mirowski, 2002, p. 60), sees signals as additive and as independent of the cognitive properties of the receiver. This separation between cognition and information, as well as the notion that the latter can be seen as signals upon which market actors transact, are present in the structural treatment of markets as networks too (White, 2002, pp. 100–101). Network ties themselves are signals for third-party actors, while circulating other signals at the same time. The assumption of shared frames of perception, as well as of given classifications (produced by information intermediaries), does not question the cognitive processes through which data are processed by financial actors and transformed into meaningful information. The market's analogy with a telephone switchboard is expanded into one of multiple switchboards that are ranked according to the trust in the signals they send and the strength of this signal. At the same time, these switchboards are partially disconnected from each other. The 'better' switchboards do not constantly exchange signals with the 'lesser' switchboards. This social structuring of information leads to the coexistence of different patterns of volatility on different switchboards, as well as to specific dynamics across these patterns.

5. Financial Markets as Social and Political Institutions

While the social-structural approach to markets emphasizes the role of quasi-closed networks of relationships with respect to price volatility, it is worth asking whether financial markets should not be considered in their broader social, political and cultural contexts, in connection to institutions such as the state or the legal system. After all, the impact of markets goes well beyond the allocation of material and monetary resources: their influence on modern, developed societies can be located in domains such as social policy (e.g. pension systems), ethics,[9] or culture (witness here, among others, a long literary tradition dealing with financial speculation). This implies an enlarged perspective with respect to the spectrum of explanatory variables and of the effects under investigation: that is, departing from the narrower focus on securities prices and asking questions about how financial markets shape modern societies beyond allocation processes.

Perhaps not surprisingly, this widening of sociological perspectives has been promoted by organizational sociology; since the late 1970s, it has emphasized the role of belief systems in shaping organizational activities.[10] This has led to a re-working of the notion of rational actor and to a departure from the a-historical perspective on economic rationality implicit in normative assumptions about human behaviour. Whereas the traditional approach to organizations was that of relentless rationalization and efficiency (inspired by a certain reading of Max Weber's thesis about the iron law of capitalist development), sociologists of organizations such as Charles Perrow (2002), Walter Powell, Paul DiMaggio (Powell and DiMaggio, 1991) or Niklas Luhmann (1990), among others, argued that organizations develop rituals and belief systems as a mode of justifying their existence and of ensuring their reproduction and stability. Rituals and belief systems do not work according to (universal) criteria of rationality, but are centred on producing shared meanings via the use of symbols; with respect to these latter, questions about universal, ever expanding rationality do not necessarily appear as primordial. Market transactions can be seen as embedded in complex organizational arrangements; therefore, transactions cannot be separated from rituals, symbols and belief systems.

This argument has at least two sets of consequences: on the one hand, it requires the investigation of how concrete rituals and symbols shape the behaviour of financial actors such as traders and investors. On the other hand, it requires examining the connection between financial markets and other social institutions (such as the state), in order to highlight the ways in which political belief systems, for instance, spill over to markets and influence their rules. Conversely, one can examine how belief systems initiated within financial markets influence other economic sectors (such as corporate life, for instance), as well as political institutions. As mentioned above, this requires a departure from the understanding of markets as quasi-closed systems and a reorientation towards their role in and impact upon the larger society.[11]

In his ethnography of Wall Street bond traders, Mitchel Abolafia (1996) set out to examine how beliefs and rituals influence trading strategies, as well as the relationships among traders.[12] His starting point is that economic behaviour, implying the maximization of personal gain, is pursued for more than one reason. While the accumulation of personal wealth is a dominant goal for bond traders, it is by far not the only one (and not necessarily the ultimate one). In interacting with each other, traders engage in social games that produce a hierarchy or ranking among them. Accumulating personal wealth is one way of securing a position within this hierarchy. Other ways may include landing a particularly successful trade, or demonstrating resilience in the market. These games imply both hyperrational behaviour and opportunism (Abolafia, 1996, p. 19). Opportunism includes offering incomplete information and/or actively distorting information; this is countered by the traders' vigilance, making them engage in a continuous search for information, as well as in information checks and evaluation of its relevance (Abolafia, 1996, p. 25). The search for information, a key feature of trading financial securities, appears in this perspective not as driven primarily by objective, interaction-external uncertainties, but by uncertainties generated in the games traders play with each other.

This work partly covers topics similar to those investigated by Charles Smith in his ethnographic work on traders and on auctions (Smith, 1999, 1989). Working in the tradition of symbolic interactionism, Smith (who also builds on his own trading experience) argues that the uncertainties related to the valuation and pricing of objects (including financial securities) cannot be processed but in orderly face-to-face interactions, interactions which must be made visible to outside observers. Such interactions, however, are grounded in common rituals and shared symbols, which Smith highlights by comparing auctions on the floor of the stock exchange with other types of auctions (such as art or race horses auctions). Consequently, pricing processes cannot be seen as consisting exclusively in calculations about how to gain advantages in the trading game, but are anchored in such symbols and rituals. There is a significant difference here between conceiving market actors as playing a fundamentally rational game (which systematically produces distorted or incomplete information) and conceiving transactions as moored to rituals, which are essential with respect to valuation processes.

From the perspective of the individual trader, there is a distinction between interaction-oriented frames of valuation and pricing (such as rituals) and frames of valuation that have more to do with how other market actors are perceived. Since perception operates with categories, it follows that not only securities but also traders are ordered by their peers along categories of action, or 'psychological types'. Smith (1999, p. 141) distinguishes four such categories[13] (economic/instrumental, political/interpersonal, ordering/ideational and libidinal/expressive). They help traders produce overviews of the market, used for evaluating future price movements as well as general market trends. By combining the uses of these categories with respect to other traders and with respect to oneself, Smith identifies 15 types of traders (the sixteenth combination being contradictory), arguing that market transactions cannot be reduced to a single, dominant psychological type (Smith, 1999, p. 143). This conclusion, which is very similar to Ezra Zuckerman's thesis of structural incoherence (discussed above), sees financial markets as fragmented along a classificatory system concerning not only securities but also market actors.

If information is something traders constantly use and modify to their advantage, can it still be conceived as analogous to electric impulses and as network specific? While not denying the role of social networks in building up trust, Abolafia tends to take a more individualistic view, according to which traders engage in games both within and outside networks. Ranking social competitors appears thus as more important than building up networks of total trust. While this encourages opportunism, institutional rules contribute to keeping it in check. First, institutional rules establish social distinctions on the floor of the exchange and thus reduce social competition. These distinctions are tied to specific identities that limit opportunistic behaviour. For instance, the role of the specialist as it existed on the New York Stock Exchange implied mechanisms of social control that kept competition among traders within certain limits (Abolafia, 1996, p. 110). Moreover, status positions such as that of the market maker contribute to maintaining liquid transactions: they conduct (continuous) auctions observed by other market actors (Carruthers and Stinchcombe, 2001, p. 109). Second, both institution-internal and external rules create a framework in which the traders' games can take place: they establish what is legitimate and is illegitimate, what is legal and what is not. In a more restricted sense, (formal) rules reduce uncertainties and contribute to creating liquidity in financial markets (Carruthers and Stinchcombe, 2001, p. 125). Therefore, opportunism is always socially restrained and controlled. In order to understand financial transactions and their specific outcomes, one has to grasp the sets of rules framing these transactions, as well as the ways in which traders play their games within this framework. The emphasis here is not so much on networks as on social games, and not on information as signals but on the procedures through which information is processed, checked and evaluated.

In his more recent work, Abolafia investigates the interpretive procedures used in monetary policy, procedures through which data are agreed or disagreed upon as meaningful by policy makers. Examining the transcript of the Open Market Committee (OMC) of the Federal Reserve, Abolafia (2005) argues that policy making itself is framed by interpretive politics – that is, by the epistemological assumptions, interests and interactions of the OMC members. Re-examining the interplay between opportunism and institutional constraints, he maintains that interpretive policies are characterized by competition among policy makers, with regard to turning constraints into resources that will advance particular agendas, as well as to controlling the definition of market conditions (Abolafia, 2005, p. 227). Once again, information (be it statistical data, or data about political and economic events) appears as uncertain in value and significance before entering interpretive procedures. At the same time, uncertain data are but one of the resources used in the interpretive processes characterizing monetary policy making. The interaction constraints present during committee meetings as well as broader worldviews of the participating actors are used as policy-making resources too.

6. Political Institutions and Financial Markets

While the intra-institutional behaviour of individual actors (such as traders) is characterized by engaging in social games with other actors, the outcome of which is a ranking or hierarchy, what can be said about financial institutions as such? In the same way in which rules constrain and control opportunistic behaviour at the individual level, political constraints control institutional opportunism. In this perspective, the state (and, more generally, political institutions) appears not as the antonym of markets, but as deeply intertwined with them. The theoretical underpinnings of this position are developed, among others, by Neil Fligstein (1996), who argues that states create markets by setting in place regulatory frames that comprise property rights, governance structures and rules of exchange. These are mechanisms of social and political control without which markets would become unstable (Fligstein, 1996, p. 660). This argument is very similar to the one made by Bruce Carruthers (1996) in his historical investigation of the connections between politics and the rise of financial markets in eighteenth century England. Carruthers's point is that while economic considerations may influence political actions, the opposite is also true. Modern financial markets, the emergence of which is inextricably tied to state debt, are characterized by the mingling of political with economic interests. Political interests do not designate here simply the state's interests, but also those of various groups, which can be organized in political parties. They will determine the adoption of a specific legal frame (with important consequences for market liquidity, for instance), as well as specific patterns of shareholding.

Not only that political interests play a role in the adoption of specific legal frames for financial transactions; on a more micro-institutional level, such interests appear as instrumental with respect to the adoption of the product categories with which institutional actors operate. While structural analysis (discussed above) saw financial intermediaries as akin to literary critics, operating with categories that were sometimes clear-cut and sometimes disputed, the investigation of how such categories are produced reveals the role played by group interests in their establishment and adoption by the financial services industry. In their investigation of how the mutual funds industry adopted the product categories it operates with, Michael Lounsbury and Hayagreeva Rao (2004) argue that these categories are not produced according to technical criteria shared by all mutual funds, but emerge rather in the interaction between specialized agencies (which publish surveys of mutual funds) and powerful incumbents in the field.

Consequently, (financial) markets are characterized not so much by (perfect) competition as by niche carving, by orientation towards peers within the same segment and by the accommodation of specific group interests. This view attempts at reconciling the neo-institutionalist tenet about the relevance of historically evolved belief systems in organizational life with the structural approach, according to which markets are quasi-closed networks of relationships. Market rules are political in nature, in the sense of being the outcome and the expression of power relationships, of being shaped by the interaction between market actors and political institutions. These rules create stability by encouraging if not triggering market-internal differentiation into niches and segments, to the effect that competing firms orient themselves to each other within a given segment. Within this frame, the structural examination of pricing processes discussed in the previous sections retains its validity.

This focuses the inquiry upon the links between financial markets and political institutions, upon transaction-governing rules and the role played by financial actors in the larger economy. The notion of information understood either as signals or as determined by shared (or negotiated) interpretive frames recedes from view, being replaced by the notion of power as central with respect to the place taken by financial markets within economic life and, more generally, within society. This builds upon Max Weber's insight that financial markets are political institutions too, and that financial trading cannot be separated from interests and power relationships (Weber, 1924 [1894], p. 316). Generally speaking, power is understood in this context as the reproduction of specific (group) interests by political and cultural means, a process that confers a self-referential logic upon these means.

With respect to financial markets, the consequence is that the cultural means used by market actors in order to attain, stabilize and reproduce specific interests become self-sustaining and generalized, being perpetuated in disjunction from the specific interests that may have initially supported them. Cultural means can take the form of a particular rhetoric about market efficiency, or of discourses about the interests of shareholders. Examples in this sense are provided in the work of Frank Dobbin and his collaborators (e.g. Dobbin, 1994; Zorn, 2004; Zorn et al., 2005). While in his earlier work Dobbin (1994) has shown how political principles have been transferred into various railroad policies during the nineteenth century, with the consequence of different financial strategies, the more recent investigations have centred on the effects of financial markets upon corporate structures and policies. Starting from the case of the chief financial officer, a top-level position that has emerged in the late 1960s in US corporations as held by accountants (Zorn et al., 2005, p. 279), these sociologists show how, since the early 1980s, it has shifted away from accounting and towards managing investor relationships.

This shift is interpreted as the result of a successful redefinition of group interests as being synonymous with the general interests of investors, a redefinition promoted by takeover firms, institutional investors and securities analysts. For various reasons (having mostly to do with their valuation practices) these groups favoured focused firms over conglomerates (the dominant business model in the 1960s). Takeover firms, analysts and institutional investors have become more and more important in financial markets since the early 1980s; they promoted stock price as a corporate metric (Zorn et al., 2005, p. 276) and the focused firm as the business model corresponding to shareholder interests. Prominent takeovers during the 1980s as well as changing patterns of acquisitions contributed to the imposition of a business model characterized, among other things, by the prominence of the chief financial officer (usually occupied by a person with close connections to financial markets) in charge of investor relationships. In time, this business model became self-legitimating, with the added benefit of *post hoc* economic rationalizations for its existence. Thus, it is less the efficiency of one business model over another that contributes to its dominant position; the success of business models is given by the ability of given groups to impose them and provide a rationalization acceptable to the larger society.

Neil Fligstein (Fligstein and Shin, 2003) contends that the business model propagated by specific financial actors not only dominated the sector of publicly held corporations, but spread across various industrial sectors in the USA. The widespread use of computer technologies in corporate settings, regarded by many as a source of increases in productivity and hence of economic growth, was, according to Fligstein, 'not an exogenous change in American business but part and parcel of "maximizing shareholder value"' (Fligstein and Shin, 2003, p. 25). In a more general frame, the successful imposition of business models, the increased role played by financial activities as an autonomous profit centre within corporations, together with the widespread perceived legitimacy of discourses about shareholder value can be seen as indicators of a wider process of 'financialization' of advanced economies (Krippner, 2005). This closes the argumentative circle: while the neo-institutionalist approach to financial markets has started by asserting a transfer of belief systems from political to financial institutions, it asserts now that such systems are produced by groups situated within finance, from where they spread into the economy at large, affecting political activities too.

Methodologically speaking, there are some significant differences between structural analysis and neo-institutionalism. Structural analysis has been preoccupied with the construction of general formal models of markets-as-networks (as exemplified, for instance, in the work of Harrison White), but less with their direct empirical testing. Nevertheless, there are some important exceptions here: Joel Podolny's (2005) theory of status groups aims at elaborating an empirically testable, overarching view of how economic information affects transactions. We can also find empirical tests of formal relationships in the work of Wayne Baker or Ezra Zuckerman, for instance, tests using both primary and secondary data. Statistical analysis is supplemented in some cases (especially in Zuckerman's work) with additional insights gained from interviewing field actors (e.g. securities analysts).

By comparison, neo-institutionalist research on financial markets relies on a broader mix of qualitative and quantitative methods. Highlighting the tensions between the opportunistic behaviour of traders, on the one hand, and institutional constraints, on the other hand, requires methods focusing the context-bound, interaction-oriented aspects of such behaviour. Methods of direct, *in situ* observation, even if not conducive to generalizations, are more able to capture such aspects than statistical analyses. They have featured prominently in the work of Mitchel Abolafia, for instance, being complemented by (or supplanted with) interviews in other cases. With a major neo-institutionalist tenet being that of path dependency – that is, of present systems of beliefs and rules of action being the result of historical developments – historical analysis, combining statistical with qualitative techniques, has taken a central place in the work of authors such as Frank Dobbin or Bruce Carruthers, for instance.

At this point, the question can be raised which methodology should be able to capture best the production, processing, distribution and valuation of information. Since this concept is central within both the economics frame and the sociological one, this appears as relevant. However, it is to be acknowledged here that these approaches do not operate with a notion of information as the basis on which to build a sociological theory of price formation within financial markets. While they acknowledge the role of perception frames (for instance, belief systems can be seen as perception and interpretive frames), these approaches do not investigate their formation close-up. The conceptual core of the analysis is provided by power (as determined by group interests combined with persuasion tools), allowing thus an opening toward organizational and macro-social processes. While the neo-institutionalist approach explicitly tries to accommodate notions such as cognition and culture (e.g. by acknowledging the role played by shared frames of perception and belief systems), the question about the fine-grained processes through which financial knowledge is produced, stabilized and diffused does not receive an answer here.

7. Financial Information and Cognition as Objects of Sociological Investigation

It would not be too hazardous to claim that financial information has been made into an object of systematic, micro-analytic investigation only recently, in relation to the emergence of the social studies of finance as a new subdiscipline since the late 1990s. While incorporating insights from disciplines such as political economy, cultural anthropology and human geography, social studies of finance[14] have been decisively influenced (including the name borrowing) by social studies of science, a direction of research established since the 1970s with the aim of systematically investigating how scientific knowledge (with its specific epistemic traits, including truth claims) is produced, stabilized and distributed within and outwith scientific communities. This influence is expressed, among other ways, in the fact that since the late 1990s several known scholars from the social studies of science have re-focused their research interests on financial markets. Letting aside various individual motivations, this reorientation emerged against the renewed prominence gained by financial markets in the 1990s, after the fall of the Iron Curtain, and, at least as important, against the accelerated process of market technologization experienced in this period, as well as against the growing prominence of formal models in financial trading.

It could be ventured here that preoccupations with how scientific information is generated, with the relationship between information and cognition, have played a formative role for the ways in which social studies of finance deal with financial information. A long line of empirical investigations about how information is produced in scientific (and technological) settings underscores the role of tacit skills in the processing of raw inputs into relevant information, the cooperative nature of this process, as well as the role played by artefacts (e.g. measuring and observation devices) in this process (e.g. Latour, 1988; Hutchins, 1995; Pickering, 1995; Collins, 2001). The methodology through which these insights have been gained underscores direct, close-up, longitudinal observation of information-producing processes in natural settings, coupled with estrangement procedures – that is, the observer's bracketing out of all assumptions about the natural, given or expected character of any of these processes. This methodology is less oriented towards elaborating formal models and testing them against empirical data, but stresses procedures of direct, field observation, not entirely dissimilar from those used by natural field scientists. Consequently, methodological accuracy (concerning, among other things, how to achieve unbiased, 'uncontaminated' observation) becomes even more important in close-up field research.

In parallel with investigating how market actors produce information, social studies of finance investigate how information itself is made into a central concept in financial economics, by tracing the concept's career and metamorphoses within the economics profession. In this respect, the work of Philip Mirowski on conceptual transfers from physics to economics (Mirowski, 1989) and on the introduction of the notion of information into economic theory (Mirowski, 2002) plays a seminal role. Mirowski shows how, under the influence of operations research, post-WWII economic theory adopted a concept of information understood as meaningful patterns of signals detectable from more general 'noise' (Mirowski, 2002, pp. 7, 21). Recent work in social studies of finance, concerned with the 'performativity of economics' (to be discussed in more detail below) actually overlaps at least in part with Mirowski's programme of research by showing how pricing formulae incorporate specific, selected information which then changes the practices of market actors.

A central aspect in the investigation of financial information is provided by securities prices, not only because a central tenet of the EMH is that prices incorporate all the information available to market actors (Stigler, 1961; Woelfel, 1994, p. 328; Shleifer, 2000, pp. 1–3), but also because prices in themselves constitute crucial information for financial transactions. This implies that market actors are able to distinguish between relevant and irrelevant information, between (meaningful) signals and noise without recourse to issues of cognition.

Yet, what does it mean – from the viewpoint of market actors – to use price information? Prices are not abstract, given or spontaneously generating themselves, without any interference from human actors. They appear to market participants as data, obtained in specific interactions, requiring specific activities from the actors (e.g. observation), as well as the use of specific recording, storage and transmission technologies. This perspective requires abandoning the notion of price as something abstract in favour of price data, produced in specific settings under specific conditions. Concomitantly, it opens up a programme of research about (a) the assumptions of veridicality, robustness and reliability implied in the production of price data; (b) the cognitive activities – such as observation, classification, memorization – without which data production cannot take place; (c) the technologies that endow data with specific properties. In short, price data are treated as a practical problem for market actors and not as the given or natural basis of financial transactions. Moreover, the question can be raised here whether financial economics, by generally leaving price data unquestioned,[15] does not share a basic set of assumptions with financial practice – in short, whether they are different types of rationality or not.

The veridicality, robustness and reliability of price data are not independent of cognitive activities such as observation and memorization, or of the technologies allowing data recording, observation and storage. These are also two of the main research themes in social studies of finance, as exemplified by micro-analytical field studies of how traders observe price data, as well as of price-recording and display technologies. To start with observation: an analysis of how traders observe securities prices displayed on computer screens may benefit from the comparison with how scientific observation is conducted in settings such as the laboratory. Social studies of science have long argued that scientific observation is a complex, collective work, involving the spatial and temporal coordination of several actors (e.g. Lynch *et al.*, 1983; Lynch, 1985), as well as the processing of raw inputs into meaningful data. In their fieldwork on currency trading, Karin Knorr Cetina and Urs Bruegger (2002, pp. 923–924) show how the observation of currency prices involves the temporal coordination of traders who are dispersed over several time zones; this coordination, which takes the form of conversational interactions, makes it possible for traders to regard their screen displays not as artful arrangements of pixels, but as meaningful, action-conducive data. For instance, currency traders request feedback from each other over the 'right' price and communicate price data to each other in ritualized form, both online and offline. The collaborative character of data production is reiterated in subsequent field studies (e.g. Zaloom, 2003; Beunza and Stark, 2005) showing that traders rely on feedback from and interaction with other traders in their observations of price data and their subsequent interpretation. Caitlin Zaloom (2003, p. 263) stresses the role of bodily interaction in making price data meaningful: the significance of price and volume data communicated among traders depends on their bodily posture, pitch of voice and attitude. While on the floor traders are visible to each other, in automated trading, where names are not displayed on the screen, traders have developed methods for guessing the identities of their counterparts from the price and data volume displayed on screen (Zaloom, 2003, p. 267).[16]

This, among other things, suggests that technology is not neutral with respect to what constitutes price data as well as other trading-relevant information. The properties of such data, as well as the traders' response to them, appear to be influenced by the technologies used for recording, memorizing and transmitting prices. One way of investigating how technology endows data with specific properties and how traders react to these properties would be a historical examination of the emergence and evolution of price-recording technology. The stock ticker was perhaps the first successful, custom-made recording technology used in financial markets (Preda, 2006): introduced on the New York Stock Exchange in December 1867, it was adopted on the London Stock Exchange in 1872 and continued to be used throughout the twentieth century (albeit in electronic form since the 1960s). Before the ticker machine was invented by Edward Calahan, stock exchanges used messenger boys to record and circulate securities prices on paper slips. This technique made price recording unreliable, susceptible to gaps and to data losses, and encouraged the existence of parallel markets within the same location. The introduction of the stock ticker allowed for a continuous recording in near real time. It allowed, if not encouraged, the unification of markets that previously coexisted in the same location, and required continuous attention on the part of market actors. Moreover, the stock ticker encouraged a reorganization of the trading floor based on the differentiation among trading posts specialized in certain classes of securities. It supported the production of visualization instruments such as minute price charts, which in their turn required expert interpretation. Around the turn of the twentieth century, some brokers and traders switched from trading to the commercialization of price chart interpretations, starting what became later an institutionalized branch of financial analysis (Preda, 2007). On a broader scale, the existence of mechanically recorded price data was used as an argument by the US Supreme Court in declaring financial markets as fraught with public interest, a definition that opened the way to public regulation of market transactions.

According to this empirical evidence, a technology like the stock ticker is not neutral with respect to the properties of price data and to the ways market actors use these data. While not predetermining user behaviour, price-recording technologies elicit reactions from their users, ranging from internal reorganizations of the stock exchange to the ways in which data are perceived and interpreted. These technologies can trigger unforeseen and unplanned changes, such as a reconsideration of the legal status of financial transactions or the emergence of a new form of expertise.

From a complementary perspective, Fabian Muniesa (2000, 2003) examined the social processes that led to the automation of the Paris Bourse (now part of the Euronext exchange), as well as the assumptions grounding the design of its automated trading system. He shows how in the mid-1980s the Paris Bourse embarked on the automation project not because of efficiency concerns, but because of a concern for offering customers distinctive features with regard to its main competitors. By adopting and adapting a system introduced without success on the Toronto Stock Exchange in the 1970s (CATS, or Computer Assisted Trading System), the Paris Bourse was confronted with the problem of assumptions about fairness and equilibrium that should underlie the design of the trading algorithm software. The design of the double auction algorithm, however, emerged not as the implementation of a theoretical blueprint but as the result of internal debates about what constitutes a 'just' price that will reduce chances for price manipulation (Muniesa, 2000, p. 306). Thus, argues Muniesa, considerations about what is socially legitimate inform this design, while aspects such as volatility may be left unaffected. Securities prices, as realized in such an automated trading system, 'are the result of translations, negotiations and efforts of all kinds that give them a specific "form"' (Muniesa, 2000, p. 307). Automated trading technologies are the outcome of complex social negotiations among groups with various interests rather than the direct translation of theoretical models.

With respect to the relationship between information and cognition, the studies discussed above stressed the impossibility of separating the two. They show that a notion of information as signals passively received by users does not fit the actual processing of raw inputs into meaningful data. Financial cognition appears here as a set of complex, interlocked processes, ranging from perception and memorization to classification and the calculation of trading operations, and implying not isolated individuals, but group work, actors as well as technologies. While classification appears as an important aspect of financial cognition, it is not the only one, being dependent on features such as observation and memorization. This is relevant with respect to the neo-institutionalist treatment of classification as the major (if not the only) cognitive operation shaping financial transactions. In this perspective, field studies of financial cognition and technologies represent a departure from the notion(s) of information present used by structural analysis and neo-institutionalism. These studies depart from the notion of signal, while at the same time expanding and specifying the general concept of perception frame usually found (under varying names) in neo-institutionalist studies, by showing how such frames are constituted, as well as their irreducibility to classification processes.

More generally, the theoretical implications are that market incoherence is not due only to the coexistence of fuzzy and clear-cut categories for classifying financial securities, or of various networks carving niches for themselves. Incoherence is as much cognitive as it is structural: in their search for informational advantages, market actors modify and adapt perception frames in ways which are not predetermined, hoping to thus get an edge over their competitors.[17] However, since information cannot be seen as independent of such frames, it follows that changing the latter automatically implies modifying the meaning of the former. Market actors creatively use the tools and resources at their disposal in order to create information differences and to trade on their basis. This means that trading rests on a continuous process of generating such differences. Perfect information, characterized by completeness, general availability and full reflection in prices, may not be the best fitting description for this process. First, prices themselves constitute data that can be (and are) interpreted differently. Second, from the perspective of market actors, informational differences appear more important than completeness.

8. The Uses of Formal Models in Trading

Continuing this line of reasoning, one can see formal models of price variations not only as having a representational function, but also as constituting information that can be used by market actors in their transactions. While sociologists traditionally have distinguished between formal theoretical models and the (social or natural) phenomena they represent, social studies of finance see such models from the perspective of their use by practitioners. The blurring of the distinction between (academic) formal representation, on the one hand, and practical uses of representations outside the context of their production, on the other hand, has been one of the strategies through which social studies of science investigate the transfer of scientific knowledge across practical settings (e.g. Henderson, 1999; Pinch, 2003).

Within social studies of finance, the examination of the relationship between theoretical models and market transactions has taken shape in the performativity argument (e.g. Callon, 1998, 1999, 2007; MacKenzie and Millo, 2003; MacKenzie, 2006a). In a nutshell, the performativity argument claims that formal economic models do not simply represent economic phenomena (such as market transactions), but can create them too. In his initial formulation of this thesis, Michel Callon (1998) wanted to distance himself from the sociological debates about the (in)existence of homo oeconomicus by arguing that the latter is not just an abstract model, but a series of behavioural scripts put into practice by implementing theoretical models of market transactions. One of Callon's favourite examples was that of the strawberry auction market in Fontaines-en-Sologne (Garcia, 1986), which has been reshaped according to the plans drafted by an economist; the new auction market substantially differed from the old one, which was based on webs of personal relationships among producers and buyers. Therefore, argued Callon, economic models are performative in the sense of changing, and not just describing, empirical market transactions.

This concept of performativity bears resemblance with the sociological concept of agency, understood as the capacity of actors to open up avenues of action that are not predetermined, to rise above given routines and act in novel ways. Social studies of science have repeatedly argued that agential capacities cannot be exclusively ascribed to human actors, but are distributed across constellations of humans and artefacts. In other words, working (and interacting) with artefacts appears as essential with respect to such agential capacities. Within this frame, theoretical agency designates the ways in which theoretical models can transform not only the academic context in which they are produced, but also contexts of practical use. This sends us to the issue of the boundaries between scientific and vernacular forms of knowledge: the transfer of theoretical models into contexts of practical action is affected by the users' vernacular knowledge, so that in practical situations we do not necessarily encounter 'pure', unadulterated theoretical models. Another aspect implied in this concept is that of calculation: if the use of theoretical models changes the behaviour of market actors, can it be said that such models make actors more rational and prone to using formulae?[18] Hence, performativity implies investigating at least theoretical and calculative agencies,[19] as well as boundaries between academic and other forms of expert knowledge.

Donald MacKenzie and his collaborators (e.g. MacKenzie and Millo, 2003) have expanded, modified and applied the notion of performativity to the study of financial markets. Their prime case is that of the Black–Scholes–Merton formula and the rise of the derivatives markets since the early 1980s. Reconstructing the uses of this formula on the floor of the Chicago Board of Trade (CBOT) and its adoption by traders, MacKenzie and Millo argue, in a vein similar to Muniesa's, that the CBOT was exploring possibilities of branching into new forms of transactions. The Chicago Mercantile Exchange (CME) and the CBOT decided to expand into derivatives trading, pushing for regulatory changes disentangling derivatives from gambling and seeking legitimacy from economics (MacKenzie, 2006b, p. 147). Against this background, traders started using the Black–Scholes–Merton formula in spite of the fact that its theoretical prices did not fit empirical data. They adopted it because it was freely available, simple, came from academia and the theoretical prices it generated could be printed on rolled paper sheets and taken on the floor of the exchange. Traders used these paper sheets (containing theoretical prices) as a means of coordinating their actions and as a guide to trading. Repeated use of theoretical prices generated empirical price data, which fit the predictions, confirming thus the validity of the formula.

In his subsequent work, Mackenzie (2006a, b, p. 17) distinguishes among four forms of perfomativity: generic, effective, Barnesian[20] (named after the sociologist

Barry Barnes) and counter-performativity. Generic performativity designates the use of theoretical models as tools by market actors. Effective performativity designates situations where the practical use of an aspect of economics modifies economic processes. Barnesian performativity designates the situation where the nature of the modification is to make those processes more like how economics posits them as being. Counter-performativity designates situations where market practitioners imitate each other's data production in such a way that the use of a theoretical model does not constitute a cognitive advantage anymore, but is turned into a disadvantage. Imitation of data production (such as in copying trades done by competitors) eliminates advantages and can send the market into an unravelling spiral. A case in point here (studied in MacKenzie, 2005) is that of Long-Term Capital Management (LTCM): its competitors imitated LTCM's trades, creating a situation in which in a crisis there were no counterparties left, except at distress prices. Lack of counterparties (and hence of liquidity) coupled with highly leveraged trades sent the market downwards.

Concepts such as performativity and calculative agency are not without critics within the community. Among the objections raised in this respect are that relationships of power remain out of sight when the adoption (and modification) of theoretical models is investigated, that in some cases models are adopted only as a *post hoc* justification of privatization processes (called market creation) and that not all users adopt such models (e.g. Mirowski and Nik-Kah, 2007).[21]

How do investigations of performativity relate to the cognitive programme in social studies of finance? More importantly perhaps, is there a specific notion of information supported by these investigations and, if yes, where do the similarities and differences lie with the notions discussed above? On a first level, performativity seems to take a macro-analytical turn, being oriented more towards examining aspects such as the interplay between regulatory frames and the adoption of formal models, the various groups promoting these models and the group impact of model adoption. Methodologically speaking, studies of performativity have been historical reconstructions anchored in interviews and document analysis, sometimes with the added benefit of descriptive statistical data. On a further level, performativity studies and field studies of financial cognition share the insight that information is not reducible to signals and that cognitive processes such as observation, memorization, classification and calculation play an important role in endowing data with specific properties. Both acknowledge technology as intrinsic to this process. While field studies of financial cognition stress local variability, but do not give privilege to formal models in the constitution of information, performativity studies operate with more nuanced distinctions among various types of financial expertise and stress the links between economic theory and economic practice. Intrinsic to this link is investigating how assumptions and notion(s) of information present in formal models on financial economics are transferred into and affect market practices. Conversely, the question can be raised about whether vernacular notions of information, as used by market actors, influence the construction of theoretical models.

As the notion of information seems to get biological underpinnings in economic theory, as exemplified by the recent emergence of neuroeconomics as a
subdiscipline, it becomes even more important to be aware of (and examine) the
intellectual transfers from biology to economics and their consequences, both within
the academic field and with respect to market practitioners.

9. Conclusion

What I have discussed here as the sociology of financial markets comprises a
variety of approaches, some of which are subfields of economic sociology and
organization studies, while some others operate at the intersection of economic
sociology, social studies of science and social studies of cognition. Theoretically and
methodologically, we find both divergence and overlapping but, generally speaking,
it can be argued that all these approaches, ranging from structural analysis to field
studies of financial cognition and performativity, stress the role of social interactions
with respect to price formation and volatility. While this general formulation may
seem unsurprising, it is often the detail that makes such arguments interesting:
interactions are not seen as homogeneous and conforming to a general pattern of
rationality but as quasi-closed, inward-looking and differentiated, characterized by
specific cognitive properties and dynamics, features that impact upon securities
prices and volatility. There is variation, however, in the ways in which social
interactions are understood, ranging from networks of social relationships to micro-
analytic, direct interactions.

If we are to look for one basic concept underlying all these approaches, then
it is the concept of information: social interactions are understood both as information in themselves and as channels through which information circulates. The
understanding of information, though, ranges from signals analogous to electric
impulses to cognitively determined, community-agreed objects (see Table 1).

Reflecting upon the relevance of the sociology of financial markets, the following
can be said: on a broader level, this subfield of sociology highlights both the
centrality of financial markets as modern institutions and their irreducibility to
mechanisms of resource allocation. The societal impact of markets has always
gone beyond this, and it is sociology's task to analyse how (financial) markets
connect with other social institutions (e.g. the state, the media), how they affect
people's lives in ways other than economic and how they are perceived by the
larger society. On a second, more restricted level, the sociology of financial markets
can formulate insights useful not only for the history of financial economics, but
also for better understanding actors' behaviour in economic settings, as well as
the elements underlying financial cognition. In this respect, there is certainly the
possibility of a dialogue with behavioural finance, a possibility that has begun taking
concrete shapes. While behavioural finance usually refers to laboratory- or survey-
based psychological studies of human behaviour, studies of financial cognition are
conducted *in situ* and are thus able to offer additional insights. Structural analysis
and neo-institutionalism provide us with valuable conceptualizations of the link
between social ties and price volatility too.

Table 1. The Concept of Information in the Sociology of Financial Markets.

	Character of interactions	Character of information	What is information	Methodology
Structural analysis	Networks of social relationships Status groups	Signals analogous to electric impulses	Relationships are signals and relays for the transmission of signals Signals are classified into categories Categories provide frames for signal interpretation	Formal modelling Quantitative analysis
Neo-institutionalism	Rule oriented Path dependent Framed by belief systems	Determined by perception frames Information is manipulated by market actors Rules restrain manipulation Rules are shaped by power structures	Signals interpreted according to rules Concept of power has primacy	Both quantitative and qualitative
Field studies of financial cognition	Oriented to local resources and constraints Characterized by cognitive features Collective work implying coordination with other actors and with artefacts	Result of cognitive processing: observation, memorization, classification, calculation Undergoes internal differentiations	Raw inputs are cognitively processed into information Material objects (e.g. screen displays, formulae on paper, etc.) Processing techniques confer specific properties	Qualitative Inductive analysis Historical reconstruction
Performativity studies	Experts interact with practitioners Formal models are adopted and adapted by practitioners according to specific interests	Information is a tool used in practical actions Not restricted to data; includes abstract models, formulae Use of information generates information Dependent on cognitive processes	Material objects	Historical reconstruction Qualitative

If I were to track now future developments, at least the following areas of research can be highlighted in this context.

1. The expansion of computer-supported trading and the impact of technology upon trading behaviour: since the start of the new millennium, technology has made great inroads into financial markets and we witness now an accelerated shift from the more traditional floor-based trading to electronic trading. This raises a whole series of interesting issues both at the macro-analytical and at the micro-analytical level. At the macro-analytical level, these issues concern at least the role of regulators in the new, transcontinental, electronic trading environment, and the shape, organizational structure and rules of the new emerging exchanges. At the more micro-analytical level, the widened non-professional participation in electronic trading brings about questions about the similarities and differences in trading behaviour between professionals and non-professionals.
2. The relationships among various forms of financial expertise and their uses by practitioners: The rise of electronic trading has highlighted the role played by various forms of financial expertise in market transactions; it becomes therefore necessary to pay closer attention to how this expertise affects trading behaviour and how it is integrated in the new electronic environment.
3. The broader social and cultural relevance of financial markets: With increased social visibility, financial markets acquire broader meanings. As mentioned above, they affect people's lives in ways going beyond resource allocation: for instance, they affect families' planning for the future, professional choices, can affect how society is understood and can contribute to the individualization processes characterizing advanced societies. Widened participation in financial transactions, in its multiple forms (e.g. through electronic trading, personal investments and the like), can contribute to processes such as individualization. It is one of the profession's important challenges to investigate such changes.

Notes

1. David Stark (2000) makes the argument that the sociologists' lack of interest about market transactions can be followed back to the division of academic labour promoted by Talcott Parsons in the 1950s: while economists study value, sociologists should investigate values – that is, the transactions-external web of social relationships supporting market exchanges.
2. Mark Granovetter's embeddedness argument continues and expands on Karl Polanyi's (1957 [1944]) thesis that economic exchanges cannot be sustained outside webs of social relationships. A complementary sociological perspective is provided by Émile Durkheim's argument (1984 [1893], pp. 150–151) against the Rousseauist view of rational contracts as providing the basis of modern social life and, implicitly, of economic exchanges. In order to have any force, (economic) contracts need to be anchored in a series of tacit assumptions shared by partners, assumptions concerning reliability and trustworthiness. Therefore, relationships of trust emerge as a fundamental condition of economic transactions; such relationships cannot be

limited to transactions, but extend into (and blend with) the larger spheres of social life. The attempt at separating the domain of economic transactions as purely rational and contrasting it with the irrationality of other aspects of life proves futile. In fact, it is exactly this blurring of the boundaries that makes economic transactions possible. Durkheim's critique of the notion of contract opens up an important direction of research about the anchoring of economic transactions in trust relationships, a direction represented both in social-structural research on markets and in the neo-institutionalist approach.

3. Granovetter's embeddedness argument, which proved so influential until the end of the 1990s, has recently come under attack exactly on the grounds that it separates social relationships from transactions and sees the latter as being only embedded in the former (Krippner, 2001). Concomitantly, Harrison White's innovative view on markets as networks of social relationships, which are at the same time signalling systems, has become more and more influential.

4. White's arguments bear close resemblance to those of the late German sociologist Niklas Luhmann (1988), whose theory of social systems conceives economic exchanges as a closed system organized around the code of monetary value.

5. While dealing mainly with producer markets, very generally understood, White seems to be more ambiguous on financial markets. On the one hand, as mentioned above, he uses producer markets as a template: any kind of transaction in which an object (be it material or intellectual, including obligations and promises) changes hands for money falls within this category. At the same time, financial markets are seen by White as a kind of secondary-order markets, arising out of the entrepreneurial need to raise cash (White, 2002, pp. 246–247).

6. The role of computerized trading technologies and their influence on traders' behaviour has been examined by the social studies of finance, which I discuss in the following sections.

7. While Zuckerman's approach provides us with a functionalist explanatory frame for fundamental analysis, which classifies financial securities along various economic categories, it is less helpful with respect to technical analysis, or Chartism, which claims to forecast price movements without resorting to such classifications.

8. In this perspective, existing webs of social relationships can not only process uncertainties, but also put the brakes on innovative approaches and novel initiatives. This resonates with Ronald Burt's (1992) idea that creativity can emerge in 'structural holes' – that is, in situations where social relationships are less dense.

9. An example in this sense is provided by the current discussions about what constitutes 'just' compensation for top executives, discussions triggered time and again by announcements about the yearly bonuses of traders. On Continental Europe, these discussions have been concretized, for instance, in proposals to limit these compensations by law (i.e. to introduce a 'maximum wage' in addition to the already existing minimum wage requirements). Another example is provided by debates (in the wake of the dotcom crash) about stock options as just or efficient compensation for executives.

10. This direction of research, known as neo-institutionalism, acknowledges intellectual indebtedness to cultural anthropological work on belief systems. Mary Douglas's *Purity and Danger* (1966), for instance, is explicitly paid tribute to as a major source of intellectual inspiration.

11. This opening reinvigorates the sociological tradition that saw financial markets as not only economic institutions, but political as well. Not only Karl Marx (1964

[1894]) but Max Weber (1978 [1921], 2000 [1894]) too saw markets as irreducible to allocation systems.

12. The ethnographic fieldwork on which Abolafia's book is based was conducted in the late 1980s and the early 1990s; since then, computerized trading technologies have considerably affected trading procedures and strategies. How technology shapes trading behaviour is discussed in the next section of this paper. Moreover, new regulations with respect to the handling of information have been put in place since the 1980s, regulations that affect trading directly.

13. Sociologists cannot fail to notice here the strong similarity between Smith's types and Talcott Parsons's four fundamental values that lay the basis of any social system: adaptation, goal attainment, integration and latency (Parsons, 1951).

14. Social studies of finance have generated several publications (books as well as articles) and attracted doctoral students; they have become featured at the yearly conferences of the profession and have hosted several international conferences. For the purposes of this discussion, I distinguish here between two branches of social studies of finance: field studies of financial cognition and performativity studies.

15. This does not mean, of course, that the veridicality or reliability of some price data cannot be questioned in specific situations. Such situations, however, are indicative of a temporary crisis that must be overcome rather than of a permanent and radical questioning of all data. For instance, when statistically processing price data, which have been mechanically recorded, the reliability and particular properties of the price-recording technology remain unquestioned.

16. Ethnographic observations suggest, indeed, that in automated trading institutional actors try to hide their identities by slicing up and dispersing large trades, while other traders try to guess their identities from past patterns of price movements. While this game of hide and seek is important with respect to the traders' strategies, fieldwork suggests that at least some online traders are not interested in any deeper knowledge about the identity of other market actors or in maintaining social relationships with them. This seems to depart from the notion of network as determining pricing processes and as circulating information.

17. For instance, traders and analysts custom tailor their spreadsheets; they select the 'relevant' data in such a way as to gain a perceived advantage over the competition and they place a premium on building their own indices and measures (e.g. Mars, 1998).

18. An important direction of investigating calculative practices is provided by ethno-accountancy – a branch of economic sociology concerned with how financial data are produced and invested with formal qualities (e.g. Vollmer, 2003; Kalthoff, 2005).

19. Michel Callon (2004, p. 123; Barry and Slater, 2002, p. 181) defines calculative agency as being characterized by (a) framing, (b) disentanglement and (c) performativity. Framing means a set of distinctions between what is calculable and what is not. Disentanglement means drawing boundaries between what is relevant and what is irrelevant with respect to calculability, while performativity indicates the use of technologies (including abstract models) in market transactions.

20. Initially, the term used was Austinian performativity. The very notion of performativity is indebted to J.L. Austin's (1962) distinction between performative and constative utterances. Austin pays special attention to a class of utterances that do not have a truth value and do not describe a state of things but, when uttered

under certain circumstances (called felicity conditions), effect a change in the state of the world. Common examples of such utterances are baptism and marriage formulae.

21. Interviews with traders (both professional and independent) done by this author suggest that not all of them use the Black–Scholes–Merton formula in their trades. Some regard it as irrelevant, while others assert that they cannot gain any informational advantage by using this formula. It appears that such uses are not generalized, but can be ignored or resisted by market practitioners.

References

Abolafia, M. (1996) *Making Markets. Opportunism and Restraint on Wall Street.* Cambridge, MA: Harvard University Press.

Abolafia, M. (2005) Interpretive politics at the Federal Reserve. In K. Knorr Cetina and A. Preda (eds), *The Sociology of Financial Markets* (pp. 207–228). Oxford: Oxford University Press.

Austin, J.L. (1962) *How To Do Things with Words.* Oxford: Oxford University Press.

Baker, W. (1984) The social structure of a national securities market. *American Journal of Sociology* 89: 775–811.

Barry, A. and Slater, D. (2002) Introduction: the technological economy. *Economy and Society* 31(2): 175–193.

Beckert, J. (1996) What is sociological about economic sociology? Uncertainty and the embeddedness of economic action. *Theory and Society* 25: 803–840.

Beunza, D. and Stark, D. (2005) How to recognize opportunities: hierarchical search in a trading room. In K. Knorr Cetina and A. Preda (eds), *The Sociology of Financial Markets* (pp. 84–101). Oxford: Oxford University Press.

Burt, R. (1992) *Structural Holes. The Social Structure of Competition.* Cambridge, MA: Harvard University Press.

Callon, M. (1998) Introduction. In M. Callon (ed.), *The Laws of the Markets* (pp. 1–57). Oxford: Blackwell.

Callon, M. (1999) Actor–network theory – the market test. In J. Law and J. Hassard (eds), *Actor–Network Theory and After* (pp. 181–195). Oxford: Blackwell.

Callon, M. (2004) Europe wrestling with technology. *Economy and Society* 33(1): 121–134.

Callon, M. (2007) What does it mean to say that economics is performative? In D. MacKenzie, F. Muniesa and L. Siu (eds), *Do Economists Make Markets? On the Performativity of Economics* (pp. 311–356). Princeton, NJ: Princeton University Press, forthcoming.

Carruthers, B. (1996) *City of Capital. Politics and Markets in the English Financial Revolution.* Princeton, NJ: Princeton University Press.

Carruthers, B. and Stinchcombe, A. (2001) The social structure of liquidity. Flexibility in markets, states, and organizations. In A. Stinchcombe (ed.), *When Formality Works. Authority and Abstraction in Law and Organizations* (pp. 100–139). Chicago, IL: University of Chicago Press.

Collins, H. (2001) What is tacit knowledge? In T. Schatzki, K. Knorr Cetina and E. von Savigny (eds), *The Practice Turn in Contemporary Theory* (pp. 107–119). London: Routledge.

Dobbin, F. (1994) *Forging Industrial Policy. The United States, Britain, and France in the Railway Age.* Cambridge: Cambridge University Press.

Douglas, M. (1966) *Purity and Danger. An Analysis of Concepts of Pollution and Taboo.* London: Routledge & Kegan Paul.

Durkheim, É. (1984 [1893]) *The Division of Labor in Society.* New York: Free Press.

Fligstein, N. (1996) Markets as politics. A political-cultural approach to market institutions. *American Sociological Review* 61(4): 656–673.

Fligstein, N. (2004) The transformation of the American economy, 1984–2001. Theory and research in comparative social analysis. Department of Sociology, UCLA, 16. Downloaded at http://repositories.cdlib.org/uclasoc/trcsa/16, 30 April 2007.

Fligstein, N. and Shin, T.-J. (2003) The shareholder-value society. *Indicators* 2(4): 5–43.

Franke, G. and Hess, D. (2000) Information diffusion in electronic and floor trading. *Journal of Empirical Finance* 7: 455–478.

Garcia, M.F. (1986) La construction sociale d'un marché parfait: le marché au cadran de Fontaines-en-Sologne. *Actes de la recherche en sciences sociales* 65: 2–13.

Granovetter, M. (1985) Economic action, social structure and embeddedness. *American Journal of Sociology* 91(3): 481–510.

Henderson, K. (1999) *On Line and on Paper. Visual Representations, Visual Culture, and Computer Graphics in Design Engineering.* Cambridge, MA: MIT Press.

Hutchins, E. (1995) *Cognition in the Wild.* Cambridge, MA: MIT Press.

Kalthoff, H. (2005) Practices of calculation: economic representation and risk management. *Theory, Culture and Society* 22(2): 69–97.

Klein, J.L. (2001) Reflections from the age of economic measurement. In J.L. Klein and M.S. Morgan (eds), *The Age of Economic Measurement. History of Political Economy* 33. (supplement): 111–136.

Knorr Cetina, K. and Bruegger, U. (2002) Global microstructures: the virtual societies of financial markets. *American Journal of Sociology* 107(4): 905–950.

Krippner, G. (2001) The elusive market. Embeddedness and the paradigm of economic sociology. *Theory and Society* 30: 775–810.

Krippner, G. (2005) The financialization of the American economy. *Socio-Economic Review* 3: 173–208.

Latour, B. (1988) *The Pasteurization of France.* Cambridge, MA: Harvard University Press.

Lounsbury, M. and Rao, H. (2004) Sources of durability and change in market classifications: a study of the reconstitution of product categories in the American mutual fund industry, 1944–1985. *Social Forces* 82(3): 969–999.

Luhmann, N. (1988) *Die Wirtschaft der Gesellschaft.* Frankfurt: Surhkamp.

Luhmann, N. (1990) *Essays on Self-Reference.* New York: Columbia University Press.

Lynch, M. (1985) Discipline and the material form of images. An analysis of scientific visibility. *Social Studies of Science* 15: 37–66.

Lynch, M., Livingston, E. and Garfinkel, H. (1983) Temporal order in laboratory work. In K. Knorr Cetina and M. Mulkay (eds), *Science Observed: Perspectives on the Social Study of Science* (pp. 205–238). London: Sage.

MacKenzie, D. (2005) How a super-portfolio emerges. Long-Term Capital Management and the sociology of arbitrage. In K. Knorr Cetina and A. Preda (eds), *The Sociology of Financial Markets* (pp. 62–83). Oxford: Oxford University Press.

MacKenzie, D. (2006a) Is economics performative? Option theory and the construction of derivatives markets. *Journal of the History of Economic Thought* 28(1): 29–55.

MacKenzie, D. (2006b) *An Engine, Not a Camera. How Financial Models Shape Markets.* Cambridge, MA: MIT Press.

MacKenzie, D. and Millo, Y. (2003) Constructing a market, performing a theory: the historical sociology of a financial derivatives exchange. *American Journal of Sociology* 109: 107–145.

Mars, F. (1998) Wir sind alle Seher. Die Praxis der Aktienanalyse. Unpublished PhD thesis, Bielefeld, Germany.

Marx, K. (1964 [1894]) *Das Kapital. Kritik der politischen Ökonomie.* Dritter Band, Buch III: *Der Gesamtprozeß der kapitalistichen Produktion.* Berlin: Dietz.

Mirowski, P. (1989) *More Heat than Light. Economics as Social Physics, Physics as Nature's Economics.* Cambridge: Cambridge University Press.

SOCIOLOGICAL APPROACH TO FINANCIAL MARKETS 121

Mirowski, P. (2002) *Machine Dreams. Economics Becomes a Cyborg Science*. Cambridge: Cambridge University Press.
Mirowski, P. and Nik-Khah, E. (2007) Markets made flesh: performativity, and a problem in science studies, augmented with consideration of the FCC auctions. In D. MacKenzie, F. Muniesa and L. Siu (eds), *Do Economists Make Markets? On the Performativity of Economics* (pp. 190–224). Princeton, NJ: Princeton University Press, forthcoming.
Muniesa, F. (2000) Performing prices: the case of price discovery automation in the financial markets. In H. Kalthoff, R. Rottenburg and H.-J. Wagener (eds), *Facts and Figures: Economic Representations and Practices* (pp. 289–312). Marburg: Metropolis.
Muniesa, F. (2003) Des marchés comme algorithmes. Sociologie de la cotation électronique à la Bourse de Paris. PhD dissertation, Ecole des Mines, Paris.
Parsons, T. (1951) *The Social System*. London: Routledge & Kegan Paul.
Perrow, C. (1986) *Complex Organizations. A Critical Essay*. New York: Random House.
Perrow, C. (2002) *Organizing America. Wealth, Power, and the Origins of Corporate Capitalism*. Princeton, NJ: Princeton University Press.
Pickering, A. (1995) *The Mangle of Practice. Time, Agency, and Science*. Chicago, IL: University of Chicago Press.
Pinch, T. (2003) Giving birth to new users: how the Minimoog was sold to rock and roll. In N. Oudshoorn and T. Pinch (eds), *How Users Matter. The Co-Construction of Users and Technologies* (pp. 247–270). Cambridge, MA: MIT Press.
Podolny, J. (2001) Networks as the pipes and prisms of the market. *American Journal of Sociology* 107(1): 33–60.
Podolny, J.M. (2005) *Status Signals. A Sociological Study of Market Competition*. Princeton, NJ, and Oxford: Princeton University Press.
Polanyi, K. (1957 [1944]) *The Great Transformation*. Boston, MA: Beacon Press.
Powell, W. and DiMaggio, P. (eds) (1991) *The New Institutionalism in Organizational Analysis*. Chicago, IL: University of Chicago Press.
Preda, A. (2006) Socio-technical agency in financial markets. The case of the stock ticker. *Social Studies of Science* 36(5): 753–782.
Preda, A. (2007) Where do analysts come from? The case of financial chartism. In M. Callon, F. Muniesa and Y. Millo (eds), *Testing Markets*. Oxford: Blackwell, forthcoming.
Shleifer, A. (2000) *Inefficient Markets: An Introduction to Behavioral Finance*. Oxford: Oxford University Press.
Smith, C.W. (1989) *Auctions. The Social Construction of Value*. New York: Free Press.
Smith, C.W. (1999) *Success and Survival on Wall Street. Understanding the Mind of the Market*. Lanham, MD: Rowman & Littlefield.
Stark, D. (2000) For a sociology of worth. *Working Paper Series*, Centre on Organizational Innovation, Columbia University. Available online at http://www.coi.columbia.edu/pdf/stark_fsw.pdf, downloaded 30 April 2007.
Stigler, G. (1961) The economics of information. *Journal of Political Economy* 69(3): 213–225.
Uzzi, B. and Lancaster, R. (2004) Embeddedness and price formation in the corporate law market. *American Sociological Review* 69(3): 319–344.
Velthuis, O. (2005) *Talking Prices. Symbolic Meanings of Prices on the Market for Contemporary Art*. Princeton, NJ, and Oxford: Princeton University Press.
Vollmer, H. (2003) Bookkeeping, accounting, calculative practice: the sociological suspense of calculation. *Critical Perspectives on Accounting* 3: 353–381.
Weber, M. (1924 [1894]) Die Börse. In *Gesammelte Aufsätze zur Soziologie und Sozialpolitik* (pp. 256–322). Tübingen: J.C.B. Mohr (Paul Siebeck).

Weber, M. (1978 [1921]) *Economy and Society. An Outline of Interpretive Sociology.* Berkeley, CA: University of California Press.

Weber, M. (2000 [1894]) Stock and commodity exchanges [Die Börse]. *Theory and Society* 29: 305–338.

White, H. (1981) Where do markets come from? *American Journal of Sociology* 87(3): 517–547.

White, H. (2002) *Markets from Networks. Socioeconomic Models of Production.* Princeton, NJ: Princeton University Press.

Woelfel, C. (1994) *Encyclopedia of Banking and Finance.* Chicago, IL: Irwin.

Zaloom, C. (2003) Ambiguous numbers: trading technologies and interpretation in financial markets. *American Ethnologist* 30(2): 258–272.

Zorn, D. (2004) Here a chief, there a chief. The rise of the CFO in the American firm. *American Sociological Review* 69(3): 345–364.

Zorn, D., Dobbin, F., Dierkes, J. and Kwok, M.-S. (2005) Managing investors. How financial markets reshaped the American firm. In K. Knorr Cetina and A. Preda (eds), *The Sociology of Financial Markets* (pp. 269–289). Oxford: Oxford University Press.

Zuckerman, E. (1999) The categorical imperative: securities analysts and the illegitimacy discount. *American Journal of Sociology* 104(5): 1398–1438.

Zuckerman, E. (2004) Structural incoherence and stock market activity. *American Sociological Review* 69: 405–432.

6

WORKERS' SAVINGS AND THE RIGHT TO MANAGE

Donald A.R. George

Edinburgh School of Economics, University of Edinburgh

1. Introduction

The collapse of communism in Eastern Europe and the former Soviet Union appears to solve the central issue of political economy. Surely it proves that capitalism really is the only viable economic system and that socialist alternatives, with their bureaucratic, over-centralised, economies can never be efficient. The political concomitant of capitalism is, of course, democracy, so we should expect to see a transition towards democracy, parallel with the transition to capitalism. It may arrive quickly (as in Hungary), it may be delayed (as in China) or adopt some kind of transitional form (as in Russia), but democracy must surely arrive eventually. The political Right has apparently won the argument, leaving the Left with a huge problem: are they to be reduced to arguing for progressive taxation, better health and safety legislation, and similar matters? Is the argument now about how best to manage capitalism rather than how it can be radically transformed? Such an argument would be largely technical, and could safely be left to neutral technical experts such as mainstream economists. At last the value-free scientific approach of economic theory could be extended to economic policy.

On closer examination the argument is more complex than this. Arguments for capitalism (and against socialism) usually turn out to be arguments for the market (and against central planning). Adam Smith argued for the market partly as a democratising force which would weaken the landed aristocracy in favour of the emerging merchant class. By analogy the transition from communism to the market will surely democratise the formerly one-party states of the communist world, weakening the *nomenklatura* in favour of the people as a whole. Arguments about markets and planning explain well why the informational and incentive properties of central planning are likely to lead to fatal inefficiencies and eventual collapse. But capitalism is not primarily a market system and, conversely, a market economy need not be capitalist. Perhaps worryingly, the most ardent enthusiasts for central planning are the multinational capitalist corporations,[1] and anyone who has had to deal with the customer services department of a privatised utility will confirm that private sector bureaucracies can be just as bad as (or even worse than) public sector ones. First and foremost capitalism is a system of private ownership and control. Capitalists themselves do not particularly like markets and try to abolish them wherever possible: markets mean competition and most capitalists are well aware of the advantages of monopoly. And they do not especially favour democracy either. German capitalists were delighted to cooperate with Hitler, having no difficulty with his abolition of German democracy or with the introduction of central planning.[2] While the apologists for capitalism (if not the capitalists themselves) may well advocate political democracy, they usually baulk at industrial democracy. The government is elected, can be criticised freely and is answerable to those it seeks to govern. By contrast, managers are not, in general, elected nor answerable to those they seek to manage, and the mildest criticism can be dangerous (even in institutions such as universities which pay lip service to free speech[3]). Most Western capitalist institutions are islands of fascism in a sea of democracy.

The key feature of capitalist private ownership is that ownership of capital confers the right to manage capital or to appoint agents to manage it on the owners' behalf. This right to manage includes the right to

- decide what and how much to produce
- decide on how the product is priced
- decide what techniques of production to adopt
- decide what research and development to carry out
- decide on making new investments and scrapping existing ones
- allocate workers to tasks
- allocate internal rewards such as promotion
- hire and fire workers.

On this basis the economies of the former Soviet Union and Eastern Europe should be regarded as state capitalism rather than socialism. They were not economies without property but rather economies with state property. The state owned capital and appointed agents to manage it: there was as little democracy within the Soviet firm as there is within the capitalist firms of the West. The question then arises 'can the link between ownership and control be broken while retaining (or even strengthening) the market as the primary mechanism of resource allocation?' This paper answers this question in the affirmative. In so doing it also advocates the strengthening of democracy by introducing it from the sphere of politics, into the firm, to create a *self-managed firm*, that is, one where

- the right to manage rests with workers not owners
- management is democratic not hierarchical
- workers' rewards are linked to the firm's performance in some way (perhaps by a share of profits, revenue or income per worker), and not by a fixed wage.

This definition of self-management is not without difficulties. For example the 'right to manage', as conventionally conceived, includes the right to hire and fire, and to award internal promotions. How workers could democratically exercise these rights is not immediately obvious. This point is returned to in Section 3.2 below.

2. Savings, Investment and Pensions

Capitalism has engulfed Russia and Eastern Europe, and it will soon spread to the rest of the former Soviet empire and to China. It is doubtful if even Cuba and North Korea will avoid its embrace. This process of economic transition has run in parallel with, and has contributed to, a new wave of globalisation, with international trade and capital movements expanding much more rapidly than world GDP in the post World War II period. International labour mobility has also increased since World War II but still remains at a lower level than it was in 1914 (see Crafts (2000) for evidence on this). Any economic system must produce a surplus for investment: a growing population must be equipped with a stock of capital appropriate for efficient production, capital goods wear out physically and must be replaced, and technical progress must be embodied in new capital goods. Socialist planning had a tendency to over-accumulate capital and under-invest in technical progress, except when it directly benefited the State, as with military hardware (see, for example, Gregory and Stuart, 1990). Investment under capitalism is a more subtle process. All capital goods are of course produced by workers, but they do not generally own or control capital and have little influence over the accumulation process. As discussed above the defining features of capitalism do not concern its use of the market mechanism; instead they are

- private ownership of capital
- the right to manage stems from ownership and nowhere else.

To reproduce itself successfully, a capitalist economy must devote enough productive capacity to investment without allowing workers any meaningful ownership or control of capital. Thus investment must be sharply separated from workers' savings. Under modern capitalism this is achieved by ensuring that most investment is undertaken from retained profits[4] and that workers' savings are managed by institutions such as banks and pension funds. This not only reduces the rate of return on workers' savings but also ensures that these savings confer no power over the processes of accumulation or production. The resulting mechanism of accumulation in the mature capitalist economies has operated with extreme inefficiency during the post-war period, and even prior to that. Keynes (1936) comments: 'When the capital development of a country becomes a by-product of the activities of a casino, the job is likely to be ill-done'. Drucker (1976) developed this idea and suggested that pension funds might hold the key to solving these problems. Perhaps tongue in cheek, he referred to 'pension fund socialism' and implied that the United States, with its extensive system of pension funds, was 'the first truly socialist country in the world'.

But in the mature capitalist economies of the West populations are ageing. Birth rates have fallen below replacement rates (e.g. see Blackburn, 2003) and increasing affluence together with medical progress have increased life expectancies (to approximately 80 years in Western Europe). This has created a sense of alarm and crisis.[5] Pension funds seem incapable of meeting their obligations as dependency ratios rise. To provide incomes for the retired, workers either will have to dramatically increase their private or occupational savings, or will have to pay radically increased taxes. In the UK final salary occupational pension funds are closing to new members, or even being wound-up and replaced with money purchase pensions, which reduce costs to employers and shift risk to individual pensioners (see, for example, Blackburn, 2003). Bankrupt firms are seemingly entitled to renege on their pension commitments and shedding the 'legacy costs' of these commitments is often an important aspect of takeovers. The alternative to increased savings (voluntary or forced) is to give up the standard retirement age (usually 65) and continue working into older age.

In fact this so-called crisis is nothing like as bad as it has been made to appear. In the UK, for example, there are approximately 2 million people between the ages of 50 and 65 who are out of work. Of these, 250,000 are actively seeking work and a further 750,000 are 'discouraged workers' who would like to work. A recent survey (HSBC, 2005) across 10 countries shows that the vast majority of currently employed workers would like to continue working (possibly part-time) beyond their contracted retirement age. The problem for these people is as much ageism as pensions provision. A detailed analysis of ageism in the workplace is beyond the scope of this paper, but is at least partially understandable as a management failure. Managing the capitalist labour process is a fairly crude business, involving a mixture of threat and reward. The worker has no direct interest in the performance of his employer's firm (up to the point of its bankruptcy) and, on a fixed wage, has an incentive to shirk as much as possible. So the employer must monitor the labour process, reward the hard workers and sack the idle, all of which is costly. Capitalist firms devote considerable resources to line management, supervisors, foremen, 'human resource' departments and elaborate internal labour markets. The techniques which work to motivate young workers are less effective for older ones. They have a shorter time horizon and are unlikely to be particularly concerned about promotion. With some savings and low mortgages, the threat of dismissal is less serious than it would be to a younger worker with more commitments. So employers need to develop new management techniques which work effectively with older workers: thus far they have (with some honourable exceptions) completely failed to do this.

Most capitalist economies have responded to the pensions 'crisis' not by strengthening State provision, nor by preventing employers from reneging on their commitments, nor by tackling ageism in the workplace. Instead they have turned to the market for financial services, now as globalised as most other markets. The trend is towards privatised pensions: individuals must make their own arrangements for their retirement savings via the global market for financial services. The argument is the standard argument for markets: individuals surely know their own (inter-temporal) preferences better than any State planner or bureaucrat. The well-known tendency for mainstream economists to ignore inconvenient empirical evidence is discussed in George, 'Consolations for the Economist' (this volume), and true to form, the case for privatised pensions remains undented by the British pensions mis-selling episode (see, for example, Blackburn, 2003). Moreover there is evidence from Australia (see Pierson, 1998) that people want to be forced by the State to save for their retirement. How this finding can be incorporated into mainstream economic theory remains to be seen.

3. Self-management

3.1 Self-management and the 'Pangloss Theorem'

As discussed in Section 1, most capitalist institutions (especially firms) are islands of fascism in a sea of democracy. Their internal structure is based on threat and bribery. Most capitalist workplaces are hardly shining examples of personal freedom where each individual can develop their abilities and potential, for the common good. The call-centre workers who have to ask permission to go to the lavatory, the bullying (and often incompetent) boss, the persecuted whistle-blower are all the stuff of legend. There are countless psychological studies demonstrating how the workplace can make workers mentally ill. Even more remarkable is the extensive research (see Blumberg, 1968) which shows that labour productivity dramatically increases with job satisfaction. Surely that alone would induce employers to improve the quality of working life and treat workers with some respect. But that line of argument ignores the nature of the capitalist labour process. 'Industrial democracy' has gained some ground in the capitalist economies, but primarily in the middle-class professions. Law firms, accountancy firms and medical practices are often partnerships, but extending any measure of worker influence (never mind control) into large scale industry would threaten the capitalist right to manage. If workers discovered that they are quite capable of managing the firm without help from the bosses, where would it all end? (See Marglin (1975) for a discussion.)

Firms which approximate to self-management are workers' cooperatives under Western capitalism or the firms of the former Yugoslavia. And this provides a standard empirical argument against self-management: the economic performance of the former Yugoslavia was hardly spectacular (see Sirc, 1979) and the country finally disintegrated in a vicious civil war. In fact the evidence shows that the Yugoslav economy could only be described as (approximately) self-managed over the period 1965–1974 and that economic performance was relatively good from 1965 until 1979. Most of Yugoslavia's economic problems post-1979 can be traced back to the country's undemocratic one-party state and its petty nationalism rather than its self-managed firms (see George (1993) for further discussion).

The opponents of self-management have a more powerful, seemingly knock down, argument, namely the notorious 'Pangloss theorem'. This asserts 'what is, is optimal' and has the important corollary 'no reform is necessary or desirable'. The theorem and its corollary apply to any economic institution including self-management. In this context the theorem simply states that there is no need to 'promote' self-management, because it would emerge naturally in a 'free' economy if it genuinely offered benefits to workers superior to those available elsewhere. After all, in such an economy, there is nothing to stop workers from forming a cooperative if they wished, so the fact that they rarely do so simply reveals a preference for orthodox forms of economic organisation. There are two broad approaches to justifying the Pangloss theorem. First, economic institutions can be treated as the outcome of maximising behaviour in much the same way as prices and quantities. Second, appeal may be made to an evolutionary argument, according to which existing institutions are the outcome of 'natural (economic) selection'. Economists have developed some ingenious explanations for the paucity of self-managed firms under capitalism[6] (see, for example, Dow, 1993; Kahana and Nitzan, 1993), but ultimately none of them circumvent the Pangloss theorem.

The first approach to the Pangloss result is decisively rejected by at least one mainstream economist (Weitzman, 1983).

> I do not subscribe to the (tautological) philosophy that every existing economic convention, institution or contract must have a *raison d'être* in terms of economic theory. To explain everything this way is to turn [mainstream] economic theory into a game which explains nothing. When it comes to system wide socio-economic conventions, good economic theory can sometimes be used to provide legitimate historical explanations, but the pure inertia of social tradition is a strong independent force which discourages tampering [with economic institutions]. (Weitzman, 1983; remarks in square brackets added)

The 'pure inertia of social tradition' may often be best thought of in political terms. Very few economic reforms are Pareto improvements; they inevitably make some groups worse off and others better off. Even those reforms which are Pareto improvements can rarely be achieved in a sequence of Pareto-improving steps. The groups which anticipate being made worse off have a strong incentive to mobilise politically to block the relevant reforming step. This is a major problem for the economic reformers of Russia and Eastern Europe. (See Dewatripont and Roland (1997) for the distinction between 'optimal' and 'politically feasible' transition strategies.) There are powerful interest groups such as professional managers and trade unions which might well feel threatened by the emergence of a substantial self-managed sector under capitalism and which have the political and economic means to frustrate it (see George (1997) for a discussion). There is a further difficulty for the Pangloss approach to institutions. Along with most mainstream economics it is based on the assumption that preferences are exogenous to the economic system: they can therefore be revealed by observing choice, and are invariant with respect to evolutionary change. This view treats the Pangloss result as a form of that ultra-conservative doctrine, beloved of mainstream economists, the principle of 'revealed preference'. Mainstream economists have 'proved mathematically' that, under certain mild assumptions, preferences can be deduced by observing choice. In fact it is more credible to assume endogenous preferences. A study by Greenburg (1984), for example, shows how the value placed by American workers on participation increased dramatically after they had worked for some time in a cooperative.[7] The political feasibility and endogenous preference arguments apply with as much force to the evolutionary interpretation of Pangloss as to the revealed preference version. But in any event, much 'evolutionary economics' is based on a false application of a biological principle to economics (see Hodgson (1996) for a detailed discussion).

Although the Pangloss theorem accords well with mainstream economic theory, it fails once non-mainstream considerations such as political feasibility and endogenous preferences are taken into account. Nonetheless the mainstream analysis of self-management does help to explain the paucity of self-managed firms under capitalism, and helps to suggest a policy response. We now review that mainstream analysis and consider its implications.

3.2 The Ward–Vanek–Meade Model

The textbook model of self-management can be traced back to Ward's (1958) seminal paper on the firm in Illyria. The model proposed by Ward was developed by Vanek (1970) and Meade (1972). The form of the model conforms to economic orthodoxy: firms are treated as objective functions plus production functions and their behaviour is 'modelled' as constrained maximisation. The main unusual feature of the model at this stage is that the self-managed firm is assumed to maximise income per worker instead of profits. The idea is that workers receive a share of the firm's income net of non-labour costs, including capital rental charges. Behind the model lies the assumption that the conventional bundling of capitalist property rights can be 'unbundled', so that the owners of capital receive a 'normal' return on it but have no right to manage (they are called 'basic owners'). Vanek (1977a) draws the important distinction between 'users' ownership' and 'basic ownership' of capital. The former entails the right to manage and to appropriate net income (i.e. excluding rent). The latter entails the right receive rent reflecting the scarcity of capital in the economy. Under self-management, users' ownership must rest with the workers in the firm, while basic owners could be anyone, including the State, private banks or even the workers themselves. In the latter case the status of workers as users of capital must be clearly differentiated from their status as basic owners. The essential features of users' ownership and basic ownership are summarised in Table 1.

Initially then, assume that the firm rents capital from basic owners at a given rental rate (r) (or equivalently that it is fully externally financed). Risk, for the moment, is ignored. There can be no labour market in a self-managed economy and therefore no wage rate (this point is returned to below). Suppose the firm has a production function (f) relating its output (Q) to labour (L) and capital (K):

$$Q = f(L, K) \qquad (1)$$

Much of the mainstream analysis involves comparing the behaviour of a self-managed firm with that of a capitalist (profit-maximising) firm facing the same prices and with the same technology (known as its 'capitalist twin'). In true mainstream fashion, this analysis is often presented as pure theory, but it is best treated as a source of testable predictions about the comparative behaviour of capitalist and self-managed firms. For simplicity assume that all workers supply the same amount of labour, so that the number of workers can be identified

Table 1. Users' Ownership and Basic Ownership (Adapted from Vanek, 1977a)

	Owners	Rights	Obligations	Transferability and taxability
Users' ownership	Members of firm*	Democratic management* Inalienable right* Appropriation of net income (excluding rent)*	Capital maintenance rule Pay scarcity-reflecting rent*	Taxable Transferable without charge to another firm
Basic ownership	Anyone, e.g. State, banks, individual members	Receive scarcity rent* Receive depreciation charges Inalienable right*	Refinance fully depreciated assets	Taxable Can be sold to another basic owner without agreement of users

*Essential features of self-management.

with the amount of labour used by the firm. It may therefore be treated as maximising

$$R = \frac{pf(L, K) - rK}{L} \tag{2}$$

Maximising (2) subject to (1) allows some potentially interesting conclusions to be drawn. Treating labour as variable in the short run and both factors variable in the long run we can deduce the following.

- Both factors receive their marginal value products, in the short run for labour and the long run for capital.
- In the short run the self-managed firm will adopt a higher capital/labour ratio than its capitalist twin, making positive supernormal profits.
- In a self-managed economy inter-firm differences in labour income will not be competed away in the short run as they would in a capitalist economy with a competitive labour market.
- In the long run, with capital-renting or full external finance, the self-managed firm and its capitalist twin will be in an identical equilibrium, which is Pareto-efficient and technically efficient. For the capitalist economy this requires a free-entry condition, while for the self-managed economy it does not.

This analysis presupposes that the labour input is freely variable upwards and downwards in the short run. This may be plausible for variations which can be brought about by changes in hours worked, with the firm's 'membership' fixed. But a reduction in the labour input which required a reduction in membership might be particularly difficult for a self-managed firm: would such a firm be likely to sack some of its members for purely economic reasons? Ward (1967) argued that a membership reduction of less than 50% could be brought about by majority voting without specifying rules (such as 'last in first out') to determine who gets the sack. It has been suggested, however (see Steinherr and Thisse, 1979[8]), that such membership reductions would require, prior to the vote, the identification of those members liable for dismissal. Steinherr and Thisse argue further that there are only two types of membership reduction which are 'fair' to all members. The first is full compensation, so that any member is indifferent between leaving and staying. The second is random selection of those to be dismissed, with each member assigned an equal probability of dismissal.

3.3 General Equilibrium of the Self-managed Economy

Dreze (1989) has applied general equilibrium analysis to the self-managed economy, adopting the Ward–Vanek–Meade assumption that self-managed firms maximise income per worker. Following the orthodox approach, he established the existence of general equilibrium for such economies, along with the two central theorems of neoclassical welfare economics. These two theorems show that every general equilibrium is Pareto-efficient and every Pareto-optimum can be decentralised as an equilibrium. An obvious problem arises for the self-managed economy in that no labour markets exist in such an economy. This accounts for the problem, mentioned above, that inter-firm differences in labour income would not, in the short run, be competed away under self-management. The general equilibrium approach, in effect, substitutes the free formation and closure of firms for a competitive labour market. The Dreze analysis follows the conventional general equilibrium route, slightly modified to reflect self-management. These modifications amount to assuming that self-managed firms use only rented capital and, in equilibrium, such firms are formed efficiently. In particular the definition of 'general equilibrium' now includes the following clauses:

- There is no discrimination between members of any given firm. That is, within each firm members supplying the same quantity and quality of labour are paid the same income.
- No group of individuals can form a firm paying at least as much income to everyone and more to at least one of them.
- Rentier institutions receive savings and buy capital goods which they rent to firms. The rental rate is equal to the interest rate plus the depreciation rate so that the rentier institutions make zero profit.

With these modifications to the standard definition of 'general equilibrium' it is relatively easy to establish the existence of such an equilibrium, which is identical to that of a capitalist (profit-maximising) economy with the same utility functions, technology and initial endowments (and which, therefore, is Pareto-efficient). *Without* the capital-renting assumption above, general equilibrium under self-management is *not*, in general, Pareto-efficient.

3.4 *Financing the Self-managed Firm*

The capital-renting assumption made above is clearly unrealistic and the analysis of finance for the self-managed firm must clearly go beyond the simplifying assumption of full external finance. This topic has generated a great deal of controversy (see, for example, Bonin and Putterman, 1987). The three critical issues, for the purpose of this paper, are

- the Furubotn–Pejovich effect
- the Vanek effect
- the risk-sharing effect

Furubotn and Pejovich have repeatedly argued that self-management is fatally flawed by its failure to allocate property rights appropriately. This approach forms the nucleus of what has come to be known as the 'Texas school'. In particular Furubotn and Pejovich (1970) have argued that the collective nature of property rights in a self-managed firm's capital will induce it to under-invest. In taking investment decisions in a self-managed firm, members will be influenced by the fact that they may leave the firm during the economic lifetime of newly acquired capital. Since this capital is collectively owned, such members would not be able to recoup 'their part' of the principal and would forgo some of the return. Self-managed firms cannot issue shares to outside shareholders because they would transfer some of the right to manage to these shareholders, and the firm would cease to be self-managed. Moreover there is generally no market in membership rights. Under these circumstances the internal rate of return required for the investment to take place would be biased upwards and the level of investment correspondingly biased downwards.

Vanek (1977a) put forward a different but related argument. He argued that, under internal financing, self-managed firms will not pay a scarcity-reflecting rent for the use of capital, thus changing its maximand. He shows that this will lead to the firm operating at an inefficiently low scale. Figure 1 depicts equilibrium outcomes for external and internal financing, assuming both Furubotn–Pejovich and Vanek effects at work. They lead the self-managed firm to operate (in the long run) at too low a capital labour/labour ratio and too low a scale. This is Pareto-inefficient and would cause the self-managed firm to lose a competition with its capitalist twin.

Both Vanek and Furubotn–Pejovich effects would disappear under full external financing, but the standard capitalist method of doing this is not available to the self-managed firm. Of course such a firm could issue bonds, but this approach has limits. First, bond financing imposes all the risks of an investment project on the firm and none on the lender. Workers would then have to bear capital risks in addition to risks associated with employment, a situation often unfavourably compared with the allegedly efficient allocation of risk under capitalism. However, these comparisons ignore the fact that, apart from the unlikely case of full employment, workers under capitalism will be concerned about the risk of unemployment[9] as well as about risks associated with income variations. In addition to this, there remains the problem of 'increasing risk'. Even though bonds carry a fixed and certain rate of interest, there

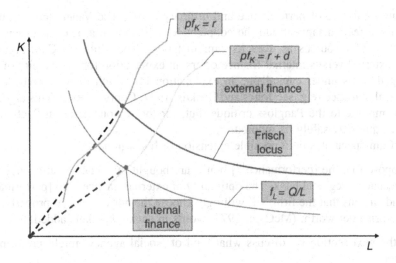

Figure 1. Internal versus External Finance for the Self-Managed Firm.

remains the possibility of default, and the probability of the lender suffering a loss increases as the proportion of equity capital in the financial structure decreases. The lender therefore demands a higher rate of return and the cost of bond-financed capital rises at the margin. In addition, a fixed commitment to interest and principal repayments gears the risk to residual claimants, who in a self-managed firm are its members, thus reducing their willingness to undertake further borrowing. This collection of problems will be referred to as the 'risk-sharing' effect.

The capitalist firm has an obvious route out of these difficulties, namely the issuing of shares. As mentioned above, this option is not open to the self-managed firm, because shareholders would require some measure of control over the firm which would therefore cease to be self-managed. Self-management requires external financing to be efficient, but in a capitalist financial environment the means are not generally available to achieve this. There are some exceptions, however. The Mondragon system of cooperatives, for example, is partially financed via a specialised bank, the Caja Laboral Popular (see Thomas and Logan, 1982), while Danish cooperatives are, to some extent, financed externally, via trade union and labour movement institutions (see George, 1982).

Vanek (1977b) and McCain (1977) have suggested that successful self-management requires the introduction of a new kind of financial asset into the economy, namely a 'performance bond'. Such a bond is simply a title to a dividend, the amount of which varies with the firm's 'performance'. In Vanek's version the dividend is a fixed proportion of value added, while in McCain's it is a fixed proportion of workers' income. Performance bonds would carry no voting rights or other power to influence the firm's management. McCain shows that, under uncertainty, when the option of performance bond financing is available to the cooperative, it will choose not to finance itself from retained earnings but rather to issue a mixture of performance and ordinary bonds. The Vanek and Furubotn–Pejovich effects disappear and the cooperative will achieve at least as efficient an allocation of resources as does its capitalist twin. The Vanek/McCain argument about external versus internal finance offers an explanation for the paucity of self-managed firms under capitalism, an explanation for which there is considerable empirical evidence (e.g. see Jones and Backus, 1977; George, 1982). This argument is not immune to the Pangloss critique, but, for the reasons given in Section 3.1, that critique may safely be ignored.

McCain speculates on a possible extension of his argument:

> Suppose that the [performance[10]] bonds are bought by some social agency such as a state or regional bank. The optimality of external finance with [performance] bonds means that the firm will willingly choose the norm of social property, zero enterprise net worth. (McCain, 1977; words in square brackets added)

In the next section we discuss what kind of 'social agency' might perform this function.

4. Wage-earners' Investment Funds

4.1 Workers' Capital Accumulation

The important role of pension funds for the capitalist accumulation process was discussed in Section 2. This section will argue that some kind of enhanced pension fund would be an appropriate 'social agency' to hold the Vanek/McCain performance bonds. During the World War II, Keynes (1940) proposed a system of state-administered savings out of wages. The purpose of his proposed system was to reduce private consumption to allow for war-time production requirements in as equitable a way as possible (see Maital (1972) for a discussion). Keynes saw implications of his proposal well beyond the needs of the British war-economy. He suggested that:

> the accumulation of working class wealth under working class control [could induce] an advance towards economic equality greater than any we have made in recent times. (Keynes, 1940; words in square brackets added)

During the post-war period proposals for wage-earners' investment funds, similar to those proposed by Keynes, have been widely discussed in Europe, for example in Germany, the Netherlands, Denmark, Sweden, the UK and Italy. The only such funds actually implemented were set up in Sweden in 1984 and wound up in 1991.

A wage-earners' fund would receive contributions from a tax levied for example on wages or profits and would accumulate capital, mostly in the form of shares, on behalf of wage-earners. The fund might operate as a savings vehicle for individuals, allowing the holding of individual saving certificates. Alternatively it might have an obligation to contribute to the state pension system, which in most capitalist countries is in need of bolstering for the reasons discussed in Section 2 above. Funds could be administered by the government, trade unions, independent managers, an elected management board or by various combinations of these. Wage-earner funds might be seen as, at least partially, restoring the link between investment and workers' savings, a link decisively broken under modern capitalism for the reasons discussed in Section 2 above. They represent an alternative to enterprise-level forms of financial participation such as profit-sharing and workers' share-ownership schemes. As originally conceived, wage-earner funds operate by transferring ownership to workers rather than by redefining the right to manage. This might be seen as running counter to the principles of self-management, but it will be argued in this paper that a wage-earner fund could hold performance bonds as well as shares. In so doing it could provide external finance for self-managed firms and, over time, help to promote the growth of a self-managed sector under capitalism.

4.2 European Policy Proposals

During the 1950s the German trade union economist Bruno Gleitze proposed a wage-earner investment fund for Germany, to be financed from a profits tax and administered by the unions (Gleitze, 1968). This proposal was developed by the German Social Democrats and trade unions. In 1974 a proposal was advanced which would institute a system of funds, none of which would be confined to a particular sector or region, and among which individuals would be free to choose. There was union opposition to the proposal (particularly from the metalworkers' union IG Metall) and no legislation materialised. The idea of wage-earner funds was supplanted by a system of enterprise-level codetermination (Mitbestimmung). Capital ownership was not seen as a prerequisite for the unions' real objective, namely a substantial degree of managerial participation within conventional firms.

In Denmark as well as Germany, the debate on wage-earner funds was bound up with issues of managerial participation within firms. In contrast to Germany, a degree of collective worker ownership of capital was seen as complimentary to other measures designed to establish industrial democracy. In 1973 a Bill on wage-earner funds was presented to the Danish parliament in tandem with a Bill on codetermination. The codetermination Bill passed into law while the funds Bill was rejected. The Danish proposal was for a fund financed from a wage tax, which would increase in steps for 10 years to a maximum of 5%. The proposed fund would operate a degree of private redemption of savings by issuing non-negotiable certificates to individuals, who would be allowed to redeem them after a minimum seven year period (though the unions wanted a five year redemption period). Two-thirds of each contribution was to be made in the form of equity (which the fund would be obliged to retain), with the remainder in cash (available for investment in the Danish economy). The fund would not be permitted to hold more than 50% of the equity in any single firm. The fund's management council would consist of 36 members appointed by unions and 24 appointed by the Minister of Labour.

Sweden is the only country to have actually implemented a system of wage-earner funds. The Swedish funds were a development of the 'Meidner plan' (Meidner,

1978) advanced in 1975. Under this plan, funds would receive contributions purely as scrip issue and would act in a purely redistributive role, rather than pursuing an active stock market policy. Five funds were set up in 1984 and wound up in 1991 in the face of political pressure. The funds were organised along nominally regional lines and received contributions from a 20% profits tax and a 0.2% payroll tax in each of the years 1984–1990. Redemption arrangements were purely collective, with each fund obliged to pay a 3% real return to the state pension system. By 1990 the funds together owned approximately 5% of the Swedish stock market, making each fund equal in size to many private institutional shareholders. No fund was entitled to hold more than 8% of the voting rights in any one firm and they were obliged to transfer half their voting rights to local unions upon request. The management board of each fund was appointed by the government and consisted of nine members, at least five of whom were to 'represent the interests of employees' (most of these were trade unionists).

One objective of the Swedish funds was to strengthen the policy of wage solidarity. The Swedish economy is highly unionised and wage bargaining takes place in a highly centralised manner between a small number of agents, typically the union organisation LO and the employers' organisation SAF. This bargaining process tends to equalise wages in a given occupation across the economy regardless of firm profitability. Of course there is a degree of wage-drift at firm level, but nonetheless unions are faced with a dilemma. If they exert wage restraint they will help to achieve policy objectives such as limiting inflation and protecting profitability, but the fruits of that restraint will accrue to employers in the form of enhanced profits. The funds would admit the possibility of taxing profits and using the proceeds to finance capital accumulation under workers' control, thus providing a quid pro quo for wage restraint.

A second objective was to increase worker influence both within firms and over the process of capital accumulation. The transfer of voting rights to local union organisations is an obvious way to achieve the former effect but clearly there is no reason why a wage-earner fund should not hold bonds and performance bonds as well as shares. Thus it could play the role of McCain's 'social agency', discussed in Section 3.4, and direct resources towards self-managed firms. We return to this possibility below. A third objective was to strengthen the state pension system. In contrast to the private pension arrangements discussed in Section 2, wage-earner funds would strengthen rather than weaken the link between investment and workers' savings.

Wage-earner funds provoked a vigorous and colourful debate in a country known for its consensual (and usually rather dull) politics. Employers and the political Right opposed the funds vigorously. Lars Nabseth, director-general of SAF (Swedish employers' federation) said during the 1982 election campaign:

The most acute problem facing Swedish industry is the threat of collective wage-earner funds. They would completely revolutionise our economic system and severely worsen the conditions on which industry functions in Sweden.

A leading Swedish mainstream economist resigned from the political party promoting the funds (the Social Democrats) saying:

I left the party in protest. [Wage-earner funds] will mean the collectivisation of society. Palme [Social Democrat Prime Minister] has been pushed into this by the unions. (Remarks in square brackets added)

Opposition to the funds took a number of different forms. It was suggested that the funds would lead to a command economy of East European type (still largely unreformed in 1982) and ultimately to some sort of totalitarianism. Failing this frightening possibility there was still the danger that the funds could become major agents in the capital market, possibly gaining a controlling stake in several firms, including some large and important ones. A dangerous increase in the power of trade unions was predicted and possibly a catastrophic stock market collapse. There was less strident opposition, along German and Danish lines, putting forward firm-level profit-sharing, share-ownership and worker participation schemes. Since the funds together only owned a maximum of 5% of the Swedish stock market, the wilder threats to the Swedish economy never materialised, and in fact there was a mild stock market boom following their introduction.

4.3 Wage-earner Funds: Summary of Policy Issues

From the European policy debate on wage-earner funds, six key policy issues emerge.

- *Structure of fund contributions.* Should the base of the contributions tax be the wage bill, the profits bill, or a combination of the two? If profits were adopted as the tax base the question of definition arises. Should profits be defined to exclude a 'normal' return to capital? If so the role of supernormal profits in influencing the allocation of capital would presumably be attenuated. The burden of the contributions tax may of course be shifted. (George (1987) analyses a case in which the burden of a contributions tax levied on wages is shifted, in the short run, to profits.) It is also necessary to decide on the proportion of contributions made in cash as opposed to scrip issue.
- *Redemption arrangements.* Should these be individual (as in the Danish proposal) or collective (as in the Swedish case)? If individuals were allowed to hold stakes in the fund would a minimum holding period be imposed before they could be redeemed? Perhaps redemption of savings would be allowed only at retirement as with a pension fund. Under a purely collective arrangement, wage-earner funds could be explicitly linked to the state pension system, for example by requiring them to pay a return to a state pension fund.
- *Stock market policy of the fund.* Fund managers could be placed under an obligation to seek the maximum rate of return, or to invest only domestically, or to pursue objectives such as employment, regional or environmental policy. They could be restricted in the voting rights they may hold in any particular firm.

- *Scope and coverage of the fund.* Which wage-earners would be covered and which sectors of the economy? For example, would public sector workers be covered and, if so, would the public sector make fund contributions?
- *Regional/branch funds.* Should there be a single central fund or a system of funds? In the latter case should the funds compete with each other or should each be confined to a particular geographical region or branch of the economy? Should individuals have a choice as to which fund should hold their savings?
- *Worker participation.* How would workers exercise control over the process of capital accumulation and how should the fund promote worker influence within firms?

5. Conclusions

The possibility emerges of a radical approach to the reform of capitalism which

- introduces democracy from the political to the economic sphere, giving workers power over their working lives and improving the quality of working life;
- increases productivity by economising on monitoring costs and reducing the disutility of work;
- unbundles capitalist property rights, assigning 'users' ownership' to workers and 'basic ownership' to a potentially wide range of agents, including wage-earners' investment funds – this re-assignment of property rights would create a system of ownership different from 'private' and 'public' ownership, as at present understood;
- retains or even strengthens the role of markets;
- strengthens the pensions system, thus helping to deal with the so-called 'pensions crisis';
- allows workers some degree of influence over capital accumulation and other policy objectives such as regional or environmental policy.

A wage-earner investment fund (or system of funds) would recycle workers' savings without breaking the link between those savings and the investment to which they give rise. By holding bonds and performance bonds as well as shares, the fund could provide external finance for a self-managed sector and thus overcome the Vanek, Furubotn–Pejovich and risk-sharing effects which can prove fatal to self-management.

George (1993) conducts a simulation exercise to gauge the likely size of a self-managed sector promoted in this way. Table 2 shows the output of a simulation run, showing the proportion (x) of the total capital stock allocated to the self-managed sector after 20 years. The fund simulated here is assumed to receive contributions from a wage tax at rate t, and invest half its available income in the self-managed sector and half in the private sector. Results are shown for different values of t and s (the savings propensity of the fund). Table 2 reveals relatively low values of x, ranging from 4.1% to 27.4%.

Table 2. Simulated Values of x after 20 Years (George, 1993).

t	s		
	0.2	0.5	0.8
0.05	0.041	0.072	0.108
0.10	0.057	0.113	0.172
0.20	0.088	0.186	0.274

The proposals of this paper would threaten the interests of private capital owners and so, like most economic reforms, would not be Pareto-improving. They would require decisive political action, and can thus be sharply differentiated from voluntary, enterprise-level schemes for introducing profit-sharing, employee share-ownership or industrial democracy.

Notes

1. The Communists copied central planning from the capitalist corporation in the first place. Lenin was a great admirer of Taylorism and wanted to turn the entire economy into a single, gigantic firm.
2. It is often said that the main difference between Stalin and Hitler was that the former operated five year plans while the latter preferred four year ones.
3. The antipathy of mainstream economists to pluralism and open discussion is discussed in 'Consolations for the Economist: the Future of Economic Orthodoxy', this issue.
4. Most stock market transactions facilitate capital re-structuring via mergers, de-mergers and takeovers rather than new investment.
5. Media alarmism on this topic is curiously contradictory. One day there will be a newspaper article or television report on how we are just not saving enough for our old age, the next day we learn that we are not *consuming* enough and a high street recession is looming.
6. There are more cooperatives in Western Europe and the United States than is commonly supposed including several thousand in Scandinavia, Italy and France. However, they account for a small proportion of GDP in those countries.
7. Given the large quantities of resources devoted by capitalist firms to advertising and marketing, even conventional preferences over bundles of goods would be better treated as endogenous. If preferences are endogenous the vast bulk of mainstream welfare economics collapses.
8. This paper discusses the notorious result, first advanced by Ward, that the self-managed firm may have a backward sloping supply curve.
9. The 'efficiency wage' analysis of unemployment (see Shapiro and Stiglitz, 1984) suggests that equilibrium wages under capitalism will not clear the labour market, because unemployment is necessary to discipline the workforce. This argument is based on the idea, discussed in Section 1, that the capitalist labour process involves high costs of monitoring and supervising the workforce. These costs are likely to be significantly lower under self-management.
10. McCain calls them 'participation bonds'.

References

Blackburn, R. (2002) *Banking on Death*. London: Verso.

Blumberg, P. (1968) *Industrial Democracy, the Sociology of Participation*. London: Constable.

Bonin, J.P. and Putterman, L. (1987) *Economics of Cooperation and the Labor-Managed Economy*. East Tyler, TX: Harwood.

Crafts, N. (2000) Globalization and growth in the twentieth century. *IMF Working Paper no. 00/44*.

Dewatripont, M. and Roland, G. (1997) Transition as a process of large scale institutional change. In D. Kreps and K. Wallis (eds), *Advances in Economic Theory*, Vol. 2. Cambridge: Cambridge University Press.

Dow, G.K. (1993) Why capital hires labor: a bargaining perspective. *American Economic Review* 83: 118–134.

Dreze, J.H. (1989) *Labour Management, Contracts and Capital Markets*. Oxford: Basil Blackwell.

Drucker, P. (1976) *The Unseen Revolution: How Pension Fund Socialism Came to America*. New York: Harper and Row.

Furubotn, E.G. and Pejovich, S. (1970) Property rights and the behaviour of the firm in a socialist state: the example of Yugoslavia. *Zeitschrift fur Nationalokonomie* 30: 431–454.

George, D.A.R. (1982) Workers' cooperatives in Denmark. *Managerial and Decision Economics* 3: 205–212.

George, D.A.R. (1987) Wage-earners' investment funds: theory, simulation and policy. *International Review of Applied Economics* 1: 109–123.

George, D.A.R. (1993) *Economic Democracy: The Political Economy of Self-Management and Participation*. London: Macmillan.

George, D.A.R. (1997) Self-management and ideology. *Review of Political Economy* 9: 51–62.

Gleitze, B. (1968) *Sozialcapital und sozialfonds als Mittel der Vermogenspolitik*. Cologne: Bunderverlag.

Greenburg, E.S. (1984) Producer cooperatives and democratic theory: the case of the plywood firms. In R. Jackall and H.M. Levin (eds), *Worker Cooperatives in America*. Berkeley, CA: University of California Press.

Gregory, P.R. and Stuart, R.C. (1990) *Soviet Economic Structure and Performance*. New York: Harper Collins.

Hodgson, G.M. (1996) Organisational form and economic evolution: a critique of the Williamsonian hypothesis. In U. Pagano and R. Rowthorn (eds), *Democracy and Efficiency in the Economic Enterprise*. London: Routledge.

HSBC (2005) *The Future of Retirement*. http://www.hsbc.com/public/groupsite/retirement_future/en/_overview_future_of_retirement.jhtml

Jones, D.C. and Backus, D.K. (1977) British producer cooperatives in the footwear industry. *Economic Journal* 87: 488–510.

Kahana, N. and Nitzan, S. (1993) The theory of the labour-managed firm revisited: the voluntary interactive approach. *Economic Journal* 103: 937–945.

Keynes, J.M. (1936) *The General Theory of Employment, Interest and Money*. London: Macmillan.

Keynes, J.M. (1940) *How to Pay for the War*. London: Macmillan.

Maital, S. (1972) Inflation, taxation and equity: how to pay for the war revisited. *Economic Journal* 82: 158–169.

Marglin, S. (1975) What do bosses do? The origins and functions of hierarchy in capitalist production. *Review of Radical Political Economy* 6: 60–112.

McCain, R. (1977) On the optimal financial environment for worker cooperatives. *Zeitschrift fur Nationalokonomie* 355–384.

Meade, J.E. (1972) The theory of labour-managed firms and of profit-sharing. *Economic Journal* 82: 402–428.

Meidner, R. (1978) *Employee Investment Funds: An Approach to Collective Capital Formation*. London: Allen and Unwin.

Pierson, C. (1998) Globalisation and the changing governance of welfare states: superannuation reform in Australia. *Global Society* 12: 31–48.

Shapiro, C. and Stiglitz, J.E. (1984) Equilibrium unemployment as a worker discipline device. *American Economic Review* 74: 433–444.

Sirc, L. (1979) *The Yugoslav Economy under Self-Management*. London: Macmillan.

Steinherr, A. and Thisse, J.F. (1979) Is there a negatively-sloped supply curve in the labor-managed firm? *Economic Analysis* 13: 23–33.

Thomas, H. and Logan, C. (1982) *Mondragon, and Economic Analysis*. London: Allen and Unwin.

Vanek, J. (1970) *The General Theory of Labour-Managed Market Economies*. Ithaca, NY: Cornell University Press.

Vanek, J. (1977a) Some fundamental considerations on financing and the form of ownership under labor management. In *The Labour-Managed Economy: Essays by Jaroslav Vanek*. Ithaca, NY: Cornell University Press.

Vanek, J. (1977b) Uncertainty and the investment decision under labor-management and their social efficiency implications. In *The Labor Managed Economy: Essays by Jaroslav Vanek*. Ithaca, NY: Cornell University Press.

Ward, B. (1958) The firm in Illyria: market syndicalism. *American Economic Review* 48: 566–589.

Ward, B. (1967) *The Socialist Economy: A Study of Organisational Alternatives*. New York: Random House.

Weitzman, M. (1983) Some macroeconomic implications of alternative compensation systems. *Economic Journal* 93: 763–783.

7

A NEW VISION OF THE KNOWLEDGE ECONOMY

Brian Chi-ang Lin

National Chengchi University

There are changes in other spheres too which we must expect to come. When the accumulation of wealth is no longer of high social importance, there will be great changes in the code of morals . . . . Of course there will still be many people with intense, unsatisfied purposiveness who will blindly pursue wealth – unless they can find some plausible substitute. But the rest of us will no longer be under any obligation to applaud and encourage them. (Keynes, 1963, pp. 369–370)

1. Introduction

The present interpretation of the knowledge economy (or knowledge-based economy) focuses mainly on the important role of knowledge or human capital in long-term economic growth (e.g. Grossman and Helpman, 1991; Freeman and Polasky, 1992; Jones, 1995; OECD, 1996; Aghion and Howitt, 1998; Neef, 1998; Mokyr, 2002; Paganetto, 2004; Carlaw *et al.*, 2006).[1] According to an OECD report (1996), it is estimated that more than half of the GDP in the major OECD countries is now knowledge based. Yet the unifaceted exposition of the knowledge economy from the perspective of increased production and accumulation has been far from perfect. Despite the fact that the share of knowledge production in GDP has been increasing over the past several decades, our human societies have been concurrently characterized by serious phenomena such as growing economic inequality (e.g. World Bank, 1997; United Nations, 2005) and environmental degradation (e.g. Yi, 2001; Murray and Cook, 2002; Diamond, 2005; Meadows *et al.*, 2005).

To resolve the aforementioned problems and lead socioeconomic progress towards a sustainable society, it is necessary to develop a pluralistic perspective of the knowledge economy. Since the Brundtland Report was released in 1987, we have begun to inquire into the possibility of global sustainability through successive generations. Fundamental to this holistic perspective is the recognition that human generations are interrelated and that intergenerational issues such as equity, environmental externalities, allocation of (environmental) resources and policies for social optimality ought to be critically addressed (e.g. Howarth and Norgaard, 1990; Howarth, 1991; Babu *et al.*, 1997; Farmer and Randall, 1997; Dasgupta, 1998; Ansuategi and Escapa, 2002; Farmer, 2005).

To thoroughly investigate the growth-oriented exposition of the knowledge economy, Section 2 first reviews the Austrian analysis of knowledge and the knowledge industries, which are considered the inspiration of the mainstream exposition. Section 3 examines the new growth theory, which considers knowledge and technological spillovers as the main sources of economic growth. Then, Section 4 analyses the lacunae of the knowledge economy, such as the growth of income and wealth inequality, and Section 5 briefly assesses the Austrian and mainstream approaches. To develop an alternative new vision of the knowledge economy, Section 6 analyses the evolution of knowledge and its impact on human development. Section 7 introduces indigenous knowledge, a unique intellectual knowledge system, which has been increasingly recognized as critical for sustainable development. Section 8 argues that the notion of sustainable development has in its roots John Stuart Mill's *stationary state*, an ideal and sustainable society compatible with Keynes's vision described in his *Economic Possibilities for Our Grandchildren* (1930). Section 9 offers a value-committed vision of the knowledge economy that helps emancipate the present growth-oriented capitalism, and Section 10 concludes.

2. The Inception of Knowledge Industries: The Austrian Exposition of Knowledge

The present interpretation of the knowledge economy emphasizes the significance of production, distribution and use of knowledge for economic growth. As early as 1962, Fritz Machlup, a late president of the American Economic Association (AEA) and an eminent Austrian economist, first analysed and coined the phrase the 'knowledge industry' in his pioneering book entitled *The Production and Distribution of Knowledge in the United States*. Later, Machlup published some other relevant works, including *Knowledge and Knowledge Production* (1980), *The Branches of Learning* (1982) and *The Economics of Information and Human Capital* (1984).[2] His ideas have highlighted the significance of knowledge accumulation or production for economic growth in modern economies and have stimulated subsequent research into the knowledge economy. For instance, 1979 Nobel Laureate T.W. Schultz has applied Machlup's (1962) concepts of education in his important book entitled *The Economic Value of Education* (1963), which later became an underlying basis of the new growth theory developed by his Chicago colleague Robert Lucas in the 1980s.

2.1 *Fritz Machlup's Analysis of Knowledge Production*

Machlup's 1962 book represents the first major scholarly promulgation of the 'information revolution' and the 'knowledge society' (Langlois, 1985). According to Machlup (1962, pp. 21–22; 1980, p. 108), knowledge can be classified into the following five classes: (1) practical knowledge,[3] (2) intellectual knowledge, (3) small-talk and pastime knowledge, (4) spiritual knowledge and (5) unwanted knowledge.[4] In addition, Machlup (1962, 1980, Ch. 14) classified knowledge production into six major knowledge industries and branches: (1) education, (2) research and development (R&D), (3) artistic creation and communication, (4) media of communication, (5) information services and (6) information machines. According to some preliminary estimates provided by Machlup (1962, pp. 354–357), total knowledge production for the USA in 1958 was $136,436 million, with $60,194 million in education, $10,990 million in R&D, $38,369 million in media of communication, $8,922 million in information machines and $17,961 million in information services.[5] The ratio of knowledge production to adjusted GNP in 1958 was almost 29%.

In the 15 years after Machlup's research, Porat and Rubin (1977) took up and extended Machlup's (1962) work to complete a nine-volume report entitled *The Information Economy*, frequently referred to as the Commerce study. The main difference between Machlup's (1962) work and the Commerce study is that the Commerce study rigidly used the data compiled by the Bureau of Economic Analysis in the official national income accounts. For his work, Machlup (1962) took some of the activities into account that are not part of the national income accounts. According to the Commerce study, the primary information sector accounted for 25.1% of GNP in 1967 and the secondary information sector accounted for an additional 21.1% of GNP. Overall, 46.2% of US GNP could be attributed to the activities of the information sector in 1967 and the USA had become the *de facto information economy*.[6]

Rubin *et al.* (1986) further provided updated US statistics on the production of the knowledge industry presented by Machlup (1962) up to 1980. Their major findings indicate that total expenditures for knowledge production have steadily increased from 1958 to 1980, rising from $138,825 million in 1958 to $201,080 million in 1963, $290,809 million in 1967, $432,261 million in 1972, $700,971 million in 1977 and $967,909 million in 1980. The *knowledge industry*, as a result, accounted for 28.6% of adjusted GNP in 1958 to 31.0% in 1963, 33.3% in 1967, 33.9% in 1972, 34.2% in 1977 and 34.3% in 1980.

Machlup is a defender of the neoclassical micro-theory. His investigation of knowledge and economics 'extended only to the role of knowledge as a commodity that can be bought, sold, and invested in', and his Knowledge Project is methodologically more of 'a semantic exercise than an economic analysis' (Langlois, 1985, p. 233). Clearly, Machlup's methodological position is best understood from his scholarly background, that is, the Austrian School.[7] In this regard, Vaughn (1994) has pointed out that, to be part of the greater academic community, it had become necessary for eminent Austrian economists such as Fritz Machlup, Joseph Schumpeter, Oskar Morgenstern and Gottfried Haberler (who had left Austria for America during the 1920s or 1930s) to examine their Austrian themes using neoclassical language and techniques. Indeed, Machlup's 1962 work has been called 'an Austrian theme in a neoclassical setting' (Vaughn, 1994, p. 36).

2.2 F. A. von Hayek and the Knowledge Problem

From an Austrian perspective, one of the driving features of the market process is the fact that 'knowledge is a multifaceted, heterogeneous, disaggregated, often private or tacit and imperfect phenomenon' (Vaughn, 1994, p. 4). Historically, the Austrian exposition of the knowledge subject can be traced far back to the early work of the founder of the Austrian School, Carl Menger, in his *Principles of Economics* first published in 1871 (Vaughn, 1990, 1994; Langlois, 1991; Baetjer, 2000). In the 1930s and 1940s, Hayek, who would become the best known Austrian economist of the second half of the twentieth century,[8] explicitly advanced one of his most significant ideas – the role of the 'division of knowledge' (which later became known as the *knowledge problem*) – and emphasized the importance of dispersion of knowledge and information among masses of people (Machlup, 1976, pp. 36–37).

The knowledge problem is a central topic of the Austrian analysis (Kasper and Streit, 1998, Ch. 3.1). In his 1937 paper 'Economics and Knowledge', and subsequently in his 1945 paper 'The Use of Knowledge in Society', Hayek attacked the conventional assumption of complete knowledge and stressed the nature of the economic problem:

> But in our analysis, instead of showing what bits of information the different persons must possess in order to bring about that result, we fall in effect back on the assumption that everybody knows everything and so evade any real solution of the problem. . . . It has become customary among economists to stress only the need of knowledge of prices, apparently because – as a consequence of the confusion between objective and subjective data – the complete knowledge of the objective facts was taken for granted. (Hayek, 1937, p. 49)

> The economic problem of society is thus not merely a problem of how to allocate 'given' resources – if 'given' is taken to mean given to a single mind, which deliberately solves the problem set by these 'data'. It is rather a problem of how to secure the best use of resources known to any of the members of society, for ends whose relative importance only these individuals know. Or, to put it briefly, it is a problem of the utilization of knowledge not given to anyone in its totality. (Hayek, 1945, pp. 519–520)

That is, Hayek recognized that the lack of (perfect) knowledge – human ignorance – is constitutional. In essence, the economic problem is concerned with how heterogeneous individuals with limited knowledge carry out their actions and execute their plans over time through exchanges with each other. The concept of competition, to Hayek, means decentralized planning by heterogeneous individuals with limited knowledge (i.e. heterogeneous individuals who possess differential knowledge). His notion of equilibrium, in this context, implies a specific situation in which all heterogeneous individuals' plans are synchronized. More importantly, the interactions of all these heterogeneous individuals (best known as the market process or a *catallaxy*) can lead to the creation or discovery of new knowledge.

Later, in his first volume of *Law, Legislation and Liberty*, Hayek integrated into his previous analyses the concept of tacit knowledge – we know more than we can tell – developed by Polanyi (1958) and stressed a new feature of the market process:

> Although still an unfamiliar conception, the fact that language is often insufficient to express what the mind is fully capable of taking into account in determining action, or that we will often not be able to communicate in words what we well know how to practise, has been clearly established in many fields. (Hayek, 1973, pp. 76–77)

Thus, it is not difficult to infer that the market process is a trial-and-error process, and it is not surprising to observe that people are wrong in their decisions from time to time. Hayek himself did not further investigate the implications of tacit knowledge in market economies, but the role of knowledge has become a major theme of the Austrian analysis (Vaughn, 1994, p. 122).

In his 1974 Nobel Prize lecture, Hayek again warned that economists pretended to know what was in practice not fully known or measurable, and they inevitably risked giving false advice. He said:

> To act on the belief that we possess the knowledge and the power which enable us to shape the processes of society entirely to our liking, knowledge which in fact we do *not* possess, is likely to make us do much harm. (Hayek, 1974)

All in all, the market is instrumental and necessary for the realization of individual freedom, the solving of economic problems and the gestation of new knowledge. The central planners and/or boards characterized by their limited knowledge cannot predict the final outcomes of individual actions in the unknown future. They cannot just issue authoritative orders to solve the economic problems existing in society. People learn by doing and acquire new knowledge through the competitive market process. The market is an institution for the coordination, exchange and utilization of the differential knowledge of individuals. From an Austrian perspective, the competitive market process has led to beneficial interaction among market participants.

2.3 *The Impact of Antitrust and Intellectual Property on the Competitive Market Process*

The Austrian analysis of the competitive market process consists of the following three key concepts: (1) the entrepreneurial role, (2) the role of discovery and (3) rivalrous competition (Kirzner, 1997). An Austrian perspective emphasizes that entrepreneurs can operate to 'change price/output data' and it is 'entrepreneurial boldness and imagination' that drives the market process. An entrepreneur is always ready to be surprised in an open-ended, uncertain world and also prepared to take actions to profit by such surprises. Entrepreneurs compete with other entrepreneurs and the competitive process refers to a series of discoveries generated by that 'entrepreneurial boldness and alertness' (Kirzner, 1997, pp. 70–73).

In contrast, some government-enforced policy such as antitrust regulation and intellectual property rights (IPRs) protection (such as patent rights, copyrights, semiconductor chip protection and trademark protection for the USA) might interfere with the Austrian market-process world of entrepreneurial discovery. Thus, a further investigation of the Austrian position on antitrust and intellectual property has become consequential. One might promptly anticipate a plentitude of work on the subjects of antitrust and intellectual property to be found in the Austrian literature. Surprisingly, however, the Austrian School economists have so far offered very few analyses of these aspects.

In a global society, the IPRs system has become prevalent and dominant in controlling access to knowledge, the dissemination of knowledge and also the trading of knowledge-related goods and services.[9] The emergence of the intellectual property system such as a patent creates a monopoly price (or a heavy tax) on the use of knowledge. In this regard, Austrian economists have, from time to time, explained the abuse of patent data as indicators for innovation and technical change and suggested the abolition of the patent system for promoting the market process (see Oakman, 1986; Desrochers, 1998, for example).

In relation to antitrust, the following statements seem to be quite consistent with the Austrian notion of the competitive market process:

> The antitrust prohibition of price discrimination, merging, price fixing, and even free-market monopolization prevents freely contracting parties who hold legitimate rights to property from making, or refusing to make, certain contractual arrangements that they believe to be in their best interests.... [P]rivate and peaceful activities such as price discrimination, merging, tying, and price fixing violate no property rights in the ordinary sense of the term; that is, they do not necessarily involve force, fraud, or misrepresentation. Yet, from a strictly natural-rights perspective, the antitrust laws themselves which regulate private and peaceful trade are inherently violative of property rights. (Armentano, 1999, pp. 99–100)

To Austrian economists, the freedom of an individual's participation in economic activities to profit is an essential ingredient of human (private) property rights. Turning to their concern, the intervention of antitrust policy clearly decreases the market value of asset titles and substantially circumscribes private property rights.

3. The New Growth Theory: Knowledge, Technology and Innovation as the Sources of Growth

Although the Austrian School economists investigated the general subject of knowledge much earlier and made a significant contribution, it was a group of Chicago School economists – T.W. Schultz, Gary Becker and particularly Robert E. Lucas and Paul M. Romer[10] – who technically incorporated more direct knowledge into their theories and models and promoted the research domain of growth theory to the academic frontier. Romer (1986) and Lucas (1988) initiated the research wave in the mid-1980s and the burgeoning growth literature that followed. According to the new growth theory, the advance of knowledge is a crucial determinant of long-term economic growth. The current revival of interest in growth theory, to a considerable extent, stems from a lack of good aggregate-level models to capture facts that have long been acknowledged by growth theorists (Romer, 1994).

3.1 Background and Spillover Models

1. There are many firms in a market economy.
2. Discoveries differ from other inputs in the sense that many people can use them at the same time.
3. It is possible to replicate physical activities.
4. Technological advances come from things that people do.
5. Many individuals and firms have market power and earn monopoly rents on discoveries.
   (quoted from Romer, 1994, pp. 12–13).

Romer (1994) has argued that the neoclassical growth model developed by Solow (1956) only captured the aforementioned facts 1, 2 and 3. In both the Romer model (1986) and the Lucas model (1988), fact 4 (but not fact 5) is considered, and the technology is endogenously provided. In effect, based upon their conceptual nuances, explanations for sources of sustained growth in the new growth literature can be further divided into two major strands, that is, technological spillovers and human capital spillovers (or normally termed knowledge spillovers).[11] In his model, Romer (1986) assumed that the aggregate production function could be expressed as $Y = A(R)F(R_i, K_i, L_i)$. In this expression, A denotes the public stock of knowledge that is a function of aggregate expenditure on research and development, R, by firms. K_i and L_i denote the level of capital and labour by firm i. Romer's breakthrough was to assume that it is (technological) spillovers from private research activities that lead to advancement in the public stock of knowledge.

Lucas (1988) considered the *external effects* of human capital built on the concept of human capital developed by Schultz (1963) and Becker (1964).[12] These effects are seen as spillovers from one person to another, and to some extent contribute to the productivity of all factors of production.[13] Technically, his formulation of equilibrium path with external effects directly follows from Arrow (1962) and Romer (1986).[14] The engine of growth in the Lucas model (1988) is human capital (spillovers). It seems that output for firm i takes the form $Y_i = A(H)F(K_i, H_i)$, where the level of technology A is a function of human capital H. Lucas (1988, p. 19) repeatedly emphasized that 'human capital accumulation is a *social* activity, involving *groups* of people in a way that has no counterpart in the accumulation of physical capital'.

3.2 The Schumpeterian Framework

Another line of growth inquiry points to endogenous technological change and innovation as the engine of growth (e.g. Romer, 1990; Grossman and Helpman,

1991; Aghion and Howitt, 1992). Many of the subsequent R&D-based models in the new growth literature (and certainly some referenced above) cited Joseph Schumpeter as an inspiration. Schumpeter (1975, pp. 82–83) argued that 'in dealing with capitalism we are dealing with an evolutionary process .... The fundamental impulse that sets and keeps the capitalist engine in motion comes from the new consumers' goods, the new methods of production or transportation, the new markets, the new forms of industrial organization that capitalist enterprise creates .... This process of Creative Destruction is the essential fact about capitalism.' Schumpeter emphasized that innovation is a central element of economic activity, and development propelled by innovation is an evolutionary process.

The Schumpeterian perspective on growth influenced to a great extent some recent work such as Aghion and Howitt (1998) and Nelson (1996). According to Nelson (1996, pp. 109–113), in a Schumpeterian or evolutionary context a firm has three features: its strategy, its structure and its core capabilities. A firm defines and rationalizes its objectives based on a set of broad commitments. In practice, it is formidable for a firm to actually figure out a best strategy. A firm, however, will not survive for very long if it only produces a given set of products with a given set of processes. To survive in the long run, a firm must innovate and requires a set of core capabilities in R&D that it can carry on. In a rapidly changing environment, firms will eventually choose somewhat different strategies, subsequently leading to development of different structures and core (R&D) capabilities.

3.3 *Frontline Appeal and Comparative Assessment*

Romer (1986) and Lucas (1988) were the primary developers of the new growth theory and their works have generated tremendous influence in the mainstream literature. In addition to receiving numerous significant awards, Romer was also named one of America's 25 most influential people in 1997 by *TIME* magazine for his new growth theory, which, according to the magazine, might 'revolutionize the study of economics'. Lucas was awarded the 1995 Nobel Prize for his rational expectations thesis. It was even predicted that he might be awarded a second Nobel Prize because of his influential 1988 paper 'On the Mechanics of Economic Development'.[15] A thoughtful investigation of the development and interpretation of the new growth theory might lead one to inquire into the following questions. Do the key elements of the new growth theory represent an intellectual breakthrough from an epistemological perspective? In addition, does any relationship exist between the Austrian analysis of knowledge and the new growth theory? It has been widely recognized that Austrian economics is almost entirely focused on microeconomics.[16] Thus, in the first place one might be unaware of the nexus between the (micro) Austrian analysis of knowledge and the (macro) new growth theory. After further examination, one might find some evidence that the Austrian analysis of knowledge and the macro analysis of the new growth theory are related to some extent.

Baetjer (2000) has pointed out, from an Austrian perspective, that capital is embodied knowledge and, consequently, capital development is a social learning (and ongoing) process. The key concepts and results such as 'knowledge as the basic form of capital' (Romer, 1986, p. 1003), 'endogenous technological change' (Romer, 1990) and 'growth rates increasing over time' (Romer, 1986, p. 1002) do not differ from the Austrian analysis of knowledge. The main difference between the Austrian perspective and Romer's work centres on their distinct views on 'what factors slow these tendencies to increasing rates of growth' (Baetjer, 2000, p. 169). From an Austrian perspective, Romer (1986, 1990) inappropriately regarded output as an additively separable function of all the distinct types of capital goods, and failed to comprehend the process by which technological change occurs. The real challenge for exponential growth is how to maintain capital complementarities in an environment of incomplete and vastly changing knowledge.

It would appear that the Austrian predilection for market-oriented knowledge (for growth) and the mainstream analysis of knowledge-driven growth, despite their remaining disagreements and some diverse foci, are analytically compatible and sequentially connected to a great extent.[17] Austrians criticize the neoclassical assumption of given knowledge and emphasize the constitutional ignorance of human existence. However, one might initiate appropriate institutional arrangements such as educational reform to ease human ignorance and facilitate the accumulation of knowledge. Over time, the accumulation of knowledge can lead to long-term economic growth.

It has become customary for new growth theorists to make simplified assumptions in order to keep their models tractable. Technically speaking, the present interpretation of the new growth theory that emphasizes the importance of knowledge to long-run growth can be viewed to some extent as the restructuring of the microfoundations of mainstream macroeconomics towards the Austrian School. In this regard, Romer (1986) and Lucas (1988) can best be understood as pioneers in constructing mathematical models of knowledge. Nevertheless, their concepts and insights are absolutely not novel if one takes a close review of the Austrian literature. Note, for example, that the following statements of strong Austrian flavour were actually made by Romer (1994) in his concluding remarks:

> We will be able to address the most important policy questions about growth: In a developing country like the Philippines, what are the best institutional arrangements for gaining access to the knowledge that already exists in the rest of the world? In a country like the United States, what are the best institutional arrangements for encouraging the production and use of new knowledge? (Romer, 1994, p. 21)

A special note on Schumpeter seems to be necessary for completing the analysis in this section. If Schumpeter is counted as an Austrian economist, the overall Austrian insights into economic growth will become more significant. Schumpeter's academic lineage, however, is not unambiguous. Although he is frequently regarded as an economist in the Austrian School tradition (see Ekelund and Hébert, 1997, Ch. 20, for example), others such as Landreth and Colander (1994, pp. 390–391) classify Schumpeter as a quasi-institutionalist. Due to his renowned emphasis on the 'evolutionary process' of capitalist development, perhaps it is better to recognize

Schumpeter as one of the early founders for creating new work in 'evolutionary economics'.[18]

4. The Growth of Income and Wealth Inequality

4.1 *The Lacunae of the Growth-oriented Knowledge Economy*

Although we now live in a knowledge economy, this economy has also brought an increase in income inequality (Atkinson and Court, 1998; Thurow, 1999).[19] According to the evidence shown in the US Census Bureau's Historical Income Inequality Tables,[20] inequality in household income in the USA has been significantly on the rise over the past two decades. The Gini coefficients remained at the 0.39–0.40 level from 1967 to 1981. Then, the coefficients increased from 0.41 in the early 1980s to 0.43 in the early 1990s, to 0.45 in the mid-1990s, and to 0.46 since 2000. Keister's (2000) study has further pointed out that wealth is much more unequally distributed than income in the USA. In 1989, the share of the top 1% of income recipients was about 16% of all income. In contrast, the wealthiest 1% of all households owned 39% of all assets. Barlett and Steele (1994) have shown that the USA is a two-tax, two-class society. More and more in taxes are being paid by the middle-income taxpayers, while less and less in taxes are being paid by corporations. The wealthiest individuals frequently take advantage of generous write-off provisions. US politicians, especially congressmen, have, according to Barlett and Steele (1994), championed and reinforced the arguments for tax cuts to benefit the wealthy at the expense of the middle class.

In fact, it is a class war that 'Middle America' has lost, and several studies have examined the decline of the US middle class. Newman (1988, 1993) conducted in-depth interviews with ordinary Americans mainly to explore the socioeconomic characteristics of the middle class. She clearly found that the American middle class was facing the bitter problem of downward mobility (i.e. the gradual loss of decent jobs and a reliable income). Strobel (1993) also argued that, due to the general economic decline, the American middle class had been under tremendous living pressure. Peterson (1994) pointed out that the shrinking of the middle class in the 1980s was a major consequence of the USA's silent depression that had been ongoing. Strobel and Peterson (1997) further explained that the shrinking size of the American middle class was due to lower real wages, lost middle-class jobs and increased financial burdens. Unfortunately also for the poor, Galbraith (1992) pointed out that the underclass (the working and non-working poor) exhibited a lower voter turnout and had handed over the control of government to the 'contented', that is, the more financially secure group.

Tachibanaki (2006) examined inequality and poverty in Japan and warned that Japan had entered a critical period. The degree of inequality had been increasing, and its level had also become one of the highest among advanced industrialized countries. Burniaux *et al.* (1998) studied 13 OECD countries and found that inequality (measured in disposable income) had risen in most of them between the mid-1970s and the mid-1990s.[21] Indeed, growing inequality has become a global phenomenon not confined to the OECD countries. For China, the benefits of growth have been primarily absorbed by urban areas and the coast, and income distribution has become increasingly unequal since economic reforms were initiated in 1978 (World Bank, 1997). According to the United Nations (2005) *Report on the World Social Situation*, 80% of the world's GDP belongs to the 1 billion people living in the developed countries, while the 5 billion people living in developing countries share the remaining 20%. Their analysis of the reliable World Income Inequality Database, with a sample of 73 countries, further indicates that within-country income inequality rose in 48 countries (approximately two-thirds) between the 1950s and the 1990s. Overall, the prospect of meeting global commitments to reducing inequality, as outlined in the 1995 World Summit for Social Development in Copenhagen and endorsed in the United Nations Millennium Declaration, is bleak.

4.2 *The Insights of Professors Gunnar Myrdal and Kenneth E. Boulding*

Gunnar Myrdal, a 1974 Nobel Laureate and a well-known institutionalist, investigated the South Asia region (including Pakistan, India, Indonesia, Burma, the Philippines, Thailand, Ceylon and Malaya, and occasionally South Vietnam, Cambodia and Laos as well) and published a three-volume book entitled *Asian Drama: An Inquiry into the Poverty of Nations* in 1968. To pursue the goal of a sustainable society, some of his penetrating insights of almost five decades ago deserve further attention. The entire third volume of *Asian Drama, Problems of Population Quality*, was devoted to the study of health, education and the social system as a whole, with an application of his analysis to government action.

From a holistic perspective, a social system in each South Asian country is composed of a large number of conditions that can be classified into the following six broad categories: (1) output and incomes, (2) conditions of production, (3) levels of living, (4) attitudes towards life and work, (5) institutions and (6) policies (Myrdal, 1968, pp. 1859–1864). The first three categories represent 'economic factors', and categories 4 and 5 represent 'non-economic factors'. Category 6 is a mixture and can be considered to belong to the 'economic factors' when the purpose of the policies is to induce changes in the first three conditions. In a social system, all the aforementioned conditions are causally interrelated and economic conditions do not have precedence over the others.

Myrdal, for instance, pointed out that the South Asian people have not only been insufficiently educated but have also been miseducated to a great extent (due to their past colonial rule). Thus, educational reforms needed in these now independent countries are far more than the popular suggestion of increased 'investment in education'. The main reason is that 'existing educational establishments are part of a larger institutional system, which includes social stratification; and this system is supported by people's attitudes, which themselves have been moulded by the institutions' (Myrdal, 1968, p. 1649). Influential vested interests in these countries have been embedded in the educational and institutional systems, and they resist or warp reform policies.

To Myrdal (1974, p. 729), development means 'the upward movement of the entire social system'. Unfortunately, 'development was commonly understood as simple economic growth, regularly accounted for in terms of very questionable statistics on gross national product or income ... . What the poor do need are radical institutional reforms' (Myrdal, 1978, p. 782). Kenneth E. Boulding, a late AEA president and also a well-known institutionalist, notes on this point:

> One area where economists have a good deal to be humble about is in the field of economic development of the poor countries. In the rich countries we have done fairly well; in the poor countries our record is distinctly spotty. (Boulding, 1966, p. 11)

It is well known that the burden of poverty has fallen heavily on women and children. This phenomenon is particularly significant for developing countries. In particular, people in poverty, due to their more limited access to health care and services, exhibit a worse health status (OECD, 2003; WHO, 2006). Indeed, poverty has become a chronic phenomenon and can be better understood only from a broad institutional perspective. Poverty, for instance, is frequently entangled with phenomena such as contagious diseases and criminal activities,[22] which cause a great negative impact on other individuals and communities. Thus, reducing poverty is essential for achieving a sustainable community if poverty reduction induces greater public health and security. From a global perspective, the reduction of poverty is even more significant if it contributes to disease eradication and global peace, both of which are crucial for global sustainability.[23]

5. An Assessment of Austrian and Mainstream Views

Landreth and Colander (1994, p. 407) have pointed out that 'it remains difficult to find an Austrian who is not a conservative; most simply assume the market is desirable and necessary for achievement of individual freedom'.[24] Obviously, the Austrian analysis of the market-oriented knowledge is far from perfect and one might simply present the Austrians with two basic questions. First, it is not a problem to admit that people are to some extent ignorant. However, why do people possess differential knowledge? In other words, why does the Austrian School regard individuals with differential knowledge as a given in their analysis? It is clear that the Austrian analysis methodologically rationalizes the existing *heterogeneous* knowledge structure of the capitalist system. It is not difficult to imagine, however, that the profits or losses from market activities and, accordingly, the distribution of income and wealth of the society are closely related to the differential knowledge of economic agents. Since differential knowledge is a key element in deciding market winners and losers, the study of the formation of the knowledge structure for market participants is vital. The Austrian analysis, however, takes the existing *heterogeneous* knowledge structure of society for granted without further examination of its causes and far-reaching consequences. Not surprisingly, the discovery and production of knowledge are greatly extolled, but the coexistent phenomena such as growing income inequality have been reduced to triviality in the Austrian analysis.

Second, why does the implementation of free market institutions cater to all the interests of differential people and communities? In his analysis of the Austrian and Chicago schools, Hunt (1992, pp. 572–584) has shown that these two schools purport to be a value-free science and claim that their theory fits all people at all times. In contrast, institutionalists who consider their economic discipline to be the original institutional economics (OIE) or economists greatly influenced by the OIE have emphasized a value commitment to study economics (cf. Myrdal, 1958, 1981; Boulding, 1969; Söderbaum, 1999).[25] Myrdal, for instance, overtly remarked:

> Valuations are always with us. Disinterested research there has never been and can never be. Before we can have answers there must be questions. There can be no view except from a viewpoint. In the questions raised and the viewpoint chosen, valuations are implied. (Myrdal, 1981, p. 44)

Indeed, the choice of a free market along with its institutions is merely an option and the paramount propaganda of the free market structure unleashed by the Austrians remains dubious. Differential people and communities should have wide latitude in choosing and building economic institutions catering to their specific interests such as pursuing economic equality for social justice or developing a self-reliant type of economy with limited external trade, and so on. The concept of economic freedom should be expanded not only to include the concept of free market competition but also to incorporate the choice of other economic institutions created for satisfying different groups of people.

The limitations imposed by the mainstream's narrow analysis of the knowledge economy are also evident. Knowledge is largely regarded as the central impetus to economic growth. Yet one might ask the following question: Can knowledge be regarded as the central element for promoting socioeconomic progress such as creating a sustainable society? As soon as this type of question is asked, some critical issues emerge. For example, many poor people relentlessly die of hunger or disease every day. According to the United Nations 2005 *Report on the World Social Situation*, the wealthiest 20% on earth occupy 86% of all private consumption, while the poorest enjoy just above 1%. The pressing issue, indeed, is not to produce more but to seek a *knowledgeable* allocation and distribution (to alleviate poverty).

Moreover, the mainstream underlying emphasis on the *competitiveness* of a single person or country is very shortsighted, which will not fulfil the goal of long-term development of humans.[26] From a global perspective, we can intuitively consider that there exists only one human society on earth. It can be fairly understood that our human society will not develop for very long if competition exists between different generations. As an older generation controls the society, it will not allocate enough resources to enhance the competitiveness of the younger generation. The younger generation, as a result, will become *weaker* over time and the society as a whole will eventually come to an end.[27] Thus, the concept of competition (or competitiveness) is *de facto* insufficient for dealing with the nature of long-term development of human societies.

6. The Evolution of Knowledge: Knowledge and Human Development

Human life is collective, cumulative and evolutionary in character. It is reasonable to state that an ordinary individual living in the twenty-first century may not be any more clever than a person living in the first century. Many well-known facts can immediately justify this statement. Just take the phenomenal Egyptian pyramids for example. So far, modern scientists have not figured out exactly how they were built. However, we realize that the average person lives better and longer nowadays. Why? The truth is that knowledge has accumulated over time and spread from generation to generation. That is, the knowledge fund has grown and modern people have consequently been endowed with greater intellectual capacity and capital. To better understand this point, we might hypothetically imagine the existence of *a knowledge barn* (or *commons*) for human society from an overlapping-generations perspective. In primitive and ancient times, the knowledge barn only accommodated a small quantity of knowledge. When our human ancestors went into the knowledge barn, they found few pieces of knowledge available for use. As time went on, more pieces of knowledge were piled up in the barn as each human generation made its marginal contribution to the accumulation and spread of knowledge. Thus, the existing generations have to recognize that they are very fortunate. Knowledge has accumulated and spread across the world generation by generation. This long-term process of gestation to some extent benefits *all* of us.

Let us consider a very basic (but important) piece of knowledge. That is, one plus one equals two ($1 + 1 = 2$). In relation to this *simple* piece of knowledge, the various kinds of symbols ($1, 2, +, =$) and the addition rule were previously designed and created by our human ancestors. This piece of knowledge is their legacy and is collectively inherited by all of us. We can easily understand that accountants could not do bookkeeping without it. Without it, Bill Gates's programmers would not be able to write computer programs and help Bill Gates establish his Microsoft empire. In fact, astronauts would not have landed on the moon without this piece of knowledge. As a matter of fact, a *pure* inventor or creator does not exist from an intellectual sense.

It is also known that R&D activities are central to the generation of new knowledge. R&D activities are dispersed across individual workrooms, private profit and non-profit organizations, academic institutions and governmental agencies. If one wants to measure, for example, the total cost of R&D activities, one has to take the monetary and non-monetary outlays of the parties involved into account. Thus, it can be expected that the costs to society as a whole will be extraordinarily high at first. The benefits that society can derive from the enormous amounts of money, time and effort expended on R&D activities are normally low in the initial stages, but are expected to increase over the long run. This phenomenon is particularly significant for basic research.

Figure 1 summarizes the aforementioned arguments and shows the evolution of knowledge from a long-term perspective.[28] The bottom left-hand quadrant shows that knowledge accumulates and spreads from generation to generation over time; the basic unit of the time span, depending on different types of knowledge (for

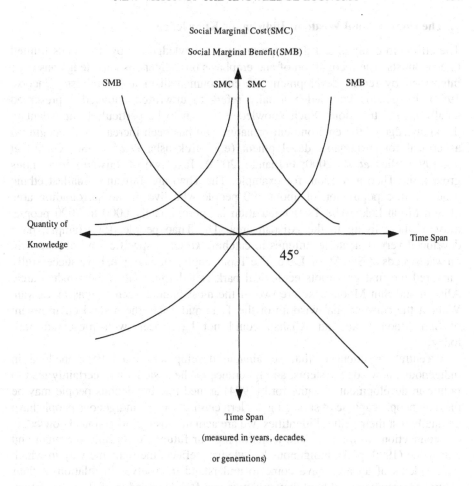

Figure 1. The Evolution of Knowledge.

further analyses), can be measured or denoted in terms of years, decades or generations. From an overlapping-generations perspective, the top two quadrants show that, corresponding to each generation, the social marginal costs decrease and the social marginal benefits increase as the quantity of knowledge accumulates.

Each human generation enjoys the benefits of knowledge transmitted from the preceding generations and, consequently, passes the accumulated benefits (i.e. the preceding benefits plus the marginal benefits created by the existing generation) to the immediate subsequent generation. In this respect, one might be aware that knowledge is a special type of international public good. An international public good, in principle, can benefit all countries, all people and all generations. Although each human generation is mortal, its knowledge exists and continues to expand in society. That is, the collective knowledge is still living and is vital to the long-term development of humans.

7. The Conventional Wisdom: Indigenous Knowledge

The efforts to comprehend the importance of knowledge are by no means limited to economists. The recognition of and emphasis on indigenous knowledge has been intensified by recent developments in environmentalism and feminism (Jacobs, 1994). Indigenous knowledge usually refers to unwritten knowledge preserved locally in oral traditions. Such knowledge is seen to be particularly abundant in the knowledge of the environment or nature and has been increasingly recognized as critical for sustainable development (e.g. Brokensha *et al.*, 1980; Gadgil *et al.*, 1993; Ellen *et al.*, 2000; Fernando, 2003). Take two of Taiwan's indigenous groups, the Thao and Tsou, for example. The Thao are Taiwan's smallest ethnic group, with a population of about 300 people who live in the surrounding area of Sun Moon Lake. The Tsou population is approximately 6000 to 7000 people, most of them living in the Alishan area. The Thao people, for example, have developed very delicate techniques in catching *kiluat*, a specific kind of lake fish, on waterweeds of Sun Moon Lake. The Tsou people, for example, have successfully furthered the first grassroots ecological park called *Tanayiku* in the Alishan area. Alishan and Sun Moon Lake are two of the most famous scenic areas in Taiwan. Without the conventional wisdom of the Thao and Tsou, the natural environment of Sun Moon Lake and Alishan could not have been well preserved until today.

A central argument is that sustainable development must be embedded in indigenous knowledge systems, and ignorance of the systems will certainly lead to failure in development. Weatherford (1994) argued that indigenous people may be the only people capable of salvaging modern civilization. As indigenous people have gradually lost their cultural identities, we are actually losing indigenous knowledge, our connections to the past, and jeopardizing our future. According to Semali and Kincheloe (1999, p. 3), indigenous knowledge 'reflects the dynamic way in which the residents of an area have come to understand themselves in relation to their natural environment and how they organize that folk knowledge of flora and fauna, cultural beliefs, and history to enhance their lives'.

The following is another real example of indigenous knowledge. The Onge people make up an aboriginal tribe with a population of less than 100 people. They live on Little Andaman Island (India) in the Bay of Bengal. They possess indigenous knowledge encompassing medicine, biology and nature (Norchi, 2000). They rely on their knowledge of a specific plant to treat fever and gastrointestinal disorders. This same plant is also effective in dealing with malaria and, consequently, the Onge people no longer suffer from that disease. Now, scientists have been conducting tests on the medicinal plants used by the Onge people, and pharmaceutical companies have also shown an interest in reaching an agreement with the patentee. In addition, all 96 Onge people survived the tsunami in December, 2004, which left around 300,000 people missing or dead in or around the Indian Ocean, including residents of the Onge people's nearby town of Hut Bay. Before the tsunami, the Onge people fled into the jungle for protection after they found that the water in the creek had suddenly run out to sea.

The work of protecting and promoting indigenous knowledge, however, is challenging. The following urgent issues need to be examined and evaluated. First, it is important to conduct research on how people can preserve the natural environment of the indigenous people, since indigenous knowledge and their natural habitats go hand in hand. Second, whether the existing IPRs system can be applied or extended to indigenous knowledge remains highly controversial (Marinova and Raven, 2006). In this regard, Darrell A. Posey, an influential figure for his advocacy of the rights of the indigenous people, emphasized that the development of traditional resource rights (TRRs) can protect the interests of indigenous peoples and strengthen the practice of their self-determination (Plenderleith, 2004, Ch. 14). Third, a unique institutional system for the advancement of indigenous knowledge needs to be developed. The US Tribal Colleges were created in the late 1960s and the early 1970s in response to the higher education needs of American Indians. There are currently over 30 Tribal Colleges located in Indian reservations around the USA. The Tribal Colleges are different from standard community colleges or mainstream four-year colleges due to their cultural identities, and are relatively involved in a broad range of community services – including education, counselling and economic development initiatives – that are specifically focused on communities that would otherwise be isolated from such resources. So far, the Tribal Colleges have not drawn enough attention from either academia or the general public, and have been persistently under financial pressure.

8. John Stuart Mill and the Stationary State

Now it is time to seriously reconsider the knowledge issue from the perspective of our position in human history. Boulding describes the epistemological problem as follows:

> There are, of course, a number of epistemological questions, some of which lie more in the province of the philosopher than they do the economist or the social scientist. The one with which I am particularly concerned here is that of the role of knowledge in social systems, both as a product of the past and as a determinant of the future. (Boulding, 1966, p. 1)

What is the role of knowledge in human development? Knowledge is critical not only to economic growth but also to our society's long-term development. In light of this, what does a sustainable society look like? Following Myrdal's erudition, sustainable development of a society could be portrayed as a *sustainable upward movement of the entire social system*. At the very least, the current growth-oriented exposition of the knowledge economy in mainstream literature is not only monistic but also partial, which will not fulfil the goal of sustainable development. In this respect, John Stuart Mill's concept of *the stationary state* outlined in his *Principles of Political Economy* (first published in 1848) is compatible with contemporary analysis of a sustainable society and is worth further review.

Daly (1973, 1977, 2005) traced his exposition of a sustainable economy, a steady-state economy (SSE), back to Mill's notion of the stationary state. The SSE is a *physical* concept that refers to an economy whose scale (i.e. resource throughput, equal to population multiplied by per capita resource use) remains at a constant level. This level neither depletes the materials from the environment beyond its regenerative capacity nor pollutes the environment beyond its absorptive capacity. Indeed, Daly's concept of SSE has not been void of practice. Most indigenous tribes organized as a closed group with a common property have practised SSE for (tens of) thousands of years on earth. O'Connor (1997) investigated Mill's concepts of a private property-based liberal society as well as a stationary-state society, and argued that the writings of Mill represent a prototype for ideals of a 'sustainable development'.

Lin (2006) also stated that Mill's concept of the stationary state is conceptually consistent with the modern exposition of sustainable development. It can be widely observed that the rich communities (nations) have tended to waste resources, whereas the poor communities (nations) have tended to destroy resources. Due to a rising inequality of wealth all over the world and limited resources on earth, the global community has become less and less sustainable. To maintain a sustainable society with an efficient use of resources, it is necessary to achieve a more equitable distribution of wealth. Although greatly influenced by David Ricardo, Mill's stationary state was not the dismal scenario that Ricardo visualized. Mill took a different view of his desirable society and outlined his desires for a good future. In his chapter on the stationary state, in which he discussed the long-run tendencies of the economy, he said:

> But the best state for human nature is that in which, while no one is poor, no one desires to be richer, nor has any reason to fear being thrust back by the efforts of others to push themselves forward. . . . There would be as much scope as ever for all kinds of mental culture, and moral and social progress; as much room for improving the Art of Living, and much more likelihood of its being improved, when minds ceased to be engrossed by the art of getting on. (Mill, 1965, pp. 748–751)

Looking at the economic and social conditions of his time, Mill felt that the mass of society was bypassed by the materialistic development of the Industrial Revolution and wondered whether a country with a growing economy was a desirable living place. He envisioned that the stationary state would result in an improvement in the art of living:

> It is only in the backward countries of the world that increased production is still an important object: in those most advanced, what is economically needed is a better distribution. . . . On the other hand, we may suppose this better distribution of property attained, by the joint effect of the prudence and frugality of individuals, and of a system of legislation favouring equality of fortunes, so far as is consistent with the just claim of the individual to the fruits, whether great or small, of his or her own industry. (Mill, 1965, p. 749)

As this passage suggests, Mill's stationary state might be narrowly interpreted as a society with *no (or limited) growth in physical output*. Alternatively, it should be best understood as a society with unlimited growth in mental culture and improvements in economic equality (by means of wealth redistribution). In this regard, Mill's concept of the stationary state is in line with contemporary analysis of a sustainable society and is very close to the *ethical-utopian* perspective on sustainable development. According to van den Bergh (1996, p. 59), the ethical-utopian perspective emphasizes 'new individual value systems (respect for nature and future generations, basic needs fulfilment) and new social objectives (steady state); ... long-run policy based on changing values and encouraging citizens (altruistic) behavior as opposed to individual (egoistic) behavior'.

Surely, the transition from a growth-oriented economy towards Mill's stationary state, a final stage of civilization, will not be an easy task. Mill's vision was far, far ahead of his time. Eighty-two years later, Mill's sanity was echoed by his great fellow British economist, John Maynard Keynes. It seemed untimely, as the Great Depression was under way, that Keynes envisaged the future of our economic progress in his short essay, *Economic Possibilities for Our Grandchildren*.[29] In 1930, looking into the future, Keynes discerned the following state of affairs:

> There are changes in other spheres too which we must expect to come. When the accumulation of wealth is no longer of high social importance, there will be great changes in the code of morals.... Of course there will still be many people with intense, unsatisfied purposiveness who will blindly pursue wealth – unless they can find some plausible substitute. But the rest of us will no longer be under any obligation to applaud and encourage them. (Keynes, 1963, pp. 369–370)

Keynes concluded that the time for our destiny of economic bliss had not yet come, because 'avarice and usury and precaution must be our gods for a little longer still' (Keynes, 1963, p. 372). However, he encouraged mankind to change gradually and to make preparations for our destiny.

9. A Value-committed Vision of the Knowledge Economy: An Emancipation of the Growth-oriented Capitalist Society

9.1 *Promoting Green Politics for Sustainable Development*

Winch (2004, p. 111) points out that Mill is one of the earliest green thinkers, whose 'defense of a zero-growth society conveys the substance of his environmentalist concerns'. Mill's virtuous stationary-state (zero-growth) society, according to Winch (2004, p. 122), is 'a continuous state of dynamic equilibrium' in which all improvements in new technologies can be redirected towards redistribution of wealth and the promotion of life quality. Do there exist any possibilities of developing Mill's high-minded mental culture (and Keynes's vision of economic bliss)? In the first place, we had better rid ourselves of growth mania. This is a formidable task and requires abandonment of the dominant emphasis on economic growth.[30] Take the USA for example. Typical middle-class Americans now do have significantly higher physical products (than their counterparts living in the affluent 1950s and 1960s) but few realize that 'the more we achieve at this point yields us little in the way of enduring satisfaction' (Wachtel, 1998, p. 264).[31] To achieve the goal of a sustainable society, Harris (2000) suggests that it is necessary to develop new and more democratized avenues to the formulation of values, beliefs and knowledge. Fortunately, many people and groups worldwide such as green consumption activists have taken steps to steer people's attitudes and behaviours towards a sustainable future.[32]

Green politics is a lively mobilization of a variety of ideas, values and reform proposals for promoting environmental conservation, civic engagement, peace and social justice, and leading socioeconomic progress to a state of sustainable development (Lin, 2008b). In principle, the development of green politics is ecologically based and shares a common concern for environmental justice and equity and has been seen as forward-looking movements for resolving deficiencies of traditional democracy. Green politics has been in gestation for many years in most Western societies and has gained some political success through organizing green parties, especially in the European countries. However, the emergence of green politics is in no way of purely political significance (for promoting green parties). Instead, it could also substantially enrich the public debate on pressing environmental issues (such as climate change and global warming), help us to better understand the relationship between economic growth and the environment and help to advise the government to implement forward-looking environmental policies.

Nearly all green activists have not merely questioned material consumption of modern societies, but also overtly addressed spiritual or metaphysical issues to steer people's attitudes and values towards new social objectives. In May 1972, the world's first national-level green party, the Values Party, was launched at Victoria University of Wellington, New Zealand. For instance, the Values Party's 1972 manifesto claimed that 'New Zealand's peculiar malady is not physical poverty; it is spiritual poverty' (Rainbow, 1993, p. 25). Founded in Coventry in 1973 as the 'People' or, as it was later known, the Ecology Party, the British green party is amongst the oldest in Europe. The British Ecology Party stresses that the values of conventional politics are fundamentally flawed and has created the first edition of a *Manifesto for a Sustainable Society*.

It might be stressed here that the USA was the world's environmental policy leader in the 1970s. The USA established a national environmental protection agency (EPA) in 1970 and passed landmark legislation on clean air and water in subsequent years. Over the past decade, citizens living outside the USA, however, have become more aware of the growing discrepancies in the attitude of the US government towards trade and the environment. On the one hand, the US government has shown aggressive leadership in promoting trade liberalization and free trade agreements. On the other hand, it has expressed persistent unwillingness to make an international commitment to environmental protection. The Kyoto Protocol came into force on 16 February 2005 with a total of more than 160 countries having ratified the agreement. The two major countries currently opposed to the

Kyoto agreement are the USA and Australia.[33] Many environmentalists outside the United States 'bemoan the inability of America's environmental movement to sway its own government' (Conca, 2001, p. 32).

9.2 *Developing Academic Pluralism for Sustainable Development*

In his book, *Development Betrayed: The End of Progress and a Coevolutionary Revisioning of the Future*, Norgaard (1994, p. 62) identified 'atomism, mechanism, universalism, objectivism, and monism' as the dominant philosophical roots of Western modernism, and noted that development had been betrayed by each of these tenets. The prevalence of the aforementioned philosophical premises has caused the exclusion of other metaphysical and epistemological premises that are better for comprehending the degradation of environmental systems and more conducive to cultural diversity. Norgaard (1994, p. 73) argued forcefully that, by publicly agreeing to monism, we not only give up a public basis for using the knowledge of other cultures, but also arbitrarily throw out answers that might be just as good and reliable.

As early as the 1970s, two influential green writings challenged mainstream economics and greatly inspired subsequent green economists. In 1972, *The Limits to Growth* report warned that our earth's carrying capacity would be exceeded within 100 years if the present growth trends in population, pollution, production and resource use persisted (Meadows *et al.*, 1972). Then, in his low-frequency, well-remembered *Small is Beautiful*, E.F. Schumacher suggested, for example, a return to ecologically sound agricultural techniques and communal ownership for a better society, and challenged mainstream economics:

> Economists themselves, like most specialists, normally suffer from a kind of metaphysical blindness, assuming that theirs is a science of absolute and invariable truths, without any presuppositions.... Buddhist economics must be very different from the economics of modern materialism, since the Buddhist sees the essence of civilisation not in a multiplication of wants but in the purification of human character.... A Buddhist economist would consider ... consumption merely a means to human well-being, the aim should be to obtain the maximum of well-being with the minimum of consumption. (Schumacher, 1973, Ch. 4)

Three decades ago, Nicholas Georgescu-Roegen, a pioneer in the field of ecological economics and a lone maverick in his day, advocated the abandonment of two pillars of mainstream economics, discounting the future and maximizing utility, and pessimistically uttered that, with regard to future generations, 'our policy toward natural resources must seek to *minimize regrets*' (Georgescu-Roegen, 1977, p. 375). Emerging as a dismal green economist, Georgescu-Roegen's intellectual inquiry has inspired economists to some extent. Indeed, many economics students have not been merely insufficiently educated; they have been miseducated on a huge scale (see, for example, the Post-Autistic Economics Network). Undoubtedly, more and more academics will join the green movements to take their shared responsibility for the earth. The latest emergence of green economics is a promising sign of such concerns and endeavours (Lawson, 2006; Wall, 2006).

More importantly, the narrow academic circles must be expanded to consider the significance of indigenous knowledge to advance the global knowledge commons (Dei *et al.*, 2000). The global village on earth is composed of numerous (but finite) knowledge economies. The scope or dimension of each economy can range from a small community of a country (such as the Onge people of India) to a regional integration of many countries (such as the European Union). To expand the global knowledge commons, we have to fully acknowledge and protect the characteristics of each unique knowledge system (such as indigenous knowledge possessed by a small tribe), and then help each knowledge commons develop into a specific set of economic institutions that interact with each other in a global environment. That is, each knowledge economy is best developed based upon its characteristics that are distinct from others. Once knowledge prevails in a global society, each community (whether a small tribe or a regional integration) can improve its own development by absorbing knowledge from the global commons. In addition, it can expand the global commons by injecting knowledge into it. Gradually, this process will contribute to the emergence of new economic institutions compatible with the long-term development goals of each community (such as developing a self-reliant economy with limited external trade or pursuing economic equality for social justice), and lead to sustainable development in a global environment.

10. Conclusions

This paper has shown that the unifaceted exposition of the knowledge economy from the perspective of increased production and accumulation has been far from perfect and cannot fulfil our goal of a sustainable future. Both the Austrian analysis of the knowledge subject and the mainstream exposition of the knowledge economy have been grounded on the concept of market competition and purported to be value-free. This paper emphasizes that the conventional concept of competition is insufficient for promoting the long-term development of human societies, and proposes that the concept of economic freedom should be expanded to incorporate the choice of other economic institutions (more than free market institutions) created for satisfying different groups of people.

Global sustainability is a *de facto* shared responsibility of overlapping generations. Fundamental to this holistic perspective is the recognition that human generations are interrelated and ought to be examined as an integrated whole. One can easily observe that the global community has become less and less sustainable due to rising economic inequality and environmental degradation. To maintain a sustainable society with an efficient use of resources, it is necessary to achieve a more equitable distribution of wealth. In this regard, this paper has argued that the notion of sustainable development has in its roots John Stuart Mill's stationary state, a value-driven vision of a good future. Mill is one of the earliest green thinkers and his stationary state is an ideal society with an emphasis on unlimited growth in mental culture and improvements in economic equality (by means of wealth redistribution), a vision that is in line with contemporary analysis of a sustainable society.

This paper also stresses the significance of indigenous knowledge for promoting a sustainable society. Indigenous knowledge is seen to be particularly abundant in the knowledge of the natural environment and is critically important to the sustainable use of resources and balanced development. Thus, it is preferable to recognize that our earth is composed of numerous knowledge economies. In this perspective, each knowledge economy is best developed based upon its characteristics that are distinct from others. To help emancipate the current growth-oriented capitalist society and lead socioeconomic progress to a state of global sustainability, this paper concludes that we have to take active participation in promoting green politics to steer peoples' values towards new social objectives and in developing academic pluralism to advance the global knowledge commons.

Acknowledgements

This paper is an enhanced and extended version of three of my articles: 'A Sustainable Perspective on the Knowledge Economy: A Critique of Austrian and Mainstream Views', 'Human Capital and Knowledge' and 'Green Politics'. The research leading to this paper has been primarily financed by the US Fulbright program and conducted under the auspices of Augustana College, South Dakota. Earlier versions of this paper were presented at a seminar in the Department of Agricultural Economics at Michigan State University on 16 June 2005, in the US Society for Ecological Economics (USSEE) Third Biennial Conference in Tacoma, Washington, 20–23 July 2005, and at the European Association for Evolutionary Political Economy (EAEPE) 17th Annual Conference in Bremen, Germany, 10–12 November 2005. The author would especially like to thank Donald George and anonymous reviewers for their helpful comments and suggestions.

Notes

1. In the economics literature, 'human capital' and 'knowledge' are frequently used interchangeably and broadly refer to people's acquired or innate abilities that are conducive to productivity and economic growth. An embryonic emphasis on human capital or knowledge can be seen as far back to the early works of Adam Smith and David Ricardo (Kurz, 1997; Nerdrum, 1999, pp. 15–19). See Lin (2008a) for an encyclopaedic examination of human capital and knowledge.
2. Machlup died on 30 January 1983 and did not finish his monumental inquiry, the Knowledge Project (which as planned was to cover 10 volumes).
3. Practical knowledge can be further subdivided into six types: (1) professional knowledge, (2) business knowledge, (3) workman's knowledge, (4) political knowledge, (5) household knowledge and (6) other practical knowledge.
4. Unwanted knowledge is not related to a person's interests. It is acquired by chance and retained purposelessly.
5. The data for the information services were incomplete.
6. The term 'information economy' has been occasionally recognized as a synonym for 'knowledge economy'. However, it conveys relatively limited content and primarily refers to the importance of information and communication technology for economic growth. For the latest studies of the information economy, see OECD (2002) and Varian et al. (2004). For a critical review of the historical development

and progress of the information economy, see Babe (1994) and Lamberton (1994).

7. Landreth and Colander (1994, Ch. 14) have identified five groups of American heterodox economic schools based on political viewpoints that range from liberal to conservative, namely, the Radicals, Institutionalists, Post-Keynesians, Public Choice Advocates and Neo-Austrians (or simply the Austrian School). Important economists in the Austrian School include Ludwig von Mises, Friedrich Hayek, and their students Murray Rothbard, Israel Kirzner and Ludwig Lachman.

8. For a thorough review of Hayek's intellectual journey and work, see Caldwell (2004).

9. In recent years, the ideas of IPRs and the enforcement of trade-related aspects of intellectual property rights (TRIPS), which integrated IPRs into global trade, have attracted increased attention and debate. Proponents of the IPRs, on the one hand, believe that the current system not only can protect the process of invention and innovation but can also provide economic incentives for creative activities. Opponents, on the other hand, generally hold the view that the protection of IPRs has been implemented at the expense of the public knowledge domain. Richards (2002) examines justificatory arguments in defence of IPRs based on the philosophical writings of Locke, Hegel and Bentham, and finds that their defences for private property rights do not hold up well when applied to intellectual property. Boldrin and Levine (2002) think that intellectual property might be better referred to as 'intellectual monopoly' and argue that the extent of current copyrights has been excessive. See also Lessig (2001) for a similar conclusion. Hui and Png (2002) studied the impact of a change in the US copyright law in 1998 in relation to movie production and found that the Sonny Bono Act has only had a small impact on new creative activity.

10. Romer is currently teaching at Stanford University. He obtained his doctorate from the University of Chicago and has also taught there.

11. For a survey of the new growth theory up to the mid-1990s, see the symposium papers (Grossman and Helpman, 1994; Pack, 1994; Romer, 1994; Solow, 1994) that appeared in the *Journal of Economic Perspectives*.

12. See Nerdrum (1999) for a description of the development of the human capital theory. For a review of different approaches to measuring human capital in the growth literature, see Wößmann (2003) and Le *et al.* (2003).

13. Carlaw and Lipsey (2003) have recently argued that total factor productivity is not a good measure of technological change and proposed a growth model driven by general purpose technology.

14. In Arrow's (1962) paper on learning by doing, he constructed a model with physical capital spillovers. For a comparison with Romer (1986) and Lucas (1988), Romer (1994) assumed that output for firm i in the Arrow model can be expressed as $Y_i = A(K)F(K_i, L_i)$. In this expression, the level of technology, A, is a function of aggregate stock of capital.

15. A more apt title might be 'On the Mechanics of Economic Growth'.

16. Horwitz (2000) has recently offered an exposition of what Austrian macroeconomics would look like.

17. Even though Hayek (1945, p. 521) emphasized that 'scientific knowledge is not the sum of all knowledge' and identified the kind of 'knowledge of the particular circumstances of time and place' and further elaborated his analyses through Polanyi's introduction of *tacit knowledge*, it all became the purpose for illustrating the competitive market process. In the current growth-oriented atmosphere, it might be

mentioned here that the *discovery* of tacit knowledge has linked it to another inquiry pertinent to growth or competitiveness (e.g. Leonard and Sensiper, 1998; Lawson and Lorenz, 1999; Maskell and Malmberg, 1999; Desrochers, 2001; Langlois, 2001; Howells, 2002).

18. For a discussion of the development of evolutionary economics, see Hodgson (1999, Ch. 6).

19. Sen (1992) has argued that traditional income inequality measures are inadequate measures for both egalitarian gains and failures. Even so, these measures can still be regarded as close substitutes for the perfect measures that might be developed in the future.

20. See http://www.census.gov/hhes/www/income/histinc/ineqtoc.html (Table IE-6).

21. These countries are Australia, Belgium, Canada, Denmark, Finland, France, Germany, Italy, Japan, the Netherlands, Norway, Sweden and the USA.

22. Using the WHO statistics, Stevens (2004, p. 4) estimates that diseases associated with poverty account for about 45% of the disease burden in the poorest countries.

23. Both disease eradication and global peace are actually considered important international (or global) public goods (Kaul *et al.*, 1999; Ferroni and Mody, 2002). A pure international public good, in principle, can generate benefits that spill over borders, regions, ethnic groups and generations. It is quite conceivable that the provision of international public goods remains insufficient in the absence of an international government. In his presidential address to the AEA entitled 'International Public Goods without International Government', Kindleberger (1986, p. 11) commented that 'the system should be run at all times by rules, including regimes, not people'.

24. For Schumpeter, he was also a conservative but he 'acknowledged the power of Marx's vision of historical change' (Landreth and Colander, 1994, p. 390).

25. The field of 'institutional economics' claimed by the institutionalists to be their economic discipline can be divided into two strands: 'original' institutional economics (OIE) and 'new' institutional economics. The research of the OIE scholars extends back to the early works of Thorstein B. Veblen and John R. Commons. The new institutionalists are more associated with the mainstream neoclassical tradition and include several well-known scholars such as Ronald Coase, Douglass North and Oliver Williamson. For a detailed examination of the two major traditions of institutionalist thought in economics, see Rutherford (1994).

26. The lack of discussion of green accounting is a clear example of the mainstream's narrowness. Leading undergraduate macro texts such as Dornbusch *et al.* (2001) and Mankiw (2000) do not even mention a word on green accounting or green GDP. Leading graduate macro texts such as Barro and Sala-i-Martin (2004) and Blanchard and Fischer (1989) are preoccupied with mathematical models in dealing with the growth issue, not to mention the trivial green GDP (in their opinion).

27. To *escape* competition, the best strategy for older generations is the decision to use all the society's resources and not have any offspring. Obviously, this scenario has not yet occurred in human history.

28. I am grateful to Chiaen J. Wu for suggesting this figure.

29. This essay was collected in Keynes's work *Essays in Persuasion* (1963).

30. Daly (1996) provides a discussion about the conflict between long-term economic growth and the carrying capacity of the environment.

31. At the same time, many Americans have become more obese and suffer from associated diseases because of overeating and over-use of television and automobiles.

The negative impact of over-consumption on the environment has long been recognized by environmentalists (see, for example, Jacobs, 1997). The mainstream literature has recently begun to explore this issue (Arrow *et al.*, 2004).

32. Check the 'World Earth Day' (http://www.earthday.net) and the 'International Buy Nothing Day' (http://www.ecoplan.org/ibnd/ib_index.htm) movements, for example. The first Earth Day was organized by Denis Hayes and the late US Senator Gaylord Nelson in 1970 to raise public awareness to environmental crises. To date, Earth Day international network has now reached more than 12,000 organizations in 174 countries, while the US program has kept over 3000 groups and over 100,000 educators coordinating countless community development and environmental protection activities.

33. Indeed, before the Kyoto Protocol was to be negotiated in December 1997, the US Senate unanimously passed the Byrd–Hagel Resolution (S. Res. 98), sponsored by Democratic Party Senator Robert Byrd and Republican Party Senator Chuck Hagel, with a 95–0 vote in July 1997. The Resolution states that 'the United States should not be a signatory to any protocol to, or other agreement regarding, the United Nations Framework Convention on Climate Change of 1992, at negotiations in Kyoto in December 1997, or thereafter, which ... would result in serious harm to the economy of the United States' (S. Res. 98).

References

Aghion, P. and Howitt, P. (1992) A model of growth through creative destruction. *Econometrica* 60(2): 323–351.

Aghion, P. and Howitt, P. (1998) *Endogenous Growth Theory*. Cambridge, MA: MIT Press.

Ansuategi, A. and Escapa, M. (2002) Economic growth and greenhouse gas emissions. *Ecological Economics* 40(1): 23–37.

Armentano, D.T. (1999) *Antitrust: The Case for Repeal* (revised 2nd edn). Auburn, AL: Ludwig von Mises Institute.

Arrow, K.J. (1962) The economic implications of learning by doing. *Review of Economic Studies* 29(3): 155–173.

Arrow, K., Dasgupta, P., Goulder, L., Daily, G., Ehrlich, P., Heal, G., Levin, S., Mäler, K.-G., Schneider, S., Starrett, D. and Walker, B. (2004) Are we consuming too much? *Journal of Economic Perspectives* 18(3): 147–172.

Atkinson, R.D. and Court, R.H. (1998) *The New Economy Index: Understanding America's Economic Transformation*. Washington, DC: Progressive Policy Institute.

Babe, R.E. (1994) The place of information in economics. In R.E. Babe (ed.), *Information and Communication in Economics* (pp. 41–67). Boston, MA: Kluwer Academic.

Babu, P.G., Kumar, K.S.K. and Murthy, N.S. (1997) An overlapping generations model with exhaustible resources and stock pollution. *Ecological Economics* 21(1): 35–43.

Baetjer, H., Jr (2000) Capital as embodied knowledge: some implications for the theory of economic growth. *Review of Austrian Economics* 13(2): 147–174.

Barlett, D.L. and Steele, J.B. (1994) *America: Who Really Pays the Taxes?* New York: Simon & Schuster.

Barro, R.J. and Sala-i-Martin, X. (2004) *Economic Growth* (2nd edn). Cambridge, MA: MIT Press.

Becker, G. (1964) *Human Capital: A Theoretical and Empirical Analysis, with Special Reference to Education*. New York: National Bureau of Economic Research.

Blanchard, O.J. and Fischer, S. (1989) *Lectures on Macroeconomics*. Cambridge, MA: MIT Press.

Boldrin, M. and Levine, D.K. (2002) The case against intellectual property. *American Economic Review, Papers and Proceedings* 92(2): 209–212.

Boulding, K.E. (1966) The economics of knowledge and the knowledge of economics. *American Economic Review* 56(1/2): 1–13.

Boulding, K.E. (1969) Economics as a moral science. *American Economic Review* 59(1): 1–12.

Brokensha, D., Warren, D.M. and Werner, O. (eds) (1980) *Indigenous Knowledge Systems and Development.* Lanham, MD: University Press of America.

Burniaux, J.-M., Dang, T.-T., Fore, D., Förster, M., d'Ercole, M.M. and Oxley, H. (1998) Income distribution and poverty in selected OECD countries. *OECD Economics Department Working Papers 189,* March.

Caldwell, B. (2004) *Hayek's Challenge: An Intellectual Biography of F.A. Hayek.* Chicago, IL, and London: University of Chicago Press.

Carlaw, K.I. and Lipsey, R.G. (2003) Productivity, technology and economic growth: what is the relationship? *Journal of Economic Surveys* 17(3): 457–495.

Carlaw, K., Oxley, L., Walker, P., Thorns, D. and Nuth, M. (2006) Beyond the hype: intellectual property and the knowledge society/knowledge economy. *Journal of Economic Surveys* 20(4): 633–690.

Conca, K. (2001) Green politics in the Bush era: anti-environmentalism's second wave. *Dissent* 48(3): 29–33.

Daly, H.E. (1973) The steady-state economy: toward a political economy of biophysical equilibrium and moral growth. In H.E. Daly (ed.), *Toward a Steady-State Economy* (pp. 149–174). San Francisco, CA: W.H. Freeman.

Daly, H.E. (1977) *Steady-State Economics: The Economics of Biophysical Equilibrium and Moral Growth.* San Francisco, CA: W.H. Freeman.

Daly, H.E. (1996) *Beyond Growth: The Economics of Sustainable Development.* Boston, MA: Beacon Press.

Daly, H.E. (2005) Economics in a full world. *Scientific American* (Special Issue) 293(3): 100–107.

Dasgupta, P. (1998) Population, consumption and resources: ethical issues. *Ecological Economics* 24(2–3): 139–152.

Dei, G.J.S., Hall, B.L. and Rosenberg, D.G. (eds) (2000) *Indigenous Knowledges in Global Contexts: Multiple Readings of Our World.* Toronto: University of Toronto Press.

Desrochers, P. (1998) On the abuse of patents as economic indicators. *Quarterly Journal of Austrian Economics* 1(4): 51–74.

Desrochers, P. (2001) Geographical proximity and the transmission of tacit knowledge. *Review of Austrian Economics* 14(1): 25–46.

Diamond, J. (2005) *Collapse: How Societies Choose to Fail or Succeed.* New York: Viking.

Dornbusch, R., Fischer, S. and Startz, R. (2001) *Macroeconomics* (8th edn). New York: McGraw-Hill.

Ekelund, R.B., Jr and Hébert, R.F. (1997) *A History of Economic Theory and Method* (4th edn). Singapore: McGraw-Hill.

Ellen, R., Parkes, P. and Bicker, A. (eds) (2000) *Indigenous Environmental Knowledge and its Transformation: Critical Anthropological Perspectives.* Amsterdam: Harwood Academic.

Farmer, M.C. (2005) Environmental consequences of social security reform: a second best threat to public conservation. *Ecological Economics* 53(2): 191–209.

Farmer, M.C. and Randall, A. (1997) Policies for sustainability: lessons from an overlapping generations model. *Land Economics* 73(4): 608–622.

Fernando, J.L. (2003) NGOs and production of indigenous knowledge under the condition of postmodernity. *Annals of the American Academy of Political and Social Sciences* 590: 54–72.

Ferroni, M.A. and Mody, A. (eds) (2002) *International Public Goods: Incentives, Measurement, and Financing*. Boston, MA: Kluwer Academic.

Freeman, S. and Polasky, S. (1992) Knowledge-based growth. *Journal of Monetary Economics* 30(1): 3–24.

Gadgil, M., Berkes, F. and Folke, C. (1993) Indigenous knowledge for biodiversity conservation. *Ambio* 22(2–3): 151–156.

Galbraith, J.K. (1992) *The Culture of Contentment*. Boston, MA: Houghton Mifflin.

Georgescu-Roegen, N. (1977) Inequality, limits and growth from a bioeconomic viewpoint. *Review of Social Economy* 35(3): 361–375.

Grossman, G.M. and Helpman, E. (1991) *Innovation and Growth in the Global Economy*. Cambridge, MA: MIT Press.

Grossman, G.M. and Helpman, E. (1994) Endogenous innovation in the theory of growth. *Journal of Economic Perspectives* 8(1): 23–44.

Harris, J.M. (2000) Introduction to part 2: power, knowledge, and institutions in development practice. In J.M. Harris (ed.), *Rethinking Sustainability: Power, Knowledge, and Institutions* (pp. 141–150). Ann Arbor, MI: University of Michigan Press.

Hayek, F.A. (1937) Economics and knowledge. *Economica* 4(13): 33–54.

Hayek, F.A. (1945) The use of knowledge in society. *American Economic Review* 35(4): 519–530.

Hayek, F.A. (1973) *Law, Legislation and Liberty*, Vol. 1: *Rules and Order*. Chicago, IL: University of Chicago Press.

Hayek, F.A. (1974) The pretence of knowledge. The Nobel Prize Lecture, 11 December.

Hodgson, G.M. (1999) *Evolution and Institutions: On Evolutionary Economics and the Evolution of Economics*. Cheltenham: Edward Elgar.

Horwitz, S. (2000) *Microfoundations and Macroeconomics: An Austrian Perspective*. New York: Routledge.

Howarth, R.B. (1991) Intertemporal equilibria and exhaustible resources: an overlapping generations approach. *Ecological Economics* 4(3): 237–252.

Howarth, R.B. and Norgaard, R.B. (1990) Intergenerational resources rights, efficiency, and social optimality. *Land Economics* 66(1): 1–11.

Howells, J.R.L. (2002) Tacit knowledge, innovation and economic geography. *Urban Studies* 39(5–6): 871–884.

Hui, K.-L. and Png, I.P.L. (2002) On the supply of creative work: evidence from the movies. *American Economic Review, Papers and Proceedings* 92(2): 217–220.

Hunt, E.K. (1992) *History of Economic Thought: A Critical Perspective* (2nd edn). New York: HarperCollins.

Jacobs, J.M. (1994) Earth honoring: western desires and indigenous knowledges. In A. Blunt and G. Rose (eds), *Writing Women and Space: Colonial and Postcolonial Geographies* (pp. 169–196). New York: Guilford Press.

Jacobs, M. (ed.) (1997) *Greening the Millennium? The New Politics of the Environment*. Oxford: Blackwell.

Jones, C.I. (1995) R&D-based models of economic growth. *Journal of Political Economy* 103(4): 759–784.

Kasper, W. and Streit, M.E. (1998) *Institutional Economics: Social Order and Public Policy*. Cheltenham: Edward Elgar.

Kaul, I., Grunberg, I. and Stern, M.A. (eds) (1999) *Global Public Goods: International Cooperation in the 21st Century*. New York: Oxford University Press.

Keister, L.A. (2000) *Wealth in America: Trends in Wealth Inequality*. New York: Cambridge University Press.

Keynes, J.M. (1963) *Essays in Persuasion*. New York: W.W. Norton.

Kindleberger, C.P. (1986) International public goods without international government. *American Economic Review* 76(1): 1–13.

Kirzner, I.M. (1997) Entrepreneurial discovery and the competitive market process: an Austrian approach. *Journal of Economic Literature* 35(1): 60–85.

Kurz, H.D. (1997) What could the 'new' growth theory teach Smith or Ricardo? *Economic Issues* 2(2): 1–20.

Lamberton, D.M. (1994) The information economy revisited. In R.E. Babe (ed.), *Information and Communication in Economics* (pp. 1–33). Boston, MA: Kluwer Academic.

Landreth, H. and Colander, D.C. (1994) *History of Economic Thought* (3rd edn). Boston, MA: Houghton Mifflin.

Langlois, R.N. (1985) From the knowledge of economics to the economics of knowledge: Fritz Machlup on methodology and on the knowledge society. In W.J. Samuels (ed.), *Research in the History of Economic Thought and Methodology: A Research Annual*, Vol. 3 (pp. 225–235). Greenwich, CT: JAI Press.

Langlois, R.N. (1991) Knowledge and rationality in the Austrian school: an analytical survey. In J.C. Wood and R.N. Woods (eds), *Friedrich A. Hayek: Critical Assessments*, Vol. IV (pp. 118–140). London and New York: Routledge,

Langlois, R.N. (2001) Knowledge, consumption, and endogenous growth. *Journal of Evolutionary Economics* 11(1): 77–93.

Lawson, C. and Lorenz, E. (1999) Collective learning, tacit knowledge and regional innovative capacity. *Regional Studies* 33(4): 305–317.

Lawson, R. (2006) An overview of green economics. *International Journal of Green Economics* 1(1/2): 23–36.

Le, T., Gibson, J. and Oxley, L. (2003) Cost- and income-based measures of human capital. *Journal of Economic Surveys* 17(3): 271–307.

Leonard, D. and Sensiper, S. (1998) The role of tacit knowledge in group innovation. *California Management Review* 40(3): 112–132.

Lessig, L. (2001) *The Future of Ideas: The Fate of the Commons in a Connected World*. New York: Random House.

Lin, B.C.-A. (2006) A sustainable perspective on the knowledge economy: a critique of Austrian and mainstream views. *Ecological Economics* 60(1): 324–332.

Lin, B.C.-A. (2008a) Human capital and knowledge. In P.A. O'Hara (ed.), *International Encyclopedia of Public Policy*, Vol. 4: *Social, Environmental and Corporate Governance*, forthcoming. Perth: GPERU.

Lin, B.C.-A. (2008b) Green politics. In P.A. O'Hara (ed.), *International Encyclopedia of Public Policy*, Vol. 4: *Social, Environmental and Corporate Governance*, forthcoming. Perth: GPERU.

Lucas, R.E., Jr (1988) On the mechanics of economic development. *Journal of Monetary Economics* 22(1): 3–42.

Machlup, F. (1962) *The Production and Distribution of Knowledge in the United States*. Princeton, NJ: Princeton University Press.

Machlup, F. (1976) Hayek's contribution to economics. In F. Machlup (ed.), *Essays on Hayek* (pp. 13–59). New York: New York University Press.

Machlup, F. (1980) *Knowledge: Its Creation, Distribution, and Economic Significance*, Vol. I: *Knowledge and Knowledge Production*. Princeton, NJ: Princeton University Press.

Machlup, F. (1982) *Knowledge: Its Creation, Distribution, and Economic Significance*, Vol. II: *The Branches of Learning*. Princeton, NJ: Princeton University Press.

Machlup, F. (1984) *Knowledge: Its Creation, Distribution, and Economic Significance*, Vol. III: *The Economics of Information and Human Capital*. Princeton, NJ: Princeton University Press.

Mankiw, N.G. (2000) *Macroeconomics* (4th edn). New York: Worth Publishers.

Marinova, D. and Raven, M. (2006) Indigenous knowledge and intellectual property: a sustainability agenda. *Journal of Economic Surveys* 20(4): 587–605.

Maskell, P. and Malmberg, A. (1999) Localised learning and industrial competitiveness. *Cambridge Journal of Economics* 23(2): 167–185.

Meadows, D.H., Meadows, D.L., Randers, J. and Behrens, W.B. III (1972) *The Limits to Growth*. New York: Universe Books.

Meadows, D., Randers, J. and Meadows, D. (2005) *Limits to Growth: The 30-Year Update*. London: Earthscan.

Mill, J.S. (1965) *Principles of Political Economy with Some of Their Applications to Social Philosophy* (edited with an introduction by W.J. Ashley, first published in 1848). New York: Augustus M. Kelley.

Mokyr, J. (2002) *The Gifts of Athena: Historical Origins of the Knowledge Economy*. Princeton, NJ: Princeton University Press.

Murray, G. and Cook, I.G. (2002) *Green China: Seeking Ecological Alternatives*. London and New York: RoutledgeCurzon.

Myrdal, G. (1958) *Value in Social Theory: A Selection of Essays on Methodology* (edited by P. Streeten). London: Routledge & Kegan Paul.

Myrdal, G. (1968) *Asian Drama: An Inquiry into the Poverty of Nations*, 3 volumes. New York: Pantheon.

Myrdal, G. (1974) What is development? *Journal of Economic Issues* 8(4): 729–736.

Myrdal, G. (1978) Institutional economics. *Journal of Economic Issues* 12(4): 771–783.

Myrdal, G. (1981) What is political economy? In R.A. Solo and C.W. Anderson (eds), *Value Judgement and Income Distribution* (pp. 41–53). New York: Praeger.

Neef, D. (ed.) (1998) *The Knowledge Economy*. Boston, MA: Butterworth-Heinemann.

Nelson, R.R. (1996) *The Sources of Economic Growth*. Cambridge, MA: Harvard University Press.

Nerdrum, L. (1999) *The Economics of Human Capital: A Theoretical Analysis Illustrated Empirically*. Oslo: Scandinavian University Press.

Newman, K.S. (1988) *Falling from Grace: The Experience of Downward Mobility in the American Middle Class*. New York: Free Press.

Newman, K.S. (1993) *Declining Fortunes: The Withering of the American Dream*. New York: Basic Books.

Norchi, C.H. (2000) Indigenous knowledge as intellectual property. *Policy Sciences* 33(3–4): 387–398.

Norgaard, R.B. (1994) *Development Betrayed: The End of Progress and a Coevolutionary Revisioning of the Future*. London and New York: Routledge.

Oakman, B. (1986) Patents: an Austrian perspective. *Economic Papers* 5(1): 74–81.

O'Connor, M. (1997) John Stuart Mill's utilitarianism and the social ethics of sustainable development. *European Journal of the History of Economic Thought* 4(3): 478–506.

OECD (1996) *The Knowledge-Based Economy*. Paris.

OECD (2002) *Measuring the Information Economy*. Paris. http://www.oecd.org/sti/measuring-infoeconomy, accessed July 2005.

OECD (2003) *DAC Guidelines and Reference Documents: Poverty and Health*. Paris.

Pack, H. (1994) Endogenous growth theory: intellectual appeal and empirical shortcomings. *Journal of Economic Perspectives* 8(1): 55–72.

Paganetto, L. (ed.) (2004) *Knowledge Economy, Information Technologies and Growth*. Burlington, VT: Ashgate.

Peterson, W.C. (1994) *Silent Depression: The Fate of the American Dream*. New York: W.W. Norton.

Plenderleith, K. (ed.) (2004) *Indigenous Knowledge and Ethics: A Darrell Posey Reader*. New York and London: Routledge.

Polanyi, M. (1958) *Personal Knowledge: Towards a Post-Critical Philosophy*. Chicago, IL: University of Chicago Press.

Porat, M.U. and Rubin, M.R. (1977) *The Information Economy*, 9 volumes. Washington, DC: US Government Printing Office.

Rainbow, S. (1993) *Green Politics*. New York: Oxford University Press.

Richards, D.G. (2002) The ideology of intellectual property rights in the international economy. *Review of Social Economy* 60(4): 521–541.

Romer, P.M. (1986) Increasing returns and long-run growth. *Journal of Political Economy* 94(5): 1002–1037.

Romer, P.M. (1990) Endogenous technological change. *Journal of Political Economy* 98(5): S71–S102.

Romer, P.M. (1994) The origins of endogenous growth. *Journal of Economic Perspectives* 8(1): 3–22.

Rubin, M.R., Huber, M.T. and Taylor, E.L. (1986) *The Knowledge Industry in the United States: 1960–1980*. Princeton, NJ: Princeton University Press.

Rutherford, M. (1994) *Institutions in Economics: The Old and the New Institutionalism*. New York: Cambridge University Press.

Schultz, T.W. (1963) *The Economic Value of Education*. New York: Columbia University Press.

Schumacher, E.F. (1973) *Small is Beautiful: Economics as if People Really Mattered*. London: Abacus.

Schumpeter, J.A. (1975) *Capitalism, Socialism, and Democracy* (first published in 1942, with a new introduction by Tom Bottomore) (1st Harper Colophon edn). New York: Harper & Row.

Semali, L.M. and Kincheloe, J.L. (eds) (1999) *What Is Indigenous Knowledge? Voices from the Academy*. New York and London: Falmer Press.

Sen, A.K. (1992) *Inequality Reexamined*. New York: Russell Sage Foundation.

Söderbaum, P. (1999) Values, ideology and politics in ecological economics. *Ecological Economics* 28(2): 161–170.

Solow, R.M. (1956) A contribution to the theory of economic growth. *Quarterly Journal of Economics* 70: 65–94.

Solow, R.M. (1994) Perspectives on growth theory. *Journal of Economic Perspectives* 8(1): 45–54.

Stevens, P. (2004) *Diseases of Poverty and the 10/90 Gap*. London: International Policy Network.

Strobel, F.R. (1993) *Upward Dreams, Downward Mobility: The Economic Decline of the American Middle Class*. Lanham, MD: Rowman and Littlefield.

Strobel, F.R. and Peterson, W.C. (1997) Class conflict, American style: distract and conquer. *Journal of Economic Issues* 31(2): 433–443.

Tachibanaki, T. (2006) Inequality and poverty in Japan. *Japanese Economic Review* 57(1): 1–27.

Thurow, L.C. (1999) *Building Wealth: The New Rules for Individuals, Companies, and Nations in a Knowledge-Based Economy*. New York: HarperCollins.

United Nations (2005) *Report on the World Social Situation: The Inequality Predicament*. New York: Department of Economic and Social Affairs.

Van Den Bergh, J.C.J.M. (1996) *Ecological Economics and Sustainable Development: Theory, Methods and Applications*. Cheltenham: Edward Elgar.

Varian, H.R., Farrell, J. and Shapiro, C. (2004) *The Economics of Information Technology: An Introduction*. New York: Cambridge University Press.

Vaughn, K.I. (1990) The Mengerian roots of the Austrian revival. *History of Political Economy* (supplemental issue) 22: 379–407.

Vaughn, K.I. (1994) *Austrian Economics in America: The Migration of a Tradition*. New York: Cambridge University Press.

Wachtel, P.L. (1998) Overconsumption. In R. Keil, D.V.J. Bell, P. Penz and L. Fawcett (eds), *Political Ecology: Global and Local* (pp. 259–271). London and New York: Routledge.

Wall, D. (2006) Green economics: an introduction and research agenda. *International Journal of Green Economics* 1(1/2): 201–214.

Weatherford, J.M. (1994) *Savages and Civilization: Who Will Survive?* New York: Crown Publishers.

WHO (2006) *Health and Economic Development in South-Eastern Europe.* Paris: WHO Regional Office for Europe and Council of Europe Development Bank.

Winch, D. (2004) Thinking green, nineteenth-century style: John Stuart Mill and John Ruskin. In M. Bevir and F. Trentmann (eds), *Markets in Historical Contexts: Ideas and Politics in the Modern World* (pp. 105–128). New York: Cambridge University Press.

Wößmann, L. (2003) Specifying human capital. *Journal of Economic Surveys* 17(3): 239–270.

World Bank (1997) *Sharing Rising Incomes: Disparities in China.* Washington, DC.

Yi, Z. (2001) *China's Ecological Winter* (in Chinese). Hong Kong: Mirror Books.

8

EVOLUTIONARY AND NEW GROWTH THEORIES. ARE THEY CONVERGING?

Fulvio Castellacci

Norwegian Institute of International Affairs

1. Introduction

The crucial role of innovation for economic growth has been increasingly recognized in the last two decades. Taking inspiration from the works of Schumpeter (1934, 1939, 1943), a surge of interest in the study of innovation and growth started at the beginning of the 1980s with the seminal contributions in modern evolutionary economics (Dosi, 1982; Freeman *et al.*, 1982; Nelson and Winter, 1982). The new wave of theorizing was motivated by the unsatisfaction with the stylized view of technological change presented by the Solow model (1956). Sharing a similar criticism, new growth theorists made a great effort to refine the Solovian view by building up models of innovation-driven endogenous growth (Romer, 1986; Lucas, 1988; Aghion and Howitt, 1992).

Evolutionary and new growth theories have rapidly developed in the last two decades. The great surge of interest in the new growth tradition, in terms both of formal endogenous models and of the related econometric work, is well known, and there already exist various comprehensive surveys of the field (Temple, 1999; Islam, 2003; George *et al.*, 2004). The development of evolutionary economics has also been remarkable, and various critical discussions point to the strong similarities existing between the different strands of research within the evolutionary paradigm (Andersen, 1994; Nelson, 1995; Archibugi and Michie, 1998; Nelson and Winter, 2002).

Both evolutionary and new growth scholars have repeatedly recognized Schumpeter's work as a major source of inspiration. Evolutionary scholars have frequently pointed to the strong connections between Schumpeter and modern evolutionary economics (Hodgson, 1997; Fagerberg, 2003). New growth theorists have also been invoking Schumpeter as their main source of inspiration. Endogenous growth models have increasingly incorporated some of the Schumpeterian ideas on the process of technological competition and innovation-based growth, with the consequence of making the outcomes of the new growth models closer and closer to the ones of evolutionary models (Aghion and Howitt, 1998).

This leads to some major questions: given that the Schumpeterian insights into the process of economic development constitute the main source of inspiration for both evolutionary and new growth theories, how similar are the two approaches? Can we observe *theoretical convergence* between the two, as is often argued (Heertje, 1993; Romer, 1994; Ruttan, 1997; Sarkar, 1998), on the basis of the Schumpeterian flavour of both theories? These are the questions that this paper intends to answer. This paper carries out a critical survey of evolutionary and new growth theories with the purpose of analysing whether some kind of theoretical convergence is taking place between the two paradigms.

This paper differs from previous critical surveys of the field in two main respects. First, the comparison between evolutionary and new growth theories will not simply be carried out by focusing on the formal growth models developed in the two traditions, but will also include other strands of empirically oriented and non-formal studies. The latter constitute, in fact, an increasingly important part of growth theorizing, and provide inspiration and new insights for the development of modelling exercises. By enlarging the scope of the comparison, this paper will argue, it is possible to shed new lights on the similarities and differences between the two theoretical paradigms.

Second, the comparison will not be made in terms of the properties and results of evolutionary and new growth models, but it will analyse, at a more general level, the *theoretical foundations* of the two paradigms. By theoretical foundations we mean the theoretical characteristics that may be defined as the major building blocks of growth theorizing. This paper will consider six main theoretical foundations, and analyse them by discussing the following questions.

(1) What is the main level of aggregation on which the theory focuses?
(2) Is it based on the notion of representative agent or on the one of heterogeneous individuals?
(3) What is the mechanism of creation of innovation and new variety?
(4) What is the dynamics of the growth process? How is history conceived?
(5) Is the growth process deterministic or unpredictable?
(6) Does economic growth tend towards equilibrium, or is it a never ending process?

Section 2 will present these six questions in further detail, and it will define the main concepts used in the survey. Section 3 will use such theoretical questions as a framework to discuss the basic characteristics of the different streams of evolutionary economics developed in the last two decades, namely the neo-Schumpeterian long wave theory, the technology-gap approach, Nelson and Winter-like evolutionary theorizing, and the national innovation systems framework.[1] In these evolutionary strands of theory, technological change is the main engine of economic growth, which is regarded as a complex process of transformation and qualitative change.[2] The section will suggest that, to a large extent, these approaches share the same theoretical foundations, and may then be regarded as different strands of research within the same evolutionary paradigm. It will also point, though, to the existing tensions and formidable challenges currently faced by evolutionary economics. Section 4 will consider new growth theory by briefly looking at both formal models and econometric works, and by discussing their theoretical foundations. Finally, Section 5 will conclude the survey by pointing out the great differences still existing between evolutionary and new growth theories, and by claiming that no theoretical convergence is taking place between the two paradigms.

2. The Theoretical Foundations for the Study of Innovation and Growth

This section presents the six theoretical questions that we will use to discuss and to compare evolutionary and new growth theories in this paper. We believe that these six aspects constitute the major theoretical foundations for the study of innovation and growth, and thus represent the relevant characteristics that it is necessary to look at in order to compare different approaches. The section defines the main concepts used in the survey, and it briefly points to the origin of each concept in the history of economic thought. The reference to classical authors (e.g. Smith, Marx, Veblen, Schumpeter) will be brief and stylized, as the purpose is not to carry out an articulated discussion of the theoretical origins of modern theories of innovation and growth, but rather to define some important concepts and to introduce the analysis to be developed in the following sections.

2.1 What is the Main Level of Aggregation?

A first important distinctive feature of theories of innovation and economic growth is the level of aggregation chosen as the fundamental starting point to build up the theory. Three major positions may be distinguished in the history of economic thought.[3]

  (i) *Methodological individualism*: This is the approach typical of classical and neoclassical economists, as well as Schumpeter.[4] According to this, the aggregate properties of the economy must be studied by starting from the analysis of the microeconomic behaviour of consumers and firms. The whole economic system must be analysed by looking at its component parts; the macroeconomic theory must necessarily be microfounded.

 (ii) *Methodological holism* (Hodgson, 1993, p. 238): This is the approach typical of Karl Marx, and later frequently adopted in economic sociology and heterodox macroeconomics.[5] Here, it is the social and macroeconomic structure to determine the behaviour of economic agents. The component parts of the economic system can only be studied by analysing the whole; the microeconomic element depends to a large extent on the macroeconomic structure.

(iii) *Non-reductionism*: The previous two positions are both said to be 'reductionist', in that they only consider a one-way relationship between different levels of aggregation: either the micro determines the macroeconomic element, or the latter affects the former. An alternative to these reductionist views, not fully developed yet in modern economic theory, was proposed long ago by Veblen

(1899, 1919).[6] He suggested that important interrelationships exist between
the formation of individuals' habits of thought and aggregate institutional
regularities. In his view, the macroeconomic and social regularities are
determined by the behaviour of individuals, but economic agents are in turn
greatly affected by the macrostructure in which they live. This tentative
description of a co-evolution between different levels of analysis may be
labelled 'non-reductionism' (Hodgson, 1993, pp. 246–248), in that there does
not exist a single dominant level of aggregation, but each level interacts
with the others. As Section 3 will point out, modern evolutionary economists
frequently call for some form of non-reductionism in the attempt to analyse
the co-evolution across different levels of analysis (Dosi and Winter, 2000),
although no significant advance in this respect has been obtained yet since
the times of Veblen.

2.2 *Representative Agent or Heterogeneous Individuals?*

This question refers to the way in which (micro) economic agents are represented in
the theoretical framework. In the history of economic thought, we may distinguish
between some major different approaches.

(i) *Neoclassical typological thinking*: This is the position adopted by neoclassical
economics since the marginalist revolution, according to which economic
agents can be studied by analysing the behaviour of a 'representative agent'.
In the simplest and most standard version of the neoclassical metaphor, the
economic agent is typically described as a rational maximizer of utility/profits
under given constraints and perfect information.

(ii) *Smithian typological thinking*: According to Adam Smith and, later, Herbert
Spencer economic agents are genetically similar and homogeneous, but the
production process and the division of labour bring differentiation in skills
and tasks because individuals learn 'by doing'. Heterogeneity, in this case,
is not a precondition but a consequence of the process of economic growth.
It is not a genetic attribute of economic agents, but a characteristic acquired
during their working life.

(iii) *Marxist typological thinking*: Karl Marx pointed to the existence of a fundamental opposition between two different social classes, the capitalists and
the proletarians. These two classes are defined in terms of their relationship
to the means of production, and have permanently different interests and
purposes. However, within each class, individuals are homogeneous. In other
words, Marx implicitly assumes the existence of a duality between social
classes at the macroeconomic level, but not heterogeneity of individuals at
the microeconomic.

(iv) *Schumpeterian typological thinking*: In Schumpeter (1934, 1939), the microeconomic description of economic agents is rather peculiar. On one hand,
there is a group of individuals, the entrepreneurs, genetically endowed with
special psychological characteristics; they are the ones to determine the

growth process, the real source of change. On the other hand, however, all the other economic agents are ordinary and undifferentiated individuals, not dissimilar from the representative agents of neoclassical theory, who react in a deterministic way to the changes of the process over time. This appears as an intermediate position between neoclassical typological thinking and evolutionary biology's 'population thinking'.

(v) *Veblen's population thinking*: Heterogeneity of economic agents is an essential characteristic of an evolutionary approach to economic change, an early example being the work of Veblen (1899). Inspired by the developments of evolutionary biology, Veblen believed in the existence of a fundamental element of heterogeneity in individuals' cognitive processes and in the formation of habits of thought, and originally pointed out that this variety is an important precondition for the process of economic growth and social change. Applying the biological metaphor to economics, 'population thinking' means that economic theory cannot ignore the heterogeneity in the population of economic agents, but must necessarily be built on that, as variety is the major source of novelty (innovation) in the process of economic development.[7]

2.3 What is the Mechanism of Creation of Innovation and New Variety?

In modern theories of innovation and growth, the mechanism through which innovation and new variety are introduced in the economic system is the main source of economic growth, and it thus constitutes a key element in the theoretical framework. Referring to classical authors, we may briefly outline these different mechanisms of technical change.[8]

(i) *Manna from heaven*: The neoclassical representative firm, in its simplest description, is assumed to have perfect and complete knowledge about the best technology available at any given time, and to always be able to adopt it. Technological knowledge is static, perfectly codifiable and independent of the economic context and situation in which firms make their technological choices. All firms, then, can easily imitate and adopt advanced techniques used by more innovative firms. Knowledge is regarded as a public good, promptly available to all economic agents without further constraints. Technical change, in the most simplified version of the neoclassical metaphor, is exogenous and unexplained.

(ii) *Learning by doing*: This is the mechanism originally suggested by Adam Smith. The production process brings deeper division of labour and increasing specialization, and economic agents learn 'by doing' things and by producing goods during their working activities. Innovation, being a necessary consequence of the productive process, is therefore endogenous, and mainly incremental and continuous.

(iii) *Labour saving technical change*: This is the mechanism pointed out by Marx, according to which capitalists introduce labour saving technical innovations to decrease labour costs and to expand their profits. However, it remains unclear in the Marxian view how the new technology is invented, selected and adopted by capitalists.[9] The real mechanism of technical change is then exogenous and unexplained.

(iv) *Schumpeterian innovation*: Schumpeter was the first author to use a broad concept of innovation which encompassed technical as well as organizational changes, and to give it a central role in the explanation of economic development. Focusing on radical rather than incremental innovations, he put forward the idea that 'new combinations' are introduced by the entrepreneurs, which are individuals endowed with special psychological traits and creativity (Schumpeter, 1934). Later in his life, he suggested that the innovative process is systematically organized and performed by research and development (R&D) laboratories within large firms (Schumpeter, 1943), rather than introduced by creative entrepreneurs.

(v) *Veblen's idle curiosity*: Veblen suggests the existence of an important source of variety which continuously opposes the inertial nature of habits of thought and institutions, namely the 'human tendency towards experimentation and creative innovation' (Hodgson, 1993, p. 127). Veblen called this tendency 'idle curiosity', and regarded it as a genetic human attitude that is a precondition for the process of growth, and not a consequence of it (as in Smith and Spencer). Veblen conceived 'idle curiosity' as analogous to mutations in Darwinian evolutionary biology, and thus as an ongoing and permanent source of change and renewed variety in the economic system.

2.4 *What is the Dynamics of the Growth Process? How is History Conceived?.*

This characteristic refers to the type of dynamics of the growth process, and it is closely related to the way in which history is conceived in the theoretical framework. A brief look at the history of economic thought suggests that we may distinguish between some major different ways of conceiving economic dynamics.

(i) *Transitional dynamics*: The focus of neoclassical theory is on the static allocation of resources at a given time, and dynamic analysis is conceived as an extension of the equilibrium metaphor to the long run. Economic dynamics is regarded as a process of transition towards a new state of equilibrium. History may therefore be thought of as a process of uniform-speed transitional dynamics towards long run equilibrium, rather than a process of irreversible and qualitative change.

(ii) *Increasing complexity*: This is the position adopted by Adam Smith and Herbert Spencer, who were both deeply interested in issues of transformation and dynamics, rather than resource allocation in a static context. They both argued that socio-economic change proceeds towards an increasing degree of specialization and complexity, and that it is a process of qualitative change. History was then conceived as a (uniform-speed) gradual evolution towards higher states of complexity and differentiation.

(iii) *Revolutionary and dialectic dynamics*: Marx conceived the dynamics of economic and social change as revolutionary, violent and disruptive. Growth is not a slow process of incremental and continuous change, but rather a discontinuous and radical jump from one stage of development to a better one. In his view, history may be conceived as the succession of different phases that proceed in a dialectic and revolutionary manner, until the final state of rest, communism, ultimately sets in.

(iv) *Saltationist dynamics*: Schumpeter argued that 'social phenomena constitute a unique process in historic time, and incessant and irreversible change is their most obvious characteristic' (Schumpeter, 1954, p. 435). Such a definition of evolution points to the historical dependent unicity and irreversibility of the process of change, which is meant to be qualitative as well as quantitative change. According to him, evolution may be thought of 'more like a series of explosions than a gentle, though incessant, transformation' (Schumpeter, 1939, p. 102). This 'saltationist' characterization of the process of economic evolution is in many respects similar to Marx, and it is in sharp contrast with the more 'gradualist' character of other classical economists as well as neoclassical economics.

(v) *Gradualist evolutionary dynamics*: Gradual, continuous and incremental qualitative change is not only the characterizing element of Smith and Spencer, but also of the evolutionary theory of Veblen. According to him (Veblen, 1899, 1919), the coexistence of forces driving towards change ('idle curiosity') and inertial forces (the persistence of 'habits of thought' and 'institutions') determines a process of gradual evolution. History is an evolutionary process of qualitative change and cumulative causation.

2.5 *Is the Growth Process Deterministic or Unpredictable?*

Another important feature in economic growth theorizing is whether the process described is deterministic and predictable, or rather non-deterministic and unpredictable. Although many intermediate positions could be discussed, it is useful to point out the two major (opposite) views.

(i) *Mechanistic, deterministic and predictable process*: The economic world is understood and represented in terms of cause–effect mechanisms, in which there is no space for purposeful behaviour and free choice. Inspired by the developments of classical physics and astronomy, the mechanistic view in economics has been dominant since the time of classical economists (including Marx), marginalist and neoclassical economics. The mechanistic view implies that, given the initial conditions at the present time and the law of motion of the economic system, any future state can be perfectly foreseen. Mechanism, therefore, implies determinism and predictability of future economic outcomes.[10]

(ii) *Non-mechanistic, non-deterministic and unpredictable process*: The mechanistic metaphor, according to a different view, is not appropriate to describe the evolution of a complex system. Purposeful behaviour, deliberate choice and creativity of individuals introduce a fundamental element of non-mechanism and unpredictability in the economic world. This is the view adopted, more or less explicitly, by German Historicists, Old American Institutionalists (e.g. Veblen) and, to a certain extent, by Schumpeter. In this view, the process of innovation and economic growth is characterized by genuine and pervasive uncertainty, rather than mere computable risk. This distinction was originally put forward by Knight (1921), according to whom 'the practical difference between the two categories, risk and uncertainty, is that in the former the distribution of the outcome in a group of instances is known (either through calculation *a priori* or from statistics of past experience), while in the case of uncertainty this is not true, the reason being in general that it is impossible to form a group of instances, because the situation dealt with is in a high degree unique' (Knight, 1921, III.VIII.2). In an economic world characterized by radical uncertainty, rather than computable risk, given the initial conditions at the present state, it is not possible to predict with certainty what the future state of the economic system will be. The economic process is non-deterministic and fundamentally unpredictable.

2.6 *Towards Equilibrium or Never Ending?*

Where does the economic process lead to? Does it tend towards a final state of long run equilibrium, or does it change continuously and go on moving forever without any definite final point? By and large, it is possible to point out two main different views on this fundamental characteristic of economic theory.

(i) *Towards equilibrium*: The process of economic growth tends towards a final state of rest, equilibrium and greater economic welfare. This was the view adopted, in different forms, by Adam Smith and Herbert Spencer, as well as Marx (for which 'communism' is a final state of rest in which all conflicts and dualisms ultimately cease). The equilibrium view became more explicitly dominant in economics after the marginalist revolution, since the last decades of the nineteenth century. More recently, the neoclassical theory of growth (e.g. Solow, 1956) extended the static concept of equilibrium to the analysis of the dynamics of the long period, by assuming the existence of a 'steady state' towards which the economic system will tend in the long run.

(ii) *Never ending process*: The equilibrium view has frequently been criticized outside the economic mainstream. Economic growth, it has been argued, is a never ending and ever changing process; it does not tend towards a steady state of balanced growth. This is the view expressed in the past, among others, by German Historicists, Schumpeter and Veblen. Using Veblen's words, economic evolution is 'a continuity of cause and effect. It is a scheme of blindly cumulative causation, in which there is no trend, no final term, no consummation [...], a theory of the process of consecutive change, realized to be self-continuing or self-propagating and to have no final term' (Veblen, 1919, pp. 36–37).

3. Evolutionary Growth Theorizing

After having defined the main concepts that will be used in this survey, we will now discuss the major strands of research within modern evolutionary economics. This section will consider in turn the main approaches, namely the neo-Schumpeterian long wave theory, the technology-gap approach, Nelson and Winter-like evolutionary theorizing, and the national innovation systems framework. Each subsection is composed of two parts: the first presents a brief overview of the approach, while the second part analyses its theoretical foundations by answering the six questions presented in Section 2. The discussion will point out that these four approaches share, to a large extent, the same theoretical foundations, so that they may be conceived as different strands of research within the evolutionary economic paradigm. The analysis will also argue, though, that although important advances have been realized in evolutionary economics in the last two decades, there still exist great challenges ahead.

3.1 *Neo-Schumpeterian Long Wave Theory*

The neo-Schumpeterian approach to economic growth takes great inspiration from Schumpeter's book *Business Cycles* (1939), in which the author put forward a theory about the existence of long waves of economic growth. His original point was to focus on the importance of basic (radical) innovations in creating such long waves, because, he argued, they have potentially a deep impact on the whole economy. The Schumpeterian insights into the central role of radical innovations in the macroeconomic growth process did not affect significantly the development of economic thought in the following four decades. Since the mid-1970s, however, there started to be greater criticism on the way in which mainstream economics approached the relationships between technical change and economic growth, and a renewed interest in the central role of innovation as the major source of economic growth.

The debate started with Kuznets's (1940) review of Schumpeter's *Business Cycles* (1939). His long wave theory, Kuznets argued, did not explain either the reasons for the timing of occurrence of basic innovations in the depression phase of the wave, or why they tend to cluster over time. Mensch (1979) put forward the idea that radical innovations tend to cluster in the depression phase of the long wave because this is the time in which the lag between invention and innovation is shortened (so-called depression-trigger hypothesis). A rich body of empirically oriented literature (among others Kleinknecht, 1981; Van Duijn, 1983) focused on the timing of clustering of basic innovations. The empirical results of these works have been heavily debated. On the whole, as pointed out by Freeman *et al.* (1982), the empirical evidence on the clustering of basic innovations in the depression phase of the wave is rather weak and not conclusive.

After this empirical debate, a second stream of neo-Schumpeterian literature flourished during the 1980s, providing a number of concepts and ideas useful to give a stronger theoretical foundation to long wave theory. These more conceptually oriented contributions started with the publication of the book *Unemployment and*

Technical Innovation (Freeman *et al.*, 1982), and was followed by the works of Freeman (1983, 1984, 1987), Perez (1983, 1985) and Freeman and Louçã (2001).

As Perez (1983) points out, the Schumpeterian process of development 'unfolds within the economic sphere conceived as a self-regulating organism which provokes its own disturbances (innovations) and absorbs its impacts by constantly striving towards new higher equilibria'. The social conditions and institutional framework are excluded from the causation mechanism that drives the primary cycle. This is the reason she argues that 'Schumpeter does lay the foundations for a theory of the cyclical nature of the capitalist economy but not of long waves' (Perez, 1983, p. 359). Based on these considerations, neo-Schumpeterian scholars conceive the capitalist system as formed by two related sub-systems: the techno-economic and the socio-institutional. It is the joint evolution of these sub-systems to determine the 'mode of development', and consequently the rise and fall of long waves.

According to this view, it is not important *when* a set of basic innovations is introduced, but rather that these radical innovations are strictly interrelated and pervasive, i.e. that they may drive the growth of many fast growing sectors of the economy. Such a family of interrelated basic innovations may be called 'technological system' (Freeman *et al.*, 1982), 'technological paradigm' (Dosi, 1982) or 'technological style' (Perez, 1983). This concept is arguably quite similar to that of 'general purpose technologies', although the latter is more frequently used in new growth theories (see Section 4). When a new technological style arises, there is a big impulse in the techno-economic sub-system to adopt the new best practice technology with high profit prospects. However, the techno-economic system is more ready to accept and adopt changes, while the socio-institutional one may take a longer time before making the changes required by the new technological style. The mismatch between the two sub-systems may retard the large-scale introduction of the new paradigm, precisely because social, organizational and institutional changes are necessary before it can diffuse to the whole economy. As the socio-institutional system evolves, the 'harmonic complementarity' between the two systems gradually restores, and a new mode of development eventually sets in. This may determine a long wave pattern similar to the primary cycle described by Schumpeter (1939): rapid diffusion of the new paradigm, incremental innovations over its 'natural trajectory' (Nelson and Winter, 1977), creative destruction and, consequently, the upswing and prosperity phases of the long wave. Later on, increased competition and market saturation, decreasing revenues from the new technologies and decline of profits, characterize the recession and depression phases of the long wave.

3.1.1 *Discussion*

The first question that our critical review considers refers to the level of aggregation of the approach. In this respect, neo-Schumpeterian long wave theory is a macroeconomic approach to the study of innovation and growth, the focus of the analysis being the evolution of a country (or a group of countries) over time. Great attention is devoted to the study of sectoral differences, focusing in particular on more technologically advanced and fast-growing sectors, which are those that drive the overall growth of the economy. The sectoral analysis, though, is primarily carried out with the purpose of understanding the implications and effects of sectoral patterns on national and international macroeconomic growth. Differently from Schumpeter, then, neo-Schumpeterian theory is not explicitly microfounded. It shows that the main features of Schumpeterian macroeconomics can be obtained without necessarily following methodological individualism.

Consequently, as there is no description of the microeconomic level, the notions of heterogeneity and population thinking are not explicitly considered in this approach. However, the fundamental role of heterogeneity and, more generally, the evolutionary foundation of such an approach, are increasingly recognized by recent long wave studies (Freeman and Louçã, 2001). An evolutionary type of modelling in which the interactions of heterogeneous agents determine long wave patterns has already been proposed in the works of Iwai (1984) and Silverberg and Lehnert (1994). The future extension of this class of models could make the evolutionary foundation of neo-Schumpeterian studies more explicit than it is at the present stage.

Similarly to all the other theoretical frameworks considered in this paper, innovation is the main source of economic growth. The historical and institutional context in which technical and organizational innovations take place is considered with great accuracy in neo-Schumpeterian works. On one hand, the innovative process is exogenous, because it depends on the science and technology system, which is pointed out as important but not explicitly investigated. On the other hand, though, innovation is an endogenous activity, determined by R&D investments of firms and, in a later phase of the long wave, linked to demand and production growth through learning by doing, dynamic economies of scale, and embodied technical progress.

Innovation is arguably the major source of economic growth in this framework, but this does not justify the often-made claim that neo-Schumpeterian long wave theory is a technological deterministic approach. Such a criticism is based on the fact that when a new technological paradigm emerges, it is the evolution of the techno-economic system to determine the socio-institutional characteristics that are required to compete in the new long wave period. So, transformations in the techno-economic system affect greatly the characteristics of the new mode of development. However, in the downswing phase of the long wave, innovations are more likely to be introduced in the market because firms and consumers are more willing to risk and to try out new solutions. It is in the downswing phase that consumers' expectations, firms' animal spirits, and social and political changes facilitate the introduction and diffusion of a new technological paradigm. Therefore, changes in the socio-institutional system may also affect the techno-economic, so that it is not appropriate to argue that neo-Schumpeterian long wave theory is based on a simple one-sided and technological deterministic view of the process of economic change.

The creation and diffusion of interrelated innovations determine long waves of economic growth, each characterized by an initial speed up (upswing) and then a slowing down phase (downswing). The dynamics of the process is saltationist, disruptive, irregular, and characterized by structural and irreversible change, as in

Schumpeter's view. Precise regularity and strict periodicity are not assumed in long wave theory; the process repeats itself over time but in a rather irregular way (Freeman *et al.*, 1982). According to this interpretation of history, the recurrence of long waves does not imply that the waves are all the same. The only recurrent mechanism is the co-evolution between technological and socio-institutional changes and its importance for economic growth, but the precise form that they take in each historical phase is ever changing and always different. Every occurrence is singular and unique in historical time.

A common criticism made to the long wave approach refers to its 'mechanistic' flavour. On one hand, it is true that, once a new technological paradigm emerges, the long wave process is assumed to follow in a more or less automatic and mechanistic way, closely resembling the Schumpeterian primary cycle. On the other hand, however, in the downswing phase it is not possible to predict which technological and organizational innovations will characterize the following historical phase, and when they will come about. The outcomes of the science and technology system are not predictable with accuracy, and the same is true for the socio-institutional changes that will follow. Considering the whole long wave sequence, then, the process described may certainly be regarded as non-deterministic and non-predictable.

Finally, with respect to the sixth theoretical question that we consider in our discussion, it should be observed that the neo-Schumpeterian process of growth is ever changing and never ending; it does not tend towards the steady state. Similarly to Schumpeter, the economic system is never in equilibrium; there are always forces determining further disequilibrating movements. It is innovation that continuously breaks the circular flow of economic activity, and that determines the inherent disequilibrium nature of the economic system.

3.2 *The Technology-gap Approach*

While neo-Schumpeterian scholars study the process of economic development *within each country*, technology-gap theorists focus on technological and economic differences *between countries*. The approach has originated from the contributions of historically oriented economists, which investigated the process of catching up and overtaking of some advanced (leader) countries in the last two centuries by focusing on the creation of new technologies and on its international diffusion (Veblen, 1915; Gerschenkron, 1962; Habakkuk, 1962; Landes, 1969; Abramovitz, 1986, 1994; Freeman, 1987). These historical contributions, different as they may be, all point out that two broad sets of factors are necessary for succesful catching up and rapid growth in the long run: techno-economic and socio-institutional factors. The crucial point is thus that catching up is a complex process, so that its investigation cannot only look at economic factors, but also at the important technological, social and institutional aspects related to the development process.[11]

Originating from these historically oriented studies, a modern strand of technology-gap theory has developed since the 1980s. These more quantitative-oriented applied studies aim at explaining the historical evidence on catching up by adopting a Schumpeterian perspective on the importance of innovation and international diffusion for economic growth. The Schumpeterian idea that firms compete in the market by upgrading their technological capabilities is then applied to the macroeconomic level, where countries are assumed to compete for the economic leadership through their technological capabilities, absorptive capacities and innovating activities. Econometric works in this tradition typically investigate differences in economic growth rates and trade performances by using indicators of national technological activities, such as R&D and patent statistics. The strong correlation generally found between technological and macroeconomic performance (e.g. Fagerberg, 1987, 1988; Dosi *et al.*, 1990) is then taken as an indication of the fundamental role played by the creation and diffusion of technologically advanced products and processes for explaining growth rate differences.

These econometric studies investigate differences in technological and economic performances on large samples of advanced and middle-income countries, so that, compared to the previous historically oriented contributions, the focus shifts from the study of the catching up process of single countries to the analysis of convergence and divergence in the whole sample of countries, carried out through statistical and econometric techniques. The cross-country econometric methodology is thus remarkably similar to that used in the convergence literature in mainstream economics (see Section 4).

The theoretical perspective that underlies the applied work in the evolutionary technology-gap tradition, however, is quite different from its neoclassical counterpart. As developed by Cornwall (1977), Abramovitz (1986, 1994), Fagerberg (1987, 1988, 1994) and Verspagen (1991, 1993), the modern technology-gap approach to economic growth assumes that innovation and the international diffusion of new technologies are the main sources of differences in growth rates between countries. Follower countries have a technology-gap (or technological distance) that separates them from the leader country, and they can therefore try to exploit their backward position by imitating and using advanced technologies developed by the leader country, instead of creating them from scratch. The process of imitation and diffusion of new technologies is costly, though, and it requires the existence of social and institutional capabilities that not all the follower countries have (Archibugi and Michie, 1998). This explains why catching up and convergence are not automatic and common outcomes.

Considering the conditions that are necessary for successful imitation and catching up, two broad sets of factors have been stressed. First, following Abramovitz (1994, p. 24), it is important to consider the 'technological congruence' of a country. This is defined by various factors: (i) the 'technological interrelatedness', i.e. how much a country is committed to the old technological paradigm, and therefore how difficult it is to make the jump into the emerging one; (ii) the country's natural resources and factors endowment; (iii) consumers' demand and tastes; (iv) market size and scale; (v) transportation and infrastructure; (vi) facilities for structural change, i.e. how rapidly the economic system is able to shift resources from the old to the new paradigm; (vii) general macroeconomic conditions and the rate of growth of demand. Second, turning to the broad set of social, cultural and institutional factors, Abramovitz (1994, p. 25) defines the 'social capability' of a country, characterized by (i) its level of education and technical competence; (ii) skills of the entrepreneurial class; (iii) commercial, industrial and financial institutions; (iv) political and social characteristics that influence the risks and incentives of economic activity; (v) science–technology links in firms and public research centres.

Considering them together, techno-economic congruence and social capability differ between countries in each technological paradigm, and these structural differences may explain why some countries manage to succesfully catch up with the technological leader, while some others fall behind. The major difference between this theoretical perspective and technology-gap models in the neoclassical tradition (or north–south models, see Chui *et al.*, 2002) is that the evolutionary view stresses the importance of the social and institutional structure to determine the social capability of a country (Abramovitz, 1986) and its ability to imitate foreign technologies.

3.2.1 *Discussion*

Similarly to the neo-Schumpeterian long wave theory previously discussed, the technology-gap approach is a macroeconomic approach. Applied works in this tradition are not based on the concept of aggregate production function, and the approach is therefore not explicitly microfounded, as there is no description of the behaviour of economic agents that may determine the aggregate outcomes. The Schumpeterian insights into innovation, diffusion and technological competition are transferred from the individual to the aggregate level of analysis: such as firms compete in the market for their market shares and profits, countries compete in the international arena for the technological and economic leadership. The main unit of analysis, then, is the country (some recent works focus on the regional level instead; see Fagerberg and Verspagen, 1996; Cappelen *et al.*, 2003).

As the approach is not microfounded, heterogeneity of individuals and population thinking are not explicitly considered in this framework. It is argued that countries are fundamentally and structurally different, particularly from a social and institutional point of view, but this variety at the macroeconomic level is assumed, and not explained by focusing on the interactions in a population of heterogeneous agents. Some formal evolutionary models (Dosi and Fabiani, 1994; Dosi *et al.*, 1994), however, show that the interactions of heterogeneous agents in an evolutionary framework may generate situations of catching up and falling behind, and reproduce the empirical patterns of convergence and divergence that applied studies have found. More work of this kind is needed in the future. The study of the aggregate properties of microfounded evolutionary models is a fascinating challenge for future research in this field, and it may provide a bridge between the applied work in the technology-gap tradition with the formal analysis of Nelson and Winter-like evolutionary models (discussed in Section 3.3).

Technological change is the main source of economic growth, but its mechanism, rate and direction are not investigated. Although innovation and diffusion of technologies are conceived as fundamental conditions for catching up, the way in which they are introduced in the economic system is not analysed further. The focus is on the structural and institutional factors that may facilitate or hamper the process of international diffusion, but not on the factors that may explain a differential rate of creation of innovations in different countries. The approach does not shed any new light in this respect.

The dynamics implicitly assumed in technology-gap studies is mainly saltationist. The approach argues in fact that when a new technological paradigm sets in, there is a strong technological push in the economic system, which may turn to have important consequences for the patterns of convergence/divergence. In times of radical changes, leader countries can more easily invest in the new technologies, and are therefore likely to grow faster than follower countries, so that greater divergence between rich and poor countries may follow. After some decades, when catching up countries start to imitate and use the new technologies on a large scale, convergence in the whole sample may be a more common result. So, the dynamics of convergence/divergence between countries does not proceed at uniform speed, but rather it follows the paradigmatic, saltationist and discontinuous character of technological change.

Moreover, the process of catching up and falling behind is conceived as non-deterministic and non-predictable. The reason is that as technological change is fundamentally an uncertain phenomenon, it is not possible to predict which new technological system will prevail in the future. Therefore, it is hard to predict with accuracy the countries that will be more likely to catch up in the future, and those that will fall behind. The applied works in this tradition show the changing character of the catching up and convergence process over time. The more recent evidence points out that, while it was relatively easier to imitate and import foreign technologies in the age of Fordism and mass production, the scope for catching up has significantly decreased in the last two decades. The catching up process of follower countries requires now a greater effort for the creation and improvement of national technological capabilities (Fagerberg and Verspagen, 2002). The technology-gap process of growth is then ever changing and never ending; it is a process of qualitative change and transformation, rather than a transition towards the steady state.

3.3 *Nelson and Winter-like Evolutionary Theorizing*

The possible use of the biological evolution metaphor in economic science was originally suggested by Veblen and Marshall more than a century ago, but the development of modern evolutionary economics is relatively recent, tracing back to Nelson and Winter's (1982) book *An Evolutionary Theory of Economic Change*. Nelson and Winter-like evolutionary theorizing is currently the most influential and rapidly developing branch in the evolutionary economic paradigm.

Three complementary streams of literature have recently extended in various directions Nelson and Winter's theory of economic change: (i) microeconomic evolutionary theory of consumers, firms and organizations, closely connected to cognitive psychology, business and organizational studies;[12] (ii) sectoral studies on the historical evolution of particular industries, and related analyses of industrial dynamics and sectoral systems of innovation;[13] (iii) formal models of economic growth.[14] Although the three streams focus on different aspects of the evolutionary process at various levels of aggregation (firms, sectors and countries, respectively), they all conceive economic evolution as driven by the interactions between heterogeneity, selection and innovation processes. Figure 1 shows a simplified scheme of these interactions.

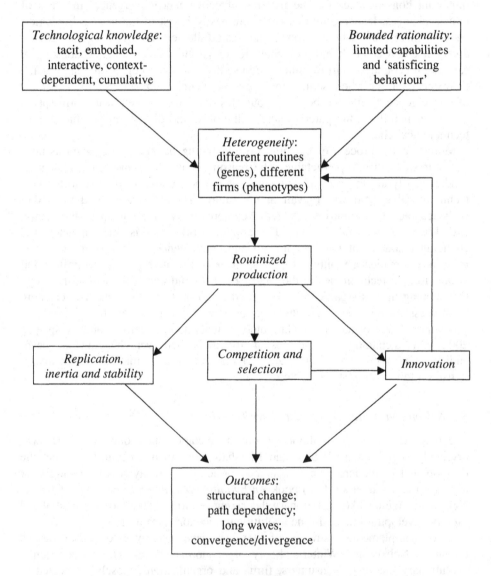

Figure 1. Main Relationships in Nelson and Winter-like Evolutionary Economics.

Heterogeneity (or variety) of economic agents is a fundamental feature of the evolutionary economic world. The latter is characterized by complex evolving knowledge, bounded rational agents and radical uncertainty. In such an uncertain world, individuals follow routines and habits of thought in their economic activities. Routines are regarded as the counterpart of genes in biological evolution. The reason for this analogy is threefold: routines are embodied in the minds and production activities of economic agents; they greatly differ among the various units of the population; and they can be transmitted from one individual to another, so that they may take account of the regularities sustaining stable and inertial patterns of production over time.

Within the same firm, production can be conceived as guided by routines at different levels, driving the standard operating procedures, the investment behaviour, and the deliberate search for new routines or solutions when the old ones prove to give unsatisfactory results in terms of market shares and profits. Routine-guided firms may thus be thought of as the counterpart of phenotypes in biological evolution, because their behaviour is the result of the interactions of their genetic endowment (individual skills and organizational routines) with a given economic and institutional environment.

Since Nelson and Winter's (1982) seminal work, several evolutionary models of economic growth have tried to formalize this idea of routine-guided heterogeneous firms within a disequilibrium framework. These models assume that firms differ with regard to the techniques that they use (Iwai, 1984; Conlisk, 1989; Silverberg and Lehnert, 1994), their behaviours and strategies (Chiaromonte and Dosi, 1993; Dosi et al., 1994; Fagiolo and Dosi, 2003; Silverberg and Verspagen, 1994a, b, 1996), or the characteristics of the sectors in which they operate (Winter, 1984; Verspagen, 1993).

Evolutionary analytical models, therefore, aim at reproducing the idea that the 'routinized' character of the productive process carried out by a population of heterogeneous firms may generate a relatively stable pattern of economic activities and relationships over time. The important point, however, is that such inertial forces and inherent persistency are continuously counteracted by dynamic forces that push the economic system towards evolution, change and transformation. These dynamic forces are technological competition and selection, on one hand, and innovation on the other.

In the same way as animal species compete for their survival in the natural environment, heterogeneous firms compete in the market by trying to employ more advanced techniques, and to produce at lower costs and better quality than their competitors. The selection mechanism in evolutionary models typically depends on the profits realized by each firm. Firms that are able to obtain high profits increase their market shares; firms with inferior technological capabilities realize lower profits, lose market shares and will ultimately be driven out of the market. The idea of selection-based growth, put forward in different forms in the past by Schumpeter (1939), Alchian (1951) and Winter (1964, 1971), is usually represented in recent formal models through the use of replicator (or Lotka–Volterra) equations in which the firm's market share (or production level) is assumed to evolve over time as a function of its technological capability and profitability.

An important qualification, made by the growing number of studies of sectoral patterns of innovation (Pavitt, 1984; Malerba, 2002), is that the competition–selection process works differently in different industries of the economy. Each sector is characterized by the complex interactions between heterogeneous agents, economic structure, institutions and technological characteristics. The latter, in particular, determine the 'technological regime' in which competition and selection take place. The technological regime may be conceived as the technological environment in which innovative activities take place in different industries of the economy. Such an environment differs in terms of technological opportunities, properties of the knowledge base, cumulativeness and appropriability conditions. Formal models and econometric evidence show that the characteristics defining technological regimes may generate the different patterns of industrial dynamics originally identified by Schumpeter (i.e. the so-called Schumpeter Mark I and II; see Winter, 1984; Malerba, 2005).

Over time, competition and selection tend to consume and to reduce the initial heterogeneity. Without the creation of new variety, the process of evolution would soon come to an end. The fundamental point about the evolutionary economic world is precisely that there is an ongoing introduction of novelty, so that heterogeneity and variety are continuously renewed, and evolution is a never ending process. In particular, two main different sources of novelty have been stressed in the literature. The first is a kind of 'unintended' innovation that arises when new routines are created as an automatic and non-deliberate consequence of routinized production within firms. This is for example the case when the firm expands its production scale by hiring additional workers or buying new machines. The additional workers and equipment can never exactly replicate what the old were doing, so that a firm's routines can be randomly modified at any time (Nelson and Winter, 1982, Ch. 5). Moreover, the old routines applied to a larger scale can be improved simply because workers learn by doing and by producing. Dynamic economies of scale assume then an important role in an evolutionary environment, as is the case for example in the model by Silverberg et al. (1988).

A second important source of novelty comes from a deliberate search for new technical solutions whenever the old one does not lead to efficient outcomes and satisficing profits. Nelson and Winter's (1982) formal model assumes that when the profit rate falls below a certain threshold, the firm will engage in a process of search for a better technique by imitating other firms or by creating innovation. Winter (1984) and Malerba (2002) point out that the probability that a firm chooses to imitate or to innovate depends on the characteristics of the technological regime in which it operates, and in particular on the possibility to appropriate the innovation profits, which determines the technological spillovers that it is possible to exploit in a given sector of the economy. A later class of evolutionary models (Silverberg and Verspagen, 1994a, b, 1995, 1996) has introduced the idea that firms may change their strategies and routines by learning from past experience, so that evolution not only implies technological change but behavioural learning as well.

In a nutshell, evolutionary economic theory explains growth in terms of the dynamic interactions between heterogeneity, competition, selection and innovation, where the latter leads to renewed heterogeneity and thus to perpetuating the growth process. From a theoretical point of view, the evolutionary description of the economic world appears as a novel contribution to growth theory. Its empirical relevance, though, is still difficult to evaluate, and the relationship between formal models and econometric work in this tradition has not been made explicit yet. In particular, what kind of empirical stylized facts may be generated as outcomes of evolutionary models?

Although evolutionary economics has not yet agreed on a standard set of assumptions and results, important empirical trends have been generated as 'emergent properties' of different classes of evolutionary models, i.e. (i) structural change and creative destruction (as in the studies of industrial dynamics, history-friendly models and recent studies on 'sectoral systems of innovation'; see Malerba, 2005); (ii) path dependency (in models where the coexistence of random events and increasing returns may generate path dependent phenomena of the kind described by David, 1985; Arthur, 1994); (iii) long waves and fluctuations without fixed periodicity (Silverberg and Lehnert, 1994; Silverberg and Verspagen, 1994a, b, 1995, 1996), reproducing the predictions of the neo-Schumpeterian literature discussed in Section 3.1; (iv) endogenous specialization patterns and uneven international trade (e.g. Verspagen, 1993); (v) patterns of convergence/divergence between countries at the macroeconomic level (Chiaromonte and Dosi, 1993; Dosi et al., 1994), closely related to the predictions of the technology-gap approach discussed in Section 3.2. The examples above indicate that an important future challenge for Nelson and Winter-like evolutionary modelling is to reach a closer link between formal models and econometric studies, as this may also provide a more explicit bridge with the other evolutionary traditions considered in this paper.

3.3.1 *Discussion*

Evolutionary models are explicitly microfounded on a population of heterogeneous agents (population thinking). The theory is bottom-up built; it considers it necessary to start from the microeconomic level to derive the macroeconomic implications. Aggregate phenomena are defined as 'emergent properties', i.e. 'the collective and largely unintentional outcome of far-from-equilibrium micro interactions' (Dosi and Winter, 2000, p. 5). Individuals' skills and firms' routines are the basic units of microeconomic analysis. However, the way in which routines and habits of thought of economic agents may in turn be shaped and affected by the macroeconomic and institutional environment in which they operate has not been made explicit yet. A co-evolution across different levels of analysis is in fact often called for, but not systematically introduced yet in evolutionary modelling. Arguably, future evolutionary models may assume the same non-reductionist character as verbal and non-mathematical studies of evolutionary economic change. Non-reductionism appears therefore as an important challenge for future research in evolutionary economics.

The population of heterogeneous firms is analysed in terms of the interactions between variety, competition, selection and innovation. The latter is the fundamental source of renewed variety and economic growth, without which evolution would ultimately cease. Novelty can take the form of the unintended and automatic consequence of routinized production, or of deliberate search by firms for new technologies (through innovation and imitation). In both cases, the focus of evolutionary modelling is on an incremental type of innovation, while Schumpeterian radical innovations have not yet found a decisive role in this strand of research.

As a consequence, the dynamics of the economic system is prevailing gradualist, characterized by slow and continuous change and transformation, rather than drastic jumps as in the case of neo-Schumpeterian and technology-gap approaches. History may be conceived as an evolutionary process of gradual and continuous growth and qualitative change, which does not necessarily pass through the succession of different paradigmatic phases. The focus on routinized production and routine-guided innovation gives the theory a bias towards continuity and gradual evolution, in which radical technical and institutional changes can hardly emerge from the inertial quality of routines and habits of thought.

Similarly to the other evolutionary strands of research, economic growth is seen as a non-predictable process, because fundamental sources of uncertainty exist in the economic system. In particular, uncertain and non-deterministic innovative activity is represented in formal models by assuming that the arrival rate of innovation follows a stochastic process (e.g. a Poisson random variable). This formalization, though, appears more suitable to represent an economic environment characterized by computable risk rather than the strong and pervasive uncertainty of the evolutionary world.

The coexistence of random and systematic factors driving economic evolution (Nelson, 1995; Verspagen, 2005), together with the coexistence of inertial and dynamic forces, determine the outcomes of the models: structural change, path dependency, aggregate growth, endogenous specialization patterns and convergence/divergence across countries. All of these phenomena are explained as the result of far-from-equilibrium microinteractions. Differently from the neoclassical metaphor of a steady state, then, evolutionary economics theorizes an ever changing and never ending process of growth and transformation.

3.4 *The National Innovation Systems Framework*

The previous sections have already made clear that the heart of evolutionary growth theorizing is the investigation of the innovative process. Many feedbacks and complex interactions are involved in the creation of technical and organizational innovations, between individuals within the same firm, between different firms, between producers and users of the new technology, between public and private organizations. Towards the end of the 1980s, it was increasingly recognized that such complex links could not be studied within a linear framework, and a 'systemic' approach to the study of innovation was developed.

Freeman (1987) was the first to use a systemic perspective in his national case study on Japan. The national innovation system (NIS) (defined as 'the network of institutions in the public and private sectors whose activities and interactions initiate, modify and diffuse new technologies'; Freeman, 1987, p. 1), he argued, is arguably the most important factor behind the spectacular economic performance of Japan after World War II. From his neo-Schumpeterian perspective, Freeman conceived the national innovation system as a subset of the 'socio-institutional' one. The case of Japan showed how important it is for a country to have an active and well-organized innovation system.

Conceiving the innovation system in a more narrow way than Freeman, Porter (1990) studied the factors behind the different economic performance of 10 industrialized countries. He argued that innovative activities greatly vary in firms of different countries for the existence of differences in the following aspects: (i) factor and resource conditions, including natural resources as well as labour; (ii) demand conditions; (iii) related and supporting industries; (iv) firms' strategies and industry structure. These four elements must be considered together, as a part of an interactive whole. The focus of Porter's analysis is the innovative activity of firms, and the various economic factors that may explain innovative activity and output in different countries.

Porter's strictly economic approach to NIS is different from that of Nelson (1993). In his book containing national case studies of the innovation systems of 15 different countries, Nelson divided them into three groups: large high-income, smaller high-income and lower income countries. In the concluding chapter, Nelson (1993, p. 518) argues that 'it is inevitable that analysis of innovation in a country sometimes would get drawn into discussion of labor markets, financial systems, monetary fiscal and trade policies, and so on. One cannot draw a line neatly around those aspects of a nation's institutional structure that are concerned predominantly with innovation in a narrow sense excluding everything else, and still tell a coherent story about innovation in a broad sense.' The fundamental difficulty for these applied studies is precisely the one stressed in the above quotation. It is rather difficult to define neatly which aspects to include or to exclude from the study of an innovation system, as private and public organizations interact within a complex institutional and economic structure. Empirical research has then proceeded in a broad and open way, given that it is hard to find universal and standard criteria to measure and compare the performance of innovation systems in different countries.

The difficulties encountered by applied research suggest that a more structured theoretical framework may be useful for the development of the approach. Closely related to Nelson and Winter-like evolutionary tradition, theoretical research in the NIS field started with the book *National Systems of Innovation: Towards a Theory of Innovation and Interactive Learning* (Lundvall, 1992), which studied the microeconomic foundations of the innovative process from an evolutionary and systemic perspective. Innovation is a complex phenomenon of a dynamic, cumulative and rather uncertain nature. It is important to consider such complexities not just from the point of view of the single individual or firm, but rather by focusing on the feedbacks and interactions between the various components of the system.

Innovations and learning are collective phenomena; they can hardly be understood without an investigation of the complex interactions between heterogeneous economic agents.

A useful distinction in the systemic theory of innovation is that between 'learning' and 'exploring'. Learning is a fundamental and ubiquitous characteristic of modern knowledge-based economies. It is, first of all, the outgrowth of the productive process, because individuals learn 'by doing' things (Arrow, 1962) and 'by using' technologies (Rosenberg, 1982). But economic agents also learn 'by interacting' with other agents (Lundvall, 1992). While learning is mainly an automatic and unaware consequence of the working activities of individuals, 'exploring' denotes a deliberate and active effort to search for new technical and organizational solutions, new products and processes. Typically, it is the R&D system, and more generally the science and technology system, which performs such an exploring activity in a systematic way. The main economic actors involved in this process are R&D professional laboratories in private firms, and research institutes and universities in the public domain.

Private and public organizations in the science and technology system, however, are not enough to define an innovation system, as there are important macro aspects that need to be considered as well. In fact, any form of learning and exploring is 'anchored in the production structure and in the linkage pattern of the system of production' (Lundvall, 1992, p. 17). So, an innovation system approach studies scientific and technological activities within the whole productive system, in which learning continuously takes place. In this respect, there are several factors that directly or indirectly affect the innovative process: the education and training system in private firms and public schools, the role of government in innovation and industrial policies, the general macroeconomic conditions, and consumers' tastes and competencies. This suggests an interesting link in the NIS framework between the microeconomic and the macroeconomic levels of analysis. The innovative behaviour of individuals and firms is affected by macroeconomic and structural characteristics, and in turn the patterns of innovative activity determine the evolution of those aggregate features over time.

This implicit interaction between the microlevels and the macrolevels of analysis within an innovation system is not only considered from a strictly economic point of view, but also from an institutional one. Institutions are conceived in a broad way as 'sets of common habits, routines, established practices, rules or laws that regulate the relations and interactions between individuals and groups' (Edquist and Johnson, 1997, p. 46). They differ from organizations, which are consciously created and have an explicit purpose. Institutions can be thought of as 'rules of the game', while organizations are regarded as 'players'. The fundamental importance of institutions in the innovative process is related to the fact that individuals are not rational agents, but follow habits of thought. Economic agents do not properly *choose* what to do, as is the case in neoclassical microeconomic theory, but rather follow predetermined rules, routines, habits of thought. When these habits are 'common to the generality of men' (Veblen, 1919, p. 239), they become 'institutions'. It follows that any kind of human knowledge and innovation is accumulated and stored through habits of thought, routines and institutions. Cognitive, learning and innovative processes at the microeconomic level are shaped by institutions and social structures; in turn, the aggregate level of analysis is continuously affected by individuals' innovative and learning processes, which tend to modify the previously adopted patterns of behaviour and habits of thought.

According to this view, institutions have an important function to perform in innovation systems, in that they help economic agents to reduce the uncertainty and complexity of the innovative process. Institutions have a stable character, which sustains and enables individual learning and incremental innovations. At the same time, however, in periods of rapid and radical technological change, there is a pressure for the old habits of thought, routines and institutions to modify and to adapt to the emerging technological paradigm. In such circumstances, some creative destruction of knowledge and institutions is necessary, so that forgetting may be as important as learning (Johnson, 1992). Countries with a higher social and institutional adaptability are more likely to enter quickly into a new techno-economic paradigm, and to have positive economic performance for a prolonged period of time, as shown by the case of Japan (Freeman, 1987).

However, although the role of institutions and their relationship with the innovative process is increasingly pointed out in the NIS approach, it must be recognized that the systemic analysis of institutional transformations is still much less developed than the corresponding analysis of technological change. The main focus of the research has so far predominantly been on the role of innovative activities performed by private and public organizations.

3.4.1 *Discussion*

In general system theory, a system is composed of its components and the relationships between them (Edquist, 2005). What gives an evolutionary flavour to the NIS approach, therefore, is not the use of system theory *per se*, but rather the way in which the components and their relationships are represented. This is discussed as follows.

As regards the relations between microactors and macrostructure, the NIS framework presents an explicit attempt to find a compromise between the two opposite views of methodological individualism and methodological holism. In a non-reductionist fashion, both levels of analysis, micro and macro, are studied in the framework. The innovative activity of private and public organizations is affected and shaped by the production structure, the macroeconomic conditions and the socio-institutional system of the country; in turn, national patterns of innovation and productivity growth are determined by the learning and searching activities of (micro) economic agents. The study of the interactions between microactors and social structure may constitute an important contribution of the NIS framework to the development of evolutionary growth theorizing. Important insights in this respect could come from a rediscovery of the work of Veblen and old American institutionalism, based on the dynamic relationships between 'habits of thought' and 'institutions' (Hodgson, 1993, 1998). Such a non-reductionist link between microlevels and macrolevels of the analysis, however, has not been made explicit yet in NIS studies, and needs to be further investigated in future research.

Focusing the attention on the microfoundations of the NIS framework, a fundamental characteristic is the heterogeneity and variety of individuals and organizations (McKelvey, 1997; Saviotti, 1997). If all economic agents had the same learning and innovative capabilities, in fact, innovation could be studied by simply analysing the behaviour of a representative agent, and there would be no need of a systemic perspective. But great complexities arise because learning and innovation are interactive activities carried out by heterogeneous agents. NIS is therefore implicitly based on population thinking.

Technical and organizational changes are the result of the complex interactions between private and public organizations, consumers and users of new technologies, macroeconomic structure and institutional framework. Innovation partly depends on learning processes (an inherent consequence of the production process) and partly on exploring activities (a deliberate effort to search for new technical solutions performed by the science and technology system). Therefore, the NIS theory of innovation points to the role played by both radical and incremental innovations. It presents an explanation of technical and organizational changes that combines the neo-Schumpeterian focus on radical innovations with the evolutionary microfounded theory based on learning and incremental changes.

Consequently, the dynamics of the economic process driven by innovation is in principle consistent with both a saltationist dynamics as in neo-Schumpeterian and technology-gap approaches, and the more gradualist view typical of Nelson and Winter-like evolutionary studies. Nevertheless, most empirical research has so far focused on the static characteristics of the innovation system in a given period, not on its process of change over time. The analytical–theoretical explanation of the process of evolution of the system over time has not been made explicit yet in the NIS framework. The study of 'complex evolving system' could constitute, according to Metcalfe (2001), a way to give a more precise evolutionary foundation to the NIS approach and to investigate the dynamic properties of evolving national systems in a more rigorous way.

What is clear is that, similarly to the other strands of research within evolutionary economics, economic change is conceived as a non-deterministic and non-predictable process. The fundamental and permanent source of uncertainty and unpredictability is constituted by the complexities of the innovative process and by the nature of interactive learning between heterogeneous individuals. Relatedly, as in all the other evolutionary perspectives considered so far, it is also clear that the evolution of the innovation system does not tend towards equilibrium, but it is assumed to be a never ending and always changing process.

4. New Growth Theory

This section shifts the focus to the other major paradigm in modern theorizing on innovation and growth, namely new growth theory (NGT). The first part of the section describes the main types of analytical models developed in the field in the last two decades, while the second part points to the major strands of applied research related to NGT. There exist already comprehensive overviews of this literature, in relation to both NGT analytical models (Aghion and Howitt, 1998; Chui *et al.*, 2002) and the related applied work (Temple, 1999; Islam, 2003). The reader is referred to these previous works for a more complete discussion of the technical issues involved, and for a more in-depth assessment of the advances obtained in this field.[15] The present section, on the contrary, does not aim at providing a complete survey of NGT. The major purpose here will be to prepare the ground for the discussion of the theoretical foundations of NGT, which will be carried out in the final part of the section. The discussion will analyse the theoretical foundations of NGT by discussing the six major questions that this paper uses as a framework of analysis, and this will make it possible to point out the great differences existing between NGT and the evolutionary economic paradigm.

4.1 *New Growth Models*

NGT models originated in the second half of the 1980s to overcome the problems left unresolved by the neoclassical model of economic growth (Solow, 1956). Two were the main sources of criticism made to the Solovian view. First, under the assumptions of constant returns to scale of each factor in the production function, and of decreasing marginal productivity of capital over time, the Solow model predicted that economic growth would have ceased in the long run. The only possible source of permanent growth in the steady state was technological change, which was exogenous and unexplained by the model. The latter was then unable to explain why GDP per capita has been continuously growing in most industrialized countries since the Industrial Revolution. Second, as technology was assumed to be a public good, freely available to all countries, the model predicted that poor and rich countries would have all converged to the same level and rate of growth of GDP per capita in the long run (given population and saving rates). This prediction was in contrast with the empirical evidence on the persistence of growth rates differences over long periods of time.

Taking these two problems into account, NGT models developed with the purpose of explaining how technological change can generate sustained growth and persistent differences between countries in the long run. The first generation of models was pionereed by Romer (1986) and Lucas (1988). Their models suggest that technological knowledge may be conceived as a non-rival good. This means that once new knowledge is produced by a firm (or by an economic agent who is accumulating human capital) this may benefit all the other firms as well. The public good characteristic of innovation introduces an important externality in the economic system, and consequently it may explain the existence of increasing returrns to scale in the aggregate production function. Differently from the Solow model, an increase in inputs of production can now have a permanent effect on the rate of growth of output, not only on its level. In the new framework, then, a positive growth rate in the long run can be explained by endogenous technical change, i.e. by the fact that there exist externalities associated with the production of technological knowledge by economic agents.[16] Moreover, an important implication of these models is that endogenous technological change and increasing returns in the aggregate production function may determine persistent differences in economic growth rates between countries, and so tackle the second question left unresolved by the Solovian model. The main problem associated with the first generation of NGT models, however, was that the reason economic agents may decide to invest in the accumulation of knowledge and human capital was not made explicit. If knowledge is a purely public good, in fact, where do individuals and firms take the incentive to invest in the accumulation of these resources?

This question was considered by a second generation of models (Grossman and Helpman, 1990; Romer, 1990). Still based on the idea that there are important externalities associated with the public good features of knowledge, these models argue that knowledge is an (at least partly) appropriable good, meaning that the fruits of technical progress may be appropriated by the producer in the form of monopoly rents. This idea is formalized by assuming that innovation is created by a separate research sector, whose purpose is to create new blueprints for the production of intermediate capital goods. Once a new blueprint is found, the producer firm can appropriate its invention by patenting it, so that it becomes a monopolist in the production of the new capital good. As a consequence, the assumption of perfect competition is released, as the intermediate goods sector is characterized by monopolistic competition. These models also assume that once a new capital good is produced, it adds to the older ones, which are not instantaneously driven out of the market. Economic growth, then, takes the form of an increasing variety of intermediate goods.

In a nutshell, the appropriability character of technological knowledge explains the microeconomic incentive to invest in innovative activities, and its non-rival feature explains aggregate increasing returns, endogenous growth and differences between countries, as in the previous generation of models. The Romer (1990) and Grossman and Helpman (1990) version of NGT, however, opens up an additional question: is it appropriate to model innovation as a deterministic and certain outcome of the activity of the research sector?

A third generation of NGT models, originating from the works of Aghion and Howitt (1992) and Grossman and Helpman (1991), proposed an answer to this question by pointing to the uncertain nature of innovative activity. Analytical models formalize the uncertainty characterizing the innovative process by assuming that new blueprints are found according to a Poisson stochastic process, whose parameter represents the productivity in the research sector. As the parameter of the stochastic process is known, it is possible to calculate an average arrival rate of innovation, and consequently an average rate of growth of the economy. The second modification introduced by this class of models is that they assume that each new blueprint makes the previous ones instantaneously obsolete, so that the previous monopolists in the intermediate good sector are driven out of the market as soon as an innovation is found. These models drop the idea that there is an increasing variety of coexisting capital goods, and point out that the process of technological competition and economic growth is characterized by Schumpeterian 'creative destruction' (or 'business stealing effect'): the monopoly power associated with a new bluprint is only temporary, and once a new intermediate capital good is introduced, the previous monopolists are driven out of the market.

Combining stochastic innovative activity, creative destruction and aggregate increasing returns, these models predict that economic growth in the long run is a function of three major factors: the amount of labour resources employed in the research sector, the degree of market power in the intermediate capital goods sector, and the productivity in the research sector.

An important empirical fact that these previous generations of endogenous growth models did not consider is the observation that innovations may have different sizes with different impacts on the economy. The distinction between radical and incremental innovations is an important one in evolutionary economics, and it was originally pointed out in the neo-Schumpeterian long wave strand of research. How can this empirical fact be represented in NGT models? How does the size of innovation matter for endogenous growth theory?

It is the most recent generation of NGT models (Bresnahan and Trajtenberg, 1995; Helpman, 1998) that put forward an answer to these questions. These works emphasize that innovations may have different sizes: they can be drastic (radical) or incremental. Some drastic innovations, in particular, may have deep impacts on the process of economic growth. According to Helpman (1998, p. 13), 'a drastic innovation qualifies as a "general purpose technology" if it has the potential for pervasive use in a wide range of sectors in ways that drastically change their modes of operation'. From this definition, it appears that the concept of 'general purpose technologies' (GPTs) is quite similar to that of 'technological paradigm' (Dosi, 1982; Freeman et al., 1982), which we have previously presented with reference to the neo-Schumpeterian long wave theory (see Section 3.1).

In this recent class of NGT models, once a new GPT arrives the radical innovation is not immediately ready to be used in the final goods sector, but it needs to be implemented in the form of a new intermediate capital good (incremental innovation). The arrival of the latter is formalized as a Poisson-distributed random variable, as in the previous Aghion and Howitt (1992) and Grossman and Helpman (1991) models.

After the introduction of the new GPT, labour resources are transferred to the research sector in order to develop the new capital goods and to appropriate the relative monopoly rents, in a phase in which the old technological paradigm still presents higher productivity than the new one. At the aggregate level, this first phase results in a slump of economic activity that may last for a few decades. Later on, once a certain number of intermediate goods embodying the new GPT are found, the profitability of the new methods of production turns out to be more evident to the firms in the final goods sector, and the GPT becomes the new dominant technological paradigm. In this second phase, the new GPT diffuses to the whole economy, and this may sustain the growth of aggregate productivity for the following decades. This two-phase cycle of growth is assumed to repeat over time, and in the long run such a cyclical trend tends towards the steady state.

The stylized description presented above clearly indicates that GPT models propose a formalization of the Schumpeterian theory of long waves. This is an interesting attempt, but modelling exercises of this type should in the future address some major questions. (i) Why does the GPT arrive at a given point in time? Is there any economic or socio-institutional factor affecting the invention of new GPTs? (ii) Is there any economic or socio-institutional factor affecting the rate of diffusion of the new technological paradigm over time and in different countries? These questions suggest possible avenues for future research in this field, and open up a possible ground for further interactions between the evolutionary long wave theory and the GPT modelling tradition.

4.2 *NGT Applied Research*

The development of new growth models has attracted a great deal of interest of empirically oriented scholars, and a huge amount of applied studies on cross-country differences in economic growth has flourished in the last 15 years. These works typically take the form of cross-section econometric regressions where the growth of GDP per capita over time is regressed on its level at the beginning of the period (a proxy for the scope for catching up), and on a set of other structural and economic characteristics, such as countries' accumulation of physical capital and levels of education and human capital.

The so-called convergence debate refers to the two different approaches and interpretations that this type of study may lead to (Temple, 1999; Islam, 2003). One set of econometric works derives growth regressions in the context of the Solow model augmented with human capital (e.g. Mankiw *et al.*, 1992). The convergence property is then interpreted, in a neoclassical fashion, as a result of decreasing marginal product of physical and human capital. Another stream of cross-country applied research, on the contrary, includes additional variables in the specification, such as political conditions, industrial structure and so on, and interprets the conditional convergence result (or lack of such) in an NGT framework, i.e. as an indication of persistent growth rate differences across countries (e.g. Barro, 1991; Barro and Sala-i-Martin, 1995). Here, conditional convergence does not depend on different rates of accumulation of physical capital, but rather on the advantages that the international diffusion of technologies may determine for catching up countries.

An important result in the growth regressions literature, though, is that convergence is not a ubiquitous phenomenon, but it depends to a great extent on the countries included in the sample under study. In a seminal paper, Baumol (1986) pointed out the existence of three different convergence clubs in the world economy (OECD countries, centrally planned economies and less developed countries), and demonstrated that the patterns of convergence greatly differ between these groups. Baumol's idea has been refined in a number of subsequent empirical studies (Baumol and Wolff, 1988; De Long, 1988; Baumol *et al.*, 1989; Baumol, 1994), which have all stressed the great variety of macroeconomic performance in the world economy, and the striking differences between the rapid growth of a restricted group of advanced economies and the static patterns of less developed countries (Pritchett, 1997).

A well-known paper by Durlauf and Johnson (1995) developed this idea further, and classified world countries into four groups according to their initial conditions (i.e. initial levels of GDP per capita and of literacy rate). Their empirical study confirmed the existence of different convergence clubs with markedly different characteristics and growth behaviour. Instead of using the common cross-country regression framework, Quah (1996a, b, c, 1997) studied the dynamics of the distribution of world income, and found evidence of 'emerging twin peaks', i.e. the existence of polarization and of increasing differences between rich and poor countries.

These applied works are all the more important in growth theory because, as observed by Temple (1999, p. 150), it is 'useful to draw distinctions between types of country. [...] It is important to move away from characterizing the "average" developing country, and work towards a deeper understanding of differences.' It is thus increasingly felt in growth theory 'the need to acknowledge heterogeneity, and move away from techniques based on "representative" economies' (1999, p. 150).

The important challenge that this strand of econometric studies presents for future research in the field is twofold. First, it shows that a wide array of different econometric methodologies may be used to shed new light on the issue of growth rate differences and to complement the traditional cross-sectional approach: panel data methods (Islam, 1995), regression trees and other clustering techniques (Durlauf and Johnson, 1995), and techniques for analysing the dynamics of the whole distribution of world income (Quah, 1996a). Second, it suggests the need for further modelling efforts to provide a theoretical explanation for the empirical findings of convergence clubs, polarization and twin peaks. One possible direction would be to extend the multiple equilibria type of models (e.g. Azariadis and Drazen, 1990; Galor, 1996), although the link between this class of model and the NGT empirical work has not been made explicit yet.

One major criticism often made to the new growth empirics is that the various econometric studies are tests of conditional convergence on a large sample of countries, and not of innovation-driven endogenous growth for each single country belonging to the sample (Fine, 2000). They are not estimation of the structural form of the analytical NGT models, but rather tests of its reduced form. As Paul Romer (1994, p. 11) argues 'the convergence controversy [...] represents a digression from the main story behind endogenous growth theory', and not a direct test of it.

Sharing this point of view, Jones (1995a, b) shifts the attention to the time series implications of new growth models, so originating a new class of empirical tests more directly aimed at testing the predictions of the endogenous formalizations. As mentioned above, NGT models predict a positive relationship between the amount of labour resources employed in the research sector and the rate of economic growth. Jones shows, however, that this prediction is in contrast with the empirical evidence, which indicates that the steady rise of R&D intensity since the 1960s has not been associated with increasing but with constant or decreasing economic growth rates.

This finding has recently inspired a new type of empirical tests of NGT models, which focuses on the time series dimension of the growth process, and on the 'scale effects' implications of the analytical models (Jones, 1999; Greiner *et al.*, 2005). This new direction of research is promising, although various methodological and data-related problems may hamper the diffusion of this type of time series tests (Temple, 1999, 2003; Islam, 2003). An interesting connection that would enrich even further this line of empirical research could be the one between time series endogenous tests and the recent class of GPT models, investigating the empirical relevance of the two-phase long wave cycle generated by the emergence of a new GPT.

4.3 *Discussion*

NGT models and the related empirical works are based on the concept of aggregate production function, meaning that the approach is macroeconomic but implicitly microfounded. Economic agents are represented as rational maximizers of an intertemporal profit or utility function. Moreover, they are conceived as fundamentally homogeneous. The use of the 'representative agent' metaphor makes it possible to study the effects of the microeconomic behaviour on the macroeconomic level of analysis by using relatively simple analytical and formal models. The approach is thus based on typological thinking, which implies a less realistic description but a greater analytical power of NGT models compared to evolutionary studies.

When NGT models formalize the ideas of 'variety of capital goods' and 'product differentiation' (Grossman and Helpman, 1990; Romer, 1990), these are rather different from the way in which heterogeneity and variety are conceived in evolutionary economics. In NGT, variety is a consequence of innovative and learning activities of economic agents (reminding us somewhat of the 'increasing complexity' of the growth process described by Adam Smith and Herbert Spencer), not an essential precondition of the process of economic growth (as in evolutionary economics).

In NGT models, innovation is a major source of economic growth. Technological knowledge is formalized as a non-rival and partly appropriable economic good produced by a separate research sector. Innovation may be explained by two kinds of complementary mechanisms: learning by doing in relation to the accumulation of knowledge and human capital (emphasized by Romer, 1986; Lucas, 1988), and 'exploring' through the R&D activity of private firms (emphasized since the model of Romer, 1990). More recently, GPT models enlarge the set of possible mechanisms explaining technological innovation and productivity growth by assuming that *radical* innovations may have particularly deep and pervasive impacts on the economy. At the present stage of development of these models, however, the arrival of a new GPT is exogenous, serendipitous, and not linked to any economic or socio-institutional factor. A field for further modelling exercises would be to endogenize the arrival of radical innovations by following some of the insights coming from the neo-Schumpeterian long wave literature (Freeman *et al.*, 1982; Freeman and

Louça, 2001; see Section 3.1). An interesting possibility, in particular, would be to model the 'depression-trigger hypothesis' by linking the rate of arrival of radical innovations to economic factors such as demand and profitability conditions in the downswing phase of the long wave cycle.

Learning by doing and exploring activities by the R&D sector determine a gradualist type of dynamics, following which the economic system smoothly proceeds towards the steady state. History, then, may be conceived as a uniform-speed transitional dynamics, rather than an evolutionary process of transformation and qualitative change. Such a gradualist view, however, may be modified in the future by the advances of the recent generation of GPT models. In this case, innovations are mainly radical and may determine saltationist dynamics and long run fluctuations. The tentative combination of gradualist and saltationist dynamics in GPT models appears to be a novel element in NGTs, and needs to be further explored in the future.

Another important theoretical feature of NGT models is the way in which uncertainty is introduced in modelling exercises. These, in fact, represent innovation as an uncertain outcome of R&D activities by assuming that its arrival rate follows a Poisson stochastic process with given parameter. This formalization suggests that the process of growth is not characterized by 'strong' and radical uncertainty as in evolutionary economics (Dosi, 1982), but rather by 'computable risk'. In fact, although a stochastic element exists in the model, it is still possible to predict on average the rate of arrival of innovations, and consequently that of economic growth. The recent class of GPT models does not constitute an exception in this respect: the two-phase cycle repeats mechanically over time, and no strong uncertainty is present in the succession of the deterministic and predictable long waves. The way in which uncertainty is represented in NGT models implies a stylized description of the growth process, but its advantage is certainly the greater tractability and stronger analytical power of NGT models compared to evolutionary works. In an emerging class of models of economic dynamics, namely *chaos models*, a deterministic system may, due to the high sensitivity in initial conditions, generate radically uncertain outcomes (Boldrin and Woodford, 1990; George and Oxley, 1999). This type of models presents a peculiar combination of neoclassical characteristics (the description and microfoundations of the deterministic system) and evolutionary outcomes (uncertain and disequilibrium behaviour). This class of models has not been applied yet to the study of innovation and growth, but its wider use in future modelling and empirical exercises may possibly constitute a bridge between the evolutionary and NGT research traditions.

Finally, the economic process represented by NGT, in formal models as well as in empirical works, tends towards a steady state of balanced growth, which may differ across countries. Differently from evolutionary economics, the impact of innovation on economic growth is therefore analysed in a dynamic equilibrium setting. In GPT models too, the economic fluctuations determined by the stochastic arrival of innovations do not permanently deviate from the long run equilibrium trend. Temple (2003) has recently argued, however, that the steady state metaphor should not be taken too literally by growth researchers, as its major purpose is to provide an analytical tool for the tractability of formal models, and not a prediction to be tested by empirical studies. Yet another challenge for future research, then, would be to shift the focus from the long run properties of the growth models towards the process of transitional dynamics, which is all the more important in terms of welfare and policy implications (George *et al.*, 2004).

5. Conclusions

This paper has presented a critical survey of two major modern approaches to the study of innovation and economic growth, evolutionary and new growth theories. The purpose has been to discuss the often-made claim that the two approaches, both inspired by Schumpeter's seminal works, are becoming more and more similar in terms of the sources and mechanisms of the growth process on which they focus. According to this argument, some kind of theoretical convergence between the two paradigms is taking place.

This paper has argued that a comprehensive comparison of these different growth theories cannot simply be done by pointing to their common Schumpeterian features, as is frequently done, or by looking at the properties and results of modelling exercises. The comparison needs to be made at a more general level of analysis, i.e. by investigating the theoretical foundations of the different approaches. By theoretical foundations we mean the theoretical characteristics that may be considered as the main building blocks of each growth paradigm.

Following this idea, Section 2 has presented the six theoretical questions that we have used as a framework to compare the two approaches. It has defined the main concepts used in the survey, and it has briefly pointed to the origin of each concept in the history of economic thought. Section 3 has analysed the basic foundations of different streams of modern evolutionary economics, namely the neo-Schumpeterian long wave theory, the technology-gap approach, Nelson and Winter-like evolutionary theorizing, and the national innovation systems framework. The section has shown that these recent streams of evolutionary economics share the same theoretical foundations, so that they can be regarded as different strands of research within the same (broadly defined) evolutionary paradigm. However, the discussion has also pointed to some existing tensions and to the great challenges ahead for the evolutionary economic paradigm.

Section 4 has turned the attention to NGT, and it has briefly discussed the main generations of analytical models, as well as the major developments in the applied tradition. The section has shown that the theoretical foundations of NGT greatly differ from those of the evolutionary approach. The main differences between the two growth paradigms can be summarized as follows (see Table 1).

(1) The aggregate properties of new growth models are derived from the analysis of the behaviour of rational economic agents, and the related cross-country econometric work is set up in a production function framework. Both of them are thus implicitly based on methodological individualism. On the contrary, evolutionary studies point to the theoretical advantages of a non-reductionist

Table 1. The Theoretical Foundations of Evolutionary and New Growth Theories.

	New growth theories	Evolutionary theories
What is the main level of aggregation?	Aggregate models based on neoclassical microfoundations ('methodological individualism')	Towards a co-evolution between microlevels and macrolevels of analysis ('non-reductionism')
Representative agent or heterogeneous individuals?	Representative agent and typological thinking	Heterogeneous agents and population thinking
What is the mechanism of creation of innovation?	Learning by doing and 'searching' activity by the R&D sector; radical innovations and GPTs	Combination of various forms of learning with radical technical and organizational innovations
What is the dynamics of the growth process? How is history conceived?	History is a uniform-speed transitional dynamics	Towards a combination of gradualist and saltationist dynamics: history is a process of qualitative change and transformation
Is the growth process deterministic or unpredictable?	'Weak uncertainty' (computable risk): stochastic but predictable process	'Strong' uncertainty: non-deterministic and unpredictable process
Towards equilibrium or never ending?	Towards the steady state	Never ending and ever changing

    theory where the microlevels and macrolevels of analysis co-evolve and interact with each other. This attempt is often called for, but it is nonetheless difficult to make operational, and the different strands of evolutionary research have not yet reached a clear and common position in this respect.

(2) 'Typological thinking' and 'representative agent' are conceived as useful principles in NGT, as they increase the analytical tractability of formal models, thus strengthening their conceptual power. In NGTs, the notion of heterogeneity is not an essential intrinsic characteristic of individuals, firms, sectors and countries, but rather a consequence of the productive process, close in spirit to the metaphor of increasing complexity associated with the growth process described in the past by Adam Smith and Herbert Spencer. In evolutionary economics, on the other hand, heterogeneity of economic agents, routines and habits of thought assumes a fundamental role in the construction of the theory, which is then close to a Veblerian type of population thinking. The latter increases the realism of the description of the growth process, but presents formidable challenges for modelling exercises.

(3) Although innovation is the main source of economic growth in both equilibrium and evolutionary views, the underlying concept of knowledge is rather different. In NGT, knowledge is conceived as a non-rival and partly appropriable economic good. Evolutionary theories, though, point out that knowledge is a more complex entity, which cannot be analysed in purely economic terms. According to evolutionary scholars (Nelson and Winter, 1982), knowledge is often tacit, and not always codified and codifiable. It is embodied in the routines of individuals and organizations, and not stored in a book of blueprints. It is interactive, collective and systemic, and not simply the result of individual learning. It tends to be highly dependent and strongly rooted in a given organizational and institutional context, and not separable from it. On the whole, the mechanisms of creation of innovation look similar in evolutionary and new growth theories, but the conceptual foundation behind them is rather different.

(4) NGT models conceive history as a uniform-speed transitional dynamics towards the steady state, not as a process of qualitative change and transformation. Evolutionary economics, on the contrary, searches for a combination of saltationist and gradualist dynamics, and stresses the role of qualitative change and permanent transformation of the growth process. In both paradigms, however, it is difficult to combine gradualist and saltationist features in a single theoretical framework, and this presents interesting challenges for future research.

(5) The new growth world is characterized by 'weak' uncertainty and computable risk, as implied by the use of random variables to formalize the arrival of innovation in the analytical models. The growth process is hence stochastic but predictable. On the other hand, the evolutionary growth process unfolds in an economic environment marked by 'strong' uncertainty and unpredictability. This is clearly argued by a large set of appreciative and non-formal type of studies, while evolutionary modelling exercises do not significantly differ from new growth models in this particular respect. The tension between appreciative and formal types of evolutionary studies poses a crucial challenge for future developments of the evolutionary paradigm.

(6) In NGTs, economic growth tends towards the steady state in the long run. The steady state metaphor, in this context, should be interpreted as a useful tool that increases the tractability and analytical power of formal models, rather than a prediction to be confronted with empirical evidence. The growth path described by evolutionary theories, on the contrary, is an ever changing and never ending process of change and transformation, much closer in spirit to the disequilibrium economic world theorized in the past by Veblen and Schumpeter.

In a nutshell, NGT combines ideas from classical authors such as Smith and Schumpeter, and interprets them in a dynamic equilibrium framework, where rational choices of economic agents lead to steady state outcomes in a stochastic way. Evolutionary economics draws inspiration from various classical authors, such as Marx, Veblen and Schumpeter, and interprets their insights in an evolutionary disequilibrium context, where interactions among routine-guided and boundedly rational heterogeneous agents determine an unpredictable and endless process of qualitative change and transformation. The former paradigm points to the advantages that formal modelling may lead to in terms of increased analytical simplicity and greater power of generalization. The latter stresses the new insights that a more realistic description of the growth process makes it possible to obtain.

On this ground, the often-claimed convergence between evolutionary and new growth theories cannot be simply justified in terms of their common Schumpeterian features. The analysis carried out in this paper leads to the conclusion that evolutionary and new growth theories greatly differ with respect to all of their theoretical foundations. No theoretical convergence between the two paradigms is taking place.

This finding should be welcomed by both evolutionary and new growth scholars, as it is not theoretical convergence that determines advances in growth theory, but rather the continuous process of interaction and give-and-take between the two paradigms. Although no theoretical convergence is taking place, in fact, there exists an intense exchange of ideas and a fruitful interaction between the two approaches. On one hand, evolutionary economics greatly benefits from the development of NGTs. The unsatisfaction with the stylized and formal type of analysis of the development process offered by endogenous growth models has proved to be a fundamental motivation to induce evolutionary economists to provide more realistic descriptions and to search for new empirical insights.

On the other hand, NGTs benefit from the development of evolutionary economics, as the latter provides new insights into the complexities associated with the innovative process and its impacts on economic performance. The re-interpretation of some of these evolutionary insights in a dynamic equilibrium framework has in fact led to the refinement of NGT models and to new empirical applications. Three specific examples may illustrate this point. The first refers to the evolutionary strand of long wave theory that flourished in the 1980s (Section 3.1). This type of historical and descriptive research has later been formalized by the recent class of GPT models, where the evolutionary insights into radical innovations, technological paradigms and Schumpeterian long waves have been re-interpreted in an endogenous growth framework. The second example relates to the technology-gap approach (Section 3.2). These types of empirical studies, that flourished during the 1980s, were originally quite close to an evolutionary and disequilibrium interpretation of the growth process. But a later strand of econometric work in NGT applied a similar idea on the relevance of innovation and the international diffusion of new technologies, and interpreted it in the context of a microfounded dynamic equilibrium setting. Finally, a third type of interaction between the two paradigms refers to the idea of variety of macroeconomic behaviour. While this has been a major point motivating evolutionary research since its outset (e.g. in the literature on national systems of innovation, see Section 3.4), mainstream growth theory did not initially acknowledge this as a major point for building up analytical models and undertaking empirical research. In the last decade, however, NGT has increasingly focused on the great variety of growth behaviour in the world economy, and investigated the existence of different convergence clubs through multiple equilibria models as well as a wide array of non-parametric econometric techniques.

In all these examples, the insights provided by evolutionary research have proved to be a crucial motivation to develop successive waves of new growth models, where the latter have re-interpreted the evolutionary insights in a mainstream dynamic equilibrium framework based on neoclassical microfoundations. The outcomes of these NGT models reproduce the same stylized facts pointed out by evolutionary studies, but, admittedly, the theoretical structure underpinning them is fundamentally different from the conceptual framework originally proposed by evolutionary theories. So, the cases mentioned above do not represent examples of theoretical convergence between the two paradigms, but they rather indicate the existence of interactions between radically different economic worlds.

The interactions between these alternative paradigms have been quite important for the development of the field in the last two decades, and they will go on playing a relevant role in the future. The crucial point is that such fruitful exchange of ideas between evolutionary and new growth theories takes place precisely because the two approaches are so different. Therefore, it is the inherent difference between the two that stimulates advances in growth theory, not their convergence to a common paradigm. The day in which different paradigms will have converged to a single framework, growth theory will cease to be such a dynamic and fascinating field of research. This day is still distant in the future.

Acknowledgements

I wish to thank Michele Di Maio, Jan Fagerberg, Arne Fevolden, Jarle Hildrum, Per Botolf Maurseth, Bart Verspagen and an anonymous referee of this journal for their helpful comments and suggestions on a previous draft of this paper. The usual disclaimers apply.

Notes

1. Following Witt (1991), Nelson (1995) and Fagerberg (2003), we will use the label 'evolutionary economics' to indicate the whole set of approaches that will be discussed in Section 3. Section 3.3, however, will focus on the more narrow set of evolutionary approaches directly linked to Nelson and Winter's (1982) influential theory of economic change that we will label 'Nelson and Winter-like evolutionary theorizing'.
2. There are some other important disequilibrium views (such as the Austrian School, post-Keynesian and institutional economics) that are indirectly related to the development of modern evolutionary economics, but are outside the scope of this survey, so that they will not be considered further.
3. A more detailed discussion of the relevance of different levels of aggregation in economic theory can be found in Hodgson (1993, Ch. 15).
4. It is well known that Schumpeter was the first to use the expression 'methodological individualism'.

5. See Swedberg and Granovetter (1992).
6. See also Hodgson (1998).
7. An extended discussion of the concept of 'population thinking' can be found in Andersen (1994) and Hodgson (1993).
8. Freeman (1994) and Dosi (1997) present critical surveys of the different mechanisms of technical change in economic theory.
9. A critical discussion of the role of technical change in the theory of Karl Marx can be found in Elster (1983) and Hodgson (1993).
10. See Hodgson (1993, Ch. 14) for a critical discussion of this issue. The brief characterization of a mechanistic, deterministic and predictable economic process pointed out here is admittedly simplistic. There exists a class of models of economic dynamics, so-called *chaos models* (Boldrin and Woodford, 1990; George and Oxley, 1999), where a deterministic system, due to the high sensitivity in initial conditions, may lead to stochastic behaviour and uncertain outcomes. However, chaos models have not been widely applied yet to the study of innovation and growth, and a discussion of them goes therefore beyond the scope of this survey.
11. The historically oriented literature on catching up and growth has been recently surveyed by Fagerberg and Godinho (2005).
12. Pavitt (2005) has recently considered some of the most important contributions in this now huge literature.
13. An overview of the main findings of the recent studies of sectoral systems of innovation can be found in Malerba (2005).
14. For a previous discussion of evolutionary models of economic growth, with special emphasis on diffusion models, see Sarkar (1998).
15. Several comprehensive surveys related to NGT have recently been presented in this journal, in relation to different aspects of growth theory, such as the role of trade for the growth process (Lewer and Van den Berg, 2003), the effects of inflation (Temple, 2000; Gillmann and Keyak, 2005) and of financial liberalization (Auerbach and Siddiki, 2004), and the role of fiscal policies (Zagler and Durnecker, 2003). Measurement and empirical issues have also been discussed, particularly in relation to different measures of human capital (Wobmann, 2003; Gibson and Oxley, 2003) and of total factor productivity (Carlaw and Lipsey, 2003). For a detailed discussion of these contributions, see George *et al.* (2004).
16. New growth models are in fact also referred to as *endogenous growth models*, due to the endogenous nature of technological change. All the models reviewed in this section share this characteristic, as they all focus on innovation as the main engine of growth. However, there exist other classes of endogenous growth models that emphasize other sources of economic dynamics than technological change (see previous note). In this type of models, which we do not consider in this survey, it is the long run growth rate, rather than innovation, that constitutes the endogenous feature of the formalization.

References

Abramovitz, M. (1986) Catching-up, forging ahead and falling behind. *Journal of Economic History* 46: 385–406.
Abramovitz, M. (1994) The origins of the postwar catch-up and convergence boom. In J. Fagerberg, B. Verspagen and N. von Tunzelmann (eds), *The Dynamics of Technology, Trade and Growth*. Aldershot: Edward Elgar.

212 CASTELLACCI

Aghion, P. and Howitt, P. (1992) A model of growth through creative destruction. *Econometrica* 60: 323–351.

Aghion, P. and Howitt, P. (1998) *Endogenous Growth Theory*. Cambridge, MA: MIT Press.

Alchian, A.A. (1951) Uncertainty, evolution, and economic theory. *Journal of Political Economy* 58: 211–222.

Andersen, E.S. (1994) *Evolutionary Economics, Post-Schumpeterian Contributions*. London: Pinter.

Archibugi, D. and Michie, J. (1998) Technical change, growth and trade: new departures in institutional economics. *Journal of Economic Surveys* 12(3): 313–332.

Arrow, K. (1962) The economic implications of learning by doing. *Review of Economic Studies* 29: 155–173.

Arthur, W.B. (1994) *Increasing Returns and Path Dependence in the Economy*. Ann Arbor, MI: University of Michigan Press.

Auerbach, P. and Siddiki, J.U. (2004) Financial liberalisation and economic development: an assessment. *Journal of Economic Surveys* 18(3): 231–265.

Azariadis, C. and Drazen, A. (1990) Threshold externalities in economic development. *Quarterly Journal of Economics* 105: 501–526.

Barro, R. (1991) Economic growth in a cross-section of countries. *Quarterly Journal of Economics* 106: 407–443.

Barro, R. and Sala-i-Martin, X. (1995) *Economic Growth*. Boston, MA: McGraw-Hill.

Baumol, W.J. (1986) Productivity growth, convergence and welfare: what the long-run data show. *American Economic Review* 76(5): 1072–1085.

Baumol, W.J. (1994) Multivariate growth patterns: contagion and common forces as possible sources of convergence. In W.J. Baumol, R.R. Nelson and E.N. Wolff (eds), *Convergence of Productivity: Cross-National Studies and Historical Evidence*. Oxford: Oxford University Press.

Baumol, W.J. and Wolff, E.N. (1988) Productivity growth, convergence and welfare: reply. *American Economic Review* 78(5): 1155–1159.

Baumol, W.J., Batey Blackman, S.A. and Wolff, E.N. (1989) *Productivity and American Leadership: The Long View*. Cambridge, MA: MIT Press.

Boldrin, M. and Woodford, M. (1990) Equilibrium models displaying endogenous fluctuations and chaos. *Journal of Monetary Economics* 25: 189–222.

Bresnahan, T. and Trajtenberg, M. (1995) General purpose technologies: 'engines of growth'? *Journal of Econometrics* 65: 83–108.

Cappelen, A., Castellacci, F., Fagerberg, J. and Verspagen, B. (2003) The impact of regional support on growth and convergence in the European Union. *Journal of Common Market Studies* 41(4): 621–644.

Carlaw, K.I. and Lipsey, R.G. (2003) Productivity, technology and economic growth: what is the relationship? *Journal of Economic Surveys* 17(3): 457–495.

Chiaromonte, F. and Dosi, G. (1993) Heterogeneity, competition, and macroeconomic dynamics. *Structural Change and Economic Dynamics* 4: 39–63.

Chui, M., Levine, P., Murshed, S.M. and Pearlman, J. (2002) North–south models of growth and trade. *Journal of Economic Surveys* 16(2): 123–165.

Conlisk, J. (1989) An aggregate model of technical change. *Quarterly Journal of Economics* 104: 787–821.

Cornwall, J. (1977) *Modern Capitalism, its Growth and Transformations*. London: Martin Robertson.

David, P. (1985) Clio and the economics of QWERTY. *American Economic Review* 75: 332–337.

De Long, J.B. (1988) Productivity growth, convergence and welfare: comment. *American Economic Review* 78(5): 1138–1154.

Dosi, G. (1982) Technological paradigms and technological trajectories. *Research Policy* 11: 147–162.

Dosi, G. (1997) Opportunities, incentives and the collective patterns of technological change. *Economic Journal* 107: 1530–1547.

Dosi, G. and Fabiani, S. (1994) Convergence and divergence in the long-term growth of open economies. In G. Silverberg and L. Soete (eds), *The Economics of Growth and Technical Change: Technologies, Nations, Agents.* Aldershot: Edward Elgar.

Dosi, G. and Winter, S. (2000) Interpreting economic change: evolution, structures and games. *LEM Working Paper 2000/08.*

Dosi, G., Pavitt, K. and Soete, L. (1990) *The Economics of Technical Change and International Trade.* London: Harvester Wheatsheaf.

Dosi, G., Fabiani, S., Aversi, R. and Meacci, M. (1994) The dynamics of international differentiation: a multi-country evolutionary model. *Industrial and Corporate Change* 3: 225–241.

Durlauf, S.N. and Johnson, P.A. (1995) Multiple regimes and cross-country growth behaviour. *Journal of Applied Econometrics* 10: 365–384.

Edquist, C. (2005) National systems of innovation. In J. Fagerberg, D.C. Mowery and R.R. Nelson (eds), *The Oxford Handbook of Innovation.* Oxford: Oxford University Press.

Edquist, C. and Johnson, B. (1997) Institutions and organizations in systems of innovations. In C. Edquist (ed.), *Systems of Innovation: Technologies, Institutions and Organisations.* London and Washington, DC: Pinter.

Elster, J. (1983) *Explaining Technical Change.* Cambridge: Cambridge University Press.

Fagerberg, J. (1987) A technology gap approach to why growth rates differ. *Research Policy* 16: 87–99.

Fagerberg, J. (1988) International competitiveness. *Economic Journal* 98: 355–374.

Fagerberg, J. (1994) Technology and international differences in growth rates. *Journal of Economic Literature* 32: 1147–1175.

Fagerberg, J. (2003) Schumpeter and the revival of evolutionary economics: an appraisal of the literature. *Journal of Evolutionary Economics* 13: 125–159.

Fagerberg, J. and Godinho, M.M. (2005) Innovation and catching-up. In J. Fagerberg, D.C. Mowery and R.R. Nelson (eds), *The Oxford Handbook of Innovation.* Oxford: Oxford University Press.

Fagerberg, J. and Verspagen, B. (1996) Heading for divergence? Regional growth in Europe reconsidered. *Journal of Common Market Studies* 34: 431–448.

Fagerberg, J. and Verspagen, B. (2002) Technology-gaps, innovation-diffusion and transformations: an evolutionary interpretation. *Research Policy* 31: 1291–1304.

Fagiolo, G. and Dosi, G. (2003) Exploitation, exploration and innovation in a model of endogenous growth with locally interacting agents. *Structural Change and Economic Dynamics* 14(3): 237–273.

Fine, B. (2000) Endogenous growth theory: a critical assessment. *Cambridge Journal of Economics* 24: 245–265.

Freeman, C. (1983) *Long Waves in the World Economy.* London: Pinter.

Freeman, C. (1984) Prometheus unbound. *Futures* October: 490–500.

Freeman, C. (1987) *Technology Policy and Economic Performance: Lessons from Japan.* London: Pinter.

Freeman, C. (1994) The economics of technical change. *Cambridge Journal of Economics* 18: 463–514.

Freeman, C. and Louçã, F. (2001) *As Time Goes By: From the Industrial Revolution to the Information Revolution.* Oxford: Oxford University Press.

Freeman, C., Clark, J. and Soete, L. (1982) *Unemployment and Technical Innovation.* London: Pinter.

Galor, O. (1996) Convergence? Inferences from theoretical models. *Economic Journal* 106: 1056–1069.

George, D. and Oxley, L. (1999) Robustness and local linearisation in economic models. *Journal of Economic Surveys* 13(5): 529–550.

George, D., Oxley, L. and Carlaw, K. (2004) *Surveys in Economic Growth: Theory and Empirics*. Oxford: Blackwell.

Gerschenkron, A. (1962) *Economic Backwardness in Historical Perspective*. Cambridge, MA: Harvard University Press.

Gibson, T.L.J. and Oxley, L. (2003) Cost- and income-based measures of human capital. *Journal of Economic Surveys* 17(3): 271–307.

Gillmann, M. and Kejak, M. (2005) Contrasting models of the effect of inflation on growth. *Journal of Economic Surveys* 19(1): 113–136.

Greiner, A., Semmler, W. and Gong, G. (2005) *The Forces of Economic Growth: A Time Series Perspective*. Princeton, NJ: Princeton University Press.

Grossman, G.M. and Helpman, E. (1990) Comparative advantages and long run growth. *American Economic Review* 80: 796–815.

Grossman, G.M. and Helpman, E. (1991) Quality ladders in the theory of growth. *Review of Economic Studies* 58: 86–91.

Habakkuk, H.J. (1962) *American and British Technology in the Nineteenth Century*. Cambridge: Cambridge University Press.

Heertje, A. (1993) Neo-Schumpeterians and economic theory. In L. Magnusson (ed.), *Evolutionary Approaches to Economic Theory*. Dordrecht: Kluwer.

Helpman, E. (ed.) (1998) *General Purpose Technologies and Economic Growth*. Cambridge, MA: MIT Press.

Hodgson, G. (1993) *Economics and Evolution: Bringing Life Back into Economics*. Cambridge, MA: MIT Press.

Hodgson, G. (1997) The evolutionary and non-Darwinian economics of Joseph Schumpeter. *Journal of Evolutionary Economics* 7(2): 131–145.

Hodgson, G. (1998) The approach of institutional economics. *Journal of Economic Literature* 36: 166–192.

Islam, N. (1995) Growth empirics: a panel data approach. *Quarterly Journal of Economics* 110: 1127–1170.

Islam, N. (2003) What have we learnt from the convergence debate? *Journal of Economic Surveys* 17(3): 309–362.

Iwai, K. (1984) Schumpeterian dynamics. An evolutionary model of innovation and imitation. *Journal of Economic Behavior and Organization* 5: 159–190.

Johnson, B. (1992) Institutional learning. In B.-Å. Lundvall (ed.), *National Systems of Innovation: Towards a Theory of Innovation and Interactive Learning*. London: Pinter.

Jones, C. (1995a) R&D based models of economic growth. *Journal of Political Economy* 103: 759–784.

Jones, C. (1995b) Time series tests of endogenous growth models. *Quarterly Journal of Economics* 110: 495–525.

Jones, C. (1999) Growth: with or without scale effects? *American Economic Review* 89: 139–144.

Kleinknecht, A. (1981) Observations on the Schumpeterian swarming of innovations. *Futures* 13: 293–307.

Knight, F.H. (1921) *Risk, Uncertainty and Profit*. Boston, MA: Houghton Mifflin.

Kuznets, S. (1940) Schumpeter's business cycles. *American Economic Review* 30: 257–271.

Landes, D. (1969) *The Unbound Prometheus. Technological Change and Industrial Development in Western Europe from 1750 to the Present*. Cambridge: Cambridge University Press.

Levine, R. and Renelt, D. (1992) A sensitivity analysis of cross-country growth regressions. *American Economic Review* 82(4): 942–963.

Lewer, J.J. and Van Den Berg, H. (2003) How large is international trade's effect on economic growth? *Journal of Economic Surveys* 17(3): 363–396.

Lucas, R. (1988) On the mechanics of economic development. *Journal of Monetary Economics* 22: 3–42.

Lundvall, B.-Å. (1992) *National Systems of Innovation: Towards a Theory of Innovation and Interactive Learning*. London: Pinter.

Malerba, F. (2002) Sectoral systems of innovation and production. *Research Policy* 31(2): 247–264.

Malerba, F. (2005) How innovation differs across sectors and industries. In J. Fagerberg, D.C. Mowery and R.R. Nelson (eds), *The Oxford Handbook of Innovation*. Oxford: Oxford University Press.

Mankiw, N., Romer, D. and Weil, D. (1992) A contribution to the empirics of economic growth. *Quarterly Journal of Economics* 107: 407–437.

McKelvey, M. (1997) Using evolutionary theory to define systems of innovation. In C. Edquist (ed.), *Systems of Innovation: Technologies, Institutions and Organisations*. London and Washington, DC: Pinter.

Mensch, G. (1979) *Stalemate in Technology: Innovations Overcome the Depression*. New York: Ballinger.

Metcalfe, S. (2001) Institutions and economic progress. *Industrial and Corporate Change* 10: 561–586.

Nelson, R.R. (1993) *National Innovation Systems: A Comparative Analysis*. New York and Oxford: Oxford University Press.

Nelson, R.R. (1995) Recent evolutionary theorizing about economic change. *Journal of Economic Literature* 33: 48–90.

Nelson, R. and Winter, S. (1977) In search of a useful theory of innovation. *Research Policy* 6: 36–76.

Nelson, R. and Winter, S. (1982) *An Evolutionary Theory of Economic Change*. Cambridge, MA: Harvard University Press.

Nelson, R. and Winter, S. (2002) Evolutionary theorizing in economics. *Journal of Economic Perspectives* 16(2): 23–46.

Pavitt, K. (1984) Sectoral patterns of technical change: towards a taxonomy and a theory. *Research Policy* 13: 343–373.

Pavitt, K. (2005) Innovation processes. In J. Fagerberg, D.C. Mowery and R.R. Nelson (eds), *The Oxford Handbook of Innovation*. Oxford: Oxford University Press.

Perez, C. (1983) Structural change and assimilation of new technologies in the economic and social systems. *Futures* October: 357–375.

Perez, C. (1985) Microelectronics, long waves and world structural change: new perspectives for developing countries. *World Development* 13: 441–463.

Porter, M. (1990) *The Competitive Advantage of Nations*. London: Macmillan.

Pritchett, L. (1997) Divergence, big time. *Journal of Economic Perspectives* 11(3): 3–17.

Quah, D.T. (1996a) Twin peaks: growth and convergence in models of distribution dynamics. *Economic Journal* 106: 1045–1055.

Quah, D.T. (1996b) Convergence empirics across economies with (some) capital mobility. *Journal of Economic Growth* 1(1): 95–124.

Quah, D.T. (1996c) Empirics for economic growth and convergence. *European Economic Review* 40: 1353–1375.

Quah, D.T. (1997) Empirics for growth and distribution: stratification, polarization, and convergence clubs. *Journal of Economic Growth* 2: 27–59.

Romer, P. (1986) Increasing returns and long-run growth. *Journal of Political Economy* 94: 1002–1037.

Romer, P. (1987) Crazy explanations for the productivity slowdown. In S. Fischer (ed.), *NBER Macroeconomics Annual*. Cambridge, MA: MIT Press.

Romer, P. (1990) Endogenous technological change. *Journal of Political Economy* 98: 71–102.

Romer, P. (1994) The origins of endogenous growth. *Journal of Economic Perspectives* 8(1): 3–22.

Rosenberg, N. (1982) *Inside the Black Box: Technology and Economics*. Cambridge: Cambridge University Press.

Ruttan, V. (1997) Induced innovation, evolutionary theory and path dependence: sources of technical change. *Economic Journal* 107: 1520–1529.

Sarkar, J. (1998) Technological diffusion: alternative theories and historical evidence. *Journal of Economic Surveys* 12(2): 131–176.

Saviotti, P. (1997) Innovation systems and evolutionary theories. In C. Edquist (ed.), *Systems of Innovation: Technologies, Institutions and Organisations*. London and Washington, DC: Pinter.

Schumpeter, J. (1934) *The Theory of Economic Development*. Cambridge, MA: Harvard University Press.

Schumpeter, J. (1939) *Business Cycles*. Philadelphia, PA: Porcupine Press.

Schumpeter, J. (1943) *Capitalism, Socialism and Democracy*. New York: Harper.

Schumpeter, J. (1954) *History of Economic Analysis*. London: Routledge.

Silverberg, G. and Lehnert, D. (1994) Growth fluctuations in an evolutionary model of creative destruction. In G. Silverberg and L. Soete (eds), *The Economics of Growth and Technical Change. Technologies, Nations, Agents*. Aldershot: Edward Elgar.

Silverberg, G. and Verspagen, B. (1994a) Learning, innovation and economic growth: a long-run model of industrial dynamics. *Industrial and Corporate Change* 3: 199–223.

Silverberg, G. and Verspagen, B. (1994b) Collective learning, innovation and growth in a boundedly rational, evolutionary world. *Journal of Evolutionary Economics* 4: 207–226.

Silverberg, G. and Verspagen, B. (1995) An evolutionary model of long term cyclical variations of catching up and falling behind. *Journal of Evolutionary Economics* 5: 209–227.

Silverberg, G. and Verspagen, B. (1996) From the artificial to the endogenous: modelling evolutionary adaptation and economic growth. In E. Helmstädter and M. Perlman (eds), *Behavorial Norms, Technological Progress and Economic Dynamics: Studies in Schumpeterian Economics*. Ann Arbor, MI: University of Michigan Press.

Silverberg, G., Dosi, G. and Orsenigo, L. (1988) Innovation, diversity and diffusion: a self-organisation model. *Economic Journal* 98: 1032–1054.

Solow, R. (1956) A contribution to the theory of economic growth. *Quarterly Journal of Economics* 70: 65–94.

Swedberg, R. and Granovetter, M. (1992) Introduction. In M. Granovetter and R. Swedberg (eds), *The Sociology of Economic Life*. New York: Westview Press.

Temple, J. (1999) The new growth evidence. *Journal of Economic Literature* 37: 112–156.

Temple, J. (2000) Inflation and growth: stories short and tall. *Journal of Economic Surveys* 14(4): 395–426.

Temple, J. (2003) The long-run implications of growth theories. *Journal of Economic Surveys* 17(3): 497–510.

Van Duijn, J.J. (1983) *The Long Wave in Economic Life*. London: Allen and Unwin.

Veblen, T. (1899) *The Theory of the Leisure Class: An Economic Study of Institutions*. New York: Macmillan.

Veblen, T. (1915) *Imperial Germany and the Industrial Revolution*. New York: Macmillan.

Veblen, T. (1919) *The Place of Science in Modern Civilisation and Other Essays*. New York: Huebsch.

Verspagen, B. (1991) A new empirical approach to catching up or falling behind. *Structural Change and Economic Dynamics* 2: 359–380.

Verspagen, B. (1993) *Uneven Growth between Interdependent Economies: Evolutionary View on Technology-Gaps, Trade and Growth.* Aldershot: Avebury.

Verspagen, B. (2005) Innovation and economic growth. In J. Fagerberg, D.C. Mowery and R.R. Nelson (eds), *The Oxford Handbook of Innovation.* Oxford: Oxford University Press.

Winter, S. (1964) Economic 'natural selection' and the theory of the firm. *Yale Economic Essays* 4: 225–272.

Winter, S. (1971) Satisficing, selection and the innovating remnant. *Quarterly Journal of Economics* 85: 237–261.

Winter, S. (1984) Schumpeterian competition in alternative technological regimes. *Journal of Economic Behavior and Organization* 5: 137–158.

Witt, U. (1991) Reflections on the present state of evolutionary economic theory. In G. Hodgson and E. Screpanti (eds), *Rethinking Economics: Markets, Technology and Economic Evolution.* Aldershot: Edward Elgar.

Wobmann, L. (2003) Specifying human capital. *Journal of Economic Surveys* 17(3): 239–270.

Zagler, M. and Durnecker, G. (2003) Fiscal policy and economic growth. *Journal of Economic Surveys* 17(3): 397–418.

9
REPETITION AND FINANCIAL INCENTIVES IN ECONOMICS EXPERIMENTS

Jinkwon Lee

Korea Environment Institute

1. Introduction

While experimental economics has been widely applied to many economic issues as an effective tool for economic research, there has been a debate on the methodological aspects. Among them, the effect of financial incentives and repetition, which have been norms in experimental economics, has been at the centre of the debate.

In this paper, we discuss the issues related to financial incentives in laboratory experiments and review some experimental studies investigating the effect of financial incentives on subjects' performance under a repetition environment. Here, *financial incentives* are defined by performance-based monetary rewards, and *repetition* means that subjects repeatedly face identical or similar tasks in an experimental session.[1] The *improvement of subjects' performance* is defined in terms of the closeness to a normative prediction or the increase of the absolute achievement for a given task. That is, the improvement of subjects' performance means that their performance converges to a normative prediction or that the number of their correct responses increases.

Investigating the effect of financial incentives can be divided into two important dimensions, that is, a comparison between hypothetical incentives and financial incentives, and a comparison between a small amount of financial incentives and a large amount of financial incentives. Here, hypothetical incentives include both non-monetary rewards and only flat monetary rewards (e.g. a flat participation fee). Experimental economists have argued against psychologists for the former, and against non-experimental economists for the latter. Many psychologists believe that financial incentives will not much improve subjects' performance. Many non-experimental economists believe that a typical small amount of monetary rewards in laboratory experiments cannot represent the real economic environment where people must make decisions. One of the critiques of experimental economics has been the argument that people will behave differently if the stakes for a task are not low as in the laboratory but significantly high enough as in real life.

Experimental economists believe that financial incentives improve subjects' performance while hypothetical incentives cannot do so.[2] At the same time, they also believe that the results from laboratory experiments where a small amount of financial incentives are typically used would not be much different even if a large amount of financial incentives were used.[3] Naturally, experimental economists have given much attention to this important empirical question, and have collected experimental evidence to support their arguments. Ultimately, the conclusion in this debate could become clear after a number of empirical results are accumulated. In due course, a review study about empirical studies to date will be definitely helpful. This could be a rationale for this review study in addition to previous review studies. In this paper, the effect of financial incentives versus hypothetical incentives is mainly dealt with, commenting occasionally on the comparison between the effects of high and low financial incentives.

A number of review studies investigating the effect of financial incentives seem to suggest that it depends on task types, the degree of difficulty of a task, and the payoff mechanism that is used (Smith and Walker, 1993a; Pelham and Neter, 1995; Jenkins *et al.*, 1998; Camerer and Hogarth, 1999; Prendergast, 1999; Bonner *et al.*, 2000; Hertwig and Ortmann, 2001, 2003). While these studies deal with the interaction between financial incentives and the task type, the degree of difficulty and/or payoff mechanisms, they have not made any distinction between a single-shot trial and repeated trials.[4] In this respect, these studies are still quite general rather than specifically addressed to the question of repetition.

A provisional conclusion from these reviews is that financial incentives do not always improve performance in all sorts of task, though they, in general, reduce the variance of performance (Smith and Walker, 1993a; Camerer and Hogarth, 1999). In this respect, the effect of financial incentives seems to be task dependent. However, suppose that these studies suggest that there is no effect of financial incentives on performance in a particular task A. Since these reviews do not make a distinction between an experiment where the tasks are repeated and one where the task is single shot, there is no guarantee that financial incentives do not affect subjects' performance under the repetition environment of the task A. That is, even if $p \rightarrow q$ under a compounded condition of H_1 and H_2, it is not always true that $p \rightarrow q$ under the condition H_1. In an empirical sense, this argument must be plausible because repetition must create new important concepts such as learning and boredom, which may not exist under a single-shot task.

If we are to investigate the effect of financial incentives on performance under repetition, we are confronted with some important topics that may not be necessary for a single-shot task. First, we must be concerned with learning. It is natural to consider learning under repetition since one of the main purposes of repetition in laboratory experiments is to give subjects an opportunity to learn something about the task.[5] Hence, one dimension of the interaction between financial incentives and repetition must be related to the relationship between financial incentives and the learning process.

Second, we must think of boredom caused by repetition. Of course, we may not be able to measure subjects' boredom, and therefore we may not be able to

Table 1. Payoff Mechanisms.

	Single-shot payoff mechanisms	Repetition payoff mechanisms[a]
Hypothetical incentives	No rewards Flat payoffs (participation fees)[b]	No rewards Flat payoffs (participation fees)
Financial incentives (performance-based payoffs)	Piece-rate payoff mechanism Quota payoff mechanism Tournament payoff mechanism Binary lottery mechanism Random person payoff mechanism (RPPM)[c]	Accumulated payoff mechanism (APM) Random round payoff mechanism (RRPM)[c]

[a]A repetition payoff mechanism means a payoff mechanism that needs to be added to a single-shot payoff mechanism due to repetition. Hence, a complete payoff mechanism for an experiment using repetition will be composed of both a payoff mechanism for each single-shot round and a payoff mechanism for the total repetition. For example, an experiment using repetition would use a piece-rate for each round (single shot) and an accumulated payoff mechanism for the overall round (i.e. accumulation of the piece-rate earnings through overall rounds).
[b]Flat payoff could be categorized to financial incentives. However, since financial incentives are defined by performance-based monetary payoffs here, it is more appropriate for the flat payoff to be included in hypothetical incentives.
[c]The more usual and comprehensive term for both RRPM and RPPM in the literature is 'random lottery procedure' or 'random lottery incentive mechanism'. However, because we need to distinguish the two payoff mechanisms, we use such specific terms in this review. Throughout this thesis, the term 'random lottery incentive mechanism' and 'random round payoff mechanism' will be used interchangeably.

make a clear distinction between learning periods and boredom periods. However, if we can assume that boredom would be more significant after a learning process is completed, the relationship between financial incentives and boredom may take another dimension for investigation.

Third, the payoff mechanisms may be important under repetition. Table 1 summarizes the widely used single-shot payoff mechanisms and repetition payoff mechanisms in laboratory experiments. Even if there is no difference between a hypothetical payoff treatment and a performance-based monetary treatment with a repetition payoff mechanism in one experiment (e.g. accumulated payoff mechanism, APM), it is not impossible that an experiment whose repetition payoff mechanism is modified (e.g. random round payoff mechanism, RRPM) results in a significant difference between treatments. In fact, whether each different payoff mechanism under a repetition environment leads to a different behaviour or not is one issue under debate. For example, a debate on whether or not RRPM can induce subjects to a decision as if they face a single-shot task is ongoing in individual decision-making contexts (Holt, 1986; Segal, 1990; Starmer and Sugden, 1991; Beattie and Loomes, 1997; Cubitt et al., 1998; Hey and Lee, 2005a, b). Hence, if we are concerned with the relationship between financial incentives and repetition, we may need to focus on the payoff mechanism under repetition.

We review, in this paper, 44 studies investigating the effect of financial incentives under a repetition experimental environment. It is found from this review that the positive effect of financial incentives on subjects' performance becomes more prevalent when subjects face a task repetitively. Learning seems to be reinforced by the financial incentives combined with repetition, and the boredom effect tends to be reduced by the financial incentives. However, the dependence of the effect of financial incentives on the task type seems to still exist even when the financial incentives are combined with repetition. While financial incentives mainly improve subjects' performance in judgement tasks, this effect is not clear in choice tasks, and in game and markets tasks. Although studies reporting the positive effect of financial incentives are still the most frequent even in choice tasks and in game and markets tasks, it would be difficult to conclude that financial incentives improve subjects' performance when subjects face a task repetitively since the number of studies reviewed in this paper is too small in these types of tasks. Interestingly, the effect of payoff mechanisms on performance seems to depend on a task type. Especially, we argue that when subjects' risk attitude is critical for performance, RRPM and APM may induce a different level of performance.

It would be appropriate that this review is regarded as a complement of the previous reviews in the sense that this study focuses on the more specific question of investigating the effect of financial incentives on subjects' performance when those are combined with repetition of a task. Considering the results of the previous reviews and this one, we conclude that if an experimenter is to use repetition as a treatment, then it will be necessary or at least safe that he or she adopts financial incentives. In addition to this, we argue that he or she needs to be careful in adopting an appropriate repetition payoff mechanism; otherwise, the data from the experiment would be impaired by unexpected biases due to the payoff mechanism itself.

In Section 2 we summarize the general results on the effect of financial incentives and a review related to the use of repetition is described in Section 3. In Section 4, the main issues from the relationship between financial incentives and repetition are discussed in more detail. We review some experimental studies that have investigated the effect of financial incentives on performance under a repetition environment in Section 5, and Section 6 deals with some miscellanies that may be related to financial incentives. In Section 7, a conclusion and a discussion follow.

2. Financial Incentives in Laboratory Experiments

2.1 *Three Arguments on the Use of Financial Incentives in Laboratory Experiments*

Economists' rationale for using financial incentives itself is an empirical question. It depends on an introspective experimentation about human rationality that people do not want to make an effort (i.e. a cognitive or physical effort) without an appropriate reward or clear incentives.

Experiments in the laboratory definitely require subjects to make efforts. Hence, experimenters must think and have thought how they can induce subjects to make an appropriate effort for a given task. Experimental economists have decided to give them extrinsic incentives for this purpose by following the reasoning described above. They especially adopt a monetary reward as the best incentive since money is value neutral and it is thought to induce monotonic utility (Smith, 1976).[6] Moreover, economists naturally believe that the monetary reward should be based on subjects' performance so that it can function as an incentive. This is often called the *salience condition* (Smith, 1976). This is the basic rationale for the use of financial incentives in laboratory economics experiments.[7]

However, psychologists, especially cognitive psychologists, argue that people often have 'intrinsic motivation' for a task. Intrinsic motivation is a kind of deep-rooted incentive inside people. This term is used as opposed to the term extrinsic incentives, which is given from outside of people. Intrinsic motivation implies that people originally have an incentive to want to perform a task well without any extrinsic incentive (Deci, 1975). For example, there is no reason why they do not reveal their true preferences in hypothetical individual decision-making tasks (Kahneman and Tversky, 1979). The feelings of achievement, self-confidence, self-satisfaction, altruism and/or reciprocity are examples of intrinsic motivation. Hence, if subjects already have a sufficient level of the intrinsic motivation to make an effort for a task, then there may be no reason why experimenters must give any extrinsic incentive to them. Moreover, some psychologists argue that the extrinsic incentive or motivation often impairs intrinsic motivation and so results in harming subjects' performance rather than improving it (Lepper *et al.*, 1973; Deci and Ryan, 1987).[8]

One more polar position exists for non-experimental economists. They argue that the results from laboratory experiments may be invalid since the monetary stakes used in a typical laboratory experiment are too modest to represent real world economic behaviour. Smith (1994) regards this as a kind of infinitive nihilism since no empirical evidence virtually can falsify this argument. Suppose an experiment comparing the effect of the size of rewards on performance with a small reward X and a large reward Y, and suppose that the results report that there is no difference. Then, is the above argument falsified? It is not: it can still be argued that if an arbitrarily larger reward Z than Y is used, then there will be a difference. Hence, this argument can never be falsified. However, the point is that an economic theory in general cannot explain the behavioural difference resulting from the differences in levels of stakes. In the sense that there is evidence for each side, it may still be useful to collect the results from experiments that compare the effects of various levels of stakes on economic performance; it could help economists to construct theories that explain the difference in behaviour due to the difference in the level of stakes (Smith, 2002).

2.2 *Some Experimental Results on the Effect of Financial Incentives*

It is natural that a number of experimental studies have been run in order to judge between these polar arguments. The result is unfortunately still indecisive. However, some contingent conclusions seem to appear from the accumulation of results of the experimental studies.

2.2.1 *Financial Incentives and Performance*

First, financial incentives in general increase the level of effort, but the increase of effort does not necessarily lead to the improvement of performance (Farber and Spence, 1953; Pelham and Neter, 1995; Camerer and Hogarth, 1999; Bonner *et al.*, 2000).

Camerer and Hogarth (1999) explain this with the 'capital–labour framework'. Subjects' performance is a kind of production, and is a function of a cognitive capital (i.e. a cognitive skill or procedural knowledge) and a cognitive effort.[9] Hence, even if a cognitive effort increases with financial incentives, performance may not be improved unless subjects have an adequate cognitive capital for a given task. This argument is a further development from Smith and Walker (1993a, b)'s 'labour theory framework'. They focused on the relationship between financial incentives and cognitive efforts. It does not seem, though, that they completely ignore the existence of cognitive capital.

> Since increasing the reward level causes an increase in effort, the new model predicts that subject decisions will move closer to the theorist's optimum and result in a reduction in the variance of decision error. But this predicted shift towards optimality is qualified if effort is already constrained by the maximum that can be supplied, which would be the case for very complex decision problems. (Smith and Walker, 1993a, p. 260)

Rather, they seem to have assumed that most subjects may have enough cognitive capital or abilities to learn the optimal decision through an experimental process such as repetition (Smith, 1962, 1965, 1976; Grether and Plott, 1979). Friedman and Sunder (1994, p. 39) support this view when they explain why university undergraduates would be the most appropriate and popular subject pool for laboratory experiments: they note that undergraduates in general show a steep learning curve.

Of course, this argument cannot devalue the important message of the 'capital–labour framework', that is, experimenters definitely and seriously have a concern with subjects' cognitive capital. A difficulty is in the fact that the kinds of experimental tasks are various and so the kinds and levels of subjects' cognitive capital required are also various. We may need to seriously check whether a particular subject pool has an adequate knowledge and skill for a particular task. A way to do this would be a thorough pilot study or the use of preliminary quizzes.

2.2.2 *Financial Incentives and Intrinsic Motivation*

Second, there seems to always exist subjects who follow their intrinsic motivation rather than extrinsic incentives (Camerer and Hogarth, 1999). Subjects' behaviours in dictator games, ultimatum games and public good games are the examples where other motivation (i.e. altruism or reciprocity) rather than the clear extrinsic incentive of monetary rewards plays a role (Straub and Murnighan, 1995; Hoffman *et al.*, 1996; Cameron, 1999; Camerer, 2003; van Winden *et al.*, forthcoming).

However, though the deviation from a normative prediction with the assumption of selfishness in these examples still exists even for quite high real stakes, the proportion tends to decrease and the behaviour approaches closer to the normative prediction of economic models when the use of high real stakes is combined with the use of repetition (Slonim and Roth, 1998; List and Cherry, 2000).[10]

Moreover, it would be an empirical question if subjects still possess the intrinsic motivation as they face identical tasks many times even if it is conceded that they have enough intrinsic motivation to do a single-shot task without any extrinsic incentive. We suspect that this question must be related to learning process and boredom.

2.2.3 *Dependence of the Effect of Financial Incentives on Other Conditions*

Third, the effect of financial incentives on subjects' performance seems to depend on the type of task, the difficulty of the task and the payoff mechanisms. Camerer and Hogarth (1999) report that financial incentives improve performance in judgement tasks and routine tasks while they do not have an effect in market trading, bargaining and gamble choice tasks. Moreover, they note that financial incentives harm performance in some tasks. Bonner *et al.* (2000) also report that the positive effect of financial incentives decreases as a task becomes more complex and difficult.[11]

This relationship between financial incentives and a task type or difficulty may be related to the cognitive capital as briefly discussed above in the sense that, as a task becomes more difficult, the possibility that subjects have an adequate knowledge for the task seems to be less (see Pelham and Neter, 1995). The conclusions of other review studies are not much different from these (Jenkins, 1986; Jenkins *et al.*, 1998; Prendergast, 1999; Hertwig and Ortmann, 2001).

Bonner *et al.* (2000) report that the single-shot payoff mechanism influences the effect of financial incentives on performance. A *quota scheme* leads to the most positive effect on performance, a *piece-rate scheme* the next, a *tournament scheme* the next and a *flat-rate scheme* was the last.[12] While the quota scheme and the tournament scheme have been widely used in the real economy, they have a shortcoming in their use in the laboratory for the purpose of incentives. For the quota scheme, subjects' behaviour may be dramatically different in the margin of the quota point. The tournament scheme may induce subjects, whose performance is not going well, to behave without attention or effort (Friedman and Sunder, 1994). Moreover, the very competitive environment induced by the tournament scheme may aggravate 'choking under pressure' suggested by Baumeister (1984).[13] These all increase biases and errors in laboratory experiments. As a result, the most widely used payoff mechanisms in laboratory experiments (at least in economics) have been variations of the piece-rate scheme.[14]

As a matter of fact, the main debate in the experimental methodology on financial incentives has been between the piece-rate mechanism and a hypothetical payoff mechanism given that subjects are paid off a flat monetary reward for participation. Of course, many psychology experiments have used a pool of subjects where subjects are psychology students required to participate in some experiments

for course credits. Although we give attention to experimental situations where
subjects receive a participation fee, it must be interesting to question if voluntary
subjects show a different behaviour from obligatory subjects.[15] Our conjecture is
that the answer may depend on the reason why voluntary subjects volunteer in an
experiment. The best candidate for the reason seems to be an extrinsic incentive (i.e.
a monetary reward) rather than intrinsic motivation (e.g. self-satisfaction) though we
cannot ignore the fact that there are always exceptions (see Camerer and Hogarth,
1999). If so, there may be a difference in the motivation between voluntary subjects
and obligatory subjects, that is, the former will show a less intrinsically motivated
behaviour while the latter are much more intrinsically motivated.

2.2.4 *Financial Incentives and Variance of Performance*

Fourth, many experimenters agree with the fact that financial incentives decrease
the variance of subjects' performance (Kahneman and Tversky, 1979; Smith and
Walker, 1993a; Camerer and Hogarth, 1999; but see Wilcox, 1993). The small
variance due to financial incentives provides a more powerful statistical test.
Moreover, assuring a small variance would be important in some contexts that are
sensitive to a variation of subjects' choice, for example, 'weak link' coordination
games or asset markets with potential for speculative bubbles (Camerer, 2003).

Especially, the round by round variance of behaviour at later rounds under
repetition would be related to the effect of boredom, and it will be discussed
in Section 4.1 in more detail where it will be argued that the fact that financial
incentives reduce the variance of a subject's choice may imply that boredom, in
general, increases the variance of the subject's behaviour.

2.2.5 *Financial Incentives and Risk Attitudes*

Fifth, financial incentives seem to induce subjects to more risk-averse preference
(Binswanger, 1980, 1981; Millner and Pratt, 1991; Kachelmeier and Shehata, 1992;
Holt and Laury, 2002). While there is no theoretical prediction on this pattern, it
implies an important message for experimenters: if a subject's risk attitude is a
critical variable in a task, for example, many games, auctions, individual decision
making or value elicitation under risk, then hypothetical incentives would bias his
or her behaviour. That is, as long as risk attitudes matter, hypothetical incentives
do not seem to represent subjects' true preferences.

Harrison and Rustrom (forthcoming) review the studies that investigate the validity of the 'contingent valuation method' (CVM) for valuing environmental damages,
which is a commonly used survey instrument in environmental resource valuations.
The CVM is hypothetical since the payoffs used in eliciting value are hypothetical
and the good being valued is not provided. They argue that the studies reporting
'no hypothetical bias of CVM' in general have methodological or statistical defects,
and conclude that it is difficult to deny the existence of the hypothetical bias in
CVM. In relation to this, there is one interesting real-life example recently having
been a social issue in South Korea: more than 60% out of about 57,000 people,

who had promised in advance to donate their bone marrow that is usually used for medical treatment of leukaemia, rejected doing so when it was actually needed (SBS, 2003). Though the reasons for the rejection may be various and complicated, it is enough to cast a doubt against the validity of hypothetical incentives or surveys especially when subjects' decision involves various kinds of risk.

When financial incentives are given, Rabin (2000)'s argument could be applied. That is, a subject must be risk neutral for the typical small amount of laboratory monetary payoffs if she is an expected utility (EU) maximizer (Pratt, 1964; Arrow, 1970); otherwise (e.g. if they are risk averse for the small amount of payoffs), they show an absurd level of risk aversion for a reasonably large stake. This theoretical prediction has been so strong that explaining laboratory subjects' behaviour in terms of risk attitudes may be abandoned. However, the range of empirical evidence consistently suggests that many subjects are risk averse even for the small amount of financial incentives. Here we observe a severe collision between the theoretical prediction and the empirical evidence. How can we resolve this? This question will be discussed in more detail in Section 4.2.

2.3 *Payoff Dominance and Flat Payoff Critique*

Discussing the debate on the validity of financial incentives (i.e. a piece-rate performance-based payoff scheme and a hypothetical payoff scheme), the concept of payoff dominance has been located at the centre of the debates. The payoff dominance condition requires that the only element that can affect subjects' utility must be a monetary reward, making the other variables negligible (Smith, 1976). Since experimenters cannot observe the other variables, the payoff dominance condition might be problematic (Friedman and Sunder, 1994).

The flat payoff critique argued by Harrison (1989, 1994) is one important example to show how an experiment fails to satisfy the payoff dominance condition though the main point is quite different from the original one suggested by Smith (1976). He argues that even if subjects are given financial incentives, there is no reason why subjects do not deviate from a point of maximized expected payoff (i.e. a normative equilibrium option) if the expected losses by deviating from it are negligible. Hence, some anomalies against a normative prediction may not be systematic but due to errors caused by the flat payoff structure. An important implication of this critique is that simply using financial incentives may not sufficiently motivate subjects. This critique brought hot debates between experimental economists (Harrison, 1989, 1992; Cox *et al.*, 1992; Friedman, 1992; Kagel and Roth, 1992; Merlo and Schotter, 1992).

3. Repetition

3.1 *What, Why and How Repetition?*

Using repeated trials has been the norm in economics experiments while, in psychology, it depends on the purpose of an experiment. Of course, there have been exceptions for this norm even in economics experiments. Hertwig and Ortmann (2001) note that the experiments on trust games, dictator games and ultimatum games have usually adopted a single-shot trial environment. However, in our knowledge, the experiments using repetition have increased even in these contexts (Roth *et al.*, 1991; Slonim and Roth, 1998; List and Cherry, 2000).

The main reason why economists use repetition is to give subjects an opportunity of learning. Experimental economists believe that subjects cannot learn only the experimental environment but also the possible strategic aspects of the task through repeated trials (Hertwig and Ortmann, 2001). Here, what repetition means needs to be specified with more details. Hertwig and Ortmann (2001, p. 387) define it as follows: 'Typically, economists implement repeated trials either as stationary replications of one-shot decision and game situations or as repeated game situations'.

That is, while the stationary replications mean repeated trials of individual decision making without interaction or repeated trials of the game situation (i.e. interacting with other subjects) with change of partner or opponents, repeated game situations mean repeated trials of the game situation with the same partners or opponents.[16] Hence, whether a strategic interaction exists across rounds or not distinguishes one from the other.

We may need to add more distinction to this according to whether 'feedback' exists or not. In general, many individual decision-making experiments, especially those on risk attitudes and risky choices, do not give feedback after each trial, while most game experiments and market experiments provide it. Of course, the main reason for using repetition in the individual decision-making context is quite different from the others: the main purpose of the use of repetition in individual decision-making experiments is usually not to give a learning opportunity but rather to test consistency of choices or to collect more data, and so repetition of an exactly identical decision-making task is rare. Rather, many similar but different tasks (e.g. different probabilities and outcomes in risky choices) are given to subjects. However, we regard this as a kind of repetition since subjects can be accustomed to the decision environment through repeatedly facing similar tasks even without feedback. This must be interpreted as a kind of learning too. Moreover, the concept of boredom could be related to even this kind of repetition.

Of course, this conjecture itself is an empirical question: what and how much can subjects learn without feedback? When the external feedback is not given, subjects are in general assumed to learn nothing (El-Gamal and Grether, 1995). However, it is still possible that they may learn something through a self-evaluation and a self-feedback. Loomes and Sugden (1998) report that subjects' behaviour patterns have evolved towards the prediction of expected utility theory (EUT) over the course of their experiment where RRPM was used and no feedback was given.

In real life, many science texts such as mathematics, economics and physics do not include the solution for an exercise problem. Students try to solve it without the existence of a direct feedback: they never know whether their solution is correct or not. However, they give feedback to themselves by contemplating, often by referring to the contents of the texts. At the end, they can have some degree of confidence about their solution. This is considered a good way to learn a topic in those sciences. In laboratory experiments, the instruction plays the role of texts, the external feedback must be the solution by the author and subjects are the students. In particular, the instructions in economics experiments are, in general, very clear regarding the payoff structure and the rules.

In this respect, we cannot be sure that there is no learning even when an external feedback is not given.[17] This conjecture is supported by a recent experimental study by Weber (2003) reporting that subjects' behaviour converges to the equilibrium even without feedback in a 'p-beauty contest game'.[18] Moreover, this line of argument may be compatible with that of Roth and Murnighan (1978) on the information about the number of rounds in economics experiments. Hence, we refer to the word 'repetition' as a stationary replication or a repeated game regardless of the existence of feedback.[19]

3.2 Repetition, Learning and Boredom

The relationship between repetition and learning has recently been an active research area. A number of experiments investigate it, and a few learning theories have been developed (Milgrom and Roberts, 1991; Roth and Erev, 1995; Weibull, 1995; Cheung and Friedman, 1997; Fudenberg and Levine, 1998; Camerer and Ho, 1999; Camerer et al., 2002a, b). However, Camerer and Hogarth (1999, p. 10) comment on the limitation of learning through repetition in laboratory experiments. 'Furthermore, useful cognitive capital probably builds up slowly, over days of mental fermentation or years of education rather than in the short-run of an experiment (1–3 hours).... However, incentives surely do play an important role in inducing long-run capital formation' (italics by the authors).

Here again, we are confronted with the question about subjects' cognitive capital. An important point is whether subjects can acquire or learn the cognitive capital (i.e. skill or knowledge) adequate to a given task through repetition or not. As with the case of the effect of financial incentives, it must be task dependent. The skills for some tasks must take long to be acquired as suggested by Camerer and Hogarth while the skills for others can be easily learned in a reasonably short time, that is, only a few repetitions. All results deviating from a normative prediction should not be attributed to the absence of an adequate cognitive capital. It would be a kind of nihilism in laboratory experiments, which is similar to the nihilism in terms of the size of financial incentives. Experimenters must be able to have a high level of confidence about whether subjects can have or at least learn a necessary skill for a given task before he or she runs a main experiment. In this respect, the pilot study, the use of practice rounds and some quizzes may be more important than they have previously been thought to be.

When an experimenter wants to use repetition, she must decide how many trials should be repeated. It may depend on previous experimental studies, may depend on how many observations she needs from that experiment or may be ad hoc.[20] In fact, the number of repeated rounds seems not to have a robust base in many experimental studies. The key question she must ask would be related to the relationships between a task, learning speed (if she believes that subjects can learn the adequate skill by repetition) and boredom.

While some economists and psychologists have argued that there is an effect of boredom in repeated trials in laboratory experiments, there has not been a concrete theoretical framework to deal with this to our knowledge (see Slovic *et al.*, 1965; Ledyard, 1995). This is partly because the question is ultimately an empirical question. However, there is no reason why a basic theoretical framework cannot be built for the purpose of making a base to implement the empirical works. Existing learning theories do not deal with the relationship between learning and boredom but do deal with the learning process itself (Fudenberg and Levine, 1998; Camerer and Ho, 1999; Goeree and Holt, 1999, 2000). If a learning process always generates boredom, then the learning theories would need to incorporate this. This must be done because an equilibrium achieved by the learning process would not be stable but fluctuate if a boredom effect exists. Hence, it may be worth theoretically and empirically checking if there is a systematic pattern for boredom in a learning process.

Boredom can arise at any point in an experiment. However, we may be able to plausibly assume that it spikes at a point of accustomization while it steadily increases in initial periods of learning or the beginning of accustomization. A learning process in an experiment would have three important phases, that is, initial periods of learning, accustomization after enough learning and boredom. Moreover, boredom may have an upper bound by its definition. This depends on the assumption that people have enough incentive to break the boredom at a marginal level of boredom. People definitely can do it. How people break boredom has never been known. When they are bored, they may either persistently choose a stable easy-to-discover strategy (Slovic *et al.*, 1965) or randomly vary the choice (Siegel, 1959). We need more empirical evidence.

Then, the best in the meantime which an experimenter can do may be to set the appropriate number of repetitions before subjects' boredom level approaches the spike point. Hence, an experimenter should be very careful when she decides the number of repeated trials given that experimental economists are usually most interested in subjects' behaviour at final rounds.

4. Financial Incentives and Repetition

4.1 *Financial Incentives, Learning and Boredom Under Repetition*

Investigating the effect of financial incentives under a repetition environment brings some important topics that would not be necessary in a single-shot trial environment. There may be multiple relationships between financial incentives and learning efforts, learning speed, boredom and the payoff mechanisms. Slonim and Roth (1998) report an experimental result that there may be an interaction between the level of stakes of financial incentives and learning. They ran experiments on ultimatum games where most studies using a single-shot trial environment find a systematic deviation from the economic normative prediction: subjects offer and reject much more than predicted by a perfect equilibrium. These results seem to be quite robust for different levels of stakes (Cameron, 1995; Straub and Murnighan, 1995; Hoffman *et al.*, 1996; Henrich *et al.*, 2001).

Slonim and Roth (1998) compared three levels of stakes and used repetition of 10 rounds. In this environment, the first round behaviour of inexperienced subjects was not significantly different from those of previous studies. However, when they pooled all results of 10 rounds, they found that subjects' behaviour comes close to the perfect equilibrium when stakes become higher. They conclude that there is an interaction between financial incentives and learning, that is, if subjects face high stakes (i.e. large amount of financial incentives) and are given enough opportunities to learn, then their behaviour may approach the normative economic prediction, that is, perfect equilibrium. This result may represent the importance of systematic research on the relationship between financial incentives and subjects' behaviour in a repetition environment.

Can financial incentives increase learning effort and so precipitate learning? Many experimental studies report that financial incentives play an important role in learning and increase learning efforts (Phillips and Edwards, 1966; Castellan, 1969; Jamal and Sunder, 1991; Irwin *et al.*, 1992; List and Cherry, 2000). However, some studies report that subjects with feedback but without financial incentives outperform or do not make any difference from those who learned with feedback and financial incentives (Hogarth *et al.*, 1991; Merlo and Schotter, 1999), and that subjects' learning effort may not be connected with performance if they do not have an adequate cognitive skill (Craik and Tulving, 1975; Camerer and Hogarth, 1999). Each argument has an important implication in the methodology of experimental economics. We will deal with each argument in more detail.

Before doing this, we first assume that subjects already have adequate cognitive skills or can learn them by repetition. This implies that we avoid addressing the third argument in this discussion. However, we do not say that the argument on the cognitive capital should and can be ignored. Rather, we are assuming that an experimenter has already resolved the problems related to subjects' cognitive capital before she runs a main experiment so that she can expect subjects to have enough cognitive skills to experience the learning process.[21] If subjects do not have enough cognitive skills adequate for a task, repetition (in typical experiments of three to four hours at most) would never help them learn something, that is, subjects' behaviour would never show a consistent pattern towards a normative prediction. However, many experiments on various types of tasks report consistent patterns of subjects' behaviour through repetition. In many cases, repetition can make subjects learn about a task, and then the learning process itself could be evidence of subjects' adequate cognitive skills for the task. This could be a rationale for our assumption. However, we stress that we make the assumption only because we want to focus on the situations where repetition can lead to learning.

By our assumption, we can focus on the effect of financial incentives on the learning process and on boredom. Financial incentives are believed to precipitate subjects' learning by making them exert more effort to learn and to mitigate boredom by giving a clear extrinsic incentive. This implies that the use of financial incentives may decrease the number of repeated trials required for completion of the learning process and decrease the error resulting from boredom in excessive repeated trials. This is the main reason why financial incentives must be used with repetition. By the same logic, under hypothetical incentives, experimenters may need more repeated trials than under financial incentives. More repeated trials would increase the possibility of boredom and hence the errors resulting from it. Many experiments report the results to support this argument. The main conclusion from these experiments is that financial incentives play an important role in the learning process. This means that financial incentives are an important factor for the learning effort.

However, there are other studies reporting that subjects, who learn without financial incentives but know that there will be a task for a real reward after learning periods, outperform those who learn with financial incentives (Merlo and Schotter, 2003). These experiments question that financial incentives in the learning process itself may limit subjects' learning process. For example, subjects with financial incentives in the learning process may be easily satisfied with a myopic or stable strategy, and so they may stop attempting to learn alternatives and more profitable strategies. Moreover, financial incentives in the learning process may give subjects more pressures and make them choke under pressure, which results in poor learning (Baumeister, 1984).[22]

The key point amongst these two seemingly opposite results is not whether financial incentives are effective in learning or not, but when they are given to subjects. They agree that financial incentives ultimately increase subjects' learning effort and hence precipitate learning. The disagreement is whether financial incentives should be given in the learning process itself or not. The former argues that they should be given in the learning process. This implies that the use of financial incentives is much more important for initial trials than for the final trials. On the contrary, the latter argues that the use of financial incentives in the learning periods, that is, in initial trials, may harm subjects' learning process. This implies that subjects can learn much more under the conditions that they know one or some real trial(s) are coming soon and they are given enough opportunities to learn without financial incentives before the real trials.

What is the practical implication in these two arguments? The former argument suggests that we must use a number of real trials with financial incentives. The latter argues that it may be better to use a number of practice trials without financial incentives and then some real trials with financial incentives.[23] This could be converted to the question of what the better way to give subjects a learning opportunity is: either many trials with small financial incentives, or many practice trials plus some trials with large financial incentives. In fact, this difference of implications cannot be resolved without enough empirical investigations. We do not yet see enough experimental studies to directly deal with these so that the issue may be resolved.

Subjects' boredom may be one important issue under a repetition environment as argued in the previous section. Subjects seem to feel boredom as the number of repeated trials increases. Boredom can be thought of as a kind of negative intrinsic motivation. Subjects will try to do something to avoid boredom. This tendency seems to be suppressed by a positive extrinsic incentive, that is, financial incentives. In economics language, the opportunity cost of deviation from a best choice in order to exit from boredom increases as financial incentives become larger. The increase of opportunity cost may prevent subjects from following a boredom-induced behaviour. Hence, it is plausible to argue that financial incentives offset the effect of boredom.

What is the effect of boredom? There are two arguments about this question. First, one could argue that boredom leads to unsystematic errors resulting in a large variance of behaviour (Siegel, 1959; Smith and Walker, 1993a). This argument implies that unsystematic deviations due to boredom under hypothetical incentives will be more frequent than under financial incentives as the number of repeated trials increases. Thus, the variance of behaviour due to boredom would be larger with hypothetical incentives than with financial incentives. Therefore, the more trials an experimenter wants, the larger are the financial incentives which he or she needs to give to subjects.

Second, Slovic *et al.* (1965) argue that boredom would induce a stable behaviour that is easy for subjects to discover. This argument implies that the variance of subjects' behaviour would be larger with financial incentives than with hypothetical incentives since the financially motivated subjects will attempt to find the best strategy rather than stick to an easy-to-discover strategy.

The finding that financial incentives tend to reduce the variance and outliers of behaviours seems to support the former argument (Smith and Walker, 1993a; Camerer and Hogarth, 1999; Camerer, 2003). Considering that the important thing related to boredom is not only the between-subjects variance of the behaviour but also the round-by-round variance of a subject's behaviour in later rounds (assuming that the learning process is completed), we will argue, in Section 5.3.2, in favour of the former argument that boredom in general leads to more variable behaviour, and that financial incentives reduce the variance.

However, an important question is when subjects feel boredom. As discussed in Section 3.2, it is ultimately an empirical question. Moreover, it would depend on the number of repeated trials and learning speed, and hence task difficulty as well as task types. Therefore, though financial incentives may offset the effect of boredom somehow, the best way, which an experimenter can do, will be to control the duration of the experiment (e.g. the number of repeated trials) before boredom approaches a significant level as long as the effect of boredom is not exactly known.[24]

4.2 *Financial Incentives and Payoff Mechanisms Under Repetition*

Another important topic in examining the effect of financial incentives under repetition is about repetition payoff mechanisms. As we briefly described in the introduction, the repetition payoff mechanism is here defined as a way by which financial incentives are given to subjects under a repetition environment while the single-shot payoff mechanism is defined as a way by which those incentives are given to them for a single-shot trial.

By using repetition, experimenters usually must choose a repetition payoff mechanism in addition to a single-shot payoff mechanism. We here focus on two repetition payoff mechanisms, that is, the APM and the RRPM.

Under APM, subjects' monetary rewards in the experiment are the sum of their monetary rewards of each trial (or round) through a whole experiment. Under RRPM, subjects are given their monetary rewards based on one or only a few randomly chosen trial(s) (or round(s)) after a whole experiment has been completed. While APM is the most widely used in economics experiments, some experiments often have used RRPM. In particular, APM has been used in most market experiments and game experiments, and RRPM has been mainly used in individual decision-making experiments, specifically when a wealth effect and the problem of portfolio composition need to be controlled. The reason is that (1) in some areas, the control of subjects' risk attitudes is crucial, and RRPM is believed to do it by controlling the wealth effect and the possibility of portfolio composition; (2) RRPM is usually believed to make experimenters' budget burden lessen (Friedman and Sunder, 1994, p. 51). An important theoretical prediction from EUT is that, if subjects are risk neutral, RRPM and APM must induce an identical behaviour though the scales of the expected payoffs are different between RRPM and APM, that is, a risk-neutral subject's behaviour will not be affected by the scale difference.[25] If we resolve the scale difference by equating the expected payoffs under RRPM to those under APM, then RRPM changes only the second or higher moments of the payoff distribution, and thus it may be considered as a kind of *mean preserving spread* of a distribution under APM (Lee, 2006).[26]

Before a further discussion of the two repetition payoff mechanisms, it must be noted that the payoff dominance problem and the flat payoff problem discussed in the previous section would have more weight in a repetition environment than in a single-shot task. Essentially, repetition requires more duration for an experiment than the same single-shot trial does, and this implies that if an experimenter wants to use financial incentives, then she must give more money to subjects. This is reasoned by the prediction that subjects demand more rewards as they are required to spend more time in order to trade off their opportunity costs. This implies that the behavioural difference between when financial incentives are given and when hypothetical incentives are used may be larger in a repetition environment than in a single-shot trial environment.

The more severe problem may be related to the flat payoff critique. Because of the budget constraint, the experimenter may reduce the difference of reward rates between one choice and another (i.e. she may reduce piece-rates) so that she can resolve the payoff dominance problem.[27] However, this may generate the flat payoff problem. Essentially, the flat payoff problem becomes serious as the number of repeated trials increases at any given budget constraints. In fact, most experiments that Harrison (1994) criticized for the flat payoff problem have used repetition. Some experimenters argue that RRPM may be useful to avoid the flat payoff problem since an experimenter needs to give subjects the monetary rewards for one or only a few round(s). However, this argument can be supported only if subjects regard each trial as a completely isolated one. If subjects regard each trial as a part of a whole task, using RRPM cannot avoid the flat payoff problem by itself since the flat payoff problem is not related to the nominal payoffs but to the expected payoffs. This concern is related to the dilution of the incentive under RRPM (Holt and Davis, 1993). It is noted that many experiments in which RRPM has been used are susceptible to the flat payoff critique.

Only a few comparative studies investigating whether RRPM induces the same behaviour as a single-shot trial or not exist in individual decision-making tasks (Starmer and Sugden, 1991; Wilcox, 1993; Camerer, 1995; Beattie and Loomes, 1997; Cubitt et al., 1998). Holt (1986) re-examined the preference reversal experiment by Grether and Plott (1979) in which RRPM was used to obviate possible wealth effects in the Becker–DeGroot–Marschak (BDM) elicitation process. He argues that the preference reversal may not come from intransitive preferences but from violation of the independence axiom since it is possible under RRPM to observe the preference reversal behaviour without intransitive preferences if the independence axiom is violated. This argument implies that if subjects who are not EU maximizers do not separate each task under RRPM, RRPM would lead them to a different behaviour from that in a single-shot task. In response to this theoretical argument, only a few experimental studies have been done mainly in the individual decision-making context. Most of those support that RRPM induces an almost identical behaviour to that in a single-shot task, that is, they find that non-EU subjects tend to separate each task under RRPM (Starmer and Sugden, 1991; Beattie and Loomes, 1997; Cubitt et al., 1998; Hey and Lee, 2005a, b).

There are only two studies empirically comparing RRPM and APM to our knowledge. Laury (2005) compares three payoff mechanisms in 10 gamble choice tasks: RRPM for low payoff, APM for low payoff and 10 × (RRPM for low payoff). She finds that there is no difference in subjects' implied risk attitudes between RRPM for low payoff and APM for low payoff while subjects were significantly more risk averse in 10 × (RRPM for low payoff) than in APM for low payoff. She concludes that RRPM whose nominal payoffs at each round are identical to those under APM could be used instead of APM without inducing a different behaviour. Lee (2006) compares APM and RRPM in a game context where subjects' risk attitudes matter. He finds that if an experimenter equates the expected payoffs under both payoff mechanisms, RRPM would induce a more risk-averse behaviour and lead to a behaviour closer to equilibrium. This result seems to be in accordance with Selten et al. (1999)'s 'background risk hypothesis', which argues that the background risk induced by RRPM would make a (risk-averse) subject behave differently under RRPM and under APM. However, it would be too early to accept this conclusion: we clearly need more evidence because this issue is ultimately an empirical one.

It is notable that there is little debate between the use of RRPM and the use of APM in game experiments. In game experiments, some experiments have used RRPM while other experiments have used APM, for the same topics. This may be due to the main tendency of game theorists' accepting the theoretical prediction of EUT that people are approximately risk neutral for reasonably low stakes (Pratt, 1964; Arrow, 1970). Hence, many game experiments assume that subjects are risk neutral in the laboratory environment where small financial incentives are typically used (Friedman and Cassar, 2004). This assumption has been applied more often to the game experiments than to individual decision-making experiments.

Especially, this assumption has been more supported by Rabin's argument that, if a person shows risk aversion for a low-stakes gamble, then she must show an absurd level of risk aversion for a reasonably high-stakes gamble given that she is an EU maximizer (Rabin, 2000). However, the debate on Rabin's argument is ongoing in a theoretical context (Cox and Sadiraj, 2001; Palacios-Huerta *et al.*, 2001; Rubinstein, 2001). The main point of the debate is on how the prizes of a lottery, that is, a consequence under uncertainty, are defined in EUT. Cox and Sadiraj (2001) and Rubinstein (2001) argue that Rabin's result critically depends on the assumption that prizes of a lottery are defined by final wealth levels rather than by wealth change. While this is a practical use of EUT by economists, the EUT axioms do not require that only final wealth must be used for the prizes, that is, the EUT of final wealth is only a kind of EUT. Hence, Rabin's result could not be evidence against EUT itself while it could be one against applicability of a kind of EUT for which it is assumed that the prizes are amounts of final wealth.

In laboratory experiments, there is no reason to assume that subjects are the maximizers of EU of final wealth. Assuming that subjects are EU maximizers does not imply that they must maximize EU of final wealth. Hence, assuming that laboratory subjects must be EU maximizers cannot be the reason why considering subjects' risk aversion must be susceptible to Rabin's argument, that is, it would be a misunderstanding to argue that laboratory subjects, who in general are given a small amount of monetary reward, cannot be risk averse according to Rabin's argument.[28] However, Cox and Sadiraj (2001) note that a few experimental studies, whose explanations depend on subjects' risk aversion, have been rejected from publication by Rabin's argument.

In fact, the empirical evidence from many experimental studies directly measuring subjects' risk attitudes in the laboratory report that most subjects are risk averse even for low stakes (Murnighan *et al.*, 1988; Millner and Pratt, 1991; Kachelmeier and Shehata, 1992; Smith and Walker, 1993a, b; Holt and Laury, 2002; Harrison *et al.*, 2003). Holt and Laury (2002) show through their hybrid power-expo utility model using the experimental data that subjects' risk aversion for a small amount of prize does not need to imply absurd levels of risk aversion for a large amount of prizes if a decreasing absolute risk aversion and an increasing relative risk aversion are assumed. Combining these empirical results with the above argument, we are not confident that subjects must be risk neutral in the laboratory environment though we assume that subjects are EU maximizers.

If we concede that subjects may not be risk neutral in the laboratory, then we have a good reason why RRPM and APM may lead them to a different behaviour in laboratory experiments: RRPM would generate a riskier payoff distribution than one under APM. This would be so even if RRPM induces the same behaviour as that in a single-shot task because a wealth effect and/or the possibility of portfolio composition would exist unless subjects are risk neutral, and because the effects of these factors may be different between RRPM and APM. This implies that the effect of financial incentives may differ according to the specific payoff mechanism that has been used in an experimental study. We may need to carefully compare various repetition payoff mechanisms as has been done on various single-shot payoff mechanisms, and to be careful when we interpret the results of an experiment.

5. Review of Studies

In this section, we review laboratory experimental studies that investigated the effect of financial incentives on performance in a repetition environment. We focus on the arguments discussed in the previous section. The questions being attempted to be answered are, *under a repetition environment,* (1) whether financial incentives are effective on performance in general, comparing between hypothetical payoffs and financial payoffs, and between low financial payoffs and high financial payoffs; (2) how the effect of financial incentives on performance is related to a task type; (3) whether financial incentives are related to learning and boredom; (4) whether repetition payoff mechanisms affect performance in experiments where financial incentives are given.

We include the studies that have used repetition among those reviewed in Camerer and Hogarth (1999), Hertwig and Ortmann (2001), and among those which appear in Holt (2000)'s 2k bibliography–methodology section. In addition to these, we include recent experimental studies in economics whose purpose is to directly investigate the effect of financial incentives under a repetition environment. The resulting number included in this review is 44 experiments from 38 studies, and these are summarized in Table A1 at the end of this paper.

Since we are more interested in the aggregate tendency of the results of the studies, we minimize the discussion on the individual study as much as possible, leaving it to the summary table. It should be also noted that the term 'the effect of financial incentives' will imply both the effect of financial incentives versus hypothetical incentives and the effect of high financial incentives versus low financial incentives. When we need to distinguish one from the other, we will specify it.

5.1 *Overall Effect of Financial Incentives*

First, we check the effect of financial incentives on performance under a repetition environment in general. Nineteen studies (43.2%) out of 44 report that financial incentives improve subjects' performance, 13 studies (29.6%) report that financial incentives do not affect subjects' performance, six (18%) studies suggest that the effect of financial incentives depends on other conditions and three (6.8%) studies find that financial incentives harm subjects' performance. The other three studies report that financial incentives affect subjects' behaviour, but there is no theoretical prediction to define improvement. This result is summarized in Table 2 and Figure 1.

Table 2. Summary of Overall Results.

	Overall frequency	Percentage	Hypothetical vs real frequency	Percentage	High vs low frequency	Percentage
Improve	19	43.2	12	50.0	7	35.0
No effect	13	29.5	7	29.2	6	30.0
Harm	3	6.8	2	8.3	1	5.0
Indecisive	6	13.6	2	8.3	4	20.0
Effect but no norm	3	6.8	1	4.2	2	10.0
Total	44	100.0	24	100.0	20	100.0

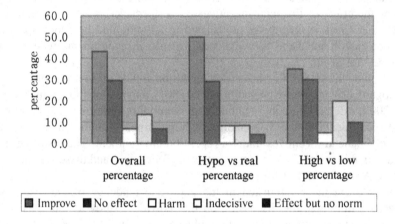

Figure 1. The Effect of Financial Incentives.

Comparing this result with that of the review study of Camerer and Hogarth (1999), we find that the major conclusion could change, that is, the positive effect of financial incentives is most commonly found under a repetition environment while their comprehensive review (in the sense of including both repetition and single-shot trial environments) finds that the most common case was 'no effect of financial incentives on performance' (45%). In their study, the positive effect was 40% and the negative effect was 15%. This suggests that there may be a relationship between financial incentives and repetition: financial incentives improve subjects' performance under repetition.

Some may argue that the improvement of performance under repetition in this review is due to feedback and learning, and not due to financial incentives. This argument is inappropriate because the financial incentive treatments are compared with each other given that the other treatments, for example, feedback and learning, are controlled to be identical. Of course, there may be an indirect effect that financial incentives influence the effect of feedback and learning and consequently improve the performance. However, this must be interpreted as the effect of financial incentives, not of feedback and learning, since the origin of the improvement is not feedback and learning but rather the financial incentives. As discussed later, the interaction between financial incentives, and feedback and learning would be one important issue that must be explored.

5.1.1 *Financial Incentives vs Hypothetical Incentives*

Second, we consider 24 studies comparing the effect of hypothetical incentives with the effect of financial incentives. As shown in Table 2, 12 studies report that financial incentives lead subjects to an improved performance over hypothetical incentives. Here, seven studies report that financial incentives do not affect subjects' performance, two studies report that the effect depends on the other conditions, two studies suggest that financial incentives harm subjects' performance and one study reports that financial incentives affect performance but there is no theoretical prediction.

This result supports an argument that there is a significant difference between a hypothetical incentive and a financial incentive (Smith, 1965, 1976; Smith and Walker, 1993a). This may show that the position of experimental economists against psychologists can be supported at least for experiments where repetition is used. In other words, it would be necessary to use financial incentives if an experimenter wants to use repetition in his or her experiment.

5.1.2 *High Financial Incentives vs Low Financial Incentives*

Third, we compare 20 studies that investigate subjects' behavioural difference between the effect of low financial incentives and the effect of high financial incentives. Seven studies report that subjects' (mean) performance with high financial incentives is significantly better than that with low financial incentives while six studies report there is no significant difference in subjects' (mean) performance between high financial incentives and low financial incentives. Subjects' performance was negatively affected by high financial incentives rather than by low financial incentives only in one study (McClintock and McNeel, 1966). Four studies find compounded effects (Wilcox, 1993; Irwin *et al.*, 1998; Slonim and Roth, 1998; List and Cherry, 2000), and two studies find an effect for which there is no theoretical prediction. This is summarized in Table 2 and Figure 1.

The effect of the size of financial incentives under repetition seems to be indecisive. This result may support experimental economists' view against non-experimental economists, that is, there is little behavioural difference between a low payoff and a high payoff, and hence a laboratory experiment could well predict real economic behaviour. However, it must be noted that the sample size for our studies is too small to draw a firm conclusion. More studies need to be done. Especially, a careful study on the relationship between learning by repetition, boredom and financial incentives across various levels of payoff seems to be promising.

5.2 *Financial Incentives and Task Types*

Fourth, we check how the effect of financial incentives on performance is related to task type. For this purpose, we divide the tasks in the reviewed studies in a few categories: memory tasks, judgement tasks, choice tasks, problem-solving tasks, and game and market tasks. If we follow Bonner *et al.* (2000)'s categorization, the difficulty of the tasks would be arranged in the order of memory tasks, judgement and choice tasks, problem-solving tasks and game and market tasks from a less difficult to a more difficult one.

The overall effects of financial incentives are summarized in Table 3 and Figure 2. Because the more important task types in economics must be game and market tasks, choice tasks, and judgement tasks, we will concentrate on discussing the results from these task types.[29]

In game and market tasks, it is notable that the two studies comparing financial incentives with hypothetical incentives report that the financial incentives improve performance (Jamal and Sunder, 1991; Irwin *et al.*, 1992) while five out of eight studies comparing low financial incentives with high financial incentives find that high financial incentives do not improve performance more than the low financial incentives do or that the effect is compounded. This seems to support experimental economists' argument that financial incentives, which are typically used in the laboratory, can improve subjects' performance and at the same time represent their real economic behaviour.

Moreover, it is also notable that two of three studies reporting 'no effect of financial incentives' (Neelin *et al.*, 1988; Roth *et al.*, 1991) and the two studies reporting that the effect of financial incentives is compounded (Slonim and Roth, 1998; List and Cherry, 2000) are on ultimatum bargaining games while three out of four studies reporting the positive effect of financial incentives are on market experiments (Smith, 1965; Jamal and Sunder, 1991; Irwin *et al.*, 1992) and the other one is on a *p*-beauty contest game (Ho *et al.*, 1998). It would be interesting to note that the decision environment for the market and *p*-beauty game experiments is much more competitive than that for the ultimatum bargaining game (and the dictator game) experiments. Then, these results may suggest that the effect of financial incentives differs according to the competitiveness of a decision environment.

Of the 17 studies on choice tasks, six report the positive effect of financial incentives on performance while five studies do not find any effect of financial incentives on performance. Three studies report that the effect interacts with other conditions, and three studies find an effect for which there is no normative prediction in terms of the definition of improvement. Grether and Plott (1979) and Cox and Grether (1996) report no effect of financial incentives on performance in preference reversal experiments. Though there are some studies reporting that financial incentives reduce preference reversals (Ordonez *et al.*, 1995), the preference reversal phenomenon has been one of the most robust anomalies irrespective of the associated treatment.

For example, Cox and Grether (1996) ran many experiments on preference reversals varying institutional mechanisms and incentive treatments. Financial incentives

Table 3. The Effect of Financial Incentives by Task Types.

	Memory	%	Judgement	%	Choice	%	Problem solving	%	Games and markets	%	Total	%
Improve	2	50.0	6	54.5	6	35.3	1	50.0	4	40.0	19	43.2
No effect	1	25.0	4	36.4	5	29.4	0	0.0	3	30.0	13	29.5
Harm	0	0.0	1	9.1	0	0.0	1	50.0	1	10.0	3	6.8
Indecisive effect	1	25.0	0	0.0	3	17.6	0	0.0	2	20.0	6	13.6
But no norm	0	0.0	0	0.0	3	17.6	0	0.0	0	0.0	3	6.8
Total	4	100.0	11	100.0	17	100.0	2	100.0	10	100.0	44	100.0

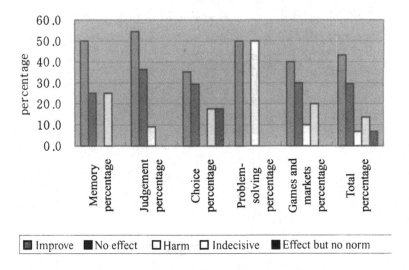

Figure 2. The Effect of Financial Incentives by Task Types.

do not significantly reduce preference reversals with the BDM mechanism and the second bid auction mechanism while they reduce those with the English clock-descending auction. Notably, repetition reduces preference reversals regardless of the kinds of incentives with the second bid auction, and reduces those for real incentives with the English clock auction. Moreover, with low real incentives, repetition reduces preference reversals with the BDM mechanism.[30]

Hogarth and Einhorn (1990) find that there is no difference in subjects' implied risk attitudes with hypothetical incentives and with financial incentives, but that subjects with high financial incentives appear to be more risk averse than those with low financial incentives. Most studies on measuring subjects' risk attitudes generally report that subjects are more risk averse with financial incentives than with hypothetical incentives, and that they are more risk averse with high financial incentives than with low financial incentives.

For the judgement task, six studies report that financial incentives improve subjects' performance, four studies find that financial incentives do not affect performance and one study reports that the effect of financial incentives on performance is negative.

In Zizzo *et al.* (2000), the effect of financial incentives on subjects' performance is isolated from the effect of feedback by comparing two groups, that is, a group with financial incentives and feedback, and a group with feedback but without financial incentives. In this study, the results are compounded: when tasks are complex, financial incentives do not improve subjects' behaviour (i.e. do not reduce the conjunction fallacy), but when tasks are simple, financial incentives do improve performance (i.e. reduce the conjunction fallacy).

In pupillary dilution tasks, Kahneman *et al.* (1968) report that a high financial incentive does not affect judgement accuracy while Kahneman and Peavler (1969) find that a high financial incentive leads to more correct recall than a low financial incentive does.[31] These quite opposite findings may be due to the use of a penalty in the former experiment. Though it is not certain that a positive financial incentive creates the so-called 'choking under pressure', it seems to be clear that a penalty, that is, a negative financial incentive, causes more tension and pressure leading to a choking behaviour.[32] This would trade off the incentive effect of a positive financial incentive.

Competition due to a tournament-type payoff mechanism would also create more tension and pressure as discussed in Section 1. The study by van Wallendael (1995) that reports 'no effect of financial incentives on judgement tasks' in an experiment where a tournament-type financial incentive is used may be subject to this criticism. Moreover, the tournament-type financial incentives may generate unexpected biases (Friedman and Sunder, 1994). Considering this argument, we may argue that only two out of four studies that report 'no positive effect of financial incentives on judgement tasks' is plausible. Then, with the fact that some previous overall review studies, which include both single-shot trial experiments and repetition experiments, report the positive effect of financial incentive in judgement tasks (Camerer and Hogarth, 1999), we may be slightly in favour of the argument that financial incentives improve subjects' performance in judgement tasks though a firm conclusion is surely postponed until enough studies are accumulated.

As is clear, the number of studies in each task-type category is not enough to draw a firm conclusion, in particular for the memory tasks, the problem-solving tasks and the game and market tasks. Though it is conceded that some studies may not be included in this review by our filtering rules or by our ignorance, a clear fact is that only a few studies exist for investigating the effect of financial incentives in some research areas.

In summary, it seems quite plausible to conclude that the effect of financial incentives is positive in the judgement tasks. For the choice tasks and for the game and market tasks, the positive effect of financial incentives is the most frequent case but there is only a slight difference from the no-effect cases. However, this is notable given that previous review studies including both single-shot trail experiments and repetition experiments report that the most frequent case is no effect for the game and market tasks. Though it is still indecisive in the choice tasks and in the game and market tasks due to the small size of samples, we conjecture that repetition may interact with financial incentives, and that the direction of the interaction effect would depend on task type. Repetition seems to reinforce the positive effect of financial incentives on performance for most task types.

5.3 *Financial Incentives, Learning and Boredom*

5.3.1 *Financial Incentives and Learning*

The above results of this review in general imply that financial incentives play a more critical role in a repetitive trial environment in an experiment, that is, the positive effect of financial incentives seems to be larger in a repetitive trial environment than in a single-shot trial environment. This suggests that there may be a relationship between financial incentives and learning.

Jamal and Sunder (1991) argue that financial incentives are essential for learning in their double oral market experiment: only subjects who are given financial incentives learned and converged to the equilibrium. Irwin *et al.* (1992), in an experiment of fifth price Vickrey auction for insurance purchase, report that subjects' bidding behaviour with financial incentives comes closer to the normative prediction than with hypothetical incentives both under 50 rounds repetition and under 150 rounds repetition. Slonim and Roth (1998), List and Cherry (2000) and Castellan (1969) suggest that higher financial incentives may lead to more effective learning than lower financial incentives.

5.3.2 *Financial Incentives and Boredom*

Most studies in this review report that the variance of subjects' behaviour decreases with financial incentives. Especially, many studies find that the variance at an equilibrium or a normative prediction decreases with financial incentives as rounds proceed. This tendency is generally consistent even for the experiments reporting that there is little difference in subjects' performance between hypothetical incentives and financial incentives. That is, it seems clear that financial incentives at least reduce the round-by-round variance of a subject's behaviour as well as the between-subjects variance of the behaviour.

If this can be regarded as evidence that financial incentives reduce the effect of boredom on subjects' performance as argued in Section 3.1, we may predict a general pattern of behaviour when subjects are bored for a given task. If boredom induces subjects to a stable behaviour as suggested by Slovic *et al.* (1965), then financial incentives will lead to more variable behaviour. If boredom induces them to a more variable behaviour, then financial incentives will lead to more stable behaviour (Siegel, 1959).

Hence, the evidence from this review supports that boredom in general induces unsystematic errors resulting in a large variance of behaviour, and that financial incentives offset the effect of boredom by reducing the variance.

5.4 *Financial Incentives and Repetition Payoff Mechanisms*

A total of nine studies in this review use RRPM while 34 studies use APM as a repetition payoff mechanism. The effects of financial incentives between both payoff mechanisms are similar as shown in Table 4 and Figure 3.

It would be interesting to compare APM to RRPM in a more specific context, for example, hypothetical incentives vs financial incentives, and high financial incentives vs low financial incentives. However, since the number of studies using RRPM is too small, it hardly seems to give useful information. While it is quite difficult to make a conclusion since the number of studies using RRPM is too small, it would be interesting to focus on comparing studies that investigate similar tasks but use different repetition payoff mechanisms.

Table 4. The Effect of Financial Incentives by Repetition Payoff Mechanisms.

	APM	%	RRPM	%	Total	%
Improve	15	42.9	4	44.4	19	43.2
No effect	11	31.4	2	22.2	13	29.5
Harm	3	8.6	0	0.0	3	6.8
Indecisive	4	11.4	2	22.2	6	13.6
Effect but no norm	2	5.7	1	11.1	3	6.8
Total	35	100.0	9	100.0	44	100.0

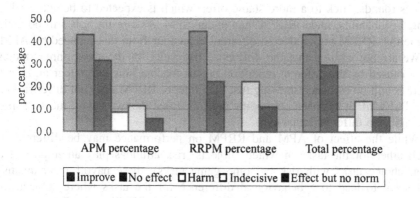

Figure 3. The Effect of Financial Incentives by Repetition Payoff Mechanisms.

List and Cherry (2000) and Slonim and Roth (1998) investigate subjects'
behaviour in ultimatum bargaining games. While the former adopts RRPM, the
latter uses APM. Ten rounds were used in each. The difference in results between
the two studies is that, in the high stakes condition, the former finds a decreasing
pattern of rejection rates across rounds whereas the latter does not. List and Cherry
(2000) attribute this to their design that allows more observations of lower offers.
However, one would argue that the difference between the two studies comes from
the difference of the payoff mechanisms, and not because of the number of lower
offers. Rejection for a positive offer is riskier under RRPM than under APM, that
is, one rejection for a positive offer under RRPM may result in zero earnings for
the whole experiment while the opportunity cost for one rejection is small under
APM. This implies that if responders are risk averse and if other conditions are
equal, responders under APM may have a larger incentive to reject than those under
RRPM do at later rounds. Hence, the fact that unconditional rejection rates decrease
as rounds proceed may be explained by the difference of the payoff mechanisms,
and not only by the number of lower offers.

Interestingly, Roth *et al.* (1991) report that the modal offers (half of the stakes)
do not change between the first round and the last round in their experiment on
the ultimatum bargaining game where RRPM and 10 rounds are used.[33] That is,

the modal offers do not decrease in this study while they do decrease in Slonim and Roth (1998).[34] This could be explained by the difference in the effects of the payoff mechanisms. It should be noted again that APM is used by Slonim and Roth (1998). Suppose that proposers are risk averse. Then, they could behave more risk aversively under RRPM than under APM since the riskiness of the decision environment (or, 'background risk') becomes larger even if their degree of risk aversion may be identical between both payoff mechanisms. Under RRPM, a risky low offer (in a sense of a high probability of rejection) would result in zero earnings for the whole experiment, while under APM the opportunity cost for the risky low offer is much smaller. Moreover, as the level of stakes increases, the opportunity cost of a risky low offer increases. These all predict that risk-averse proposers will, across rounds, stick to a more stable offer, which is expected to be accepted with a high probability, under RRPM than under APM. As a result, it is still possible to argue that RRPM may induce a different behaviour from that induced by APM.

We are not arguing that the difference in results for the above three studies is only caused by the different repetition payoff mechanisms, but rather arguing that there is still no evidence showing that the effect of RRPM does not differ from that of APM while it has been commonly presumed that the two payoff mechanisms do not induce a different behaviour.

While the effect of APM and RRPM on performance may be different from each other for the tasks in which subjects' risk attitudes play an important role (e.g. choice tasks with risk or some game tasks), these payoff mechanisms do not seem to lead to a behavioural difference for the tasks where subjects' risk attitudes do not matter. For example, Castellan (1969), Phillips and Edwards (1966) and Grether (1992) investigate subjects' probability learning behaviour. The first one uses APM while the others use RRPM. However, these studies all report that financial incentives and higher financial incentives improve subjects' probability judgement. That is, provided that a proper financial incentive is given, leaning towards a normative prediction seems to take place irrespective of the type of payoff mechanism used.

Since the number of studies adopting RRPM is small and hence there are no other studies in this review that use RRPM and APM for the same type of task, the effects of different repetition payoff mechanisms (especially, RRPM vs APM) are not exactly known. However, it may be reasonable to conclude that the effect of RRPM and APM may be different from each other and be worth investigating at least for the tasks in which the subjects' risk attitudes matter while the effects may be almost identical for the tasks in which their risk attitudes do not matter, given that the clear difference between RRPM and APM exists in the probability, that is, risk, that a payoff from a decision in a round is realized.

6. Instructions and Subject Pools

In this section, we briefly discuss two methodological issues, instructions and subject pools in laboratory experiments, which we skipped in previous sections but which may interact with financial incentives under repetition.

Using a well-structured instruction and choosing the subjects pool have been the topics of debates. Moreover, they could influence the effect of financial incentives on performance.

While a well-structured instruction is important to experimental economists, the structure of an instruction is more flexible to experimental psychologists. The norms for an instruction in economics experiments include briefness, clarity and concreteness. That is, the instruction must give subjects enough information on the experiment in a simple and clear form. In contrast, psychologists feel rather freer about the instructions than economists do. They flexibly compose the instruction according to the purpose of an experiment. Therefore, they often give subjects an incomplete instruction in the sense that it does not contain any particular information, for example, payoff rules or scoring rules. Some experiments even do not provide an instruction. This convention of psychological experiments may make psychologists feel free on the use of financial incentives, that is, if subjects are not informed of the base on which real rewards are given by an instruction (i.e. unless subjects have information how they can increase their earnings), the use of financial incentives may be meaningless in the sense that they may not function as positive incentives.

Of course, this difference between economics experiments and psychology experiments may be in the difference of the research purpose of each discipline. Roughly speaking, economics is interested in a final behaviour while psychology mainly deals with the process underlying the final behaviour.[35] Hence, economists' concern is with subjects' behaviour given that all available information for a task is given to them while psychologists are interested in subjects' decision process itself when all available information is given to them or when some information is not available to them. In our opinion, the instruction, at least in economics experiments, has to be like a very short section of a science text written in clear and unambiguous language. This may be very important in the presence of the problem related to subjects' cognitive capital, which we have discussed in the previous sections. We believe that it could be handled by both a well-structured instruction and enough practice or repetition.

The main subject pool in psychology experiments is university undergraduates who are required for a course credit while voluntary university students mainly consist of the subject pool in economics experiments.[36] A motivational difference between obligatory and voluntary subjects may make a difference in the results from an identical experiment. This difference may be larger if an experimenter uses financial incentives. The voluntary subjects' main purpose to participate in an experiment would be to earn monetary rewards while the obligatory subjects would participate in an experiment for the purpose of course credits. That is, the latter may regard the monetary reward as a bonus rather than a main motivator while the monetary reward is the main motivator for the former. This consideration predicts that there may be a behavioural difference between both subject pools even if an experimenter runs identical experiments.

7. Conclusions

This survey attempted to discuss general methodological issues in experimental economics, especially those related to the effect of financial incentives in experiments where repetition is used. Some previous reviews on the effect of financial incentives on performance in laboratory experiments have reported that financial incentives do not affect subjects' performance in many cases though they make subjects exert more effort, and that the effect depends on the type of task. However, those reviews have been done on overall experimental studies including both single-shot tasks and repetitive tasks. Considering that financial incentives increase subjects' efforts and that repetition leads subjects to learn about a task, the main conclusion about the effect of financial incentives may become different between single-shot tasks and repetitive tasks.

The main finding of this paper is that the positive effect of financial incentives on performance is more often found in repetitive task experiments than in single-shot task experiments. This result implies that if an experimenter is to use repetition, then he or she may need to use financial incentives. Hertwig and Ortmann (2001) have suggested the use of repetition and financial incentives. Our survey may give a more detailed suggestion: an experimenter who has to use repetition may need to use financial incentives. The important implication is that repetition and financial incentives may not be independent treatment variables, but may interact with each other through variables such as learning, boredom and/or payoff mechanisms. The precise mechanism of the interactions is not yet completely known. Understanding it may be important not only for the methodology of economics experiments, but also for positive economics itself, that is, our real economic behaviours are filled with repetition of similar behaviours for monetary stakes.

It seems true that many important methodological issues on experimental economics have been addressed and resolved. However, it is also true that there are a number of methodological issues that need to be clarified. The issue related to financial incentives is definitely one of them, and would be the most important one. It is not settled yet. In fact, the difficulty comes from the fact that financial incentives would be related to many other elements in laboratory experiments, for example, repetition, learning, boredom, payoff mechanisms and even the instructions and subject pools. This study attempted to tackle the complexity of the relationship between financial incentives and repetition, and of the relationship between financial incentives and payoff mechanisms.

This review suggests that the use of financial incentives may be necessary or at least preferred if subjects may need to learn about the task in which they participate and hence repetition may be necessary. Moreover, the choice of a repetition payoff mechanism may affect the result of the experiments in which subjects' risk attitudes matter.

The limitations of this study seem to be clear, and indicate the directions for some future work. First, the number of studies in the review section was not enough to draw a firm conclusion. This limitation certainly applies when we review the effect of financial incentives according to task types. This is partly because there are not many studies investigating the effect of financial incentives on performance. Moreover, since both repetition and financial incentives have been regarded as important norms rather than as empirical questions in economics experiments, the number of studies directly investigating the effect of financial incentives on performance under a repetition environment becomes much smaller. This limitation would directly imply a future direction of research: it is suggested that more studies must proceed on this issue in both economics and psychology.

Second, we could have done a quantitative review such as a meta-analysis. This could give us more precise estimates of the effect of financial incentives. However, there were some difficulties to do a meta-analysis. First, the standard for high financial incentives and low financial incentives was different from experiment to experiment, that is, there are cases where a high reward in an experiment is a low reward in another experiment. Then, the simple meta-analytical estimates would be questionable unless the high rewards and the low rewards are standardized for all experimental studies. Of course, it would not be impossible to do as Camerer and Hogarth (1999) suggest. It is believed that this meta-analytical review would be a promising future study.

Third, we could not deal with the relationship between financial incentives and a subject pool. As suggested in Section 6.2, investigating that relationship would give an interesting finding. This could give useful information on the effect of a motivational difference on an individual's behaviour, and it seems to be important not only for the experimental methodology but also for understanding economic behaviour in the real world.

Fourth, the relationship between financial incentives and repetition payoff mechanisms could be more extended. In some tasks, the effect of financial incentives may depend on the degree of certainty (or stability) of a decision environment induced by the payoff mechanism by which financial incentives are given to subjects. Such a degree may be defined by the riskiness of the decision environment. People would be more selfish or behave more risk aversively if the riskiness of the decision environment becomes larger, for example, the increase of uncertainties on payoff realization or on future status.

Acknowledgements

This paper is a revised version of a chapter in the author's PhD thesis and the revision was done when the author was affiliated with the Centre for Experimental Economics, University of York. The author is grateful to John Hey, Chris Starmer and Miguel Costa-Gomes for their comments. He is also thankful to an anonymous referee for useful comments. Any error is the author's own responsibility.

Notes

1. The definition of financial incentives is strict. In fact, a flat financial incentive (e.g. flat fee for participation) may be a kind of financial incentive compared to 'no monetary rewards'. However, since most experiments (with some exceptions in psychology experiments) generally provide a participation fee and the main

methodological debate is between hypothetical and performance-based monetary rewards given that subjects receive a flat participation fee, we use this definition.

2. Research history on the preference reversal phenomenon is an interesting example. Grether and Plott (1979), experimental economists, argued that the preference reversal phenomenon found by psychologists (Lichtenstein and Slovic, 1971) could be an artefact generated by absence of some essential experimental controls including financial incentives. They ran their own experiment using financial incentives, but they still found the phenomenon. Since then, the preference reversal has become an active research issue in experimental economics. It should be noted that the preference reversal became a serious issue in experimental economics only after its existence was shown when financial incentives were given to subjects. For further details on the debate, see Hertwig and Ortmann (2001) and various comments on it.

3. For example, the viewpoint of experimental economists on this is well represented by Smith (1994, 2002) as will be briefly discussed later in this paper. This is ultimately included in an issue of external validity of laboratory experiments and has become one of reasons why field experiments are actively run recently. For more details on the external validity, see Harrison and List (2004) and Levitt and List (forthcoming). Interestingly, Levitt and List (forthcoming) argue that laboratory experiments can be useful in terms of qualitative predictions though their quantitative prediction is not so credible.

4. Performance-based monetary rewards include various specific payoff mechanisms: piece-rate, quota, tournaments, bonus and so on. These mechanisms can be used for both single-shot and repeated environments. Since repetition necessarily requires an additional overall payoff method such as accumulated payoff or random round payoff, it may be convenient to make a distinction between the former and the latter. We will term the former *single-shot payoff mechanisms* and the latter *repetition payoff mechanism*.

5. What subjects learn is not definite. Through repetition, they may learn the rule of the task (i.e. they are accustomed to the task environment), the best strategy for the task and/or the other players' type or tendency if the task requires subjects' interaction.

6. Grade, if subjects are undergraduates, could be an alternative for monetary incentives (Friedman and Sunder, 1994; Isaac *et al.*, 1994, 2001). Of course, goods could be used for incentives as some experiments in psychology and very few in economics have done. One pitfall of this kind of incentive is the possibility of the failure to controllability, that is, some subjects may originally have a preference for a good while the others are not interested in it (but see Sippel (1997) for a case in which goods could be used for an appropriate incentive). As an example, see Hulland and Kleinmuntz (1994).

7. However, it must be noted that many experimental traditions in economics such as the use of financial incentives and the use of repetition are actually indebted to a behavioural psychologist, Sydney Siegel (Smith, 1976, 1991; Friedman and Sunder, 1994).

8. However, Cameron and Pierce (1994) suggest that the results of a meta-analytic review on 96 experimental studies report no detrimental effect of extrinsic (monetary) rewards and extrinsic reinforcement (i.e. feedback) on intrinsic motivation.

9. Knowledge can be divided two categories: declarative knowledge and procedural knowledge. Declarative knowledge is related to facts while procedural knowledge is related to operating declarative knowledge to solve a problem. See Camerer and Hogarth (1999) for more details.

10. Telser (1995), in a field study of ultimatum bargaining in Major League Baseball players contracts, argues that in a real economy where a significant amount of money is for stakes, the intrinsic motivation of altruism and reciprocity seem to disappear.

11. They define five task types: vigilance and detection, memory, production and simple clerical, judgement and choice, and problem solving, reasoning and game playing in order from less complex to more complex.

12. They define each payoff mechanism as follows: (a) flat-rate schemes: a fixed amount of reward is given, and it is not related to performance; (b) piece-rate schemes: a predefined reward is given for each unit of desired performance, and so it is related to performance; (c) variable-ratio schemes: similar to piece-rate schemes, but the reward is given only for the part of time for each unit of desired performance; (d) quota schemes: flat-rate schemes up to a given target level of performance and a bonus above this level (sometimes, the bonus is given based on piece-rate schemes); (e) the reward is given not based on an absolute performance level but based on competitive rankings of performance between people. Because variable-ratio schemes are very similar to piece-rate schemes, they combine both in their analysis of results (Bonner *et al.*, 2000, footnote 8).

13. According to Baumeister (1984), 'pressure' is defined as a factor that increases the importance of a task or performance, and 'choking' is defined as a performance decrement under such pressure circumstances. Hence, 'choking under pressure' implies the occurrence of unsuccessful performance under an important circumstance.

14. While the single-shot payoff mechanisms (or reward types as a more comprehensive definition) are related to an important topic in labour economics, organization theory, management accounting and education, the specific investigation on them is beyond the focus of this review. For more details on this issue, see Bonner *et al.* (2000), Prendergast (1999), Cameron and Pierce (1994) and Eisenberger and Cameron (1996).

15. Strictly speaking, we are not sure that a hypothetical payoff scheme given the flat participation fee must be the same as an absolutely hypothetical one (i.e. without even the flat participation fee). A kind of gift-exchange theory, which may be similar to the one by Fehr *et al.* (1998), would predict that the flat participation fee may lead to an increase of subjects' effort relative to the absolute hypothetical one. See Kagel *et al.* (1979) for a study investigating the difference between volunteer subjects and real economic agents.

16. In a game situation, the former is often called 'stranger treatment' or 'random rematching treatment', and the latter is called 'partner treatment'. The stranger treatment may include the absolute stranger treatment or so-called 'zipper treatment' according to the degree that controls indirect contamination effect. Theoretically, the indirect contamination effect may exist (Fudenberg and Tirole, 1991; Kandori, 1992), but a general stranger treatment (i.e. random rematching treatment) seems to be approximately the same as the strict stranger treatment given that the pool is large enough and anonymity is guaranteed.

17. Barron and Erev (2003) recently ran an experiment to compare a descriptive one-shot trial decision making with known payoff structure on subjects with a repetitive decision making with feedback and unknown payoff structure. The results are indecisive, that is, in some contexts, feedback improves subjects' performance while it harms subjects' performance in others. In fact, since this experiment does not combine feedback with a known payoff structure (for their purpose), it is slightly distinguished from a general sense of learning used in experimental economics while

it may shed some light on future research on learning process only by feedback. However, it should be clear that this experiment attempts to isolate the effect of feedback from others and that it may be useful to develop the study on subjects' behaviours in laboratory experiments.

18. The term 'p-beauty contest game' is also called 'beauty contest game' 'average game' or 'guessing game'. The basic logic for this term was given by Keynes (1936), and has been analysed by Moulin (1986) in a game-theoretic context. In this game, players simultaneously choose a number from an interval, say $[a, b]$, and the winner is the person who chose a number nearest to the value which is p times the average of numbers that all players chose. In general, p is predetermined and informed to players before the game begins, and the winner usually takes a fixed predetermined prize. For a brief review on the p-beauty contest game and its variations, see Nagel (1999).

19. Feedback, specifically, external feedback can have several dimensions. For example, Hogarth et al. (1991) distinguish an 'exact' feedback from a 'lenient' feedback. The exact feedback means a sensitive one to choice while the lenient feedback means a relatively insensitive one to choice. For details, see Hogarth et al. (1991).

20. If an experimenter uses repetition in order to simply increase the number of observations, then there is one important issue. What is the unit of a standard observation: an observation at each round, or an observation from each session consisting of many rounds? If we want 'independent observations', then an observation at each round may not be an adequate unit of observation in a strict sense because performances seem to be correlated through rounds mainly by a learning process. For this reason, some researchers argue that an adequate unit of observation should be based on a session. See also Friedman and Cassar (2004).

21. In fact, this assumption cannot be applied to many psychology experiments because the topics dealt with in that discipline are much broader than those of economic experiments at least in terms of cognitive difficulty. For example, let us consider experiments on short-term memory. Even if an extreme number of repeated trials are used, the digits that subjects can recall seem to be bounded at some points: they seem not to be able to recall more than 20 digits at best. Moreover, the results will not be much different even if a very large amount of financial incentives are given. This implies that, in some topics, there is a boundary due to cognitive capital under which financial incentives and repetition can make subjects' performance improve.

22. For definitions of 'pressure' and 'choke', recall note 13.

23. Of course, subjects should know before that at the beginning of the experiment the real trials with financial incentives will follow after the practice trials.

24. Repetition on different days would be one way to control the boredom effect. However, this method seems to have a large trade-off, that is, it will lose controllability for other important variables since there are periods that an experimenter cannot observe. In fact, that would mean abandonment of the merits of laboratory experiments unless the purpose of an experiment is directly related to investigating subjects' behaviour under such a circumstance.

25. RRPM may not have the same expected payoff as APM given that a subject makes an identical choice between the two because there is $1/R$ dilution of incentive under RRPM compared to APM, where R is the number of rounds in that experiment. For example, suppose that, in an experiment consisting of 10 rounds where a subject chooses option $A = (£10, 1/2; £0, 1/2)$ at every round, the expected payoff from RRPM (suppose that one random round is chosen in this example) will be $(1/10) \times$

$10 \times £5 = £5$ while it will be $10 \times £5 = £50$ under APM. Hence, the expected payoff under RRPM is 1/10 of that under APM. However, risk-neutral subjects' behaviour is not affected by this scale difference. Moreover, this scale difference can be easily resolved without losing consistency by an appropriate scale adjustment if it is necessary (e.g. if a flat payoff problem is considered or if subjects are not risk neutral but risk averse or love risk).

26. For the idea of the mean preserving spread in an individual decision-making context under uncertainty, see Rothschild and Stiglitz (1970).

27. That is, she needs to give a subject enough rewards to compensate the opportunity cost from his participation in that experiment.

28. It must be noted that Rabin questions the validity of EUT, so he does not argue that people cannot be risk averse for a small amount of money under risk.

29. Moreover, the number of studies in memory tasks and problem-solving tasks are too small to derive even a slight implication. Table A1 at the end of the paper may provide details for studies of these types.

30. For BDM mechanism, repetition was allowed only for the low financial incentive group. As they note, the sample size ($n = 20$) seems to be too small to conclude that repetition reduces the preference reversal even in the BDM mechanism.

31. In the psychology literature, pupillary dilations or pupillary changes are known to provide a highly valid index of the effort involved in mental activity.

32. For the definition of 'choking under pressure', see note 13.

33. Unfortunately, Roth *et al.* (1991) present only the pooled (high stakes and low stakes) pattern of rejection rates across rounds. Though the pooled unconditional rejection rates seem to decrease in the United States, Japan and Israel at later rounds, it is still dubious, given the results that learning may take place with high stakes.

34. There is no detailed explanation about the offer behaviour across rounds in List and Cherry (2000). Moreover, though the lower offer rates increase over all rounds, this seems to be due to the earning design rather than due to RRPM as they note (pp. 14–15). Hence, it is implausible to compare proposers' behaviour in this study with others in relation to payoff mechanisms.

35. This is related to the difference between substantial rationality and procedural rationality suggested by Simon (1987). Traditionally, the main concern of economics has been the former while psychologists are mainly concerned with the latter.

36. We consider only one issue about the subject pool. In fact, many other issues are related to the subject pool. For example, can university students properly represent people in the real economic world (Burns, 1985; DeJong *et al.*, 1988)? Is there not a difference between male and female subjects (Croson and Buchan, 1999; Eckel and Grossman, 1999; Schubert *et al.*, 1999) or between subjects' major (Carter and Irons, 1991)? For more details of these other issues, see Friedman and Sunder (1994).

References

Arrow, K.J. (1970) *Essays in the Theory of Risk-Bearing*. Amsterdam: North-Holland.

Ashton, R.H. (1990) Pressure and performance in accounting decision settings: paradoxical effects of incentives, feedback, and justification. *Journal of Accounting Research* 28: 148–180.

Bahrick, H.P. (1954) Incidental learning under two incentive conditions. *Journal of Experimental Psychology* 47(3): 170–172.

Barron, G. and Erev, I. (2003) Small feedback-based decisions and their limited correspondence to description-based decisions. *Journal of Behavioral Decision Making* 16:
215–233.

Baumeister, R.F. (1984) Choking under pressure: self-consciousness and paradoxical
effects of incentives on skillful performance. *Journal of Personality and Social
Psychology* 46: 610–620.

Beattie, J. and Loomes, G. (1997) The impact of incentives upon risky choice experiments.
Journal of Risk and Uncertainty 14: 155–168.

Berg, J.E., Daley, L.A., Dickhaut, J.W. and O'Brien, J.R. (1986) Controlling preferences
for lotteries on units of experimental exchange. *Quarterly Journal of Economics* 101:
281–306.

Binswanger, H.P. (1980) Attitudes toward risk: experimental measurement in rural India.
American Journal of Agricultural Economics 62: 395–407.

Binswanger, H.P. (1981) Attitudes toward risk: theoretical implications of an experiment
in rural India. *Economic Journal* 91: 867–890.

Bonner, S.E., Hastie, R., Sprinkle, G.B. and Young, S.M. (2000) A review of the effects of
financial incentives on performance in laboratory tasks: implications for management
accounting. *Journal of Management Accounting Research* 12: 19–64.

Bull, C., Schotter, A. and Weigelt, K. (1987) Tournaments and piece rates: an experimental
study. *Journal of Political Economy* 95: 1–33.

Burke, M.S., Carter, J.R., Gominiak, R.D. and Ohl, D.F. (1996) An experimental note on
the Allais paradox and monetary incentives. *Empirical Economics* 21: 617–632.

Burns, P. (1985) Experience and decision-making: a comparison of students and
businessmen in a simulated progressive auction. In V.L. Smith (ed.), *Research in
Experimental Economics*, Vol. 3 (pp. 139–157). Greenwich, CT: JAI Press.

Camerer, C.F. (1995) Individual decision making. In J.H. Kagel and A.E. Roth (eds),
The Handbook of Experimental Economics (pp. 587–703). Princeton, NJ: Princeton
University Press.

Camerer, C.F. (2003) *Behavioral Game Theory: Experiments in Strategic Interaction.*
Princeton, NJ: Princeton University Press.

Camerer, C.F. and Ho, T. (1999) Experience-weighted attraction learning in normal form
games. *Econometrica* 67: 827–847.

Camerer, C.F. and Hogarth, R.M. (1999) The effect of financial incentives in experiments:
a review and capital-labor production framework. *Journal of Risk and Uncertainty* 19:
7–42.

Camerer, C.F., Ho, T. and Chong, K. (2002a) Sophisticated experience-weighted attraction
learning and strategic teaching in repeated games. *Journal of Economic Theory* 104:
137–188.

Camerer, C.F., Ho, T. and Chong, K. (2002b) Strategic teaching and equilibrium
models of repeated trust and entry game experiments. Unpublished manuscript,
http://www.hss.caltech.edu/~camerer/camerer.html, accessed July 2003.

Cameron, L.A. (1999) Raising the stakes in the ultimatum game: experimental evidence
from Indonesia. *Economic Inquiry* 37(1): 47–59.

Cameron, J. and Pierce, W.D. (1994) Reinforcement, reward, and intrinsic motivation: a
meta-analysis. *Review of Educational Research* 64(3): 363–423.

Carter, J.R. and Irons, M.D. (1991) Are economists different, if so, why? *Journal of
Economic Perspectives* 5: 171–177.

Castellan, N.J., Jr (1969) Effect of change of payoff in probability learning. *Journal of
Experimental Psychology* 79(1): 178–182.

Cheung, Y. and Friedman, D. (1997) Individual learning in normal form games: some
laboratory results. *Games and Economic Behavior* 19: 46–76.

Cooper, R.W., DeJong, D.V., Forsythe, R. and Ross, T.W. (1989) Communication in battle-
of-sexes games: some experimental results. *Rand Journal of Economics* 20: 568–587.

Cox, J.C. and Grether, D.M. (1996) The preference reversal phenomenon: response mode, markets and incentives. *Economic Theory* 7: 381–405.

Cox, J.C. and Sadiraj, V. (2001) Risk aversion and expected-utility theory: coherence for small- and large-stakes gambles. *Working Paper 01-03*, Department of Economics, University of Arizona.

Cox, J.C., Smith, V.L. and Walker, J.M. (1992) Theory and misbehavior of first price auctions: comment. *American Economic Review* 82(5): 1392–1412.

Craik, F.I.M. and Tulving, E. (1975) Depth of processing and the retention of words in episodic memory. *Journal of Experimental Psychology: General* 104(3): 268–294.

Croson, R.T.A. (1996) Partners and strangers revisited. *Economics Letters* 53: 25–32.

Croson, R. and Buchan, N. (1999) Gender and culture: international experimental evidence from trust games. *American Economic Review* 89(2): 386–391.

Cubitt, R.P., Starmer, C. and Sugden, R. (1998) On the validity of the random lottery incentive system. *Experimental Economics* 1: 115–131.

Deci, E.L. (1975) *Intrinsic Motivation*. New York: Plenum.

Deci, E.L. and Ryan, R.M. (1987) The support of autonomy and the control of behaviour. *Journal of Personality and Social Psychology* 53: 1024–1037.

DeJong, D.V., Forsythe, R. and Uecker, W.C. (1988) A note on the use of businessmen as subjects in sealed offer markets. *Journal of Economic Behavior and Organizations* 9: 87–100.

Drago, R. and Heywood, J.S. (1989) Tournaments, piece rates, and the shape of the payoff function. *Journal of Political Economy* 97(4): 992–1001.

Eckel, C. and Grossman, P. (forthcoming) Differences in the economic decisions of men and women: experimental evidence. In V.L. Smith and C.R. Plott (eds), *Handbook of Experimental Economics Results*, Vol. 1. New York: Elsevier.

Eisenberger, R. and Cameron, J. (1996) Detrimental effects of reward: reality or myth? *American Psychologist* 51: 1151–1166.

El-Gamal, M.A. and Grether, D.M. (1995) Are people Bayesian? Uncovering behavioral strategies. *Journal of the American Statistical Association* 90: 1137–1145.

Farber, I.E. and Spence, K.W. (1953) Complex learning and conditioning as a function of anxiety. *Journal of Experimental Psychology* 45: 120–125.

Fehr, E., Kirchsteiger, G. and Riedl, A. (1998) Gift exchange and reciprocity in competitive experimental markets. *European Economic Review* 42: 1–34.

Friedman, D. (1992) Theory and misbehavior of first price auctions: comment. *American Economic Review* 82(5): 1374–1378.

Friedman, D. and Cassar, A. (2004) *Economics Lab: An Intensive Course in Experimental Economics*. London: Routledge.

Friedman, D. and Sunder, S. (1994) *Experimental Methods: A Primer for Economists*. Cambridge: Cambridge University Press.

Fudenberg, D. and Levine, D.K. (1998) *The Theory of Learning in Games*. Cambridge, MA: MIT Press.

Fudenberg, D. and Tirole, J. (1991) *Game Theory*. Cambridge, MA: MIT Press.

Gneezy, U. and Rustichini, A. (1999) Stochastic game theory: for playing games, not just for doing theory. *Proceedings of the National Academy of Sciences, USA* 96: 10564–10567.

Gneezy, U. and Rustichini, A. (2000) Pay enough or don't pay at all. *Quarterly Journal of Economics* 115: 791–810.

Goeree, J.K. and Holt, C.A. (forthcoming) Learning in economics experiments. In *Encyclopedia of Cognitive Psychology*. London: Macmillan Reference.

Grether, D.M. (1992) Testing Bayes rule and the representativeness heuristic: some experimental evidence. *Journal of Economic Behavior and Organization* 17: 31–57.

Grether, D.M. and Plott, C.R. (1979) Economic theory of choice and the preference reversal phenomenon. *American Economic Review* 69: 623–638.

Harrison, G.W. (1989) Theory and misbehavior of first price auctions. *American Economic Review* 79: 749–762.

Harrison, G.W. (1992) Theory and misbehavior of first price auctions: reply. *American Economic Review* 82(5): 1426–1443.

Harrison, G.W. (1994) Expected utility theory and the experimentalists. *Empirical Economics* 19: 223–253.

Harrison, G.W. and List, J.A. (2004) Field experiments. *Journal of Economics Literature* 42(4): 1013–1059.

Harrison, G.W. and Rustrom, E.E. (forthcoming) Experimental evidence on the existence of the hypothetical bias in value elicitation methods. In V.L. Smith and C.R. Plott (eds), *Handbook of Experimental Economics Results*, Vol. 1. New York: Elsevier.

Harrison, G.W., Johnson, E., McInnes, M.M. and Rustrom, E.E. (2003) Individual choice and risk aversion in the laboratory: a reconsideration. *Working Paper 3-18*, Department of Economics, College of Business Administration, University of Central Florida.

Henrich, J., Boyd, R., Bowles, S., Camerer, C., Fehr, E., Gintis, H. and McElreath, R. (2001) In search of homo economicus: behavioral experiments in 15 small-scale societies. *American Economic Review* 91(2): 73–78.

Hertwig, R. and Ortmann, A. (2001) Experimental practices in economics: a methodological challenge for psychologists? *Behavioral and Brain Sciences* 24: 383–451.

Hertwig, R. and Ortmann, A. (2003) Economists' and psychologists' experimental practices: how they differ, why they differ, and how they could converge. In I. Brocas and J.D. Carrillo (eds), *The Psychology of Economic Decisions* (pp. 253–272). New York: Oxford University Press.

Hey, J.D. and Lee, J. (2005a) Do subjects remember the past? *Applied Economics* 37(1): 9–18.

Hey, J.D. and Lee, J. (2005b) Do subjects separate (or are they sophisticated)? *Experimental Economics* 8(3): 233–265.

Ho, T., Camerer, C.F. and Weigelt, K. (1998) Iterated dominance and iterated best response in experimental 'p-beauty contests'. *American Economic Review* 88: 947–969.

Hoffman, E., McCabe, K.A. and Smith, V.L. (1996) On expectation and the monetary stakes in ultimatum games. *International Journal of Game Theory* 25: 289–301.

Hogarth, R.M. and Einhorn, H.J. (1990) Venture theory: a model of decision weights. *Management Science* 36(7): 780–803.

Hogarth, R.M., Gibbs, B.J., McKenzie, C.R.M. and Marquis, M.A. (1986) Preference reversals and the independence axiom. *American Economic Review* 76: 508–515.

Hogarth, R.M., Gibbs, B.J., McKenzie, C.R.M. and Marquis, M.A. (1991) Learning from feedback: exactingness and incentives. *Journal of Experimental Psychology: Learning, Memory, and Cognition* 17(4): 734–752.

Holt, C.A. (2000) The Y2K bibliography of experimental economics. www.people.virginia.edu/čah2k/y2k.htm, accessed October 2002.

Holt, C.A. and Davis, D.D. (1993) *Experimental Economics*. Princeton, NJ: Princeton University Press.

Holt, C.A. and Laury, S.K. (2002) Risk aversion and incentive effects. *American Economic Review* 92(5): 1644–1655.

Hulland, J.S. and Kleinmuntz, D.N. (1994) Factors influencing the use of internal summary evaluations versus external information in choice. *Journal of Behavioral Decision Making* 7: 79–102.

Irwin, J.R., McClelland, G.H. and Schulze, W.D. (1992) Hypothetical and real consequences in experimental auctions for insurance against low-probability risks. *Journal of Behavioral Decision Making* 5: 107–116.

Irwin, J.R., McClelland, G.H., McKee, M., Schulze, W.D. and Norden, N.E. (1998) Payoff dominance vs. cognitive transparency in decision making. *Economic Inquiry* 36: 272–285.

Isaac, R.M., Walker, J.M. and Williams, A.W. (1994) Group size and the voluntary provision of public goods. *Journal of Public Economics* 54: 1–36.

Isaac, R.M., Walker, J.M. and Williams, A.W. (2001) Experimental economics methods in the large undergraduate classroom: practical considerations. In R.M. Isaac (ed.), *Research in Experimental Economics*, Vol. 8 (pp. 1–23). Greenwich, CT: JAI Press.

Jamal, K. and Sunder, S. (1991) Money vs. gaming: effects of salient monetary payments in double oral auctions. *Organizational Behavior and Human Decision Processes* 49: 151–166.

Jenkins, G.D. (1986) Financial incentives. In E.A. Locke (ed.), *Generalizing from Laboratory to Field Settings* (pp. 167–180). Lexington, MA: Lexington Books.

Jenkins, G.D., Mitra, A., Gupta, N. and Shaw, J.D. (1998) Are financial incentives related to performance?: a meta-analytic review of empirical research. *Journal of Applied Psychology* 83: 777–787.

Kachelmeier, S.J. and Shehata, M. (1992) Examining risk preferences under high monetary incentives: experimental evidence from the People's Republic of China. *American Economic Review* 82(5): 1120–1141.

Kagel, J.H. and Roth, A.E. (1992) Theory and misbehavior of first price auctions: comment. *American Economic Review* 82(5): 1379–1391.

Kagel, J.H., Battalio, R.C. and Walker, J.M. (1979) Volunteer artifacts in experiments in economics: specification of the problem and some initial data from a small-scaled field experiment. In V.L. Smith (ed.), *Research in Experimental Economics*, Vol. 1 (pp. 169–197). Greenwich, CT: JAI Press.

Kahneman, D. and Peavler, W.C. (1969) Incentive effects and pupillary changes in association learning. *Journal of Experimental Psychology* 79(2): 312–318.

Kahneman, D. and Tversky, A. (1979) Prospect theory: an analysis of decision under risk. *Econometrica* 47: 263–291.

Kahneman, D., Peavler, W.C. and Onuska, L. (1968) Effects of verbalization and incentive on the pupil response to mental activity. *Canadian Journal of Psychology* 22(3): 186–196.

Kandori, M. (1992) Social norms and community enforcement. *Review of Economic Studies* 59(1): 63–80.

Karni, E. and Safra, Z. (1987) 'Preference reversal' and the observability of preferences by experimental methods. *Econometrica* 55: 675–685.

Keynes, J.M. (1936) *The General Theory of Interest, Employment and Money*. London: Macmillan.

Laury, S.K. (2005) Pay one or pay all: random selection of one choice for payment. *Andrew Young School of Policy Studies Research Paper Series No. 06-13*, Department of Economics, Georgia State University.

Ledyard, J.O. (1995) Public goods: a survey of experimental research. In J.H. Kagel and A.E. Roth (eds), *The Handbook of Experimental Economics* (pp. 111–194). Princeton, NJ: Princeton University Press.

Lee, J. (2006) Accumulated or random: an experimental investigation on the payoff mechanisms under repetition. Mimeo, Korea Environment Institute.

Lepper, M.R., Greene, D. and Nisbett, R.E. (1973) Undermining children's intrinsic interest with extrinsic reward: a test of the 'overjustification' hypothesis. *Journal of Personality and Social Psychology* 28: 129–137.

Levin, I.P., Chapman, D.P. and Johnson, R.D. (1988) Confidence in judgments based on incomplete information: an investigation using both hypothetical and real gambles. *Journal of Behavioral Decision Making* 1: 29–41.

Levitt, S.D. and List, J.A. (forthcoming) What do laboratory experiments measuring social preferences tell us about the real world. *Journal of Economic Perspectives*.

Lichtenstein, S. and Slovic, P. (1971) Reversal of preference between bids and choices in gambling decisions. *Journal of Experimental Psychology* 89: 46–55.

List, J.A. and Cherry, T.L. (2000) Learning to accept in ultimatum games: evidence from an experimental design that generates low offers. *Experimental Economics* 3: 11–29.

Loomes, G. and Sugden, R. (1998) Testing different stochastic specifications of risk choice. *Economica* 65: 581–598.

McClintock, C.G. and McNeel, S.P. (1966) Reward level and game playing behaviour. *Journal of Conflict Resolution* 10: 98–102.

Merlo, A. and Schotter, A. (1992) Theory and misbehavior of first price auctions: comment. *American Economic Review* 82(5): 1413–1425.

Merlo, A. and Schotter, A. (1994) An experimental study of learning in one and two-person games. *Working Paper RR#94-17*, C.V. STARR Center in Applied Economics, New York University.

Merlo, A. and Schotter, A. (1999) A surprise-quiz view of learning in economic experiments. *Games and Economic Behavior* 28: 25–54.

Merlo, A. and Schotter, A. (2003) Learning by not doing: an experimental investigation of observational learning. *Games and Economic Behavior* 42: 116–136.

Milgrom, P. and Roberts, J. (1991) Adaptive and sophisticated learning in normal form games. *Games and Economic Behavior* 3: 82–100.

Millner, E.L. and Pratt, M.D. (1991) Risk aversion and rent-seeking: an extension and some experimental evidence. *Public Choice* 69: 81–92.

Mookherjee, D. and Sopher, B. (1997) Learning and decision costs in experimental constant sum games. *Games and Economic Behavior* 19: 97–132.

Moulin, H. (1986) *Game Theory for Social Science*. New York: New York Press.

Murnighan, J.K., Roth, A.E. and Schoumaker, F. (1988) Risk aversion in bargaining: an experimental study. *Journal of Risk and Uncertainty* 1: 101–124.

Nagel, R. (1999) A survey on experimental beauty contest games: bounded rationality and learning. In D.V. Budescu, I. Erev and R. Zwick (eds), *Games and Human Behavior: Essays in Honor of Amnon Rapoport* (pp. 105–142). Mahwah, NJ: Lawrence Erlbaum.

Neelin, J., Sonnenschein, H. and Spiegel, M. (1988) A further test of noncooperative bargaining theory: comment. *American Economic Review* 78(4): 824–836.

Ordonez, L.D., Mellers, B.A., Chang, S. and Roberts, J. (1995) Are preference reversals reduced when made explicit? *Journal of Behavioral Decision Making* 8: 265–277.

Palacios-Huerta, I., Serrano, R. and Volij, O. (2001) Rejecting small gambles under expected utility: a comment on Rabin. *Working Paper No. 2001-05*, Brown University.

Pelham, B.W. and Neter, E. (1995) The effect of motivation of judgment depends on the difficulty of the judgment. *Journal of Personality and Social Psychology* 68: 581–594.

Phillips, L.D. and Edwards, W. (1966) Conservatism in a simple probability inference task. *Journal of Experimental Psychology* 72(3): 346–354.

Pommerehne, W.W., Schneider, F. and Zweifel, P. (1982) Economic theory of choice and the preference reversal phenomenon: a reexamination. *American Economic Review* 72: 569–574.

Pratt, J.W. (1964) Risk aversion in the small and in the large. *Econometrica* 32: 122–136.

Prendergast, C. (1999) The provision of incentives in firms. *Journal of Economic Literature* 37: 7–63.

Rabin, M. (2000) Risk aversion and expected utility theory: a calibration theorem. *Econometrica* 68: 1281–1292.

Roth, A.E. and Erev, I. (1995) Learning in extensive form games: experimental data and simple dynamic models in the intermediate term. *Games and Economic Behavior* 8(1): 164–212.

Roth, A.E. and Murnighan, J.K. (1978) Equilibrium behavior and repeated play of the prisoner's dilemma. *Journal of Mathematical Psychology* 17: 189–198.

Roth, A.E., Prasnikar, V., Okuno-Fujiwara, M. and Zamir, S. (1991) Bargaining and market behavior in Jerusalem, Ljubljana, Pittsburgh, and Tokyo: an experimental study. *American Economic Review* 81: 1068–1095.

Rothschild, M. and Stiglitz, J.S. (1970) Increasing risk I: a definition. *Journal of Economic Theory* 2: 225–243.

Rubinstein, A. (2001) Comments on the risk and time preferences in economics. Unpublished manuscript.

Salthouse, T.A., Rogan, J.D. and Prill, K.A. (1984) Division of attention: age differences on a visually presented memory task. *Memory and Cognition* 12(6): 613–620.

SBS (2003) SBS 8 News, 15 January 2003. news.sbs.co.kr/indexes/vod/8news index.html, accessed August 2003.

Schubert, R., Brown, M., Gysler, M. and Brachinger, H.W. (1999) Financial decision-making: are women really more risk-averse? *American Economic Review* 89(2): 381–385.

Segal, U. (1990) Two-stage lotteries without the reduction axiom. *Econometrica* 58: 349–377.

Selten, R., Sadrieh, A. and Abbink, K. (1999) Money does not induce risk neutral behavior, but binary lotteries do even worse. *Theory and Decision* 46: 211–249.

Siegel, S. (1959) Theoretical models of choice and strategy behavior: stable state behavior in the two-choice uncertain outcome situation. *Psychometrika* 24(4): 303–316.

Simon, H.A. (1987) Rationality in psychology and economics. In R.M. Hogarth and M.W. Reder (eds), *Rational Choice: The Contrast between Economics and Psychology*. Chicago, IL: University of Chicago Press.

Sippel, R. (1997) An experiment on the pure theory of consumer behaviour. *Economic Journal* 107: 1431–1444.

Slonim, R. and Roth, A.E. (1998) Learning in high stakes ultimatum games: an experiment in the Slovak Republic. *Econometrica* 66(3): 569–596.

Slovic, P., Lichtenstein, S. and Edwards, W. (1965) Boredom-induced changes in preferences among bets. *American Journal of Psychology* 78: 208–217.

Smith, V.L. (1962) An experimental study of competitive market behavior. *Journal of Political Economy* 70: 111–137.

Smith, V.L. (1965) Experimental auction markets and the Walrasian hypothesis. *Journal of Political Economy* 73: 387–393.

Smith, V.L. (1976) Experimental economics: induced value theory. *American Economic Review* 66: 274–279.

Smith, V.L. (1982) Microeconomic systems as an experimental science. *American Economic Review* 72: 923–955.

Smith, V.L. (1991) *Papers in Experimental Economics*. Cambridge: Cambridge University Press.

Smith, V.L. (1994) Economics in the laboratory. *Journal of Economic Perspectives* 8(1): 113–131.

Smith, V.L. (2002) Methods in experiment: rhetoric and reality. *Experimental Economics* 5: 91–110.

Smith, V.L. and Walker, J.M. (1993a) Monetary rewards and decision cost in experimental economics. *Economic Inquiry* 31: 245–261.

Smith, V.L. and Walker, J.M. (1993b) Rewards, experience and decision costs in first price auctions. *Economics Inquiry* 31: 237–244.

Starmer, C. and Sugden, R. (1991) Does the random lottery incentive system elicit true preferences? An experimental investigation. *American Economics Review* 81: 971–978.

Straub, P.G. and Murnighan, J.K. (1995) An experimental investigation of ultimatum games: information, fairness, expectations, and lowest acceptable offers. *Journal of Economic Behavior and Organization* 27: 345–364.

Telser, L.G. (1995) The ultimatum game and the law of demand. *Economic Journal* 105: 1519–1523.

van Wallendael, L.R. (1995) Implicit diagnosticity in an information-buying task. *Journal of Behavioral Decision Making* 8: 245–264.

Weber, R.A. (2003) 'Learning' with no feedback in a competitive guessing game. *Games and Economic Behavior* 44: 134–144.

Weibull, J.W. (1995) *Evolutionary Game Theory*. Cambridge, MA: MIT Press.

Wilcox, N.T. (1993) Lottery choice: incentives, complexity and decision time. *Economic Journal* 103: 1397–1417.

van Winden, F., van Dijk, F. and Sonnemans, J. (forthcoming) Intrinsic motivation in a public good environment. In V.L. Smith and C. Plott (eds), *Handbook of Experimental Economics Results*, Vol. 1. New York: Elsevier.

Yaniv, I. and Schul, Y. (1997) Elimination and inclusion procedures in judgment. *Journal of Behavioral Decision Making* 10: 211–220.

Zizzo, D.J., Stolarz-Fantino, S., Wen, J. and Fantino, E. (2000) A violation of the monotonicity axiom: experimental evidence on the conjunction fallacy. *Journal of Economic Behavior and Organization* 41: 263–276.

Table A1. Summary of Reviewed Studies.

Title	Task	Financial incentives	Rounds (trials)	Payoff mechanism	Results
List and Cherry (2000)	Ultimatum game [game and market]	Low ($20) High ($400)	10 Stranger treatment	RRPM	1. Similar behaviour across high vs low 2. As stakes increase, unconditional reject rate decreases 3. Learning takes places in the high stakes
Irwin et al. (1998)	BDM mechanism (willingness to pay) [choice]	With $10 initial endowment, Flat Steep	5 practice and 13 real rounds (not announced)	APM	1. Under incomplete feedback, payoff structure (steep vs flat) can make difference 2. Under complete feedback, payoff structure does not make difference
Beattie and Loomes (1997)	Gamble choices [choice]	Hypothetical (group 1 with flat $2) Real (group 2: RRPM)	4 trials	RRPM for group 2	1. In simple pair-wise choices, monetary incentive may not affect subjects' performance 2. For no simple pair-wise choices, hypothetical and RRPM differ from real single-shot task
McClintock and McNeel (1966)	Maximizing difference game (coordination game) [game and market]	Real (group 3, 4, 5, 6: single shot) Low: 0.05 Fr (= 0.2 cents)	100 No information about matching	APM	More cooperation in high reward than in low reward

Study	Task [type]	Reward	N	Test	Findings
Gneezy and Rustichini (2000)	Problem solving Exp 1: IQ test [problem solving]	High: 0.5 Fr (= 2 cents) Per each matrix point value; 4 groups: no mention about reward, NIS 0.1, NIS 1, NIS 3 per correct answer with flat NIS 60, respectively	50	APM	1. Poorer performance of NIS 0.1 group than that of no mention group 2. Mean correct answer was 28.4 vs 23.07 vs 34.7 vs 34.1
Burke et al. (1996)	Gamble choices (Allais' paradox) [choice]	Hypothetical with flat $5 Real: lottery 1–4, hypothetical, lottery 5, 6, real ($0, $5, $10)	6	APM Sum of outcomes of two preferred lotteries from lottery 5 and 6	Real incentives significantly reduce violation of EUT relative to hypothetical incentive (violation rate: 0.36 in hypothetical, 0.08 in real salient)
Castellan (1969)	Probability learning [judgement]	Low: 1 cent High: 10 cents Per correct prediction	300 At 180th round, half of subjects move from low to high, half of subjects move from high to low	APM	1. Improved performance under high reward relative to low reward 2. Payoffs improve performance in early training (learning), but there is another interaction between payoff and performance in later rounds
Kahneman and Peavler (1969)	Pupillary dilations (mental arithmetic) [judgement]	Low: 1 cent High: 5 cents Per correct answer	8 Each trial has 8 pairs of problems	APM	1. High reward leads to more correct recall than low reward does (55% under high, 18% under low)

(continued)

Table A1. *Continued.*

Title	Task	Financial incentives	Rounds (trials)	Payoff mechanism	Results
					2. More effort under high than under low
Kahneman *et al.* (1968)	Pupillary dilations (mental arithmetic) [judgement]	Low: 2 cents High: 10 cents Per correct answer With $1.50 flat participation fee Use of penalty	32 8 for each 4 conditions	APM	High reward does not affect accuracy (average 88% in low, 82% in high, insignificant difference)
Neelin *et al.* (1988)	Bargaining [game and market]	Low: $5–$0.07 (two–five rounds bargaining) High: $15–$0.21 (4 five rounds bargaining)	Single shot of 2–5 rounds bargaining for low 4 five rounds bargaining for high (1 for practice, 3 for real)	APM	No difference of offer and reject rate between low and high
Ashton (1990)	Decision making (bond rating) [choice]	Hypothetical Real: $100 for top 2	16 for feedback condition	Tournament	1. Financial incentive improves mean performance (4.64 vs 5.58), and feedback does so (4.64 vs 5.55) 2. Financial incentive and feedback improve mean performance (4.64 vs 5.70)

Author	Task	Incentive	Number	Type	Findings
Hogarth and Einhorn (1990)	Gamble choices [choice]	Hypothetical: $1 (small) or $10,000 (large) Real: $0.1 (small) or $10 (large) with $10 endowment	12	APM	3. Financial incentive leads to lower variance (3.57 vs 1.74) 1. No significant difference of risk attitudes under hypothetical and real 2. In real, more risk aversion in large ($10) than in small ($0.1)
Levin et al. (1988)	Gamble choices (missing information paradigm) [choice]	Gain experiment Hypothetical: $15 investment, $100–$200 outcomes Real: $0.15 investment, $1 or $2 outcomes	22	Two times of 6 complete information gambles + 5 incomplete information gambles The last 11 gambles for real	APM	Reduced effect of information frame on the likelihood of taking real gambles, as opposed to hypothetical gambles
Jamal and Sunder (1991)	Double oral auction market [game and market]	Market 1, (2) Period 1–5: flat (performance based) Period 6–9 : performance based (flat) Market 4 Period 1–9: flat Market 3: 12 periods	9–12	APM	1. Salience makes market behaviour converge to economic equilibrium 2. Inexperienced subjects learn well the equilibrium behaviour under performance-based payoff, but after learning they still behave well even under flat payoff

(continued)

Title	Task	Financial incentives	Rounds (trials)	Payoff mechanism	Results
		1–5: flat 6–8: performance based 9–12: flat Market 5 10 periods, flat Market 6: 11 periods 1–5: flat, 6–11: performance based			3. In all cases, market behaviour converges to economic behaviour under performance-based payoff
Yaniv and Schul (1997)	Selection of an answer from many alternatives [judgement]	Exp 1: no payoff Exp 2: NIS 2.0–0.1*k (k: marks including correct answer in inclusion condition or marks excluding correct answer in elimination condition)	30	APM	The accuracy of correct answer is almost identical between Exp 1 and Exp 2
Irwin et al. (1992)	Insurance purchase with 5th price Vickrey auction [game and market]	Hypothetical Real: (99/100, $1; 1/100, −$40) with $50 in 50 rounds condition and $80 in 150 rounds condition plus $5 for participation	50 rounds 150 rounds	APM	1. Stronger tendency towards normative prediction under real 2. Little evidence for the effect of experimental length (rounds) on reward type effects

Author (year)	Topic [type]	Design / procedure	Number of tasks	Model	Findings
Grether and Plott (1979)	Preference reversal [choice]	Group 1: flat $7 Group 2: flat $7 ± performance-based payoff (at least $5 guaranteed)	18 tasks (3 choice tasks – 12 pricing tasks – 3 choice tasks)	RRPM	The preference reversal phenomenon still exists for group 2
Hogarth *et al.* (1991)	Value prediction (relationship between feedback condition and financial incentives) [judgement]	Exp 1 (three rounds of 30 trials each) Hypo: no monetary incentive Real: 1 cent for each mean evaluation point above zero over 30 trials Exp 4 (three rounds of 30 trials each) Rounds 1 and 2: without monetary incentive and with framing for 'learning opportunities' Round 3: with monetary incentive	Three rounds of 30 trials (total 90 trials)	APM	1. For lenient condition, financial incentives improve performance 2. For exact condition, financial incentives harm performance 3. pp. 745–746
Slonim and Roth (1998)	Ultimatum bargaining in Slovak Republic [game and market]	Low: 60 Sk (= $1.9) Medium: 300 Sk (= $9.7) High: 1500 Sk (= $48.4)	10 rounds (stranger)	APM	1. In the first round, there was no significant difference for stakes difference

(continued)

Table A1. *Continued.*

Title	Task	Financial incentives	Rounds (trials)	Payoff mechanism	Results
		(average monthly rate in Slovak Rep was 5500 Sk)			2. When subjects have the opportunity to learn through 10 rounds repetition, and as stakes increased, (1) responders (pooled over 10 rounds) rejected offer less often, (2) there was an interaction effect between stakes and experience (learning): in the higher stakes conditions the offers decreased with experience (learning)
van Wallendael (1995)	Implicit diagnosticity [judgement]	Exp 2: no monetary rewards Exp 3: the highest scorer of each session wins $10 (10 subjects each session: expected earnings = (1/10) × $10 = $1)	12 tasks	APM + tournaments	The monetary incentive does not affect subjects' performance

Study	Topic	Incentive	Tasks	Model	Findings
Ordonez *et al.* (1995)	Preference reversal in simultaneous performance environment [choice]	Hypo Real: $5 + monetary reward from chosen gamble (real reward is 20% of the stated outcome in the gambles)	10 practice tasks + 100 tasks	RRPM	1. Financial incentives significantly reduce preference reversal 2. Without financial incentives, the systematic preference reversal seems to remain 3. Under simultaneous performance environment, financial incentives virtually eliminated preference reversal rate
Wilcox (1993)	Preference reversal [choice]	$8 + performance based Low: low probability of a task being randomly chosen ($p = 1/72$) High: high probability of a task being randomly chosen ($p = 1/8$) Single lottery treatment/two-stage version of simple lottery	8 choice pairs and 16 pricing pairs (2 choice pairs and 4 pricing pairs: high, 6 choice pairs and 12 pricing pairs: low)	RRPM	

(continued)

Table A1. *Continued.*

Title	Task	Financial incentives	Rounds (trials)	Payoff mechanism	Results
Mookherjee and Sopher (1997)	Constant sum games [game and market]	Games 1 and 2 : W = Rs. 5, L = 0 Games 3 and 4: W = Rs. 10, L = 0	40 rounds (partner, feedback)	APM	1. Significant deviation from min-max play 2. No difference of the deviation between the scale of payoffs 3. No support for decision cost theories
Salthouse *et al.* (1984)	Memory tasks (difference between young and old) [memory]	Five payoff conditions: 0, 1, 2, 3, 4 cents per correct response	Exp 1: 100 trials (two blocks of five payoff conditions with 10 trials each) Within subjects Exp 2: 200 trials (two blocks of five payoff conditions with 20 trials each)	APM Feedback	Financial incentives improve the percentage of correct response
Bahrick (1954)	Incidental learning (colour recognition) [memory]	No reward Real: 10 cents–$1.50 depending on the repetition number for correct recognitions for a sequence of 14 forms	Within subjects Un-predefined repetition		1. The learning speed of real group was faster than that of no reward group 2. But, the score of the real group was significantly lower than that of no reward group

Study	Task [domain]	Conditions	Trials	Payment scheme	Findings
Phillips and Edwards (1966)	Bayesian probability learning [judgement]	Control: no reward Group 1: real payoffs logarithmically related to probability estimates Group 2: real payoffs with a quadratic relationship to probability estimates Group 3: real payoffs linear to probability estimates	20 trials of 20 draws for each trial	In each trial, RRPM For the 20 trials, APM (with feedback)	1. As trials proceed, a small amount of learning is found from initial trials to later trials 2. All experimental groups (groups 1, 2 and 3) show more learning than the control group 3. Real payoffs decrease the amount of conservatism in probability estimation 4. The variances between subjects for deviation from Bayesian prediction were smaller in experimental groups than in control groups
Craik and Tulving (1975)	Word memory tasks [memory]	Exp 1–9: hypothetical Exp 10: 1, 3, 6 cents for correct recognition for three encoding conditions (the incentive for each encoding condition was different between three groups)	60 tasks (20 tasks in each encoding condition)	APM No feedback	1. Differential reward for each encoding condition had no effect 2. The level of recall or recognition of a word may not be decided by intention to learn or the amount of effort level

(continued)

Table A1. *Continued.*

Title	Task	Financial incentives	Rounds (trials)	Payoff mechanism	Results
El-Gamal and Grether (1995)	Ellsberg paradox [choice]	Flat: flat fee Perf-based: flat fee + $10 for correct response	14–21 tasks (no feedback)	RRPM	1. Error rate for a decision rule was lower in performance-based group than in flat group
Baumeister (1984)	Choking under pressure [choice]	Control: no pay Experimental: $1 for each trial where subjects' points are above a criterion	1 practice trial + 2 real trials	APM + quota	1. Financial incentives cause subjects to perform worse 2. Choking appeared on the first trial but not the second
Ho *et al.* (1998)	*p*-beauty contest game [game and market]	Low: $1 per round High: $4 per round		APM	High group comes slightly closer to NE
Grether (1992)	Probability judgement [judgement]	Hypothetical Real: $10 for correct choice	Unknown	RRPM	Real incentives make subjects less far from Bayesian prediction than hypothetical does
Smith (1965)	Trading in double auctions with excess supply [game and market]	RPPM: 4 out of 27 subjects APM	4–6 rounds		Rapid convergence for real group
Bull *et al.* (1987)	Effort decision making (tournament game) [choice]	Low: 0–$1.45 per round High: 0–$5.80 per round	12 rounds	APM	Numbers chosen by subjects are not different between low and high

	Task	Incentive levels	Rounds	Mechanism	Results
Cox and Grether (1996)	Preference reversals with various mechanisms [choice]	Hypothetical Low: 0.5 of high High: $60.57 of mean			
Drago and Heywood (1989)	Effort decision making (tournament game) [choice]	Low: 6.85 cents from $e = 0$ to $e^* = 37$ High: 67.2 cents from $e = 0$ to $e^* = 37$	12 rounds	APM	1. Mean number closer to prediction of 37 (48.7 for low and 37.2 for high in 12 rounds) 2. Lower variance for high
Roth et al. (1991)	Ultimatum bargaining [game and market]	Low: $10 High: $30	10 rounds	RRPM	No difference in ultimatum games. Small, insignificant difference in market games. More risk averse in high
Kachelmeier and Shehata (1992)	Gamble choice [choice]	Low: 1 yuan per trial High: 10 yuan per trial	25 rounds	APM	
Zizzo et al. (2000)	Conjunction fallacy [judgement]	Group 1: $3 per correct answer and feedback Group 2: No money but feedback Group 3: No money but hint Group 4: No money, no feedback, no hint	6 rounds	APM	1. When the task is framed easy, financial incentives improve correct judgement 2. When the task is framed difficult, financial incentives do not affect performance

INDEX